POSITION AND CHANGE

SYNTHESE LIBRARY

MONOGRAPHS ON EPISTEMOLOGY,

LOGIC, METHODOLOGY, PHILOSOPHY OF SCIENCE,

SOCIOLOGY OF SCIENCE AND OF KNOWLEDGE,

AND ON THE MATHEMATICAL METHODS OF

SOCIAL AND BEHAVIORAL SCIENCES

VOLUME 112

LARS LINDAHL

POSITION AND CHANGE

A Study in Law and Logic

D. REIDEL PUBLISHING COMPANY

DORDRECHT-HOLLAND/BOSTON-U.S.A.

ISBN 90-277-0787-1

Published by D. Reidel Publishing Company,
P.O. Box 17, Dordrecht, Holland

Sold and distributed in the U.S.A., Canada, and Mexico
by D. Reidel Publishing Company, Inc.
Lincoln Building, 160 Old Derby Street, Hingham,
Mass. 02043, U.S.A.

Printed in Sweden by Almqvist & Wiksell, Uppsala 1977

To Åke and Iris Odelberg

Preface

The present study which I have subtitled *A Study in Law and Logic* was prompted by the question of whether an investigation into law and legal systems could lead to the discovery of unrevealed fundamental patterns common to all such systems. This question was further stimulated by two interrelated problems. Firstly, could an inquiry be rooted in specifically legal matters, as distinct from the more usual writings on deontic logic? Secondly, could such inquiry yield a theory which would nevertheless embrace a strict and simple logical structure, permitting substantive conclusions in legal matters to be deduced from simple rules governing some basic concepts?

Before the development of deontic logic, W. N. Hohfeld devoted his efforts to this question at the beginning of this century. However, with this exception, few jurists have studied the interrelation between law and logic projected in this way. Nevertheless, two great names are to be found, Gottfried Wilhelm Leibniz and Jeremy Bentham—both philosophers with legal as well as logical training. Bentham's investigations of logical patterns in law have only recently attracted attention; and as for Leibniz, his achievements are still almost totally unexplored (his most important writings on law and logic have not even been translated from Latin).

My initial interest in the question was evoked by Professor Stig Kanger. Although primarily a logician and philosopher, Stig Kanger has been interested also in the fundamentals of legal theory. His writings on law and logic are among the few important contributions to the subject in recent times.

The present study is an attempt to research an area of the general theory of law which I have chosen to call the theory of *legal positions*. Although the logical apparatus used in the book is, from a logician's standpoint, quite elementary, the text might be more difficult to follow for the jurist or legal philosopher not conversant with formal logic. However, each of the two parts of the book begins with an introductory chapter (Chapters 1 and 6) where the background to the subject is presented in a largely informal manner.

On a more personal note, I would like to thank Professor Stig Kanger for his support and encouragement which made it possible for me to accomplish this study. My sincerest appreciation for her steadfast interest goes to Helle Kanger, herself a student of political science. Both, Stig and Helle Kanger, have consistently followed my endeavours and helped me to overcome various difficulties.

Dr. Ingmar Pörn whose interests encompass similar questions in the broader field of the social sciences has provided me with valuable insights. My good friend, Dr. Paul Needham, translated the book into English, and, with his philosophical and logical abilities, provided many useful suggestions for which I am very grateful. Next, I would like to give my very warm thanks to Professor Stanley Bender who scrutinised the final version of this book and with his acumen provided much important and constructive criticism. I am also very grateful for all the time, effort and interest Professor Bender devoted to helping me with numerous practical details. Then, I wish to thank Mrs. Susan Pearce for having painstakingly typed most of the book, and I am in everlasting debt to my mother and to my fiancée, Lena, for the understanding they have shown and for the many details they have helped with, too numerous to mention.

This study has been supported by a grant from the Swedish Council for Social Science Research, and I wish to take the opportunity to express my sincerest thanks and appreciation to the Council and its Secretary, Mr. Åke Bruhn-Möller, as well as to Professor Stig Strömholm, Dean of the Faculty of Law, University of Uppsala, for the kindness and patience they have shown me.

Uppsala, November 1976

LARS LINDAHL

Table of Contents

PART I

Basic Types of Legal Position

CHAPTER 1

From Bentham to Kanger

I. *Introduction*

In the analytical tradition established by Jeremy Bentham and John Austin, and continued in the twentieth century by W. N. Hohfeld and others, much attention has been given to legal concepts which are common to different systems of law and different parts of individual systems. For Bentham, the explication of such concepts fell within what he called *universal jurisprudence* (1970*a*, p. 294), and Austin adopted a similar term, *general jurisprudence*, understanding by it "the science concerned with the exposition of the principles, notions, and distinctions which are common to systems of law" (1863, III, p. 351). Hohfeld's best known work, *Some Fundamental Legal Conceptions as Applied in Judicial Reasoning*, considers "as of chief concern, the basic conceptions of the law—the legal elements that enter into all types of jural interests" (1923, p. 27).

Amongst the central concepts in this area, Bentham and Austin consider *right*, *obligation* (*duty*), *liberty* and *power* (Bentham, 1970*a*, p. 6, 295; Austin, 1863, III, p. 351). Hohfeld begins with precisely eight basic conceptions, namely *right*, *duty*, *privilege*, *no-right*, *power*, *liability*, *immunity*, *disability* (1923, p. 63).

One task for the programme Bentham and Austin had in mind is to define or explain the concepts *right*, *obligation*, etc., in terms of other concepts. A second task is to order these concepts (*right*, *obligation*, etc.) into a system in which the logical relations between the concepts are explicitly stated. Bentham has in fact contributed to the solution of both these problems: he defines or explains the concepts and also suggests the outlines of a logical systematization. The locus of Austin's work, on the other hand, is concerned with explanation and definition (without, however, much advance on Bentham's theory); so far as logical systematization is concerned, Austin's theory is less developed than Bentham's. Finally, Hohfeld does not give any definitions of his basic concepts; they are explained merely with the help of examples. Rather, he tries to systematize the concepts in question along the lines: *right* and *duty* are "correlatives", *right* and *no-right* are "opposites", and so forth.

Bentham's theory is based on a rudimentary deontic logic. With the development of formal logic, however,—and in particular in view of the work of Ernst Mally (1926) and G. H. von Wright (1951)—the possibilities of pursuing Bentham's lines of thought and developing a logic for basic legal positions were very much enhanced. Most notable among those to take advantage of the tools now available is Stig Kanger (see especially Kanger, 1963, translated into English as pp. 85–103 of Kanger & Kanger, 1966). Kanger has shown how a refined systematization of types of right can be obtained from ordinary sentential logic supplemented by a few rules for two additional concepts. Further developments under the influence of Kanger's work have been made by Ingmar Pörn (1970, 1971) and Helle Kanger (Kanger & Kanger, 1966, pp. 103–115).

The theory of basic types of legal positions set out in Chapters 3–5 below has been developed in the light of Kanger's work. The methods used are modifications of Kanger's method for generating so-called atomic types of right.

A survey of Bentham's, Austin's, Hohfeld's, and Kanger's theories is given in the present chapter with a view to introducing the theory of legal positions and to placing my own theory in its historical context. The survey is devoted mainly to distinguishing the basic types of right of the various authors and with an eye to the questions: (1) whether the types of right are defined with the help of more basic concepts; (2) whether the types of right constitute a logical system; and (3) whether the types of right are construed as relations between people.

Those concepts employed by Bentham, Austin and Hohfeld, relating specifically to *power to bring about changes in existing legal relations* will not be dealt with in this connection. Rather, the subject is taken up in a later chapter as an introduction to the theory of *ranges of legal action* which is presented in Chapters 6–9.

II. *Bentham's Theory*

1. *Aspects of a law and imperational logic*

Bentham's classification of types of right should be seen against a background of his theory of "aspects of a law" and "imperational logic".

This theory was developed by Bentham in *Of Laws in General*, published for the first time in 1945 although it is thought to have been written about 1782 (Bentham, 1945; Bentham 1970*b* is a more complete edition). The theory remained practically unknown until the 1970s, when Joseph Raz (1970), H. L. A. Hart (1971) and David Lyons (1972, 1973) drew attention to it. (See also Lysaght, 1973 and Sundby, 1973.)

2. *Aspects of a law*

The concept "aspect of a law" or "aspect of the will of a legislator" is introduced in the following statement:

> ... the aspects of a law: the aspects of which it is susceptible with relation to the articles which it is capable of taking for its *objects:* the aspects or *phases* which the will of a legislator may be considered as presenting to those objects in virtue of the different volitions, inclinations, or wishes which he may entertain concerning them ... (1970*b*, p. 93)

Bentham's doctrine of aspects can be briefly summarised in the following scheme (where L is an abbreviation for "the legislator" and *F* is a variable for action-propositions):

Case	*Aspect of the legislator's will with respect to F*	*Type of law with respect to F*
1. L wishes that *F*	decided, affirmative	command
2. L wishes that not-*F*	decided, negative	prohibition
3. Not: L wishes that *F*	undecided, negative	non-command
4. Not: L wishes that not-*F*	undecided, affirmative	permission (non-prohibition)

Each case described in the left-hand column corresponds univocally, according to Bentham, to that aspect named on the same line in the centre column (and conversely). Moreover, each of the four types of aspect is adequately expressed by a certain type of law—that indicated in the right-hand column. Conversely, each law of the type *command*, *prohibition*, etc., expresses that aspect indicated on the same line in the centre column. Since each type of aspect corresponds univocally to a certain type of law, and conversely, it is appropriate to speak of the aspect which a given law has. Thus, the aspect of a law of type *command* is decided and affirmative, and so forth.

At first glance, it might seem somewhat surprising that Bentham regards the aspect as negative in case 3 and affirmative in case 4, rather than vice versa. The explanation of this concerns, at least in part, his view of the use of the verbs "shall" and "may" for expressing different aspects of the legislator's will. Bentham's view can be represented in the following scheme (cf. 1970*b*, p. 95):

Expression	*Type of aspect with respect to F*	
It shall be the case that *F*	decided, affirmative	(Command)
It may be the case that *F*	undecided, affirmative	(Permission)
It shall be the case that not-*F*	decided, negative	(Prohibition)
It may be the case that not-*F*	undecided, negative	(Non-command)

(*F* is a variable for action-propositions.) If the aspect is decided, "shall" is used; and if undecided, "may". If the aspect is affirmative, *F* is not negated; and if negative, *F* is negated.

3. *The logic of imperation: Introduction*

Bentham's account of aspects was developed further with the help of certain logical principles. According to him, these principles belong to a certain branch of logic—the *logic of imperation* or the *logic of the will* (1970*b*, p. 15, n. h; cf. 1970*a*, p. 299, n. b2). Bentham himself claimed that he was here entering fresh ground: "a particular branch of logic, untouched by Aristotle", "a leaf which seems to be yet wanting in the book of science", "a new and unexplored province" (1970*a*, pp. 299 f., n. b2).

Before going into Bentham's logical principles, I would like to raise some general questions concerning interpretation and area of application. There are in Bentham two versions of these principles, which are somewhat different. For example, consider the following (1970*b*, p. 97):

Version A If *x* is a command with respect to *F*, and *y* is a prohibition with respect to *F*, then *x* excludes *y*.

Version B If it is commanded that *F*, then it is not prohibited that *F*.

Commands and prohibitions are, according to Bentham, *imperatives*, and the appropriate form of expression for them is either the grammatical imperative form or a statement with the word "shall" (1970*b*, p. 105). For example (cf. 1970*a*, p. 300, n. b2):

Grammatical imperative form

(1)	Kill the robber!	(Command)
(2)	Don't kill the robber!	(Prohibition)

The use of "shall"

(1′)	You shall kill the robber.	(Command)
(2′)	You shall not kill the robber.	(Prohibition)

Version A of Bentham's logical principle is concerned with the logical relation between two *imperatives*, according to which (1) and (1′), for example, exclude (2) and (2′).

The primary use of expressions such as "It is commanded that", "It is prohibited that", and so forth, is, on the other hand, to explain "the state which things are in, in consequence of the arrangements taken by the legislator". When such expressions are used from time to time in the law itself, it is an improper mode of expression:

> The legislator speaking as it were in the person of another man who is considered as explaining the state which things are in, in consequence of the arrangements taken by the legislator. (1970*b*, p. 154; cf. 1970*b*, pp. 178 f., 302 f.)

For example, consider

(3) It is commanded that you kill the robber;
(4) It is prohibited that you kill the robber.

According to Bentham, (3) and (4) describe states of affairs which are consequences of the legislator's actions.

According to version B of Bentham's logical principle, (3) is logically incompatible with (4): if things are as described in (3), then they are not as described in (4), and conversely.

No further development of the interpretation of versions A and B will be presented here. (Cf., however, Lyons, 1972, pp. 348 ff.; 1973, pp. 120 ff.) It must be pointed out, however, that there are many statements of Bentham's which lend support to the view that his logical principles were intended to hold in both versions (see Bentham 1970*b*, pp. 96 ff., 110 ff.). Henceforth the principles will be represented here in accordance with version B.

4. *Principles of the logic of imperation*

In representing Bentham's principles for the logic of imperation I shall take the liberty of allowing a certain modernisation. This is prompted by a desire to facilitate comparison of Bentham's views with more recent systems of deontic logic. The usual sentential connectives $\sim$ (not), & (and), v (or), $\rightarrow$ (If ... then) and $\leftrightarrow$ (if and only if) will be used, and *Commanded, Prohibited, Non-commanded, Permitted* are to be regarded as operators governing action-propositions, F being a variable over action-propositions. The basic principles can now be represented in the following five statements:

(1) Non-commanded $F \leftrightarrow \sim$ Commanded F;
(2) Permitted F (or Non-prohibited F) $\leftrightarrow \sim$ Prohibited F;
(3) Commanded $F \leftrightarrow$ Prohibited $\sim F$;
(4) Permitted $F \leftrightarrow$ Non-commanded $\sim F$;
(5) Commanded $F \rightarrow \sim$ Prohibited F.

Bentham regarded (1) and (2) as trivially true: "Permitted" is just another way of saying "Non-prohibited", the prefix having the same significance as negation. Statements (3) and (4) he motivates in the following way (remember that *Commanded* and *Permitted* correspond to affirmative aspects whilst *Prohibited* and *Non-commanded* correspond to negative aspects; see above, p. 6):

> A negative aspect towards a positive act is equipollent to an affirmative aspect towards the correspondent negative act. ... Of these two species of mandates then, an affirmative and a negative, each one may at pleasure be translated or converted into the other. (1970*b*, pp. 95 f.)

If F says that a certain person performs a given action and $\sim F$ that he does not perform that action, a prohibition with respect to F (negative aspect, positive act) can accordingly also be expressed as a command with respect to $\sim F$ (affirmative aspect, negative act).

Statements (1)–(4) can be jointly summarised in the following schema of equivalences:

$$\begin{array}{ccc} \text{Commanded } F & \leftrightarrow & \text{Prohibited} \sim F \\ \updownarrow & & \updownarrow \\ \sim \text{Non-commanded } F & \leftrightarrow & \sim \text{Permitted} \sim F \end{array}$$

As is apparent from the schema, Bentham's statements (1)–(4) render the concepts *Commanded, Prohibited, Non-commanded,* and *Permitted* interdefinable (cf. Raz, 1970, p. 56). Accordingly, if Bentham's logic were to be represented in a modern calculus for deontic logic, one of the operators—for example *Commanded*—could be chosen as primitive and the others defined by what would then be definitions (1)–(4).

Statement (5) has already been encountered above (p. 6) in connection with the interpretation of Bentham's logic. (5) is, given (1)–(4), equivalent to

(5′) $\quad$ Commanded $F \rightarrow$ Permitted F

and to

(5″) $\quad$ $\sim$(Commanded F & Commanded $\sim F$).

Whilst (1)–(4) deal with the relation between the four concepts (or operators) *Commanded, Prohibited, Non-commanded* and *Permitted,* and are essentially definitions, (5) is a more genuine principle of deontic logic. This is more apparent from (5″), where the statement is formulated entirely in terms of the concept *Commanded*; (5″) is clearly unlike (1)–(4) which merely allow the possibility of substituting the concept *Commanded* by other concepts. Were Bentham's logic to be represented as a modern calculus of deontic logic, (5″) would have the status of an axiom—in fact, the only axiom—in his logic. (The modern, so-called standard deontic logic contains an axiom corresponding to (5″) together with an additional axiom and a rule of inference; see below, Chapter 2.)

The conclusions Bentham draws from (1)–(5) are summarised in the following statement concerning whether a certain action is commanded, prohibited, non-commanded or permitted ("let us advert at present to the act: and let us state the condition into which it may be said to be put"):

First, it may be commanded: it is then left unprohibited: and it is not prohibited nor left uncommanded. 2. It may be prohibited: it is then left uncommanded: and it is not commanded nor permitted (that is left unprohibited). 3. It may be left uncommanded: it is then not commanded: but it may be either prohibited or permitted: yet so as that if it be in the one case it is not in the other. 4. It may be permitted: it is then not prohibited: but it may be either commanded or left uncommanded: yet so as that if it be in the one case, it is not in the other, as before. (1970*b*, p. 97)

Using the logical tools already introduced, Bentham's statements can be represented as follows (where numbers on the left correspond to the numbers in the passage just quoted):

		Deduction:
1a.	Commanded $F \rightarrow$ Permitted F (Non-prohibited F).	From (2) and (5).
1b.	Commanded $F \rightarrow \sim$Prohibited F.	=(5).
1c.	Commanded $F \rightarrow \sim$Non-commanded F.	From (1).
2a.	Prohibited $F \rightarrow$ Non-commanded F.	From (1) and (5).
2b.	Prohibited $F \rightarrow \sim$Commanded F.	From (5).
2c.	Prohibited $F \rightarrow \sim$Permitted F.	From (2).
3.	Non-commanded $F \rightarrow$ (($\sim$Commanded F & Prohibited F & $\sim$Permitted F) v ($\sim$Commanded F & $\sim$Prohibited F & Permitted F)).	From (1) and (2).
4.	Permitted $F \rightarrow$ (($\sim$Prohibited F & Commanded F & $\sim$Non-commanded F) v ($\sim$Prohibited F & $\sim$Commanded F & Non-commanded F)).	From (1) and (2).

Bentham's conclusions can be obtained from (1)–(5) with ordinary sentential logic; the right-hand column indicates which of (1)–(5) are required for the deductions.

Finally, it may be observed that for each F exactly one of the following alternatives obtains:

(i) Commanded F;
(ii) Prohibited F;
(iii) Permitted F & Non-commanded F.

Accordingly, (i)–(iii) give a partition of the logical possibilities into three mutually incompatible and jointly exhaustive alternatives. Bentham speaks of these alternatives as *command, prohibition* and *inactivity* (1970*b*, p. 111; cf. below, Chapter 3, pp. 111 ff.).

5. *A parenthetical note on Bentham and Leibniz*

Before proceeding to Bentham's theory of rights and obligations, which is the focus here, I shall conclude the discussion of Bentham's logic of imperation by noting the following: In calling attention to Bentham as a precursor of deontic logic and evaluating his claims of priority in this area (see above, p. 6), it should not be forgotten that Bentham's contribution to the subject was clearly anticipated by Gottfried Wilhelm Leibniz. Leibniz distinguished between four legal concepts or modalities corresponding to Bentham's, as shown by the following scheme:

Leibniz:	*Bentham:*
Just (or Licit)	Permitted
Injust (or Illicit)	Prohibited
Obligatory	Commanded
Omissible	Non-commanded

(See *Elementa Juris Naturalis*, probably dating from 1671, in Leibniz, 1930, pp. 465 ff.) Leibniz's view of the logic of those four concepts, as explicitly stated by him, can be summarised in the following scheme, where the concepts in each horizontal row behave logically in the same way (1930, p. 469):

Just (or Licit)	Possible	Some
Injust (or Illicit)	Impossible	No
Obligatory	Necessary	Every
Omissible	Contingent	Some not

From this scheme, considered in the setting of Leibniz's logic of the concepts *Possible—Impossible—Necessary—Contingent* and *Some—No—Every—Some not*, it is apparent that Bentham's principles of imperational logic did not, in fact, develop the subject beyond what was already contained in Leibniz's theory. Bentham's contribution, however, was clearly quite independent of Leibniz's earlier work in this field, since the aforementioned manuscript was not yet published in Bentham's time.

(Some fragments were published in the middle of the nineteenth century, see Trendelenburg, 1855, pp. 265 ff.) It may be added that further important contributions after Leibniz and Bentham were absent up to the twentieth century until, amongst others, Mally (1926) and von Wright (1951).

6. *Obligation and types of right: Introduction*

Bentham distinguishes between two basic types of right: the *right to a service* and *liberty*. Both of these are explicated in terms of the concept *obligation*, which is therefore a more basic concept than *right* for Bentham. As with his logic of imperation, the theory of the two basic types of right has only recently attracted attention (see Hart, 1973; cf. 1953, pp. 15 f. and 1962, pp. 313 ff.; also Lyons, 1969). Hart and Lyons have in particular discussed the analysis Bentham gave of each of the two basic types of right, his analysis of *right to a service* ("the beneficiary theory") being criticised by Hart but defended by Lyons.

An account of Bentham's analysis of *obligation*, *right to a service* and *liberty* is a necessary starting point for what follows. Particular emphasis, however, will be laid on the connection between this analysis and Bentham's logic of imperation described above. Precisely because Bentham's theory of obligations and rights can be seen against a background of a deontic logic—albeit a rudimentary one—it is of greater originality and interest than the theories of many who came later.

To facilitate presentation of what follows, certain variables will be introduced according to the following conventions:

(1) $p, q, r, \ldots$ are variables for persons;
(2) $A_p, B_p, \ldots$ are variables for action-propositions, where p is the agent;
(3) $A_q, B_q, \ldots$ are variables for action-propositions, where q is the agent;
etc.

Accordingly, A_p is read "p performs action A", B_q as "q performs action B", and so on.

A more refined logical apparatus for dealing with action-propositions will be introduced at a later stage in accordance with Kanger's conceptual machinery (see below, p. 38 and Chapter 2); Bentham's theory is not so sophisticated as to justify such refinements at this stage.

7. *Obligation*

I have mentioned earlier that expressions such as "it is commanded", "it is prohibited (forbidden)", etc., are used primarily, according to Bentham, in order to describe "the state which things are in, in consequence of the arrangements taken by the legislator" (see above, p. 7). The same holds for statements containing the term *obligation.* The legislator "imposes obligations" by enacting a law of type command or prohibition:

> ... where the provision of the law is a command or a prohibition, it creates an offence: if a command, it is the non-performance of the act that is the offence: if a prohibition, the performance. ... Moreover the law, in constituting any act an offence, is said to impose thereby an *obligation* on the persons in question not to perform it ... (1970*b*, p. 121)

Thus, to take an example from Bentham himself (1970*b*, p. 96), the following two statements are equivalent:

(1) It is forbidden to any mother to starve her children.
(2) Every mother has an obligation not to starve her children.

When the legislator enacts a law of type command or prohibition (and thereby imposes obligations) there is always, according to Bentham, a *party favoured by the law*—a person (or several people) "on whom it is the *intention* at least of the legislator to confer a benefit" (1970*b*, p. 55). Bentham does not deny that it is possible that a person has an obligation to do something although there is no party, not even himself, who actually is favoured by the fact that the obligation is carried out. He mentions cases where a person's obligation is "barren", "ascetic", or "useful to none" (1962, p. 181, 221; cf. Hart, 1973, p. 177). On the other hand, Bentham excludes the possibility of cases where a person has an obligation either to do or abstain from doing something although there is no one who is *intended to be favoured* (concerning the importance of this distinction, cf. Lyons, 1969, pp. 176 ff.). For each command or prohibition there is, according to Bentham, necessarily a party who is at least intended to be favoured:

... in every law there must also be some person or persons who are favoured by it: meaning a person on whom it is the *intention* at least of the legislator to confer a benefit. To suppose the contrary is to suppose the legislator to act without a motive. Possibly indeed the party favoured may be one who ought not thus to have been favoured: possibly no other than the legislator himself: still at any rate somebody who is favoured by it there must be. No effect without a cause: no act, no law without a motive. (1970*b*, pp. 55 f.; cf. p. 53, 58)

Bentham stresses as a desideratum that the legislator, when formulating a law, should make it explicit which party is intended to be favoured (1970*b*, p. 64).

The obvious move is to interpret Bentham's account in such a way that obligation is a relation between parties—between a party who is *bound* (*coerced*) and a party who is *intended to be favoured*. For example (cf. (1) and (2) above):

(3) Every mother has, in favour of each of her children (versus each of her children), an obligation not to starve it.

Possibly Bentham would hold that the relation *obligation* should have a place for a third party who may, in certain cases, be distinct from the other two: a party who is *exposed to suffer* (see 1970*b*, p. 54). However, this will be disregarded in what follows.

That an obligation in Bentham's sense is primarily a relation between a party bound and a party favoured does not exclude the possibility of using the term "obligation" without specifying the party favoured. It is possible to use a statement of the form

(4) p has an obligation to the effect that A_p,

that is to say, a statement which only specifies the party bound. Bentham's position, according to which there necessarily is a party favoured, entails, however, that the following holds:

(5) Necessarily: p has an obligation to the effect that A_p *if and only if* for some q, p has versus q an obligation to the effect that A_p.

Most frequently a party other than the party bound shall, according to the intentions of the legislator, be favoured by the carrying out of the obligation: so-called *extra-regarding* obligation (1970*b*, p. 57). In less common cases, however, the person who has the obligation has it only in his own interest: so-called merely *self-regarding* obligation (1970*b*, p. 57). The distinction between the two cases is given by the following statements:

(6) For some q such that $p \neq q$, p has versus q an obligation to the effect that A_p; (*Extra-regarding obligation*)

(7) p has versus p an obligation to the effect that A_p, but for no q such that $p \neq q$, p has versus q an obligation to the effect that A_p. (*Merely self-regarding obligation*)

8. *Right to a service*

When the legislator enacts a law of type command or prohibition and thereby imposes obligations, he simultaneously creates *rights to services*. As an illustration, the statement already mentioned above

(1) Every mother has, in favour of each of her children, an obligation not to starve it

says the same as

(2) Every child has versus its mother a right not to be starved by her.

The example shows that *right to a service* (like obligation) is for Bentham a relation between two parties: *right to a service* is a relation between a party favoured and a party bound. This relation is usually described as "correlative" to the relation *obligation* (Hart, 1973, p. 176; Lyons, 1973, p. 125). By this, it is meant that the following two statements are equivalent:

(3) p has versus q an obligation to the effect that A_p.

(4) q has versus p a right to the effect that A_p.

In (4) "obligation" has been substituted by "right", and the first two occurrences of variables over persons have been interchanged. However, if *right to a service* and *obligation* are said to be correlatives, a reservation must be made. According to Bentham's theory, an obligation does not correspond to a right to a service if it is *merely self-regarding*. Consequently, statement (3) cannot be substituted by statement (4) if p and q denote the same person. Alternatively expressed, the statement

(5) p has versus p an obligation to the effect that A_p

is, according to Bentham, a meaningful statement, whereas the statement

(6) p has versus p a right to the effect that A_p

is meaningless. Someone can have an obligation towards himself, but not a right to a service against himself.

This entails that the relation *right to a service*, as distinct from the relation *obligation*, is irreflexive. *Right to a service* is "correlative" only to a subrelation of *obligation*.

9. *Liberty: Introduction*

The other basic type of right is explained by Bentham in the following way:

> You have a *right* to perform whatever you are not under obligation to abstain from the performance of. (1962, p. 218)

This concept "right" is adopted as basic by a number of earlier philosophers in this area; for example, in Thomas Hobbes' *Leviathan* (Hobbes, 1962, p. 103, 215; cf. Pound, 1959, pp. 66 f.). "Right" can be replaced by *liberty* in both Hobbes and Bentham.

Whilst *right to a service* always concerns the action of another person, someone's *liberty* always concerns his own action. A statement about liberty has the form

(1) p is at liberty as regards A_p.

Statement (1) can be explained in terms of "obligation" or in terms of "permitted":

(2) p has no obligation to the effect that not A_p.
(3) It is permitted that A_p.

Note that according to (1) *liberty* is not a relation between two parties. I shall return to this question later (when speaking of "vested liberty").

The fact that a person is at liberty with respect to a certain action entails, according to Bentham, that he is favoured in a certain sense, although only "in a negative sort of way". He who is at liberty to do something is "favoured in point of agency" (1970*b*, p. 57).

10. *Naked and vested liberty*

A person's liberty to do something is, according to Bentham, of the type *naked* or *vested*. It is naked if it is combined with freedom for other people to prevent the action in question, and is vested if it is combined with an obligation for others not to prevent the action (1962, p. 218).

Concerning naked liberty it should be pointed out that Bentham maintains the principle that everything which is not "actively" forbidden by the legislator is permitted:

> ... every efficient law whatever may be considered as a limitation or exception, grafted on a pre-established universal law of liberty ... The non-commanding and permissive phases of the law placed side by side and turned towards the universal system of human actions are expressed by the before-mentioned universal law of liberty: a boundless expanse in which the several efficient laws appear as so many spots; like islands and continents projecting out of the ocean: or like material bodies scattered over the immensity of space. (1970*b*, pp. 119 f.)

In "the state of nature" where there are no laws enacted by a human legislator, each person has the liberty to perform or to refrain from any actions whatsoever; the concept *naked liberty* comprises all people and actions under these circumstances:

> As yet there is no law in the land. The legislator hath not yet entered upon his office. ... As yet all acts therefore are free: all persons as against the law are at liberty. (1970 *b*, p. 253)

In a society where there exists a legal order, liberties are often of the type *vested liberties*—a relation between two parties defined in the following way:

p has versus q a vested liberty with respect to $A_p =_{\text{def.}}$
p is at liberty with respect to A_p, and
p has versus q a right that q does not prevent A_p.

In this sense a person often has, according to Bentham, a vested liberty towards the so-called "subordinate powerholders" (as, for example, the authorities subordinate to the sovereign of the state; cf. Chapter 6):

... a mandate ... in the form of a prohibition is addressed to subordinate powerholders in general restraining them from breaking in upon the liberty of the party ... to which may be added in some cases a law of a particular kind including the sovereign himself under the same restriction. (1970*b*, p. 99)

A person can also have a vested liberty towards other agents:

... liberty as against those who first in consideration of the effect of their conduct upon the happiness of society, and afterwards in consideration of the course taken against them by the law, may be styled *wrong-doers*. (1970*b*, p. 254)

That vested liberty is primarily a relation between parties does not preclude the possibility of speaking simply of a person's vested liberty *simpliciter* to act or obstain fom acting. It is understood that the person in question here has a vested liberty against everybody else to act or refrain from acting in the way in question:

p has a vested liberty with respect to $A_p =_{\text{def.}}$
p is at liberty with respect to A_p, and, for each q such that $p \neq q$, p has a right versus q that q does not prevent A_p.

As an example, consider the following:

How can I possess the *right* of going into all the streets of a city? It is because there exists no obligation which hinders me, and because everybody is bound by an obligation not to hinder me. (1962, p. 181)

11. *Liberty as a right conferred by the law*

A person's liberty can, in certain cases, be a *right conferred by the law*, in which case *vested liberty* is concerned; that is, liberty combined with a prohibition against interference:

It is by creating duties and by nothing else that the law can create rights. When the law gives you a right, what does it do? it makes me liable to punishment in case of my doing any of those acts which would have the effect of disturbing you in the exercise of that right. (1970*b*, p. 249, n. b; cf. 1962, p. 181)

The question whether a person's liberty is a right conferred by the law seems, according to Bentham, to depend upon whether it is based on an "active" permission on the part of the legislator. If the legislator actively permits a certain action, a prohibition is "implied" against interference by subordinate powerholders:

In this case indeed the effect is produced not so much from the literal import of the mandate itself, as from another mandate which is so connected with it that if not expressed it may of course be looked upon as implied. I mean a mandate which in the form of a prohibition is addressed to subordinate powerholders in general restraining them from breaking in upon the liberty of the party whom the uncoercive mandate in question is meant to favour. Thus much must be inferred of course: to which may be added in some cases a law of a particular kind including the sovereign himself under the same restriction. (1970*b*, p. 99)

It is not clear whether Bentham means that an active permission from the legislator "implies" a prohibition against interference by other agents.

12. *The logic of obligations and rights*

Bentham's logic of imperation provides the basis of a logic of rights and obligations. Introducing the following abbreviations:

Obligation (p, A_p) for:
p has an obligation to the effect that A_p;
Obligation (p, q, A_p) for:
p has versus q an obligation to the effect that A_p;

the logic of rights and obligations can be represented by the following axioms and definitions:

Axioms:

B1. $\sim$(Obligation(p, A_p) & Obligation$(p, \sim A_p)$).
B2. Obligation$(p, q, A_p) \rightarrow$ Obligation(p, A_p).

Definitions:

Def. 1: Right$(q, p, A_p) =_{\text{def.}}$ Obligation(p, q, A_p) & $(p \neq q)$.
Def. 2: Liberty$(p, A_p) =_{\text{def.}}$ $\sim$Obligation$(p, \sim A_p)$.

That these axioms and definitions hold good in Bentham's theory is obvious from what has been said in earlier sections on his logic of imperation and his analysis of the concepts *obligation*, *right* and *liberty*. B1 is an instance of the axiom

$$\sim(\text{Commanded } F \ \& \ \text{Commanded} \sim F)$$

given earlier, and B2 says that

It is commanded that A_p

is a logical consequence of

It is, in favour of q, commanded that A_p.

Def. 1 says that the relation *right to a service* is "correlative" to the relation obligation in those cases where the parties are not identical. Def. 2, finally, says that the liberty to perform an action is the same as the absence of obligation to abstain from the action.

B1 and B2, together with Def. 1 and Def. 2, give a number of theorems for obligations and rights when supplemented by the usual sentential logic. I shall mention some of the more important theorems, which can be represented in the following schema (where the arrow represents truth-functional implication):

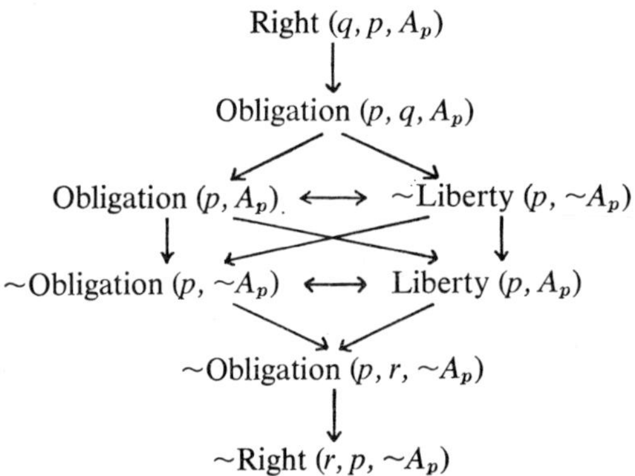

Without going into the proofs of all twelve theorems, consider by way of example

(i) $\sim \text{Liberty}(p, \sim A_p) \rightarrow \text{Liberty}(p, A_p)$

which occurs in the schema. It is easily shown that (i) is a theorem by the following steps: The negation of (i) is, given sentential logic, equivalent to

(ii) $\sim \text{Liberty}(p, \sim A_p) \ \& \sim \text{Liberty}(p, A_p)$.

Statement (ii) is equivalent, according to Def. 2, to

(iii) Obligation(p, A_p) & Obligation(p, $\sim A_p$),

and the conjunction of (iii) and axiom B1 is contradictory; hence, (i) is a theorem.

The theorems occurring in the schema are not, of course, stated by Bentham in this form; neither are they systematically collected together and explicitly stated in a single context. But the schema shows that his analysis of *obligation*, *right* and *liberty* together with his logic of imperation provides a basis, requiring only to be complemented by certain relatively trivial rules of sentential logic, from which a logical system for basic legal positions can be developed. Because Bentham's theory of obligations and rights can be seen against a background of a rudimentary deontic logic there is a sense in which his theory is more advanced than the later theories of Austin and Hohfeld.

III. *Austin's Theory*

Whilst Bentham's theory of rights remained relatively unknown until the beginning of the 1970s, Austin's theory has for a long time attracted attention and comment. However, it can be shown that Austin did not add anything essentially new to Bentham's earlier theory; in fact, his theory is less developed than Bentham's, particularly since there is no background of deontic logic.

It was shown above that Bentham distinguished between two basic types of right: the right to a service and liberty. Moreover, liberty as a right conferred by the law is a combination of liberty as such and the right to a service. These concepts and distinctions have direct counterparts in Austin's theory, which can best be shown by a number of quotations.

1. The correlation obligation—right (to a service):

A relative obligation is incumbent upon one party, and correlates with a right residing in another party. (1863, II, p. 5)

2. The definition of right (to a service) in terms of "it is commanded", etc.:

A party commanded by the sovereign to do or to forbear, and a party *towards* whom he is commanded to do or to forbear. The party to whom the sovereign expresses or intimates the command, is said to lie under a duty ... The party *towards* whom he is commanded to do or to forbear, is said to have a *right* to the acts or forbearances in question. (1863, II, p. 59)

3. Right (to a service) as a relation between parties:

... all rights reside in persons, and are rights to acts or forbearances on the part of *other* persons. Considered as corresponding to duties, or as being rights to *acts* or *forbearances*, rights may be said to avail *against* persons. (1863, II, p. 30)

4. Right (to a service) as an irreflexive relation:

Every right supposes distinct parties ... duties towards oneself and duties towards persons indefinitely, can scarcely be said to correlate with rights. (1863, II, p. 59)

5. Liberty as the absence of obligation:

... Political or Civil Liberty:—a term which, not unfrequently, is synonymous with *right*; but which often denotes simply *exemption from obligation*, conferred in a peculiar manner: namely by the indirect or circuitous process which is styled "*permission*". (1863, II, p. 3)
Civil, Political, or Legal Liberty, is the absence of Legal Restraint, whether such restraint has never been imposed, or, having been imposed, has been withdrawn. (1863, II, p. 16)

6. Liberty as a right—a combination of liberty as such and right to a service:

Liberty and Right are synonymous; since the liberty of acting according to one's will would be altogether illusory if it were not protected from obstruction. There is however this difference between the terms. In Liberty, the prominent or leading idea is, the absence of legal restraint; whilst the security or protection for the enjoyment of that liberty is the secondary idea. Right, on the other hand, *de*notes the protection and *con*notes the absence of restraint. (1863, II, p. 16)

Note that Austin's use of language in these passages is in certain respects less exact than Bentham's. Take *liberty*, for example. Austin's definition of liberty as "exemption from legal obligation" is less precise than Bentham's account, according to which the liberty to perform an action is the same as the absence of an obligation to abstain from that action, and the liberty to abstain from an action is the same as the absence of an obligation to perform the action. (Probably Austin is concerned in these passages with so-called *bilateral liberty;* that is to say, cases where a person does not have an obligation either to perform or to abstain from the action. Cf. Hart, 1973, pp. 175 f.)

Another respect in which Austin's use of language is less precise than Bentham's concerns the concept *right to a service.* When Austin speaks of a right as "correlative" to (relative) obligation, he distinguishes between a party who is "commanded by the sovereign to do or forbear" and a party "towards whom he is commanded to do or forbear". The latter party is said to have a right against the former party. Austin's expression "towards whom" is here less precise than Bentham's "*in favour of* whom". The policeman who is ordered to arrest someone is ordered to perform a certain action towards him, but not *in favour of* him. According to Bentham's usage one should say in this case that the person under arrest is *exposed to suffer* (cf. above, p. 14) whilst the *state* or the *public* is *intended to be favoured.*

Austin's obscurity on this point can, however, be supplemented with another comment indicating that his concept *right to a service* is in fact narrower than the above passage suggests; narrower than Bentham's in fact. Austin's criterion for a person's having a right to a service against someone else is that he who has the right can enforce the fulfilment of the obligation by civil action at court:

> The test of a right:—that (independently of positive provision) the acts or forbearances are not incapable of being enforced civilly or in the way of civil action: *i.e.* at the discretion or pleasure of the party towards whom they are to be done or observed. ... Right;—the capacity or power of exacting from another or others acts or forbearances;—is nearest to a true definition. (1863, II, p. 63)

(Speaking of Austin's criterion, the reader may be reminded of the fact that in English law, even where a civil action at court is allowed, the so-called specific performance is not granted unrestrictedly. See, for example, Treitel, 1962, pp. 625 ff.)

A person can have an obligation although there is no party who, according to Austin's criterion, has a corresponding right (to a service) against him; in that case the obligation is, according to Austin, *absolute* (as distinct from *relative*). In cases of this type a certain action is indeed prescribed or forbidden, but there is no person who can, by civil action at court, enforce the fulfilment of the obligation. For example:

> Jones has an obligation not to appear drunk in a public place.
> Jones has an obligation not to subject his dog to cruelty.

To such cases belong those where there is no determinate person towards whom the duty is to be observed:

> ... where there is no determinate person towards whom it [the duty] is observed, it is incapable of being enforced civilly. (1863, II, p. 63)

But in addition there are cases of this kind where the obligation is "only self-regarding":

> For to talk of a man enforcing a duty against himself is absurd. (1863, II, p. 63)

The concept of right given by this criterion of Austin's is narrower than Bentham's concept *right to a service*. It cannot be the case that a person is a claimant according to Austin's criterion although he is not intended to be favoured according to Bentham's criterion of rights. (On the distinction between claimant and beneficiary, cf. Lyons, 1969, pp. 174 f.) On the other hand, there are examples of the converse: a person can be intended to be favoured without being a claimant (see Dan. Lyons, 1965, pp. 119 ff.; Hart, 1973, pp. 191 ff., 195 f.). The relation *right* according to Austin's criterion is thus a subrelation or *subtype* of the relation defined by Bentham. Austin's definition of this subrelation is based on a number of additional concepts over and above those discussed here, namely *power* or *capacity*, *enforcing an obligation* and *civil action*.

The possibility of defining and classifying different subtypes of the general relation *right to a service* will crop up again in another connection later; there is in Kanger's theory of atomic types of right a classification of subtypes which will be presented in due course. However, Kanger does not proceed as Austin does, defining these subtypes with the help of new concepts, but rather by certain combinations of the concepts originally introduced.

IV. *Hohfeld's Theory*

1. *The basic conceptions*

Hohfeld's theory of basic types of rights is mainly concerned with the interdefinability of the four concepts within each of the following two groups:

1. Right, duty, no-right, privilege.
2. Power, liability, disability, immunity.

The concepts in the first group are closely related to the concepts *right* (to a service), *obligation* and *liberty* in Bentham and Austin. One of the examples Hohfeld considers is the following:

> ... if X has a right against Y that he shall stay off the former's land, the correlative (and equivalent) is that Y is under a duty toward X to stay off the place. ... whereas X has a *right* or *claim* that Y, the other man, should stay off the land, he himself has the *privilege* of entering on the land; or, in equivalent words, X does not have a duty to stay off. (1923, pp. 38 f.)

The concepts in the second group, on the other hand, are of a more specific character, concerning a person's ability or disability to change the legal relations prevailing between him and other people. A person can—by promising, for example—bring it about that he has a duty towards another to perform a certain action. Or by remitting a debt, a person can have the legal power of bringing it about that a certain other person no longer has a duty towards him in respect of payment of the debt. Hohfeld presents the following example:

> X, the owner of ordinary personal property "in a tangible object" has the power to extinguish his own legal interest (rights, powers, immunities, etc.) through that totality of operative facts known as abandonment; and—simultaneously and correlatively—to create in other persons privileges and powers relating to the abandoned object,—e.g., the power to acquire title to the latter by appropriating it. *Similarly*, X has the power to transfer his interest to Y, —that is, to extinguish his own interest and concomitantly create in Y a new and corresponding interest. So also X has the power to create contractual obligations of various kinds. (1923, pp. 51 f.)

The account given in the next sections of Hohfeld's theory will be concerned only with the concepts in the first group; that is, *right*, *duty*, *no-right* and *privilege*. The concept *power* together with the interrelated concepts of the second group will be considered later (Chapter 6). His theory for the concepts in the first group can be summarised in the following three points:

(i) *Right*, *duty*, *no-right*, and *privilege* are interdefinable according to a scheme of "opposites" and "correlatives".

(ii) *Right*, *duty*, *no-right* and *privilege* are relations between two parties with respect to an action of one of the parties.

(iii) *Right*, *duty*, *no-right* and *privilege* belong to "the basic conceptions of the law", "the lowest common denominators of the law" (1923, p. 27, 64).

2. *Interdefinability*

Using $p, q, r, ..., A_p, A_q, ...$ as before (above, p. 12), Hohfeld's thesis on the interdefinability between *right*, *duty*, *no-right* and *privilege* can be presented in the following schema of valid statements:

$$\begin{array}{ccc} \text{Right}(q, p, A_p) & \leftrightarrow & \text{Duty}(p, q, A_p) \\ \updownarrow & & \updownarrow \\ \sim\text{No-right}(q, p, A_p) & \leftrightarrow & \sim\text{Privilege}(p, q, \sim A_p) \end{array}$$

or

$$\begin{array}{ccc} \text{Privilege}(p, q, A_p) & \leftrightarrow & \text{No-right}(q, p, \sim A_p) \\ \updownarrow & & \updownarrow \\ \sim\text{Duty}(p, q, \sim A_p) & \leftrightarrow & \sim\text{Right}(q, p, \sim A_p) \end{array}$$

Hohfeld expresses the equivalences in this schema with the help of the notions of *opposite* and *correlative* (1923, p. 36):

Jural opposites:

$$\left\{\begin{array}{l}\text{right}\\ \text{no-right}\end{array}\right.$$

$$\left\{\begin{array}{l}\text{duty}\\ \text{privilege}\end{array}\right.$$

Jural correlatives:

$$\left\{\begin{array}{l}\text{right}\\ \text{duty}\end{array}\right.$$

$$\left\{\begin{array}{l}\text{no-right}\\ \text{privilege}\end{array}\right.$$

This schema of opposites and correlatives is somewhat misleading, not being entirely in agreement with the definitions of "opposite" and "correlative" that Hohfeld seems to have had in mind (cf. Kanger & Kanger, 1966, pp. 102 f.). That two "jural relations" T and T' are opposites apparently means for Hohfeld that, of necessity, T holds between two parties with respect to an action performed by one of them if and only if T' does not hold between the two parties with respect to the same action. In this sense *right* and *no-right* are opposites:

$$\text{Right}(q, p, A_p) \leftrightarrow \sim\text{No-right}(q, p, A_p).$$

However, *duty* and *privilege* are not opposites in this sense. Hohfeld himself points out that:

> ... always, when it is said that a given privilege is the mere negation of a *duty*, what is meant, of course, is a duty having a content or tenor precisely *opposite* to that of the privilege in question. ... as regards Y, X's privilege of entering [on X's own land] is the precise negation of a duty *to stay off*. (1923, p. 39)

In the equivalence schema above this principle is expressed by the statement

$$\text{Duty}(p, q, A_p) \leftrightarrow \sim\text{Privilege}(p, q, \sim A_p)$$

where A_p occurs on the left-hand side, but $\sim A_p$ on the right.

A similar inexactitude attaches to the schema of correlatives. That T and T' are correlatives means, apparently, that, of necessity, T holds between q and p with respect to A_p if and only if T' holds between p and q with respect to A_p. In this sense *right* and *duty* are correlatives:

$$\text{Right}(q, p, A_p) \leftrightarrow \text{Duty}(p, q, A_p);$$

but *no-right* and *privilege* are not correlatives in this same sense. Referring to Hohfeld's own example, Y's no-right against X that X shall stay off X's own land is not correlative to X's privilege against Y to stay off, but rather X's privilege against Y of *entering* (onto X's land). This is expressed in the equivalence schema by the statement

$$\text{Privilege}(p, q, A_p) \leftrightarrow \text{No-right}(q, p, \sim A_p),$$

where, as before, A_p occurs to the left but $\sim A_p$ to the right.

At the time he wrote (1913), Hohfeld's account of interdefinability, summarised in the equivalence schema above, represented a considerable step forward in respect of logical precision over other theories that were readily available then. (However, see Dickey, 1971, for some comments on Hohfeld's debt to John W. Salmond.) Compared with Bentham's theory, however—then virtually unknown—his theory is, logically speaking, the poorer. A natural addendum to the equivalence schema would be to accept as valid the following statement:

(1) $\sim(\text{Duty}(p, q, A_p) \;\&\; \text{Duty}(p, q, \sim A_p))$.

According to the equivalence schema, this can be reformulated, giving

(1′) $\text{Duty}(p, q, A_p) \rightarrow \text{Privilege}(p, q, A_p)$.

(Note that (1′) deals with duty and privilege "of the same content or tenor".)

(1) and (1′) entail excluding the possibility that someone can have both a duty to act in a certain way and a duty to abstain from acting in the same way towards one and the same person. The statements exclude the possibility of genuinely conflicting obligations towards one individual. (Regarding conflicting obligations towards different people, see below, p. 32; cf. also Chapter 2, pp. 82 ff.)

Statement (1) is valid in Bentham's theory; from

(2) $\text{Obligation}(p, q, A_p) \;\&\; \text{Obligation}(p, q, \sim A_p)$

it follows that

(3) $\text{Commanded } A_p \;\&\; \text{Commanded} \sim A_p$,

which is contradictory according to Bentham's logic. But Hohfeld offers no argument in favour of accepting (1) or (1′); he talks only of the statements "$\text{Duty}(p, q, A_p)$" and "$\text{Privilege}(p, q, A_p)$" being consistent, which does not, of course, amount to saying the latter follows from the former:

> ... if, for some special reason, X has contracted with Y to go on the former's own land, it is obvious that X has, as regards Y, both the privilege of entering and the *duty of entering*. The privilege is perfectly consistent with this sort of duty,—for the latter is of the same content or tenor as the privilege ... (1923, p. 39)

Had Hohfeld accepted (1), his theory would have been considerably enriched by a number of theorems such as:

(1a) $\text{Duty}(p, q, A_p) \rightarrow \sim\text{Right}(q, p, \sim A_p)$;
(1b) $\text{Right}(q, p, A_p) \rightarrow \text{No-right}(q, p, \sim A_p)$;
(1c) $\text{Right}(q, p, A_p) \rightarrow \sim\text{Duty}(p, q, \sim A_p)$;
(1d) $\text{Right}(q, p, A_p) \rightarrow \text{Privilege}(p, q, A_p)$;
(1e) $\sim\text{Privilege}(p, q, A_p) \rightarrow \text{Privilege}(p, q, \sim A_p)$.

3. *Right, duty, no-right and privilege as relations between two parties*

Right, duty, no-right and *privilege* are always considered by Hohfeld as relations between two parties with respect to an action or an abstention from acting on the part of one of the parties. He does not comment on statements of the kind

(1) p has a duty to perform action A,
(2) p has a privilege to perform action A,

where only one party is mentioned. Neither does his account suggest any obvious interpretation of (1) and (2). One possibility would be to interpret (1) and (2) as involving quantification along the lines

(1′) There is someone versus whom p has a duty to perform action A.
(2′) p has a privilege towards everyone to perform action A.

Given this interpretation, it is possible to derive from Hohfeld's equivalence schema the statement

$$\text{Duty}(p, A_p) \leftrightarrow \sim\text{Privilege}(p, \sim A_p)$$

which is in line with the relation between the concepts *duty* and *privilege* as understood by Hohfeld. But this interpretation of (1) and (2) excludes the possibility of *absolute obligation* (cf. above, p. 14, 23) and is not, moreover, the only conceivable interpretation (see Hansson, 1970, p. 244).

4. *Privilege and protection from interference*

As is apparent from the equivalence schema (above, p. 26), the statement

(3) *p* has versus *q* a privilege to perform action *A*

is interpreted by Hohfeld along the lines

(3′) *p* has versus *q* no duty to abstain from action *A*.

Statements (3) and (3′) are, according to Hohfeld, compatible with the following equivalent statements:

(4) *q* has versus *p* a privilege to prevent *p* from performing action *A*

(4′) *p* has versus *q* a no-right that *q* does not prevent *p* from performing action *A*.

He presents the following example:

A, B, C and D, being the owners of the salad, might say to X: "Eat the salad, if you can; you have our license to do so, but we don't agree not to interfere with you." In such a case the privileges exist, so that if X succeeds in eating the salad, he has violated no rights of any of the parties. But it is equally clear that if A had succeeded in holding so fast to the dish that X couldn't eat the contents, no right of X would have been violated. (1923, p. 41)

Thus, from (3) it is not possible to infer

(5) *p* has versus *q* a right to the effect that *q* does not prevent *p* from performing *A*.

Of course, neither can it be inferred from (3) that *p* has a "right of non-interference" against a third party:

(6) *p* has versus *r* a right to the effect that *r* does not prevent *p* from performing action *A*.

It is a familiar occurrence in legal argument that, taking (3) as the only premise (5) and (6) are inferred. But Hohfeld would say that this is a serious mistake; whether (5) and (6) are true is a "question of justice and policy" requiring a decision on the merits of the particular case:

... a privilege or liberty ... might very conceivably exist without any peculiar concomitant rights against "third parties" as regards certain kinds of interference. Whether there should be such concomitant rights (or claims) is ultimately a question of justice and policy; and it should be considered, as such, on its merits. ... It would therefore be a *non sequitur* to conclude from the mere existence of such liberties that "third parties" are under a *duty* not to interfere, etc. (1923, p. 43)

This point of Hohfeld's is important, emphasising as it does that from the premise that a certain right relation obtains between two parties p and q with respect to an action A_p, it cannot be concluded that a certain rights relation obtains between p and q with respect to a different action B_q (q's preventing p's performance of A). Hohfeld's account here is superior to either Bentham's or Austin's, which are susceptible to criticism on precisely this point. As Hohfeld himself notes, they presuppose that *liberty* as a relation between two parties always entails that the other party has an obligation of non-prevention (cf. Hohfeld's criticism of Austin in 1923, pp. 98 ff.). Bentham and Austin are led, in consequence, to make quite misleading statements which give the impression of erasing the distinction between the two basic types of right, *the right to a service* and *liberty*; for example, when Bentham says "it is by creating duties and by nothing else that the law can create rights" and when Austin says "Liberty and Right are synonymous" (above, p. 18, 22; see also Kelsen, 1945, p. 77).

5. *Relations to third parties*

From the fact that a certain right relation obtains between the two parties p and q with respect to an action A_p it is not possible, according to Hohfeld's schema, to draw any conclusions whatever about which right relation obtains between p and a third party r, even where the same action A_p is concerned. Firstly, according to his schema,

(7) $\text{Duty}(p, q, \sim A_p) \leftrightarrow \sim \text{Privilege}(p, q, A_p)$,

and consequently, the implication

(8) $\text{Duty}(p, q, \sim A_p) \rightarrow \sim \text{Privilege}(p, q, A_p)$,

also holds. However, no support can be derived from the schema for

(9) $\text{Duty}(p, q, \sim A_p) \rightarrow \sim \text{Privilege}(p, r, A_p)$,

where the variable q on the right has been replaced by r. In other words, the schema does not lead to the conclusion that the conjunction

(10) $\text{Duty}(p, q, \sim A_p)$ & $\text{Privilege}(p, r, A_p)$

is self-contradictory. That p has the duty towards q not to perform the action A is compatible with p's having the privilege against r to perform the action A. Hohfeld himself gives an example showing that (10) does indeed describe a possibility (the example concerns the shrimp salad again):

Suppose that X, being already the legal owner of the salad, contracts with Y that he (X) will never eat this particular food. With A, B, C, D and others no such contract has been made. One of the relations now existing between X and Y is, as a consequence, fundamentally different from the relation between X and A. As regards Y, X has no privilege of eating the salad; but as regards either A or any of the others, X has such a privilege. (1923, p. 42; cf. also the example in Cook, 1938, pp. 490 ff.)

Secondly, the statement (10) should, of course, be distinguished from

(11) $\text{Duty}(p, q, \sim A_p)$ & $\text{Duty}(p, r, A_p)$,

which says that p has a duty to q with respect to $\sim A_p$ and a *duty* to r of the opposite "content or tenor". (11) describes a case of genuinely conflicting obligations towards different people. Hohfeld does not, however, seem to exclude the possibility of (11) being true. (For an argument against (11), cf. below, Chapter 2, pp. 82 ff.)

6. *Right, duty, no-right and privilege as basic conceptions*

Hohfeld gives no explication of the basic concepts of right in terms of other more fundamental concepts; nor does he suggest even the possibility of such an explication. He maintains, rather, that right, duty, no-right and privilege are amongst those concepts which are "the lowest common denominators of the law" (above, p. 3, 26). These basic legal terms Hohfeld construes as *relations* between two parties with respect to an action on the part of one of the parties, and the impersonal deontic operators such as "It is commanded that", "It is permitted that" or (cf. Kanger's theory, p. 38 below) "It shall be the case that" and "It may be the case that" make no appearance in Hohfeld's theory. However, it is not implausible to interpret Hohfeld in such a way that *privilege* is a special sort of *may* concept and *duty* a special sort of *shall* concept. Such an interpretation is supported by the account of Hohfeld's theory presented by his student, the well-known American jurist Arthur L. Corbin. In order to represent Hohfeld's distinctions "in a popular way" Corbin distinguishes between, amongst others, the following questions:

(1) What *may* A (or B) do, without societal penalty assessed for the benefit of the other?
(2) What *must* A (or B) do, under threat of societal penalty assessed for the benefit of the other? (1919, p. 165)

Corbin adds that

If we determine that A *may* conduct himself in a certain way he has a *privilege* with respect to B, and B has *no-right* that A shall not so conduct himself. If we determine that A *must* conduct himself in a certain manner he has a *duty* to B, and B has a *right* against A. (1919, p. 165)

Corbin's interpretation seems plausible provided two differences between his and the usual impersonal operators *may* and *shall* are emphasised, namely

(i) Hohfeld's *privilege* and *duty* operators do not (as for example, Kanger's *may* and *shall* do) operate on arbitrary propositions, but rather only on action-propositions.

(ii) Statements of the kind "Privilege(p, q, A_p)" and "Duty(p, q, A_p)" deal, so far as Hohfeld is concerned, only with legal relations between p and q (cf. the previous section and Hansson, 1970, pp. 241 ff.). When the statements in question are rewritten in terms of *may* and *shall*, the formulation should, therefore, follow the pattern

> It may, so far as p's legal relations to q are concerned, be the case that A_p,

and

> It shall, so far as p's legal relations to q are concerned, be the case that A_p.

Note that Hohfeld's position on the relation between the concepts *duty* and *privilege* (above, p. 26) gives, according to Corbin's interpretation, a Hohfeldian counterpart to the principle of deontic logic on interdefinability between *may* and *shall*. Hohfeld's basic principle,

$$\text{Privilege}(p, q, A_p) \leftrightarrow \sim\text{Duty}(p, q, \sim A_p),$$

is a special case of the general principle (or definition)

> It may be the case that $F \leftrightarrow$ Not: it shall be the case that not F.

Hohfeld differs from the main tradition in deontic logic (Bentham, Mally, von Wright) in his choice of basic concepts, for their primitive concepts are the impersonal operators already mentioned. (However, see Hansson, 1970, pp. 241 ff., for a deontic logic using operators similar to Hohfeld's concepts.) Kanger's theory, to be considered shortly, is based on the impersonal operators of standard deontic logic. The theory was originally conceived as an explication of Hohfeld's concepts, but should perhaps rather be seen as an independent theory.

7. *Two critics of Hohfeld: Honoré and Raz*

Hohfeld and his students (particularly Corbin) have exerted a great influence amongst analytical jurists, especially in the United States. However, his theory has often been the object of misunderstanding and unwarranted criticism. More recently criticism has arisen from the distinguished jurists A. M. Honoré and Joseph Raz, and a discussion of these points will throw more light on the nature of Hohfeld's analysis.

Honoré objects to what he refers to as "two disputable axioms adopted by Hohfeld":

> The first is that a "right" means either a claim (its usual sense) or a liberty, power or immunity. No word is available in his terminology for a collection or aggregate of claims, powers, etc., still less for a variable collection of such claims, etc. The second is that a "right", so defined, is strictly correlative with a duty, or with a disability, immunity etc. What Hohfeld does not notice or does not mind is that these axioms render impossible many of the uses of "a right" to which laymen and lawyers are accustomed. (1960, p. 456)

Honoré points out that the term *right* in legal usage is often used in statements of the following kind:

(1) Smith has a right to £100 under the contract between Smith and Jones.
(2) Smith has a right to bodily security.
(3) Smith has a right of way over Blackacre.

A statement such as one of the aforementioned does not mean the same, Honoré contends, as does one of the relational statements occurring in Hohfeld's schema. Statement (1), for example, cannot be substituted by the following statement:

(4) Smith has versus Jones a right to the effect that Jones pays £100 to Smith in fulfilment of the contract between Smith and Jones.

Statement (1) could be true while (4) is false; for example if Jones is dead or bankrupt:

... the "right to £100 under the contract" might seem to be identical with a claim for £100 against the debtor. But even this is plausible only as a description of the momentary position of the right-holder. Since there are rules of law by which duties under contract are transferred on death or insolvency to persons other than the debtor, we shall sometimes be compelled to say that the right to £100 under the contract remains but that the claim securing it is not now against the debtor but against his trustee in insolvency or executor. (1960, pp. 456 f.)

Similarly, it is not correct to translate statement (2) into

(5) Smith has versus Jones a right to the effect that Jones does not assault Smith.

Clearly, statement (2) says much more than statement (5). An analysis of (2) in Hohfeld's terms requires a conjunction of several statements of rights, such as

(6) For every x, Smith has versus x a right to the effect that x does not assault Smith,

(7) Smith has versus the state a right to the effect that the state takes measures to protect Smith from being assaulted by anybody,

and so forth.

However, Hohfeld never maintained that every statement in which the expression "a right" occurs could be translated into a single statement saying that someone stands in one of Hohfeld's relations (right, privilege, power, etc.) to another with respect to a certain action. He was fully aware that many traditional legal statements where the term "right" occurs, are more complicated. For example, the analysis of statements such as (1)–(3) must be carried out in terms of a conjunction of several statements all of which need not involve the relation *right*, as Hohfeld conceived it. Some of the conjuncts might indeed involve the relation *right*, but others might involve the relation *privilege* or *power*, or some other of Hohfeld's relations. The situation is analogous to the analysis of a statement such as

(8) Smith is the owner of Blackacre.

Here the analysis is given in terms of a conjunction of statements involving the relations *right*, *power*, *immunity*, and, perhaps, a few more. (Cf. 1923, p. 51: the owner's "legal interest" consists of "rights, powers, immunities, etc.".) Hohfeld's own use of the term "right" (where *right* is a correlative of *duty*) should not be confused with what in his opinion is the correct analysis of various traditional legal statements in which the term "right" occurs.

Possibly Honoré's point is simply a verbal one concerning the appropriate usage of the word "right". Hohfeld used the word as a sign for that relation between two people which is correlative to the relation *duty*, and possibly he wanted to reserve the word "right" for this use. Honoré, on the other hand, seems to have chosen the word "right" primarily for such more complicated legal positions as those described in (1)–(3). In that case, the dispute is merely a verbal one and not of much interest. One of Hohfeld's most important contributions, however, was to have emphasised that statements such as (1)–(3) and (8) are not what he calls "clear and direct in their meaning" (1923, p. 75), since it is not apparent from the way they are formulated that they are in fact statements about relations between people. Hohfeld quotes with approval that "all rights are really against persons" and adds that

> ... since the purpose of the law is to regulate the conduct of human beings, all jural relations must, in order to be clear and direct in their meaning, be predicated of such human beings. (1923, p. 75)

The arguments made by Honoré are fundamentally joined in by Raz and it is therefore not necessary to pursue the matter in detail. However, Raz makes a further criticism which it is worth pursuing.

According to Raz, Hohfeld made a grave mistake when "he thought that every right is a relation between no more than two persons" (1970, p. 179). Raz goes on to say that

> Hohfeld's insistence that every right is a relation between no more than two persons is completely unfounded and makes the explanation of rights *in rem* impossible ... (1970, p. 180)

The gist of his argument seems to be as follows. Suppose that Smith is the owner of Blackacre, and it is true that

(9) Smith has a right *in rem* of not being prevented from using the land pertaining to Blackacre

(9) can be roughly paraphrased along the lines

(10) Smith has a right versus everybody of not being prevented from using the land pertaining to Blackacre

(cf. Austin, 1863, II, p. 32 and 1863, III, pp. 189 ff.). Raz seems to be saying that according to (10), the relation *right* holds between Smith and many others; consequently, it is incorrect to maintain that *right* is a relation "between no more than two persons".

If this is indeed what Raz intends, his argument rests upon a fallacy of elementary logic. Statement (10) can be better formulated as

(11) For every x, Smith has a right versus x to the effect that x does not prevent Smith from using the land pertaining to Blackacre.

But that (11) is true is, of course, compatible with *right* being construed as a relation between two people with respect to an action of one of them, and it does not follow that *right* is a many-place relation between Smith, Jones, Brown, White, etc. For we should then be able to argue, by analogous reasoning, that from

(12) Smith is taller than everybody else

it follows that "taller than" is a many-place relation.

V. *Kanger's Theory*

1. *Simple types of right: Introduction*

Kanger's theory of types of right can be divided into, on the one hand, the theory of *simple* types of right, and on the other hand, the theory of *atomic* types of right. Relations such as *claim*, *power*, *freedom* and *immunity* are simple types of right, and the atomic types of right are obtained by a certain method of combination of the simple types. Accordingly, the theory of atomic types of right is based on and is a further development of the account of simple types.

Kanger's account of simple types of right falls within the tradition of Bentham, Austin and Hohfeld. However, a number of important innovations are to be found in Kanger's theory. I shall begin by drawing attention to Kanger's logical apparatus and the way he constructs statements expressing rights.

2. *The basic concepts and their logic*

Kanger's theory is based on a logical apparatus which is far more powerful than the rudimentary logic used by his predecessors in this field. The logic is based on two concepts, for which explicitly formulated logical rules are given, namely the deontic concept *It shall be the case that* and the action operator *sees to it that* (Kanger, 1971, 1972) or, in an earlier version, *causes it to be the case that* (Kanger, 1957, 1963; Kanger & Kanger, 1966). These concepts occur in contexts of the kind

(1) It shall be the case that F

and

(2) p sees to it that F,

where p is a person and F a condition; for example,

(1′) It shall be the case that the window is closed

and

(2′) Smith sees to it that the window is closed.

Formally, *It shall be the case that* and *sees to it that* are operators, the first operating on conditions and the second on ordered pairs comprising a person and a condition. This is discussed in Chapter 2. In the present chapter Kanger's theory will be presented in an informal manner. Incidentally, it should be noted that the meaning of the operators, restricted according to the logical rules governing them, can be represented in set-theoretical terms along the lines of the semantic frameworks of Kanger, Saul Kripke and Jaakko Hintikka. (Concerning *sees to it that*, see Chellas, 1969, pp. 62 ff.; Pörn, 1970, pp. 9 ff., 1971, pp. 4 f. and 1974, pp. 93 ff.; Kanger, 1972, p. 121. Concerning the legal *It shall be the case that*, see Fitting, 1969, pp. 265 f. and Kanger, 1972, p. 120.)

The concepts *It shall be the case that* and *sees to it that* can be combined in a number of ways. For example,

(3) It shall be the case that *p* sees to it that *F;*
(4) *p* sees to it that it shall be the case that *F;*
(5) It shall be the case that *p* sees to it that it shall be the case that *F;*

and so forth. Kanger's account of simple types of right is based on the combination (3) together with the variations obtained from this combination by the introduction of negation. For example

(6) It shall be the case that *p* sees to it that *not F;*
(7) It shall be the case that *not: p* sees to it that *F;*
(8) It shall be the case that *not: p* sees to it that *not F;*
(9) *Not:* it shall be the case that *p* sees to it that *F;*

and so forth.

An explication of basic types of right in terms of the combination of the two concepts *It shall be the case that* and *sees to it that* (or *causes it to be the case that*) is to be found in Kanger, 1957 (pp. 11 ff.). He seems to have been the first to propose such an account, although similar ideas have been suggested subsequently by Alan Ross Anderson (1962, pp. 36 ff., cf. 1971, pp. 29 ff.) and Frederic B. Fitch (1967, pp. 269 ff.). Ingmar Pörn proposed an explication differing from Kanger's in so far as *It shall be the case that* plays no role, but rather a primitive predicate *B* for *does badly* or *suffers something bad* is used instead (1970, pp. 44 ff.).

The logical rules governing *It shall be the case that* and *sees to it that* are expressed by Kanger in terms of the long arrow $\longrightarrow$ standing for the relation of logical consequence. (Thus, $F \longrightarrow G$ is read "G is a logical consequence of F".) There are five rules (Kanger & Kanger, 1966, p. 89):

I. If $F \longrightarrow G$, then: (It shall be the case that F) $\longrightarrow$ (It shall be the case that G).
II. (It shall be the case that F & It shall be the case that G) $\longrightarrow$ It shall be the case that (F & G).
III. (It shall be the case that F) $\longrightarrow$ (Not: it shall be the case that not F).
IV. If $F \longrightarrow G$ and $G \longrightarrow F$, then: (p sees to it that F) $\longrightarrow$ (p sees to it that G).
V. (p sees to it that F) $\longrightarrow F$.

The relation of logical consequence occurring in I–V satisfies certain commonly accepted principles, of which Kanger mentions three (Kanger & Kanger, 1966, p. 88 n. 3):

(i) If F and if $F \longrightarrow G$, then G.
(ii) If $F \longrightarrow G$, then not-$G \longrightarrow$ not-F.
(iii) If $F \longrightarrow G$ and $G \longrightarrow H$, then $F \longrightarrow H$.

Rules I–III (for *It shall be the case that*) give a logic which is somewhat weaker than the standard deontic logic, which will be further commented on in Chapter 2. For the time being, note that the logic given by I–III is much stronger than Bentham's logic of imperation which contains a principle corresponding essentially to rule III, but has nothing corresponding to rules I and II (see above, p. 9).

Rules IV and V for *sees to it that* are, to the best of my knowledge, Kanger's own innovation. To illustrate their use, consider the application of rule V to the statements

(1) Smith sees to it that Jones receives White's bankbook;
(2) Smith sees to it that Jones does not receive White's bankbook.

It follows from (1) by rule V that

(3) Jones receives White's bankbook,

and from (2), by the same rule, we have

(4) Jones does not receive White's bankbook.

From the conjunction of (1) and (2) is thus derivable:

(5) Jones receives White's bankbook and Jones does not receive White's bankbook.

But since (5) is a contradiction following from (1) and (2), these assertions, according to rule V, cannot both be true. (Note that the rules for *sees to it that* do not, however, exclude the possibility of both (1) and (2) being false.)

Statement (2) is what is often referred to as the internal negation of (1). Internal negation of action statements plays an important role in Kanger's explication of types of right, and I shall return later to the question of whether any counterpart appears in the theories of Kanger's predecessors, Bentham and Hohfeld.

3. *The construction of statements expressing rights*

Kanger's construction of statements expressing rights is different from Bentham's, Austin's and Hohfeld's, who always construed the "object" of a right of a given type as an action or a statement describing an action (an action proposition). For example,

(1) Smith has versus Jones a privilege (with respect to the action) of *entering on Smith's land;*
(2) Smith has versus Jones a right (with respect to the condition) *that Jones does not enter on Smith's land.*

Thus, Bentham speaks of the right to a *service*, and he construes liberty as liberty to *act* or to refrain from *acting* (cf. 1962, p. 159). Austin speaks expressly about *acts* and *forbearances* as the "objects" of rights and duties (1863, II, p. 18, 22). And finally, Hohfeld's examples concerning *right*, *duty*, *no-right* and *privilege* were always expressed using an infinitive or present participle of a verb, or with the help of a statement saying that a person performs an action. For example,

... if X has a right against Y that he shall *stay off the former's land*, the correlative (and equivalent) is that Y is under a duty toward X *to stay off the place.* ... whereas X has a right or claim that Y, the other man, should *stay off the land*, he himself has the privilege of *entering on the land.* (1923, pp. 38 f., my italics)

Statements expressing rights are accordingly construed by Bentham, Austin and Hohfeld along the lines

$$T(p, A_p),$$
$$T(p, q, A_p),$$
$$T(p, q, A_q),$$

where T is a type of right and the last term of the relation (A_p or A_q) is always an action or (as I chose to present the theory) an action-proposition. Thus, with Bentham, for example, we have

$$\text{Liberty}(p, A_p),$$
$$\text{Obligation}(p, q, A_p),$$
$$\text{Right}(p, q, A_q).$$

Kanger, on the other hand, allows that the "object" of a right can be a condition of any kind whatever. Statements expressing rights are construed along the lines

$$T(p, q, F),$$

where T is a type of right and F an arbitrary condition—as in Claim(p, q, F) and Freedom(p, q, F). For example,

> Smith has versus White a freedom (with respect to the condition) that Jones receives White's bankbook.

The statement "Jones receives White's bankbook" does not say that Smith, Jones, White or any other person, for that matter, performs an action.

This step of Kanger's, allowing the object of a right to be any condition at all, represents, in comparison with earlier theories, a generalisation of the theory of types of right. We shall soon see that the possibility of this generalisation in Kanger's theory depends on the explication of types of right based on combinations of *It shall be the case that* and *sees to it that*.

4. *The simple types of right and their explication*

Kanger distinguishes between the following eight simple types of right (Kanger & Kanger, 1966, pp. 86 f.):

claim,	counter-claim,
freedom,	counter-freedom,
power,	counter-power,
immunity,	counter-immunity,

Kanger's explication of these simple types of right is given in the following schema, where in each case 1–8, (a) is the statement expressing the right to be explicated, (b) is the explication and (c) is a reformulation of (b) to assist reading and understanding; furthermore, "Not: it shall be the case that not" is regarded as synonymous with "It may be the case that" (1966, p. 88).

1. (a) Claim(p, q, F).
   (b) It shall be the case that q sees to it that F.
   (c) q shall see to it that F.
2. (a) Freedom(p, q, F).
   (b) Not: it shall be the case that p sees to it that not F.
   (c) It is not the case that p shall see to it that not F.
3. (a) Power(p, q, F).
   (b) Not: it shall be the case that not: p sees to it that F.
   (c) p may see to it that F.
4. (a) Immunity(p, q, F).
   (b) It shall be the case that not: q sees to it that not F.
   (c) It is not the case that q may see to it that not F.
5. (a) Counter-claim(p, q, F).
   (b) It shall be the case that q sees to it that not F.
   (c) q shall see to it that not F.
6. (a) Counter-freedom(p, q, F).
   (b) Not: it shall be the case that p sees to it that F.
   (c) It is not the case that p shall see to it that F.
7. (a) Counter-power(p, q, F).
   (b) Not: it shall be the case that not: p sees to it that not F.
   (c) p may see to it that not F.

8. (a) Counter-immunity(p, q, F).
   (b) It shall be the case that not: q sees to it that F.
   (c) It is not the case that q may see to it that F.

As is apparent from the schema, the relation between the four types *claim*, *freedom*, *power* and *immunity*, and their corresponding "counter-types" can be given by collecting them together into four pairs of synonyms thus:

$$\begin{cases} p \text{ has versus } q \text{ a counter-claim that } F, \\ p \text{ has versus } q \text{ a claim that not } F. \end{cases}$$

$$\begin{cases} p \text{ has versus } q \text{ a counter-freedom that } F, \\ p \text{ has versus } q \text{ a freedom that not } F. \end{cases}$$

$$\begin{cases} p \text{ has versus } q \text{ a counter-power that } F, \\ p \text{ has versus } q \text{ a power that not } F. \end{cases}$$

$$\begin{cases} p \text{ has versus } q \text{ a counter-immunity that } F, \\ p \text{ has versus } q \text{ an immunity that not } F. \end{cases}$$

A consequence of Kanger's explications 1–8 is that those right relations which are "correlatives" can be represented in the following schema of equivalences (where $\leftrightarrow$ is the usual sentential connective):

$$\begin{array}{ll}
\text{Claim}(p, q, F) & \leftrightarrow \text{Not Counter-freedom}(q, p, F); \\
\text{Freedom}(p, q, F) & \leftrightarrow \text{Not Counter-claim}(q, p, F); \\
\text{Power}(p, q, F) & \leftrightarrow \text{Not Counter-immunity}(q, p, F); \\
\text{Immunity}(p, q, F) & \leftrightarrow \text{Not Counter-power}(q, p, F); \\
\text{Counter-claim}(p, q, F) & \leftrightarrow \text{Not Freedom}(q, p, F); \\
\text{Counter-freedom}(p, q, F) & \leftrightarrow \text{Not Claim}(q, p, F); \\
\text{Counter-power}(p, q, F) & \leftrightarrow \text{Not Immunity}(q, p, F); \\
\text{Counter-immunity}(p, q, F) & \leftrightarrow \text{Not Power}(q, p, F).
\end{array}$$

Take, for example, the first equivalence according to which the relations *claim* and *not counter-freedom* are correlatives. Explication 1 tells us that

Claim(p, q, F)

means the same as

(1) q shall see to it that F,

and explication 6 tells us that

Counter-freedom(q, p, F)

means the same as

(2) It is not the case that q shall see to it that F.

But since (2) is just the negation of (1), it follows that

Claim(p, q, F) $\leftrightarrow$ Not Counter-freedom(q, p, F).

The remaining equivalences can similarly be shown to hold.

5. *The simple types of right as relations between parties*

All of Kanger's simple types of right, as has been made clear, are *relations between parties* with respect to a condition. The parties may be identical, so that the statements can take the form

Claim(p, p, F),
Freedom(p, p, F),

and so forth (cf., on the other hand, above p. 16, 22, concerning Bentham and Austin on *right*).

Kanger's explication of the simple types of right as relations between parties is not intended to mirror common usage. Consider, for example, the following statement thought of as an explication of a statement saying that the relation *claim* obtains between two parties with respect to a condition:

(1) Smith shall see to it that Jones receives White's bankbook.

Not just two, but three parties are named in (1)—Smith, Jones and White. Now, according to Kanger's concept of *claim*, (1) is an explication of each one of the following statements:

(2) Jones has versus Smith a claim that Jones receives White's bankbook.
(3) White has versus Smith a claim that Jones receives White's bankbook.
(4) Smith has versus Smith a claim that Jones receives White's bankbook.

Since (1) is the explication of each of (2)–(4), these statements are logically equivalent in Kanger's theory. According to legal usage, on the other hand, they are not equivalent; it is quite conceivable that (3) is true whilst (2) is false (cf. Dan. Lyons, 1965, pp. 119 ff.; Hart, 1973, pp. 191 ff., 195 ff.).

The examples raise the question whether it is possible to find criteria to supplement Kanger's explication of the simple type *claim* in order to define one or more subtypes of *claim* corresponding to common and legal usage of "claim". Bentham and Austin both tried to introduce certain criteria of this kind. Bentham used the concept "party favoured by the law" which in application to statements (2), (3) and (4) could give rise to differing truth values. To this end Austin introduced a different criterion: he who has a *right* (or *claim*) against another can enforce the fulfilment of the duty by civil action at court (see above, p. 23). Such additional criteria are not to be found in Kanger's theory of simple types of right, but they do occur in his account of atomic types of right, to be discussed shortly. Kanger distinguishes there between three subtypes of the simple type *claim;* and the remaining simple types—*freedom*, *power*, etc.—are also divided into various subtypes.

6. *Kanger's simple types of right compared with Bentham's and Hohfeld's systems*

In comparing Kanger's system of simple types with Bentham's and Hohfeld's, we should not expect to find exact counterparts. So far as Bentham is concerned, his explication of *right to a service* is built on the concept *party favoured*, which is not to be found in Kanger's account of *claim*, and the concept *liberty* (liberty as such, see above, p. 16) is not a relation between parties as are Kanger's simple types. And Hohfeld does not give any explication of his basic types of right, which makes the comparison with Kanger even more difficult. But a comparison aiming only at an approximate correspondence can have some value, if only to provide a forum for a survey of Kanger's system of concepts.

Bentham—Kanger. The nearest counterparts to Kanger's eight simple types can be represented in the following table,

TABLE I

Bentham:	*Kanger:*
Right to a positive service (Right that the other man *does act* in a certain way)	Claim Counter-claim
Right to a negative service (Right that the other man *does not act* in a certain way)	Counter-immunity Immunity
Liberty to act	Power Counter-power
Liberty not to act	Counter-freedom Freedom

where Kanger's eight concepts correspond to only four of Bentham's. For Kanger, the types *claim* and *counter-claim* concern cases where the party against whom the right is held *shall see to it* that a condition obtains (*F* and not-*F*, respectively), whereas Bentham would say that the holder of the right has a *right to a positive service* (see above, p. 15). *Counter-immunity* and *immunity* concern cases where it *shall* be that the other party *does not see to it* that a condition obtains (*F* and not-*F*, respectively), whereas according to Bentham, the holder of the right has a *right to a negative service*. With *power* and *counter-power* the holder of the right *may see to it* that a condition obtains (*F* or not-*F*, respectively), whereas according to Bentham, he has a *liberty to act*. Finally, *counter-freedom* and *freedom* concern cases where it *may be* such that the holder of the right *does not see to it* that a condition obtains (*F* or not-*F*, respectively), whereas Bentham would say that he has a *liberty not to act* (liberty to abstain from acting).

That Kanger's system provides a much richer differentiation of concepts arises from the difference in the way statements of rights are construed. Consider, for example, two statements in accordance with Bentham's approach:

(1) White has versus Smith a right that Smith delivers White's bankbook to Jones.

(2) White has versus Smith a right that Smith prevents White's bankbook from being delivered to Jones.

Statements (1) and (2) deal with the same type of right (the *right to a positive service*) and the same party; but the "object" of the right is not the same. According to (1), it is the positive action *that Smith delivers White's bankbook to Jones*, while according to (2) it is the positive action *that Smith prevents White's bankbook from being delivered to Jones.*

The action-propositions in (1) and (2), namely

(3) Smith delivers White's bankbook to Jones,
(4) Smith prevents White's bankbook from being delivered to Jones,

are for Bentham two "primitive" statements. That (3) and (4) do ultimately concern the same condition becomes apparent when (4) is considered the internal negation of (3) according to the analysis

(3′) Smith sees to it that *Jones receives White's bankbook,*
(4′) Smith sees to it that not: *Jones receives White's bankbook,*

(cf. above, pp. 40 f.). Such an analysis is not to be found in Bentham's theory, however.

According to Kanger's account, (1) and (2) would be regarded as expressing, respectively, the rights *claim* and *counter-claim:*

(5) White has versus Smith a claim that Jones receives White's bankbook.
(6) White has versus Smith a counter-claim that Jones receives White's bankbook.

The "object" of the rights is now the same, namely that Jones receives White's bankbook. This arises in Kanger's analysis as a result of his using the concept *sees to it that,* for statements (5) and (6) are explicated, respectively, as follows:

(5′) Smith shall see to it that Jones receives White's bankbook.
(6′) Smith shall see to it that not: Jones receives White's bankbook.

Ultimately, both of these statements deal with the same condition.

Hohfeld—Kanger. According to the presentation above (p. 26) of Hohfeld's theory, the relation between his and Kanger's system is much the same as that between Kanger and Bentham. The "object" of a *right* in Hohfeld's sense is that the person against whom the right is held either acts or does not act in a certain way, the right in the former case corresponding to Kanger's *claim* or *counter-claim*, and in the latter case, to Kanger's *counter-immunity* or *immunity*. A person's *privilege* can, according to Hohfeld, be a *privilege to act* or a *privilege not to act*, the former corresponding to Kanger's *power* or *counter-power*, and the latter to Kanger's *counter-freedom* or *freedom*.

In terms of the account of Hohfeld presented here, the correspondence between the two systems can be represented in the following table:

TABLE II

Kanger:	*Hohfeld:*		*Kanger:*
Claim	Right	Duty	Not counter-freedom
Counter-claim			Not freedom
Counter-immunity			Not power
Immunity			Not counter-power
Not claim	No-right	Privilege	Counter-freedom
Not counter-claim			Freedom
Not counter-immunity			Power
Not immunity			Counter-power

The concepts listed under Kanger's name are ordered so that a type occurring in the two lower groups of four is the negation of that type occurring in the corresponding place in the upper group; thus, *not claim* is the negation of *claim* and *power* the negation of *not power*. Furthermore, a type occurring in the lefthand column under Kanger's name is a correlative (or inverse, as Kanger would say) of the type occupying the corresponding position on the right-hand side. Thus, *not counter-freedom* is the correlative of *claim* (cf. the schema of correlatives above, p. 44).

Kanger has himself provided an interpretation of Hohfeld which diverges from table II in a number of respects. His table for the correspondence between his own and Hohfeld's concepts is as follows (Kanger & Kanger, 1966, p. 101; cf. also Kanger, 1971, pp. 43 f.):

Hohfeld:	*Kanger:*
Claim, Right	Claim
Duty	Inverse of claim (=Not counter-freedom)
Privilege	Freedom
No-right	Inverse of freedom (=Not counter-claim)
Power	Power
Liability	Inverse of power (=Not counter-immunity)
Immunity	Immunity
Disability	Inverse of immunity (=Not counter-power)

Hohfeld's system appears in this way very similar to Kanger's—*privilege* corresponds to Kanger's *freedom*, *power* to Kanger's *power*, and so forth. (Remember that Kanger's theory was originally intended as an explication of Hohfeld's; see particularly 1957, pp. 16 f., reprinted in 1971, pp. 43 f.). It would lead too far afield to compare in detail the two tables; suffice it to say that the following three points indicate the differences in the starting point for the two interpretations of Hohfeld:

(i) Kanger's interpretation is based on the assumption that both, he and Hohfeld, construe statements of rights in the same way (cf. Kanger & Kanger, 1966, p. 103) and that Hohfeld implicitly analyses statements expressing actions with the help of the concept *sees to it that* or something similar which allows the possibility of internal negation along the lines

p sees to it that F;
p sees to it that not F.

Table II, on the other hand, is based on the assumption that statements of rights are construed differently by each of them, and that internal negation of statements expressing an action does not occur in Hohfeld's theory (cf. above, pp. 41 f.).

(ii) Kanger always interprets Hohfeld's notion *privilege* to mean that the holder of the right may refrain from acting in a certain way. For *freedom* is explicated by Kanger thus:

$$\begin{cases} \text{Freedom}(p, q, F). \\ \text{Not: it shall be the case that } p \text{ sees to it that not } F. \\ \text{It may be the case that not: } p \text{ sees to it that not } F. \end{cases}$$

Table II, on the other hand, is based on the assumption that *privilege* sometimes entails that the holder of the right may refrain from acting in a certain way, and sometimes that he may so *act*. In the latter case Hohfeld's *privilege* corresponds to Kanger's *power*; for the explication Kanger gives of *power* is:

$$\begin{cases} \text{Power}(p, q, F). \\ \text{Not: it shall be the case that not: } p \text{ sees to it that } F. \\ p \text{ may see to it that } F. \end{cases}$$

(iii) The interpretation of Hohfeld's term *power* merits some comment. As stated above (p. 25), the term *power* as it occurs in a statement of the kind

p has versus q a power to perform action A

corresponds to Hohfeld's *power* only if the action A is a bringing about of a "legal state of affairs"; that is, that a *legal relation* obtains between p and q or p and r, etc. (Hohfeld speaks, for example, about "the power to create contractual obligations", 1923, pp. 51 f.). So far as this proviso of Hohfeld's is concerned, two positions are possible. Kanger (Kanger & Kanger, 1966, p. 102) seems to regard the restriction to the bringing about of a "legal state of affairs" only as an irrelevant and inessential narrowing of Hohfeld's concept *power*. Another, more traditional, standpoint (see, for example, Corbin, 1919, p. 165) sees it as an essential feature of Hohfeld's theory that power as a basic legal concept concerns precisely the bringing about of a "legal state of affairs". The distinction between the two standpoints has a certain connection with the question of which concepts can be used in the explication of Hohfeld's *power*. Kanger starts from the tenet that Hohfeld's power can be explicated approximately in terms of "*may* see to it that". According to the more traditional interpretation, Hohfeld's *power* should rather be explicated in terms of "*can* see to it that" (cf. for example Corbin, 1919, p. 165; Eckhoff, 1953, p. 293; Anderson, 1962, p. 47; Fitch, 1967, p. 275).

The question of *may* and *can* as tools for the explication of *power* will be dealt with later in Chapter 6. For the present, it suffices to say that the interpretation of Hohfeld's *power* in terms of *can* agrees better with the view that Hohfeld himself expressed.

7. *The relation of strength between statements of right according to Kanger's theory*

Since Kanger's simple types of right are explicated with the help of the concepts *It shall be the case that* and *sees to it that* which are governed by explicitly formulated logical rules (rules I–V above, p. 40), it can be formally shown that the relation of logical consequence holds between certain of Kanger's statements of rights as presented in the following schema (see Kanger & Kanger, 1966, p. 90, where his expression "S(X, Y)" has been replaced here by the variable *F*):

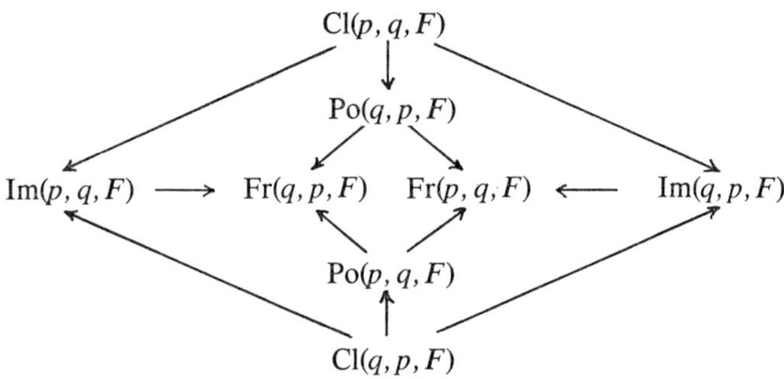

where

Cl stands for Claim,
Fr stands for Freedom,
Po stands for Power,
Im stands for Immunity,

and

⟶ stands for the relation of logical consequence.

These relations of logical consequence are easily demonstrated by replacing the statement expressing a right in the schema with its explication. Using the abbreviations

Shall for *It shall be the case that*,
May for *It may be the case that*,
Do for *sees to it that*,

the explication schema is

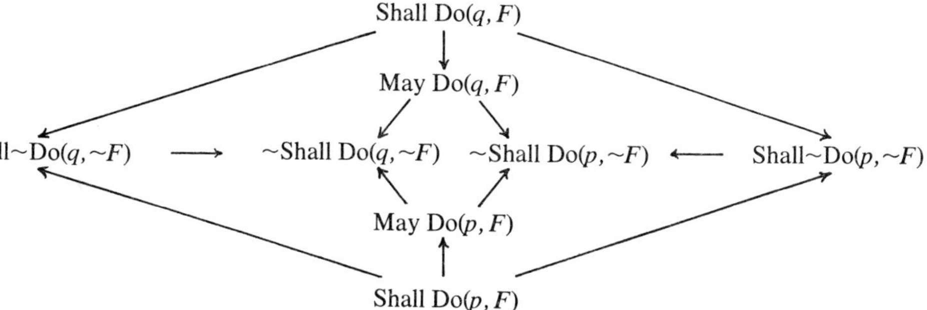

From the first schema it follows, for example, that

(1) q has versus p a power that F

has as a logical consequence

(2) p has versus q a freedom that F.

Alternatively, expressed in the terms used in the explication,

(1′) q may see to it that F

has as a logical consequence

(2′) It is not the case that p shall see to it that not F.

That (2′) is a logical consequence of (1′) can be demonstrated using rule I for *It shall be the case that* and rule V for *sees to it that*, given that the relation of logical consequence itself fulfils the rules (i)–(iii) above (p. 40). The proof is as follows:

1.	Do(q, F) $\longrightarrow F$	(rule V)
2.	$\sim F \longrightarrow \sim$Do($q$, F)	(from 1 according to rule ii)
3.	Do(p, $\sim F$) $\longrightarrow \sim F$	(rule V)
4.	Do(p, $\sim F$) $\longrightarrow \sim$Do(q, F)	(from 2, 3 according to rule iii)

5.	Shall Do$(p, \sim F) \longrightarrow$ Shall $\sim$ Do(q, F)	(from 4, according to rule I)
6.	$\sim$ Shall $\sim$ Do$(q, F) \longrightarrow \sim$ Shall Do$(p, \sim F)$	(from 5 according to rule ii)
7.	May Do$(q, F) \longrightarrow \sim$ Shall Do$(p, \sim F)$	(from 6 according to the definition of "May")

8. *Kanger's theory of atomic types of right: the twenty-six atomic types*

The theory of simple types of right serves in Kanger's later work (1963, pp. 85 ff.; 1966, pp. 90 ff.) as a basis for a more refined theory, the theory of *atomic* types of right, which are constructed by the method for building up *basic conjunctions* (see, for example, Kemeny, Snell & Thompson, 1966, pp. 15 ff.). The procedure is as follows:

I. The first step is to form the conjunction of the following statements (1)–(8):

(1) Claim(p, q, F);
(2) Freedom(p, q, F);
(3) Power(p, q, F);
(4) Immunity(p, q, F);
(5) Counter-claim(p, q, F);
(6) Counter-freedom(p, q, F);
(7) Counter-power(p, q, F);
(8) Counter-immunity(p, q, F).

Further conjunctions are then constructed by negating one or more of (1)–(8) and conjoining them with the remainder. Thus, there are eight possibilities for negating just one of (1)–(8), giving eight new conjunctions; there are twenty-eight possibilities for negating exactly two conjunctions, giving twenty-eight new conjunctions when these are conjoined with the remainder; and so on. In this way, $2^8 = 256$ conjunctions are obtained.

II. Of these 256 conjunctions, only twenty-six are non-contradictory. Amongst the self-contradictory conjunctions is the first conjunction mentioned under stage I containing no negations of (1)–(8). The contradiction is easily demonstrated, since the conjunction contains as two of its conjuncts

(1) Claim(p, q, F),
(5) Counter-claim(p, q, F),

and according to the schema of correlatives, (5) is logically equivalent to

(5′) Not freedom(q, p, F)

(see above, p. 44). Now, the schema showing the system of logical consequences tells us that

Claim(p, q, F) ⟶ Freedom(q, p, F)

(see above, p. 52), and therefore statements (1) and (5) are logically incompatible and so any conjunction containing them as conjuncts will be contradictory.

III. Within the twenty-six remaining consistent conjunctions, some of the constituent conjuncts are redundant (i.e., logical consequences of the remaining conjuncts) and these are now eliminated. For example, if a conjunction contained as conjuncts the two statements

Power(p, q, F),
Freedom(p, q, F),

the second statement is redundant and can be eliminated since from the logical consequence schema we have

Power(p, q, F) ⟶ Freedom(p, q, F).

IV. That any of these twenty-six conjunctions, stripped of redundant components, is true amounts to saying that a certain relation obtains between p and q with respect to F. This relation is an *atomic type of right.* For example, one of the twenty-six conjunctions is

Claim(p, q, F) & Not power(p, q, F).

The truth of this statement implies that a relation I shall call *Claim, not power* obtains between p and q with respect to F, and this is one of the atomic types of right.

Each of the twenty-six conjunctions generates an atomic type of right, the full list of which follows:

1. Power, not immunity, counter-power, not counter-immunity.
2. Not power, immunity, not counter-power, counter-immunity.
3. Claim, not counter-freedom.
4. Not claim, power, immunity, counter-freedom, not counter-power, not counter-immunity.
5. Power, immunity, counter-power, counter-immunity.
6. Claim, power, counter-freedom.
7. Claim, not power.
8. Power, immunity, counter-freedom, not counter-power, counter-immunity.
9. Power, immunity, counter-power, not counter-immunity.
10. Power, not immunity, not counter-power, counter-immunity.
11. Not freedom, counter-claim.
12. Freedom, not power, not immunity, not counter-claim, counter-power, counter-immunity.
13. Freedom, counter-claim, counter-power.
14. Counter-claim, not counter-power.
15. Freedom, not power, immunity, counter-power, counter-immunity.
16. Power, not immunity, counter-power, counter-immunity.
17. Not power, immunity, counter-power, not counter-immunity.
18. Not power, not immunity, not counter-power, not counter-immunity.
19. Not claim, not counter-freedom, not counter-immunity.
20. Not counter-freedom, counter-immunity.
21. Not claim, not power, immunity, not counter-power, not counter-immunity.
22. Power, not immunity, not counter-power, not counter-immunity.
23. Not freedom, not immunity, not counter-claim.
24. Not freedom, immunity.
25. Not power, not immunity, not counter-claim, not counter-power, counter-immunity.
26. Not power, not immunity, counter-power, not counter-immunity.

It can be shown that independently of how p, q and F are chosen, exactly one of these twenty-six relations obtains between p and q with respect to F, by the following argument. According to the law of contradiction:

(a) either: Claim(p, q, F),
or: Not claim(p, q, F).

(b) either: Freedom(p, q, F),
or: Not freedom(p, q, F).

(c) either: Power(p, q, F),
or: Not power(p, q, F).

(d) either: Immunity(p, q, F),
or: Not immunity(p, q, F).

(e) either: Counter-claim(p, q, F),
or: Not counter-claim(p, q, F).

(f) either: Counter-freedom(p, q, F),
or: Not counter-freedom(p, q, F).

(g) either: Counter-power(p, q, F),
or: Not counter-power(p, q, F).

(h) either: Counter-immunity(p, q, F),
or: Not counter-immunity(p, q, F).

There is just one choice for each alternative (a)–(h). Each combination of choices for all the alternatives (a)–(h) gives one of the 256 conjunctions; each correct choice gives one of the twenty-six consistent conjunctions. That at most one of these twenty-six conjunctions is true for each p, q and F follows from the fact that they are mutually logically incompatible. (If K is one of the conjunctions and K' another, then K' must contain at least the negation of one conjunct occurring in K, or conversely.)

All this is quite compatible, however, with any of the twenty-six atomic types being an empty relation. Kanger (Kanger & Kanger, 1966, p. 97) maintains that it can nevertheless be shown, by reference to examples, that for each of the twenty-six relations there is a choice of p, q and F such that the relation in question holds between them.

9. *Inverses and converses, symmetrical and neutral atomic types*

An atomic type of right T is the *inverse* of an atomic type T' provided T obtains between p and q with respect to F if and only if T' obtains between q and p with respect to F (cf. above, p. 15, 27, concerning "correlative"). For example, the atomic type no. 5

Power, immunity, counter-power, counter-immunity

is the inverse of no. 18

Not power, not immunity, not counter-power, not counter-immunity.

Thus, that no. 5 obtains between p and q with respect to F is equivalent to no. 18 obtaining between q and p with respect to F. This follows from the equivalences (see above, p. 44)

Power(p, q, F) $\leftrightarrow$ Not counter-immunity(q, p, F),
Immunity(p, q, F) $\leftrightarrow$ Not counter-power(q, p, F),
Counter-power(p, q, F) $\leftrightarrow$ Not immunity(q, p, F),
Counter-immunity(p, q, F) $\leftrightarrow$ Not power(q, p, F).

The notion of *converse* concerns the substitution of F by not-F; in particular, T is the *converse* of the atomic type T' provided T obtains between p and q with respect to F if and only if T' obtains between p and q with respect to not-F. For example, no. 3

Claim, not counter-freedom

is the converse of no. 11

Not freedom, counter-claim.

That is to say, no. 3 obtaining between p and q with respect to F is equivalent to no. 11 obtaining between p and q with respect to not-F; this follows from the equivalences

Claim(p, q, F) $\leftrightarrow$ Counter-claim($p, q, \sim F$),
Not counter-freedom(p, q, F) $\leftrightarrow$ Not-freedom($p, q, \sim F$),

(see the explication of the simple types above, p. 43).

Kanger summarised the relationships of inverse and converse amongst his atomic types as is clearly illustrated in the diagram on the following page (p. 59). In this diagram (cf. Kanger & Kanger, 1966, p. 94) the *inverse* of an atomic type T occurs in the square which is the mirror image, about the dotted diagonal line, of the square occupied by T. For example, in the lower right-hand corner, no. 24 occupies the mirror image position to no. 14's position; hence, no. 24 is the inverse of no. 14. The *converse* of an atomic type T is found by rotating the line from T's square to the centre square (occupied by no. 1) through 180 degrees.

2	7	21	18	25	14	2
20	3	19				20
8	6	4	22	10		8
5		9	1	16		5
15		17	26	12	13	15
24				23	11	24
2	7	21	18	25	14	2

Thus, starting from the square in the lower right-hand corner occupied by no. 14, and rotating through 180 degrees brings us to the square occupied by no. 7 in the upper left-hand corner; so no. 7 is the converse of no. 14.

Note that the atomic types 1, 2, 3, 4, 11 and 12 which occur on the diagonal are special cases as regards the relation inverse; they are in fact inverses of themselves, and Kanger calls these *symmetrical* atomic types. Consider, for example, the atomic type no. 3

Claim, not counter-freedom.

The statement

Claim(p, q, F) & Not counter-freedom(p, q, F)

can also be written as

Claim(p, q, F) & Claim(q, p, F)

(see above, p. 44). It is therefore easily seen that p has a right of type no. 3 against q with respect to F if and only if q also has a right of type no. 3 against p with respect to the same state of affairs F.

Furthermore, it is apparent from inspection of the diagram that types no. 1, 2, 5 and 18 are converses of themselves; these Kanger calls *neutral* atomic types. Take, for example, the atomic type no. 5

Power, immunity, counter-power, counter-immunity.

The statement

Power(p, q, F) & Immunity(p, q, F) & Counter-power(p, q, F) & Counter-immunity(p, q, F)

can also be written as

Power(p, q, F) & Immunity(p, q, F) & Power(p, q, $\sim F$) & Immunity(p, q, $\sim F$).

Thus, it is clear that p has a right of type no. 5 against q with respect to F if and only if p also has a right of type no. 5 against q with respect to the state of affairs not-F.

The six symmetrical types play an important part in Kanger's theory because all the atomic types can be constructed by what Kanger calls the *coordination* of two symmetrical types (Kanger & Kanger, 1966, p. 96). However, I shall not go into this here; the method of coordination will be thoroughly dealt with in Chapters 3 and 4.

10. *The atomic types of right as subtypes of the simple types*

The atomic types were constructed as *intersections* of certain simple types. The atomic type no. 1, for example, is the intersection of the simple types *power*, *not immunity*, *counter-power* and *not counter-immunity*. Accordingly, that p has the atomic right no. 1 against q entails (see the explication schema above, p. 43) that all the following are true:

p may see to it that F;	(*power*)
p may see to it that not F;	(*counter-power*)
q may see to it that F;	(*not counter-immunity*)
q may see to it that not F.	(*not immunity*)

It has already been remarked that Kanger's theory of simple types does not contain a criterion for allowing the possibility of different truth values of the statements

(1) *p* has versus *q* a claim that *F*,
(2) *r* has versus *q* a claim that *F*.

Both statements are explicated by Kanger in the same way, namely

q shall see to it that *F*.

The situation is the same with, for example,

(3) *p* has versus *q* a power that *F*,
(4) *p* has versus *r* a power that *F*,

statements (3) and (4) having the same explication

p may see to it that *F*.

Thus, the explication of the simple types of right does not indicate any way to distinguish whether such a relation obtains between *p* and *q* with respect to *F* but not (so far as *claim*, *counter-claim*, *immunity* and *counter-immunity* are concerned) between *r* and *q* with respect to *F* or (so far as *freedom*, *counter-freedom*, *power* and *counter-power* are concerned) between *p* and *r* with respect to *F* (cf. above, pp. 45 f.).

The situation is not the same with the theory of atomic types of right. Suppose *T* is one of the twenty-six atomic types; then the three statements

(5) *p* has versus *q* a right of the atomic type *T* with respect to *F*,
(6) *r* has versus *q* a right of the atomic type *T* with respect to *F*,
(7) *p* has versus *r* a right of the atomic type *T* with respect to *F*,

always receive different explications. In the explication of (5) there are certain conjuncts which normatively regulate *p*'s action, and certain conjuncts normatively regulating *q*'s action (cf. the explication of atomic type no. 1 just given). In the explication of (6), however, no such conjuncts regulating *p*'s action occur; just those regulating *r*'s and *q*'s action. And similarly for (7), there are conjuncts regulating *p*'s and *r*'s action, but not *q*'s action. Thus, the explication of atomic types of right always allows the parties to be distinguished, allowing the possibility of (5), (6) and (7) having differing truth values.

Since each atomic type is constituted from an intersection of simple types of right, each atomic type can be described as a *subtype* of certain simple types. Thus, the atomic type no. 3

claim, not counter-freedom

is a subtype partly of the simple type *claim*, partly of *not counter-freedom*, and represents a more refined *claim* concept than the simple type itself. Another more refined *claim* concept is represented by atomic type no. 6, and still another by atomic type no. 7 (there are exactly three atomic subtypes of the simple type *claim*). Similarly, there are twenty-three subtypes of the simple type *freedom* (all except nos. 11, 23 and 24; cf. Kanger & Kanger, 1966, p. 95). These correspond to different varieties of freedom in the sense of the simple type *freedom*.

The more refined relations of claim, freedom, and so on, that occur in various juridical contexts and everyday language (cf. above, p. 46) should thus be analysed in terms of the atomic types rather than the simple types. (Helle Kanger is using the twenty-six atomic types in a forthcoming political science thesis on the analysis of the concepts *right* and *freedom* as they occur in the United Nations' *Universal Declaration of Human Rights*.) The usual juridical concept *claim*, for example, appears to correspond most closely to the atomic type no. 6

Claim, power, counter-freedom.

This entails that, for example, the statement

(8) Smith has versus Jones a claim that Smith gets back the money that Smith has lent to Jones

is to be explicated as a conjunction of the following statements:

(a) Jones shall see to it that Smith gets back the money that Smith has lent to Jones;

(b) Smith may see to it that Smith gets back the money that Smith has lent to Jones;

(c) It may be the case that not: Smith sees to it that Smith gets back the money that Smith has lent to Jones.

(Cf. conjunct (b) with Austin's "test of a right" above, p. 23. Condition (b) constitutes the closest thing in Kanger's theory to Austin's criterion.) It can also be shown that with the help of the list of atomic types of right counterparts can be found to different variants of the concept *vested liberty* in Bentham and Austin (cf. above, p. 17, 22).

VI. *The Theory of Basic Types of Legal Positions*

In their well-known book on logico-mathematical methods, Kemeny, Snell and Thompson say that "one of the most important contributions that mathematics can make to the solution of a scientific problem is to provide an exhaustive analysis of the logical possibilities for the problem" (1966, p. 19). The result of such an analysis is a division of the set of logical possibilities into mutually incompatible and jointly exhaustive alternatives. The exhaustive analysis of logical possibilities is of great importance for problems that occur in legal theory and practice, and consequently for the topics already discussed in the present chapter. There are several contributions to such an analysis within the tradition beginning with Bentham, the most important of which is Kanger's theory of atomic types of right.

Attempts at an analysis of logical possibilities is already to be found in the theories of Bentham and Hohfeld. According to Bentham, given a person p and an action-proposition A_p ("p performs action A"), the list of alternatives is as follows:

(i) Obligation(p, A_p),
(ii) Obligation(p, $\sim A_p$),
(iii) Liberty(p, A_p) & Liberty(p, $\sim A_p$).

These alternatives are, according to Bentham's logic, mutually incompatible and jointly exhaustive. Though the principles *explicitly* formulated by Hohfeld give a weaker logic than Bentham's (see above, p. 28), a similar division into three alternatives is obtained by making a natural addition (accepting statement (1), p. 28):

(i′) Duty(p, q, A_p),
(ii′) Duty(p, q, $\sim A_p$),
(iii′) Privilege(p, q, A_p) & Privilege(p, q, $\sim A_p$).

But the statements (i)–(iii) and (i′)–(iii′) provide only a rough analysis in comparison with Kanger's theory, which represents a considerable refinement, providing not less than twenty-six different possibilities.

The theory of basic types of legal positions presented in Chapters 3–5 is a further refinement of the analysis. Three sorts of problem are distinguished. First, where it suffices to consider just one person p and a state of affairs F, the theory provides seven legal possibilities. Where it is necessary to consider two people p and q together with a state of affairs F, however, two cases are distinguished, giving us the remaining two sorts of problem. The first of these arises where the two people can be considered "individually", and thirty-five possibilities are obtained. The second arises where the two people must be considered "collectively", and in this case one hundred and twenty-seven possibilities are obtained.

Bentham, Hohfeld and Kanger emphasise the traditional legal concepts such as *obligation*, *right*, *privilege* etc., whereas the analyses presented in Chapters 3–5 are formulated directly in terms of *It shall be the case that* and *sees to it that*. I shall not be concerned to provide an analysis of the traditional concepts themselves, and they play no role in the theory.

The analyses of legal possibilities provide the basis for the next step in the theory, namely the definitions of what I call *basic types of legal positions*. If the schema $\ldots p \ldots F \ldots$ represents a statement describing one possibility for a person p and a state of affairs F, the set of ordered pairs $\langle p, F \rangle$ is constructed such that the statement $\ldots p \ldots F \ldots$ is true. Similarly, if the schema $\ldots p \ldots q \ldots F \ldots$ represents a statement describing a possibility for two people p and q and a state of affairs F, the set of ordered triples $\langle p, q, F \rangle$ is constructed such that the statement $\ldots p \ldots q \ldots F \ldots$ is true. The sets constructed in this way are basic types of legal positions, there being three collections of types corresponding to the three sorts of problem distinguished earlier, namely *one-agent types*, *individualistic two-agent types* and *collectivistic two-agent types*.

The next stage in the theory takes us to a further level of abstraction where relations between the types are discussed. In addition to the relations of *inverse* and *converse* between the types (above, pp. 57 f.), the relation *less free than* is introduced. The idea behind this is that, for example, p is *less free* if (i) or (ii) holds than p would be if (iii) holds. To see how this relation can be introduced into Kanger's differentiated system appears at first sight as not too simple a task; however, given the construction of types advocated here, it is easy to provide a precise definition of the relation *less free than* without appealing to any new concepts, and to show that the relation gives a partial ordering on the set of types of each of the three systems. Other concepts can in turn be defined in terms of the relation *less free than.*

The systematisation provided by these concepts is itself a development of the tradition of Bentham, Hohfeld and Kanger. But its main significance here lies in its application to an important area of legal problems—especially those surrounding Hohfeld's theory of *changes in existing legal relations*—which is taken up in the second part of the book (Chapters 6–9). For it is a familiar fact that the legal situation of one or more people can change from one time to another, for example by promise, contract, the decree of an authority, etc. That is to say, a pair $\langle p, F \rangle$ or a triple $\langle p, q, F \rangle$ can be moved from one type of legal position to another. For example, two people, p and q, make a contract; before the contract comes into force, $\langle p, q, F \rangle$ belongs to a certain type R, and afterwards $\langle p, q, F \rangle$ belongs to a different type R'. The problems of dealing with situations of this sort concern the "dynamics" of legal positions. This last stage in the theory of legal positions is developed in the form of a theory of what I call *ranges of legal action.* This is, perhaps, the most interesting topic taken up in the book since it deals with an area which has not received much attention.

CHAPTER 2

Symbols and Logical Rules

I. *Introduction*

The basic logical apparatus which will be used in the theory of basic types of legal positions (Chapters 3–5) is essentially the same as that used by Kanger in his theory of atomic types of right which has already been introduced in Chapter 1 (above pp. 38 ff.). The aim of the present chapter is partly to give a survey of the symbols and logical rules which I shall use, and partly to give a short commentary on the two important operators Do and Shall. The chapter is primarily aimed at readers who are not already familiar with the logic of Do and Shall.

The presentation in the following chapters involves a minimum of technicalities, and presupposes only an elementary knowledge of logic and set theory. However, certain logical rules are needed for the deduction of the results and certain symbols are needed for a clear and efficient expression of the rules, deductions and results.

In the final part of this book a more comprehensive logical apparatus will be used. Rules and symbols to complement those already presented are introduced in Chapter 7.

II. *Symbols and Logical Rules*

1. *Symbols*

The symbols are as follows:

1. Variables for agents: $p, q, r, \ldots, p_1, p_2, \ldots$
2. Variables for propositions: $F, G, H, \ldots, F_1, F_2, \ldots$
3. Symbols for truth functions:
   - $\sim$ ("not")
   - & ("and")
   - $\vee$ ("or")
   - $\rightarrow$ ("if then")
   - $\leftrightarrow$ ("if and only if")

4. Identity signs:
   $=$ ("is identical with")
   $\neq$ ("is not identical with")
5. Operators:
   Do ("sees to it that")
   Shall ("it shall be the case that")
6. Symbols for quantification:
   $\forall$ ("for each")
   $\exists$ ("for some")
7. Parentheses and comma: ( ) [ ] ,
8. Set theoretical symbols:
   $\{\ldots\}$ ("the set constituted by the elements ...")
   $\{\alpha|\ldots\alpha\ldots\}$ ("the set of all α such that ...α...")
   $\langle\ldots\rangle$ ("the ordered n-tuple of ...")
   $\cap$ ("the intersection of")
   $\cup$ ("the union of")
   $\varnothing$ ("the empty set")
   $\in$ ("is an element of")
   $\notin$ ("is not an element of")
   $\subseteq$ ("is a subset of")
   $\subset$ ("is a proper subset of")
   $\overline{\beta}$ ("the complement of the set β with respect to the universe of discourse")

Agent variables denote arbitrarily chosen agents. An agent is either an individual person or a so-called collective agent; for example, the Swedish government, such and such a company, John and Peter together, etc. The *propositional variables* denote arbitrarily chosen conditions (states of affairs). The structure of these conditions is left open. A condition can be, for example, that $2+2=4$, or that John receives £50 from Peter in his office at 1 p.m. on January 1st 1974, or that it shall be the case that p sees to it that q receives £50 from p.

Just as in the English language certain sequences of words form grammatically well-formed statements, so certain sequences of the symbols listed under 1–8 above are well-formed statements. The usual formation rules for sentential logic, predicate logic and set theory will not be listed here, but will be presupposed in what follows. However, the two operators Do and Shall are not standard symbols, and for these the following rules hold:

(1) If A is a well-formed statement and s is an agent variable, then Do(s, A) is a well-formed statement.

(2) If A is a well-formed statement, then so is Shall A.

The operator May is used in accordance with the following rule of abbreviation:

$$\text{May } A =_{\text{def.}} \sim \text{Shall} \sim A$$

(where A is an arbitrary well-formed statement).

2. *The logical rules*

The logical rules which I will be using are the usual rules of sentential and predicate logic together with those of elementary set theory and rules for the operators Do and Shall. The latter rules (cf. above, p. 40) are constituted by the following axiom schemata and rules of deduction (where A and B are arbitrary well-formed statements, s is an arbitrary agent variable and the expression "$\vdash A$" is used to say that A is a theorem, i.e., a logically valid statement, according to the rules of logic):

Rules for Do:

RI. If $\vdash (A \leftrightarrow B)$, then $\vdash (\text{Do}(s, A) \leftrightarrow \text{Do}(s, B))$.

A1. $\text{Do}(s, A) \rightarrow A$.

Rules for Shall

RII. If $\vdash A$, then $\vdash$ Shall A.

A2. $\text{Shall}(A \rightarrow B) \rightarrow (\text{Shall } A \rightarrow \text{Shall } B)$.

A3. $\text{Shall } A \rightarrow \sim \text{Shall} \sim A$.

The rules RI–RII and A1–A3 for Do and Shall give a certain precision to the vague concepts *sees to it that* and *It shall be the case that*. If the rules in question were to be rejected then the meaning of the concepts would be otherwise than presupposed here. This is not to say, however, that the rules prevent the concepts retaining a certain vagueness, and there is still room left for further precision in other ways.

A consequence of the vagueness of the basic concepts is a corresponding vagueness in the statements in which the theory's results are formulated. It should be pointed out, however, that this vagueness in the theory's statements constitutes not so much an objection to the theory, but rather shows the theory's generality. The results of the theory are formally deducible given the usual rules of sentential logic and set theory together with RI–RII and A1–A3. The theory is not, on the other hand, dependent on any special assumptions about the meaning of "sees to it that" or "It shall be the case that"; anyone is free to provide a special interpretation of these concepts. It is presupposed only that the general rules just given are accepted, in which case the results of the theory also hold for this interpretation.

III. *The Operator* Do *and Its Logic*

1. Do *and instrumental actions*

Consider the following two statements:

(1) John pays his debt to Peter.
(2) John pays his debt to Peter by sending a cheque.

The statement (2) evidently says more than statement (1). (2) gives a further specification of the action, over and above the information contained in (1), which is instrumental in John's paying his debt to Peter. (2) entails (1), but not conversely. Let us substitute (1) and (2) with the following statements where the concept *sees to it that* is introduced together with certain variables:

(1′) p sees to it that F
(2′) p sees to it that F by performing action A.

It also might well be supposed that (2′) entails (1′), but not conversely.

Without going further into the analysis of (2′), two points are noted here which provide some guidance in the discussion of certain illustrative examples given in the following chapters.

The first question concerns what kind of actions can be instrumental when a person sees to it that such and such is the case. I shall introduce here the concept *null action*.

There are usually several different descriptions of an action, all of which provide a correct specification of the actions by which a person sees to it that a state of affairs obtains. As often as not one of these correct specifications is a description of a bodily movement. The statement

(3) John sees to it that the door is closed at time t_2 by moving his left foot forward at time t_1,

for example, can be a correct specification with respect to the instrumental action of

(4) John sees to it that the door is closed at time t_2.

However it can be the case that a person sees to it that a state of affairs obtains without making any bodily movement at all. For example, suppose that the door is closed from t_1 to t_n without anyone attempting to open it. The statement

(5) John sees to it that the door is closed from t_1 to t_n

can, in such a case, be true without it being the case that John performs a bodily action at all (without John concretely "doing" anything at all) in order to keep the door closed. It happens, as a matter of fact, that the door remains closed without John needing to raise a finger, but if someone tried to open the door John would immediately intervene, for example, by going to the door and leaning against it. One might say that the instrumental action in this example is a *null action:* John sees to it that the door's condition remains as it is without actively doing anything.

Another question concerns the combination of (1′) and (2′) with the deontic concept *It shall be the case that*, *It may be the case that*, etc., and I shall briefly mention the concept *protective perimeter* introduced by Hart (Hart, 1973, pp. 179 ff.). In connection with his discussion of Bentham's notion of *liberty*, Hart draws a distinction between on the one hand, where a person's liberty to act is combined with a "correlative obligation upon others not to interfere" (cf. Bentham's concept *vested liberty*, above, p. 17) and on the other hand, where a person's liberty to act is only, as Hart says, circumscribed by a "protective perimeter":

Thus, to take a trivial example, my right to scratch my head is protected, not by a correlative obligation upon others not to interfere with my doing that specific kind of act, but by the fact that obligations to refrain from assault or trespass to my person will generally preclude effective interference to it. (Hart, 1973, p. 180)

This distinction introduced by Hart is easy to understand if one combines (1′) and (2′) with deontic concepts. For the sake of brevity, let us use the expression

$$\text{Do}(p, F, A)$$

as an abbreviation for

p sees to it that *F* by performing action *A*,

and let us express the entailment relation between (2′) and (1′) above in such a way that the following statement is logically valid:

(6) $\text{Do}(p, F, A) \rightarrow \text{Do}(p, F)$.

Then we can articulate Hart's distinction by distinguishing between the following two alternatives:

(7) $\text{May Do}(p, F)\ \&\ {\sim}\text{May Do}(q, {\sim}F)$;

(8) $\text{May Do}(p, F)\ \&\ {\sim}\text{May Do}(q, {\sim}F, A_1)\ \&$
$\quad {\sim}\text{May Do}(q, {\sim}F, A_2)\ \&\ \ldots\ \&\ {\sim}\text{May Do}(q, {\sim}F, A_n)$.

It follows immediately from (6) together with the logical rules for Shall that (8) is a logical consequence of (7). If $\{A_1, ..., A_n\}$ is only a subset of the set of all *A*, then it does not hold conversely that (7) is a logical consequence of (8). Statement (8) is, in fact, compatible with

(9) $\text{May Do}(q, {\sim}F, A_{n+1})$

from which the negation of (7) follows.

What has just now been said means that (under the assumption concerning $A_1, ..., A_n$) (7) is a stronger statement than (8). Relating this to Hart's mode of expression, according to (7) *p*'s liberty to act carries with it a correlative obligation for *q* not to interfere, whilst according to (8), on the other hand, *p*'s liberty to act is only surrounded by a "protective perimeter". The distinction between these alternatives has, as Hart remarks, been of decisive importance in a number of famous legal cases (see Hart, 1973, p. 181, n. 53).

Hart distinguishes between the case where the protective perimeter is *complete* and the case where the protective perimeter is *incomplete*. In order to throw light on this question we shall for the moment allow ourselves to quantify over instrumental actions.

A reasonable interpretation of (1′) and (2′) above would make the following statement logically valid:

(10) $\mathrm{Do}(p, F) \leftrightarrow (\exists A)\,\mathrm{Do}(p, F, A)$.

From (10) it follows immediately that:

(11) $\sim\mathrm{May\ Do}(p, F) \leftrightarrow \sim\mathrm{May}(\exists A)\,\mathrm{Do}(p, F, A)$.

In accordance with this it follows that (7) above is logically equivalent to

(12) $\mathrm{May\ Do}(p, F)\ \&\ \sim\mathrm{May}(\exists A)\,\mathrm{Do}(q, \sim F, A)$.

In other words, according to (12), p has a liberty to act and q has a correlative obligation not to interfere.

In (12) the existential quantifier is placed after the deontic operator. If the quantifier and the operator are instead positioned the other way round, we obtain

(13) $\mathrm{May\ Do}(p, F)\ \&\ \sim(\exists A)\,\mathrm{May\ Do}(q, \sim F, A)$.

(13) expresses that p's liberty to act has a protective perimeter which is *complete* (in a strong sense, cf. immediately below).

There are reasons for maintaining that the logical rules for Shall and Do should be such that (13) follows logically from (12). In that case the following statement should be valid:

(14) $(\exists A)\,\mathrm{May\ Do}(p, F, A) \rightarrow \mathrm{May}(\exists A)\,\mathrm{Do}(p, F, A)$.

The implication of (13) by (12) means, in Hart's terminology, that a prohibition of interference includes a complete protective perimeter.

When we spoke of a complete protective perimeter in accordance with (13) above, however, we used the word "complete" in a strong sense. A weaker form of completeness, which probably corresponds more closely to what Hart intends, is obtained if we allow ourselves the use of an operator Can (for "it is practically possible that"). The weaker form of completeness can then be expressed in the following statement:

(15) May Do(p, F) & $\sim(\exists A)$(Can Do(q, $\sim F$, A) & May Do(q, $\sim F$, A)).

According to (15), the protective perimeter provides protection from all instrumental actions, with respect to $\sim F$, which q *can* perform.

It is evident that (15) is a logical consequence of (13), so that the stronger form of completeness of the protective perimeter includes the weaker. However, the converse does not hold.

Summing up, we can distinguish between the following three forms of protection of a person's liberty to act:

Prohibition of interference

May Do(p, F) & $\sim$May$(\exists A)$Do(q, $\sim F$, A).

Strongly complete protective perimeter

May Do(p, F) & $\sim(\exists A)$May Do(q, $\sim F$, A).

Weakly complete protective perimeter

May Do(p, F) & $\sim(\exists A)$(Can Do(q, $\sim F$, A) & May Do(q, $\sim F$, A)).

2. Do *and intentionality*

Consider the two statements

(1) John sees to it that the door is closed;
(2) That the door is closed is a state of affairs *intended by John.*

According to everyday English usage, it is probably true that (1) entails (2). For example, if John stumbles and falls against the door so that it is closed one would perhaps not say that John *sees to it* that the door is closed. However, in reading Do as *sees to it that*, I disregard this aspect of English usage. Thus, I do not presuppose that "p sees to it that F" entails "p intends that F". On the other hand, I do not exclude the possibility of increasing the precision of "p sees to it that F" in such a way that the entailment relation obtains, provided that this is compatible with the logical rules which I have already introduced for the Do operator.

3. Do *and the use of propositional variables*

A description of an action in everyday language can be more or less specific with respect to time, place, etc. For example, compare the difference in the specification between the two statements

(1) John pays £50 to Peter;

(2) John pays £50 cash to Peter at 1 p.m. on 1st January 1974 in Peter's office for the repair of John's car.

The symbolism which I have introduced above to be used in what follows does not have the resources to make explicit the distinction of content between (1) and (2); both statements are represented by a statement of the type Do(p, F). However, the symbols I have introduced were by no means intended to make possible a translation into a formal language of all the statements which occur in a natural language. Rather, the symbols are intended as tools for the representation of a certain theory in the form of certain rules and definitions and certain theorems which can thereby be derived; this theory does not depend upon the possibility of making explicit the distinction of content between (1) and (2).

The abstracting from such distinctions as are irrelevant for the purposes at issue—a familiar method in all exact sciences—arises essentially from the use of *variables*. Statements (1) and (2) have the same logical structure in all the relevant respects, with the consequence that both statements are represented in the form Do(p, F). The distinction between statements is constituted by the variable F denoting a different *condition* when Do(p, F) represents (1) than when Do(p, F) represents (2). In (1) the condition F can be described by the statement

(3) Peter is paid £50 by John.

In (2), on the other hand, the condition can be described by the statement

(4) Peter is paid £50 cash by John at 1 p.m. on 1st January 1974 in Peter's office for the repair of John's car.

Since the distinction between conditions (3) and (4) is irrelevant to the theory presented here, it is not made explicit in the symbolism; rather, the language contains a number of variables (F, G, etc.) which denote arbitrary conditions.

Another example of how one abstracts from differences between conditions by using the Do operator is given by the following two statements:

(5) John opens the door.
(6) John keeps the door open.

Both (5) and (6) are represented in the symbolic language by a sentence of the type $\mathrm{Do}(p, F)$. In (5), F denotes the condition *that the door is opened* whilst in (6), F denotes the condition *that the door is kept open.*

4. *The logic of the* Do *operator*

According to the axiom schema A1, all the statements of the form $\mathrm{Do}(p, F) \rightarrow F$ are theorems; i.e., logically valid. A1 can be understood to say that the concept of *seeing to it that* is "effective" or "successful" (cf. Pörn, 1970, p. 11). If the statement "The door is *not* closed" is true, it is false that John *sees to it that* the door is closed. (Consider, for example, such reprimands as "The door is not closed, though I told you to see to it that it is closed".)

According to the rule RI, it holds that if

$$F \leftrightarrow G$$

is a theorem (a logically valid statement), then

$$\mathrm{Do}(p, F) \leftrightarrow \mathrm{Do}(p, G)$$

is also a theorem. RI can be explained informally in the following way. If $F \leftrightarrow G$ is a theorem then F and G denote the *same* condition, and in that case it must also hold that p sees to it that F if, and only if, p sees to it that G.

Sentential logic together with RI gives the following theorem:

$$\mathrm{Do}(p, F) \leftrightarrow \mathrm{Do}(p, (F \,\&\, (G \vee {\sim} G))).$$

That is to say, p sees to it that a given condition obtains if, and only if, p sees to it that the conjunction of both this condition and an arbitrary tautology is the case.

This theorem is completely in accordance with the informal explanation of RI just given. If F denotes a given condition then $F \,\&\, (G \vee {\sim} G)$ denotes precisely the same condition: one does not alter a condition by adding a tautology in describing the condition.

Sentential logic together with RI and A1 gives a logic for the Do operator which is considerably weaker than the logic for modal operators given by Robert Feys' so-called *System T* (for this system see, for example, Hughes & Cresswell, 1968, pp. 30 ff.). RI and A1 can be deduced within *T*, but *T* contains a number of rules of derivation or theorems which cannot be deduced from RI, A1 and sentential logic. Amongst these rules and theorems (which are not regarded in what follows as valid) are:

(I) If $\vdash F$, then $\vdash \mathrm{Do}(p, F)$.
(II) If $\vdash (F \rightarrow G)$, then $\vdash (\mathrm{Do}(p, F) \rightarrow \mathrm{Do}(p, G))$.
(i) $\mathrm{Do}(p, (F \rightarrow G)) \rightarrow (\mathrm{Do}(p, F) \rightarrow \mathrm{Do}(p, G))$.
(ii) $\mathrm{Do}(p, F) \;\&\; \mathrm{Do}(p, G) \rightarrow \mathrm{Do}(p, (F \;\&\; G))$.
(iii) $\mathrm{Do}(p, (F \;\&\; G)) \rightarrow \mathrm{Do}(p, F) \;\&\; \mathrm{Do}(p, G)$.
(iv) $\mathrm{Do}(p, (F \leftrightarrow G)) \rightarrow (\mathrm{Do}(p, F) \leftrightarrow \mathrm{Do}(p, G))$.
(v) $\mathrm{Do}(p, F) \rightarrow \mathrm{Do}(p, (G \rightarrow F))$.
(vi) $\mathrm{Do}(p, {\sim} F) \rightarrow \mathrm{Do}(p, (F \rightarrow G))$.
(vii) $\mathrm{Do}(p, F) \rightarrow \mathrm{Do}(p, (F \vee G))$.

Some of these rules and theorems are clearly incompatible with a reasonable interpretation of Do in terms of the intuitive concept *seeing to it that;* others appear, on the other hand, to be in good agreement with this concept. For example, the rule (I) clearly seems unacceptable: it follows from (I) that each person sees to it that all tautologies are the case. According to the intuitive understanding of what is meant by seeing to it that such and such is the case, a person does not see to it that a state of affairs is the case if it obtains of necessity regardless of how a person acts. On the other hand, theorem (ii) appears to be an example in accordance with the intuitive concept of *seeing to it that:* if a person sees to it that each of a pair of states of affairs obtain then he also sees to it that the conjunction of these obtains.

The rules (I)–(II) and the theorems (i)–(vii) are not needed for the theory which will be presented in what follows; the same holds for the remaining rules and theorems which do not follow from A1 and RI alone but can be deduced within the *System T.* It is not, therefore, necessary to enter further into the discussion of which of these rules and theorems are in themselves reasonable for the Do operator (cf. Pörn, 1970, p. 14 and Kanger, 1972, pp. 109 f.).

IV. *The Operator* Shall *and Its Logic*

1. Shall *as an undefined concept*

There is a long tradition in legal philosophy of trying to explicate the deontic concept "It shall be the case that" and suchlike in terms of *sanctions*. The statement

It shall be the case that *F*,

for example, is interpreted so that a sanction is imposed if *F* does not occur. By "sanction" might be understood familiar deprivations of various kinds: deprivation of freedom, money, etc. (See, for example, Bentham, 1970*b*, pp. 133 ff., and Goble, 1928, pp. 426 ff.) More recently, attempts have been made to explicate Shall along these lines in a logically well-formed language (see especially Anderson, 1956; cf. also Pörn, 1970, pp. 31 ff.).

In what follows, Shall will be treated as an undefined primitive concept. I maintain that "It shall be the case that" has an intelligible, if vague, meaning in ordinary legal usage, and no more precise interpretation in terms of sanctions will be given. (For the difficulties of actually carrying this through, see Anderson's own suggestions, 1967, pp. 345 ff.)

The meaning of Shall is determined here only by the logical rules given. As yet, we have only RII, A2 and A3; but later on, additional rules will be laid down for the combination of Shall and Do. Certain of these rules I regard as purely logical rules, whilst certain others are regarded as "rules of feasibility" (see below, Chapters 6 and 7).

2. Shall *and particular legal systems*

In 1941, Ingemar Hedenius introduced a distinction between what he called genuine and non-genuine legal statements (see Hedenius, 1941, pp. 63 ff.). This distinction has since become a standard one in legal philosophy (see, for example, von Wright, 1963, p. 105; Kanger & Kanger, 1966, p. 99; Alchourrón & Bulygin, 1971, p. 121; Stenius, 1972, pp. 114 ff.). The distinction is expressed here in terms of the distinction between genuine deontic sentences like

(1) Shall *F*, May *F*,

and meta-sentences like

(2) (Shall F) $\in S$, (May F) $\in S$,

where S is the set of deontic sentences belonging to a particular legal system at a particular time (S is, for example, the set of deontic sentences belonging to Swedish Law on 1st January, 1976).

It is important in the following chapters to distinguish between, on the one hand, the theory itself as presented, and on the other hand, the examples used in the metatheory to illustrate the theory's practical applications. The theory itself deals with genuine deontic sentences and their mutual relations; the examples, on the other hand, often make reference to particular legal systems or classes of such systems. (If Z is a genuine deontic sentence, it can be shown, for example, that Z describes a practically significant, or at least reasonable, case by making it probable that Z belongs to the deontic sentences in an existing legal system.)

3. *The principle of consequence and the paradoxes in standard deontic logic*

As rules for the Shall operator we have RII, A2 and A3, which are rules for standard deontic logic. I shall be content to argue that these rules hold for the concept Shall which is applicable in a legal context.

My argument depends on two rules which, though not postulates themselves, can be deduced from the postulates, namely

C1. If $\vdash (A \leftrightarrow B)$, then $\vdash$ (Shall $A \leftrightarrow$ Shall B).
C2. Shall $(A \; \& \; B) \rightarrow$ Shall A.

According to C1, if F is logically equivalent to G, then Shall F is logically equivalent to Shall G. If F and G are logically equivalent they express the same condition, so it would be absurd if Shall F were true and Shall G not, or if Shall F were false and Shall G true. According to C2 it is absurd that Shall(F & G) should be true and yet Shall F false: if F is part of a state of affairs that is commanded, then F itself must be commanded.

Accepting C1 and C2 is equivalent to accepting the so-called *principle of consequence*, namely

C3. If $\vdash (A \rightarrow B)$, then $\vdash$ (Shall $A \rightarrow$ Shall B).

The rule C3 can be deduced given C1 and C2, and similarly C1 and C2 follow from C3. The paradoxes usually brought to bear against acceptance of C3, namely Alf Ross' paradox, the "good samaritan" paradox, Chisholm's paradox, etc., can therefore also be used against C1 and C2.

However, these paradoxes only demonstrate the need for caution in formulating sentences of everyday language (see Wedberg, 1969, pp. 213 ff., where the better known paradoxes of this kind are discussed one by one). It is evident that there are concepts and distinctions in everyday language which cannot be articulated in our symbolic language. But this does not prevent the symbolic language being adequate for certain restricted purposes such as the development of the theory presented in this book. This theory is independent of the problems of formalisation which the paradoxes point to.

To give an example of this need for caution, I shall briefly touch upon the "good samaritan paradox" as an argument against C1 and C2. Considered as an argument against C1 and C2, the argument in question can be formulated in the following way. There are *F* and *G* such that the following three statements are true:

(1) Shall *F*.
(2) *F* is logically equivalent to (*F* & *G*).
(3) ~Shall *G*.

Given (1), (2) and (3) one can—if C1 and C2 are accepted—deduce the contradiction

(4) Shall *G* & ~Shall *G*.

Conclusion: C1 and C2 cannot both be accepted.

That (4) follows from (1), (2) and (3) given both C1 and C2 is undeniable. Thus, the argument hinges on there being as a matter of fact states of affairs such that (1), (2) and (3) are all true. Consider, then, the following example:

(1) Shall(The man who murdered John is punished).
(2) "The man who murdered John is punished" is logically equivalent to "(The man who murdered John is punished) & (There is a man who murdered John)".
(3) ~Shall(There is a man who murdered John).

The suggestion is that from (1)–(3), together with C1 and C2, it follows that

(4) Shall(There is a man who murdered John) & ~Shall(There is a man who murdered John).

The problem here, however, is that (1) is ambiguous, since a definite description is involved, and the question of scope arises. In terms of Russell's theory of descriptions, one interpretation of (1) would be

(1′) Shall$(\exists p)(\forall q)((q$ murdered John $\leftrightarrow (q=p))$ & p is punished).

Informally expressed: Shall(There is exactly one man who murdered John and that man is punished). But in this case, (1) and (3) cannot reasonably be maintained together; that is to say, under this interpretation of (1), the premises of the argument are not true. On the other hand, what is perhaps a more plausible interpretation of (1) (see Wedberg, 1969, pp. 220 f.) would be:

(1″) $(\exists p)(\forall q)((q$ murdered John $\leftrightarrow (q=p))$ & Shall(p is punished)),

where Shall no longer dominates the whole statement. Informally expressed: There is exactly one man who murdered John, and it shall be the case that that man is punished. The premises can now be maintained together, but the putative conclusion (4) no longer follows. Accordingly, the example does not constitute a counterexample to C1 and C2, but gains plausibility only by equivocating on the scope of the definite description.

4. *The logical rules for* Shall

Given that the principle of consequence, or C1 and C2, is accepted, it is easier to understand the import and motivation of the rules RII, A2 and A3.

The rule of derivation RII, namely

If $\vdash A$, then $\vdash$ Shall A,

can also be formulated as follows: if A is absurd, so is May A. The rule expresses the idea that it contradicts the meaning of Shall and May that an absurdity should be permitted.

An argument for this idea can be given in the following steps: 1. It is part of the meaning of Shall and May that in each situation certain things are permitted and others not. The logical rules for Shall ought, therefore, to be so shaped as to exclude everything being permitted. 2. From C1 and C2 it can be deduced that

C4. If $\vdash \sim A$, then $\vdash$ (May $A \rightarrow$ May B),

where B is an arbitrary well-formed statement. The rule C4 says if an absurdity is permitted then everything is permitted. 3. According to what was said in the first stage, the logical rules for Shall should be such that it is precluded that everything is permitted. However, according to C4, if the absurd is permitted, then anything is permitted. Thus, to obtain a reasonable concept of Shall, we need a rule excluding the absurd from what is permitted—a rule which says that if A is absurd so is May A. This is precisely what we achieved with rule RII.

Concerning the axiom schema A2, namely

Shall($A \rightarrow B$) $\rightarrow$ (Shall $A \rightarrow$ Shall B)

I shall again appeal to an argument relying on C1 and C2. Given C1 and C2, the following statement is a consequence of the *negation* of A2:

(1) May A & $\sim$May(A & B) & $\sim$May(A & $\sim B$).

However, the truth of (1) is incompatible with a reasonable interpretation of Shall and May. Suppose that a certain statutory law contained a statement of the form (1). If the prohibitions against the alternatives A & B and A & $\sim B$ are taken seriously, one is forced to conclude that the permission of A is only apparent; it is logically excluded that A could be true without the prohibitions being infringed. Since (1) is untenable, then, we must maintain A2.

Finally, the axiom schema A3, namely

Shall $A \rightarrow$ $\sim$Shall$\sim A$

can be motivated in the following way. Given RII and A2, it can be deduced that

(2) Shall A & Shall$\sim A \rightarrow$ Shall(A & $\sim A$),

where the antecedent is equivalent to the negation of A3 and the consequent expresses that the absurd is prescribed. Furthermore, one can, given RII and A2, deduce

(3) $\text{Shall}(A \;\&\; \sim A) \rightarrow \text{Shall}\, B$,

where B is an arbitrary well-formed statement; i.e., if the absurd is prescribed then everything is prescribed.

It turns out that the argument presented in favour of RII can be propounded, *a fortiori*, in favour of A3. If it is excluded that the absurd is permitted, it ought also to be reasonable to exclude the absurd being prescribed. And if it is excluded that everything should be permitted, it ought also to be reasonably excluded that everything could be prescribed.

5. *The Sollen-Können principle and conflicting obligations*

A3 can be considered as a version of the so-called Sollen-Können principle (cf. Lemmon, 1965, p. 47). It should be noted that A3—given RII and A2—can also be formulated as a rule of derivation as follows:

C5. If $\vdash \sim A$, then $\vdash \sim \text{Shall}\, A$.

This rule says that if A is logically impossible, then it is absurd that A should be prescribed. (Given RII and A2, C5 can be deduced from A3 and conversely.)

Bearing in mind the unacceptable results consequent upon the supposition of the negation of A3, very strong arguments indeed would be required to put A3 in question. So far as the principle corresponding to A3 for the concept Ought is concerned, there is an alleged counterexample involving *conflicting obligations* (see, e.g., Lemmon, 1965, p. 45; Danielsson, 1968, pp. 60 f.; Hansson, 1970, p. 245). However, in the case of the juridical concept Shall examples are not to be found in the well-known legal systems of genuinely conflicting obligations. That such examples are not to be found follows from the fact that these legal systems as a rule of law (or general legal principle) accept the statement

C6. $\sim \text{Possibly}\, A \rightarrow \; \sim \text{Shall}\, A$, where "Possibly" stands for *practically possible* (the principle "impossibilium nulla est obligatio"). Since any reasonable concept of Possibly must satisfy the axiom

$$\sim\text{Possibly}(A \mathbin{\&} \sim A),$$

C6 is logically inconsistent with Shall A & Shall $\sim A$—i.e., the negation of A3. If C6 is *true* relative to a given legal system, Shall A & Shall $\sim A$ is therefore *false* relative to this legal system. In a system where C6 is a rule of law (general legal principle) it is not possible to find an example of a situation which would render the statement Shall A & Shall $\sim A$ true.

As a matter of fact, a comprehensive and important part of the legal rules comprise precisely rules which give solutions for *apparently* (or *prima facie*) conflicting obligations. For example, a familiar legal situation is that a person sells the same object twice—i.e., to two people independently. Thus, suppose that John owns a car which he sells at time t_1 to Peter, but the car is not handed over at the time of purchase; rather, John promises Peter he will receive it at time t_3. However, at time t_2 John sells the car again, this time to Henry, though the car remains in John's possession, John having promised Henry he will receive the car at time t_3.

It seems in this case that John had two incompatible obligations—as though the following were true:

(1) It shall be the case that John sees to it that Peter receives the car at t_3.

(2) It shall be the case that John sees to it that Henry receives the car at t_3.

Under Swedish law, as with several other well-known legal systems, however, a solution is forthcoming since (1) is in fact true whilst (2) is false. (The so-called *principle of priority* applies in this case since neither of the purchasers has the car in his possession.) Accordingly, the conflict between the two obligations is only apparent.

In some cases the legal solution is such that a person who is apparently obliged to perform two conflicting actions, is in fact obliged to perform at least one of them, though he may perform either (so-called *alternative obligations;* cf. below, p. 94). Thus, the solution is of the kind

(3) May Do(p, F) & May Do(p, G) & Shall(Do(p, F) ∨ Do(p, G)),

where F and G are two incompatible conditions. This sort of solution is also available in the example of selling a car twice if it is assumed that John's contract with Peter is made simultaneously with the contract between John and Henry doing so (which would be the case if, for example, acceptances of John's terms arrived from both Peter and Henry in the same post). In fact this sort of solution is conceivable even in the case where G is logically equivalent with $\sim F$, in which case it takes the form

(4) May Do(p, F) & May Do(p, $\sim F$) & Shall(Do(p, F) ∨ Do(p, $\sim F$)).

(I shall return to the question of the plausibility of (4) later on, though in a different context. Cases where (4) obtains constitute counter-examples to a principle I call "the philosophy of indolence", which I shall in fact reject; see below, Chapter 3.)

CHAPTER 3

One-Agent Types

I. *Introduction*

In this and the following two chapters a theory for what I call *basic types of legal positions* is presented. The theory contains a system of *one-agent types*, a system of *individualistic two-agent types* and a system of *collectivistic two-agent types*. I begin in this chapter with one-agent types.

The theory for basic types of legal positions can be seen as a further development of Kanger's theory for atomic types of right. As in Kanger's theory, the basic principle is to construct various combinations of the two operators Shall and Do, and the methods used for the three systems depend upon the construction of so-called *basic conjunctions*.

This connection with Kanger's theory establishes an indirect link between our theory of legal positions and those of Bentham, Austin and Hohfeld. However, the traditional concepts *right*, *liberty*, etc. which play an important role for these authors will not be analysed in what follows. The basic types of legal positions which enter into the three systems are defined directly in terms of Shall and Do, and they are denoted by numbers rather than the more familiar terms.

Rather than speak of legal *position*, one might say "legal *relation*". However, the expression *legal relation*, occurring in the Hohfeld tradition, is used solely for relations which involve *exactly two parties* (cf. Corbin, 1919, p. 165). Therefore, I choose to speak of *legal position* to distinguish a relation which need not involve at least or at most two parties.

II. *The Construction of One-Agent Types*

1. *Deontic basic conjunctions*

Consider the three statements

(i) $\text{Do}(p, F)$;

(ii) $\text{Do}(p, \sim F)$;

(iii) $\sim\text{Do}(p, F) \,\&\, \sim\text{Do}(p, \sim F)$.

It is a theorem that each of these statements implies the negation of each of the others. Furthermore, the disjunction of all three is a tautology. The three statements (i)–(iii) therefore constitute a partition of logical alternatives into three mutually incompatible and jointly exhaustive alternatives.

For each of the alternatives (i)–(iii), it either *may* be the case (is *allowed*) or *may not* be the case (is *forbidden*). Thus, it holds that:

either: May Do(p, F),
or: ~May Do(p, F);
either: May Do(p, ~F),
or: ~May Do(p, ~F);
either: May(~Do(p, F) & ~Do(p, ~F)),
or: ~May(~Do(p, F) & ~Do(p, ~F)).

If a conjunction is constructed from the first statement of each pair, namely:

May Do(p, F),
May Do(p, ~F),
May(~Do(p, F) & ~Do(p, ~F)),

and then all those conjunctions obtained after first negating one or more of these three statements, eight (2^3) conjunctions result. Of these, one is self-contradictory, namely

~May Do(p, F) & ~May(~Do(p, F) & ~Do(p, ~F)) &
~May Do(p, ~F).

(A statement saying that none of the logically possible alternatives may obtain is contradictory according to the logic for Shall.) The remaining seven conjunctions are as follows:

1. May Do(p, F) & May(~Do(p, F) & ~Do(p, ~F)) &
   May Do(p, ~F).
2. May Do(p, F) & May(~Do(p, F) & ~Do(p, ~F)) &
   ~May Do(p, ~F).
3. May Do(p, F) & ~May(~Do(p, F) & ~Do(p, ~F)) &
   May Do(p, ~F).

4. $\sim$May Do(p, F) & May($\sim$Do(p, F) & $\sim$Do(p, $\sim F$)) & May Do(p, $\sim F$).
5. May Do(p, F) & $\sim$May($\sim$Do(p, F) & $\sim$Do(p, $\sim F$)) & $\sim$May Do(p, $\sim F$).
6. $\sim$May Do(p, F) & May($\sim$Do(p, F) & $\sim$Do(p, $\sim F$)) & $\sim$May Do(p, $\sim F$).
7. $\sim$May Do(p, F) & $\sim$May($\sim$Do(p, F) & $\sim$Do(p, $\sim F$)) & May Do(p, $\sim F$).

The method of construction of the statements 1–7 can be regarded as an *iterated* construction of so-called *basic conjunctions* (cf. Kemeny, Snell & Thompson, 1966, pp. 15 ff.). The first step of the construction is to take all the basic conjunctions which can be obtained from the statements

Do(p, F),
Do(p, $\sim F$).

Eliminating self-contradictory basic conjunctions and redundant components, there remain the statements

(i) Do(p, F);
(ii) Do(p, $\sim F$);
(iii) $\sim$Do(p, F) & $\sim$Do(p, $\sim F$).

The second step brings in the operator May governing each of (i)–(iii), taking all the basic conjunctions constructed from the new statements thereby obtained. Self-contradictory conjunctions are eliminated, and we are left with statements 1–7.

No constituent of the conjunctions which is redundant for each value of F remains in 1–7. However, it is apparent that statements 5–7 can be shortened. A statement, which says that all logically possible alternatives apart from one are forbidden, is equivalent to a statement saying that the last-named alternative *shall* be the case. Accordingly, it can be shown that the statements 5–7 are equivalent, respectively, to:

5′. Shall Do(p, F);
6′. Shall($\sim$Do(p, F) & $\sim$Do(p, $\sim F$));
7′. Shall Do(p, $\sim F$).

The statements 1–7 are *deontic basic conjunctions* for Do(p, F) and Do(p, $\sim F$), whereas 5′–7′ are only equivalent to such conjunctions.

2. *Disjunctions of deontic basic conjunctions*

It is easily seen that exactly one of the basic conjunctions 1–7 in the preceding section is true for a given value of p and F: the negation of the disjunction of 1–7 is a contradiction, and each of 1–7 implies the negation of each of the others. Thus, the statements 1–7 constitute a partition of the logical possibilities into seven mutually inconsistent and jointly exhaustive alternatives.

The possibility of constructing disjunctions of one or more of 1–7 is very significant in connection with the question of expressing in standardised form various statements concerning p's legal position in relation to F. I shall consider some different types of statements which can be reformulated as such disjunctions.

From the list of 1–7 it is obvious that each of the statements

(i) May Do(p, F),
(ii) May($\sim$Do(p, F) & $\sim$Do(p, $\sim F$)),
(iii) May Do(p, $\sim F$),

is equivalent to a disjunction of exactly four of 1–7. For example, the statement (i) is equivalent to the disjunction of statements 1, 2, 3 and 5 above. Similarly, each of

(iv) $\sim$May Do(p, F),
(v) $\sim$May($\sim$Do(p, F) & $\sim$Do(p, $\sim F$)),
(vi) $\sim$May Do(p, $\sim F$),

is equivalent to the disjunction of exactly three of 1–7.

The statements (iv)–(vi) are special cases of the so-called Boolean compounds of (i)–(iii). (By a Boolean compound of n statements $F_1, \ldots,$ F_n, where $n \geqslant 1$, is understood a compound of $F_1, \ldots, F_n$ constructed with the connectives $\sim$, &, v, $\rightarrow$ and $\leftrightarrow$.) Other cases of Boolean compounds of (i)–(iii) are for example

(vii) May Do(p, F) $\leftrightarrow \sim$May Do(p, $\sim F$);
(viii) May Do(p, F) $\rightarrow \sim$[May Do(p, $\sim F$) $\leftrightarrow$ May($\sim$Do(p, F) & $\sim$Do(p, $\sim F$))].

The statement (vii) is constructed from (i) and (iii) with the connectives $\sim$ and $\leftrightarrow$; (viii) is constructed from (i)–(iii) with the connectives $\sim$, $\rightarrow$ and $\leftrightarrow$.

According to a well-known theorem, every Boolean compound of one or more of n statements $F_1, \ldots, F_n$ is equivalent to a disjunction of one or more of the basic conjunctions which can be constructed from $F_1, \ldots, F_n$ (so-called disjunctive normal form). The list of 1–7 contains all of the self-consistent basic conjunctions which can be constructed from (i)–(iii). Each self-consistent Boolean compound of (i)–(iii) can therefore be formulated as a disjunction of one or more of 1–7. Thus, (vii) for example is equivalent to the disjunction of 2, 4, 5 and 7, and (viii) is equivalent to the disjunction of 2, 3, 4, 6 and 7.

As an illustration of a more complicated statement, consider

(ix) $\text{May} \sim \text{Do}(p, F) \rightarrow \text{Shall}[\sim \text{Do}(p, \sim F) \leftrightarrow (\sim \text{Do}(p, F) \,\&\, \sim \text{Do}(p, \sim F))]$.

The statement (ix) is not a Boolean compound of (i)–(iii); rather, it is a Boolean compound of the components

$\text{May} \sim \text{Do}(p, F)$,
$\text{Shall}[\sim \text{Do}(p, F) \leftrightarrow (\sim \text{Do}(p, F) \,\&\, \sim \text{Do}(p, \sim F))]$,

where the operators May and Shall govern a Boolean compound of $\text{Do}(p, F)$ and $\text{Do}(p, \sim F)$. However, (ix) is equivalent to a disjunction of statements from the list 1–7, namely 2, 5 and 6.

All of the statements (i)–(ix) so far given can be characterised in terms of a common feature as follows: each of (i)–(ix) is a *Boolean compound of one or more components in which the operators* Shall *or* May *govern one of* $\text{Do}(p, F)$ *or* $\text{Do}(p, \sim F)$, *or govern a Boolean compound of* $\text{Do}(p, F)$ *and* $\text{Do}(p, \sim F)$. It is a theorem, that every self-consistent statement which has this structure is equivalent to a disjunction of one or more of the statements 1–7.

The proof of this theorem is easily obtained by combining the theorem given above, that each self-consistent Boolean compound of (i)–(iii) can be formulated as a disjunction of one or more of the statements from the list 1–7, with a general theorem from deontic logic formulated by von Wright (1972, pp. 18 f.). Let S be a statement satisfying the characterisation in question. S can then be reformulated as a disjunction of one or more of the statements in the list 1–7 in the following stages. I. Each occurrence of Shall is replaced by $\sim$May$\sim$ as sanctioned by the definition. II. Each statement which is then governed by May (with or without a negation sign in front of May) is formulated as a disjunction of one or more of

(1) $\quad \text{Do}(p, F)$,
(2) $\quad \sim\text{Do}(p, F) \mathbin{\&} \sim\text{Do}(p, \sim F)$,
(3) $\quad \text{Do}(p, \sim F)$,

(that is to say, in disjunctive normal form). III. According to the theorem from deontic logic,

$$\text{May}(F_1 \vee \ldots \vee F_n) \leftrightarrow (\text{May } F_1 \vee \ldots \vee \text{May } F_n),$$

May is distributed in each disjunction governed by May. S has thereby been formulated as a Boolean compound of the statements (i)–(iii) above (p. 88). IV. If S is self-consistent, it can accordingly be formulated as a disjunction of one or more of the statements from the list 1–7.

As an example we can consider the statement (ix) above, i.e.,

(ix) $\quad \text{May}\sim\text{Do}(p, F) \rightarrow \text{Shall}[\sim\text{Do}(p, \sim F) \leftrightarrow (\sim\text{Do}(p, F) \mathbin{\&} \sim\text{Do}(p, \sim F))]$.

According to what has just been said, (ix) is equivalent with the disjunction of statements 2, 5, and 6 in the list 1–7. Let us consider the steps in which (ix) can be changed to such a disjunction.

Step one. For Shall we substitute $\sim$May$\sim$ and obtain

(ix′) $\quad \text{May}\sim\text{Do}(p, F) \rightarrow \sim\text{May}\sim[\sim\text{Do}(p, \sim F) \leftrightarrow (\sim\text{Do}(p, F) \mathbin{\&} \sim\text{Do}(p, \sim F))]$.

Step two. Each statement in (ix′) which is governed by May is formulated as a disjunction of one or more of (1)–(3), i.e., in disjunctive normal form. The statement $\sim\text{Do}(p, F)$ in the antecedent is equivalent to

$$(\sim\text{Do}(p, F) \mathbin{\&} \sim\text{Do}(p, \sim F)) \vee \text{Do}(p, \sim F).$$

The statement

$$\sim[\sim \mathrm{Do}(p, F) \leftrightarrow (\sim \mathrm{Do}(p, F) \;\&\; \sim \mathrm{Do}(p, \sim F))]$$

in the consequent is equivalent to $\mathrm{Do}(p, \sim F)$. We obtain therefore:

(ix″) $\mathrm{May}[(\sim \mathrm{Do}(p, F) \;\&\; \sim \mathrm{Do}(p, \sim F)) \vee \mathrm{Do}(p, \sim F)] \rightarrow$
$\sim \mathrm{May}\ \mathrm{Do}(p, \sim F)$.

Step three. The operator May is distributed giving:

(ix‴) $[\mathrm{May}(\sim \mathrm{Do}(p, F) \;\&\; \sim \mathrm{Do}(p, \sim F)) \vee \mathrm{May}\ \mathrm{Do}(p, \sim F)] \rightarrow$
$\sim \mathrm{May}\ \mathrm{Do}(p, \sim F)$.

The original statement (ix) has thus been formulated as a Boolean compound (with the connectives $\vee$, $\rightarrow$, and $\sim$) of the statements

$\mathrm{May}(\sim \mathrm{Do}(p, F) \;\&\; \sim \mathrm{Do}(p, \sim F))$,
$\mathrm{May}\ \mathrm{Do}(p, \sim F)$,

i.e., of statements (ii) and (iii) above (p. 88).

Step four. The statement (ix‴) is formulated as a disjunction of statements from the list 1–7 in the previous section (pp. 86f.), i.e., in disjunctive normal form. The statement (ix‴) is equivalent to $\sim \mathrm{May}\ \mathrm{Do}(p, \sim F)$ which, in its turn, is equivalent to the disjunction of the statements 2, 5, and 6 of the list 1–7, i.e.,

2. $\mathrm{May}\ \mathrm{Do}(p, F) \;\&\; \mathrm{May}(\sim \mathrm{Do}(p, F) \;\&\; \sim \mathrm{Do}(p, \sim F)) \;\&$
$\sim \mathrm{May}\ \mathrm{Do}(p, \sim F)$;
5. $\mathrm{May}\ \mathrm{Do}(p, F) \;\&\; \sim \mathrm{May}(\sim \mathrm{Do}(p, F) \;\&\; \sim \mathrm{Do}(p, \sim F)) \;\&$
$\sim \mathrm{May}\ \mathrm{Do}(p, \sim F)$;
6. $\sim \mathrm{May}\ \mathrm{Do}(p, F) \;\&\; \mathrm{May}(\sim \mathrm{Do}(p, F) \;\&\; \sim \mathrm{Do}(p, \sim F)) \;\&$
$\sim \mathrm{May}\ \mathrm{Do}(p, \sim F)$.

The original statement (ix) has thus been formulated as a disjunction of the statements 2, 5, and 6 from the list 1–7 in the preceding section.

With one or two minor changes this theorem also holds for deontic basic conjunctions for two or more agents (Chapters 4 and 5). Thus the theorem is of broader interest than the present considerations concerning only one agent would lead us to expect.

3. *Basic types of one-agent legal positions*

To the statements 1–7 there correspond seven *basic types of one-agent legal positions*, denoted here by $T_1, \ldots, T_7$. The types $T_1, \ldots, T_7$ are given by letting each condition expressed by the statements 1–7 define a set —the set of ordered pairs $\langle p, F\rangle$ such that statement 1 is true for $\langle p, F\rangle$, the set of ordered pairs $\langle p, F\rangle$ such that statement 2 is true for $\langle p, F\rangle$, and so forth. Each of the seven sets generated in this way is a basic type of one-agent legal position. Accordingly:

$T_1 = \{\langle p, F\rangle \mid \text{May Do}(p, F)\ \&\ \text{May}({\sim}\text{Do}(p, F)\ \&\ {\sim}\text{Do}(p, F))\ \&$
$\quad \text{May Do}(p, {\sim}F)\}$.
$T_2 = \{\langle p, F\rangle \mid \text{May Do}(p, F)\ \&\ \text{May}({\sim}\text{Do}(p, F)\ \&\ {\sim}\text{Do}(p, {\sim}F))\ \&$
$\quad {\sim}\text{May Do}(p, {\sim}F)\}$.
$T_3 = \{\langle p, F\rangle \mid \text{May Do}(p, F)\ \&\ {\sim}\text{May}({\sim}\text{Do}(p, F)\ \&\ {\sim}\text{Do}(p, {\sim}F))\ \&$
$\quad \text{May Do}(p, {\sim}F)\}$.
$T_4 = \{\langle p, F\rangle \mid {\sim}\text{May Do}(p, F)\ \&\ \text{May}({\sim}\text{Do}(p, F)\ \&\ {\sim}\text{Do}(p, {\sim}F))\ \&$
$\quad \text{May Do}(p, {\sim}F)\}$.
$T_5 = \{\langle p, F\rangle \mid \text{Shall Do}(p, F)\}$.
$T_6 = \{\langle p, F\rangle \mid \text{Shall}({\sim}\text{Do}(p, F)\ \&\ {\sim}\text{Do}(p, {\sim}F))\}$.
$T_7 = \{\langle p, F\rangle \mid \text{Shall Do}(p, {\sim}F)\}$.

The relation *converse* between basic types of one-agent legal positions is defined as follows (cf. above, p. 58):

DEFINITION. Let T, T' be variables for $T_1, \ldots, T_7$. T is the *converse* of $T' =_{\text{def.}}$ For each p and each F, $\langle p, F\rangle \in T$ if and only if $\langle p, {\sim}F\rangle \in T'$.

By a *neutral* type, I understand (in connection with Kanger) a type which is its own converse. It is easily seen that T_4 is the converse of T_2 and T_7 is the converse of T_5, whilst T_1, T_3 and T_6 are neutral.

4. *Elements of one-agent types: An illustration*

For the reasons given above, $\langle p, F\rangle$ belongs to exactly one of $T_1, \ldots, T_7$ for every value of p and F. But it has not yet been shown that none of $T_1, \ldots, T_7$ is *empty*. In other words, it has not been shown that for each $T \in \{T_1, \ldots, T_7\}$ there is a value of p and F such that $\langle p, F\rangle \in T$. It seems to me that this is to be accomplished by considering examples.

It is perhaps appropriate to begin with examples of T_1, T_2 and T_4–T_7

which are less problematic (T_3 requires extensive comment). I will suppose that John owns a property, called Whiteacre, and that Blackacre is an adjacent property. Let us consider the following states of affairs (or conditions):

F_1. that the main building on Whiteacre is painted white.
F_2. that a fence is erected at the boundary between Whiteacre and Blackacre.
F_3. that a factory building is built on Blackacre close to the border of Whiteacre.
F_4. that the electricity installations on Whiteacre are in accord with the existing security provisions.
F_5. that the main building on Blackacre is painted white.
F_6. that the requisite fire-fighting equipment does not exist on Whiteacre.

It is a natural supposition that the following should hold:

(i) $\langle \text{John}, F_1 \rangle \in T_1$.
(ii) $\langle \text{John}, F_2 \rangle \in T_2$.
(iii) $\langle \text{John}, F_3 \rangle \in T_4$.
(iv) $\langle \text{John}, F_4 \rangle \in T_5$.
(v) $\langle \text{John}, F_5 \rangle \in T_6$.
(vi) $\langle \text{John}, F_6 \rangle \in T_7$.

First, concerning (i), it is usual that an owner's so-called right of disposition over the object owned means that he is in T_1 with respect to a number of states of affairs which concern this object, and which do not essentially involve anyone else. This is exemplified in (i): John's freedom with respect to F_1 is maximal.

Statements (ii) and (iii) illustrate cases where the situation concerns the rights of others (in this case the neighbour's), and where the owner's freedom is more restricted. According to (ii), John may not prevent the erecting of a fence on the boundary of Blackacre, for such an action on his part would violate his neighbour's right. John can, however, choose between seeing to it that a fence is erected and remaining passive concerning the erection of a fence. According to (iii) John may, conversely, prevent the factory building being erected (in view of the effect the construction would have on his own property); thus he has a kind of "right of veto". He may also remain passive in respect to the construction. But he may not himself see to it that a factory building is erected on his neighbour's property.

Statements (iv) and (vi) illustrate cases of the "owner's obligations". John shall see to it that the electricity installations are satisfactory, and he shall see to it that the fire-fighting equipment is not lacking.

Finally, statement (v) illustrates a case in which John is completely unauthorised to influence the situation (since it is no business of his): John may neither bring about nor prevent the main building on his neighbour's property being painted white.

5. *Alternative obligations and one-agent type T_3*

Concerning the remaining type of our original seven, namely T_3, we might first consider the cases described by the following statement:

(1) $\text{May}\sim\text{Do}(p, F)\ \&\ \text{May}\sim\text{Do}(p, G)\ \&\ \text{Shall}(\text{Do}(p, F) \vee \text{Do}(p, G))$.

Such cases are known in law as cases of "alternative obligation". For example, consider the following quotation from Alchourrón & Bulygin (cf. above, p. 84):

> There is e.g. the well known case of Sempronius who has an obligation to give a cow or a horse to Ticius, but he has not the obligation to give Ticius a cow nor has he the obligation to give him a horse. He can fulfil his obligation by giving either of the two things, since he must give one of the two, but he is not obliged to give either in particular. (1971, p. 157)

Let p, F and G be as follows:

p: Sempronius,
F: that Ticius receives a cow from Sempronius,
G: that Ticius receives a horse from Sempronius.

Statement (1) now describes the example taken from Alchourrón & Bulygin.

The statement that interests us now,

$$\langle p, F\rangle \in T_3,$$

describes a special kind of "alternative obligation". If we substitute $\sim F$ for G in (1) we obtain

(2) $\text{May} \sim \text{Do}(p, F) \;\&\; \text{May} \sim \text{Do}(p, \sim F) \;\&$
$\text{Shall}(\text{Do}(p, F) \vee \text{Do}(p, \sim F))$.

It is easily shown that (2) is equivalent to

$$\langle p, F \rangle \in T_3,$$

that is to say, to

(2′) $\text{May Do}(p, F) \;\&\; \text{May Do}(p, \sim F) \;\&\; \sim \text{May}(\sim \text{Do}(p, F) \;\&$
$\sim \text{Do}(p, \sim F))$.

Proof

(i) $\text{Shall}(\text{Do}(p, F) \vee \text{Do}(p, \sim F)) \rightarrow \text{Shall}(\sim \text{Do}(p, F) \rightarrow \text{Do}(p, \sim F))$.

(ii) $\text{Shall}(\sim \text{Do}(p, F) \rightarrow \text{Do}(p, \sim F)) \rightarrow (\text{Shall} \sim \text{Do}(p, F) \rightarrow$
$\text{Shall Do}(p \sim F))$.

(iii) $(\text{Shall} \sim \text{Do}(p, F) \rightarrow \text{Shall Do}(p, \sim F)) \rightarrow (\text{May} \sim \text{Do}(p, \sim F) \rightarrow$
$\text{May Do}(p, F))$.

(iv) $\text{Shall}(\text{Do}(p, F) \vee \text{Do}(p, \sim F)) \rightarrow (\text{May} \sim \text{Do}(p, \sim F) \rightarrow$
$\text{May Do}(p, F))$.

(v) $\text{Do}(p, F) \rightarrow \sim \text{Do}(p, \sim F)$.

(vi) $\text{May Do}(p, F) \rightarrow \text{May} \sim \text{Do}(p, \sim F)$.

(vii) $\text{Shall}(\text{Do}(p, F) \vee \text{Do}(p, \sim F)) \rightarrow (\text{May Do}(p, F) \leftrightarrow$
$\text{May} \sim \text{Do}(p, \sim F))$.

(viii) $\text{Shall}(\text{Do}(p, F) \vee \text{Do}(p, \sim F)) \rightarrow (\text{May Do}(p, \sim F) \leftrightarrow$
$\text{May} \sim \text{Do}(p, F))$.

(ix) $\text{Shall}(\text{Do}(p, F) \vee \text{Do}(p, \sim F)) \leftrightarrow \sim \text{May}(\sim \text{Do}(p, F) \;\&$
$\sim \text{Do}(p, \sim F))$.

It follows immediately from (vii)–(ix) that (2) is equivalent to (2′).

Statements (2) and (2′) represent "alternative obligations" in a different way from that in the last-quoted example, however. In Alchourrón & Bulygin's example the conditions F and G are not logically incompatible (nor, for that matter, need they be practically incompatible). Statements (2) and (2′), on the other hand, deal with conditions which are not only logically incompatible, but *mutually contradictory:* F and $\sim F$. The example given does not, therefore, lend any support to the supposition that there are values of p and F such that statements (2) and (2′) are true for them; i.e., that T_3 is not empty.

Let us consider what it would mean to introduce a general principle that T_3 is an empty set. This is to say that the negation of (2) is true for every value of p and F. The negation of (2) is equivalent to each of the statements

(3) $(\text{May} \sim \text{Do}(p, F)\ \&\ \text{May} \sim \text{Do}(p, \sim F)) \rightarrow \text{May}(\sim \text{Do}(p, F)\ \&\ \sim \text{Do}(p, \sim F))$;

(3′) $\text{Shall}(\text{Do}(p, F) \vee \text{Do}(p, \sim F)) \rightarrow (\text{Shall Do}(p, F) \vee \text{Shall Do}(p, \sim F))$.

Thus, to say that T_3 is empty amounts to maintaining (3) and (3′) as general principles. In other words, a general principle would be introduced according to which May can be freely distributed over a conjunction of $\sim \text{Do}(p, F)$ and $\sim \text{Do}(p, \sim F)$, or equivalently, Shall can be freely distributed over a disjunction of $\text{Do}(p, F)$ and $\text{Do}(p, \sim F)$.

Considered as general principles, statements (3) and (3′) can be said to express a kind of "philosophy of indolence". According to one current interpretation, the statement (2′) means that there is at least one legally acceptable situation where p sees to it that F and at least one legally acceptable situation where p sees to it that not F, whilst there is no legally acceptable situation where p neither sees to it that F nor sees to it that not F. According to (2), (2′), therefore,

$$\sim \text{Do}(p,F)\ \&\ \sim \text{Do}(p, \sim F)$$

describes an alternative (p's "passivity" with respect to F) which from a legal standpoint is worse than both the alternative described by $\text{Do}(p, F)$ and the alternative described by $\text{Do}(p, \sim F)$. Informally expressed: p's "passivity" is worse than p's "activity", irrespective of whether the activity results in the accomplishing of F or the accomplishing of its contradictory state of affairs, not F.

It is now clear in what sense the principles (3) and (3′) express a "philosophy of indolence". (3) and (3′) each negate (2), (2′) and thereby preclude the legal preferences' being as just outlined. For each value of p and F it holds that p's passivity with respect to F is at least as good as p's seeing to it that F or at least as good as p's seeing to it that not F. Passivity is never the worst alternative.

It might be thought that "the philosophy of indolence" is an attractive principle. But it cannot be accepted as a universal principle when applied to legal systems as they are in fact constituted. Type T_3 is not empty.

By way of example, an instance of

$$\langle p, F \rangle \in T_3$$

can be such that one shows that there are p, q and F such that

(i) $\text{May}(\text{Do}(p, F) \,\&\, \text{Do}(p, \sim G))$,
(ii) $\text{May}(\text{Do}(p, G) \,\&\, \text{Do}(p, \sim F))$,
(iii) $\text{Shall}[(\text{Do}(p, F) \,\&\, \text{Do}(p, \sim G)) \vee (\text{Do}(p, G) \,\&\, \text{Do}(p, \sim F))]$,

from which it immediately follows that

(iv) $\text{May Do}(p, F) \,\&\, \text{May Do}(p, \sim F) \,\&\, \text{Shall}(\text{Do}(p, F) \vee \text{Do}(p, \sim F))$,
(v) $\text{May Do}(p, G) \,\&\, \text{May Do}(p, \sim G) \,\&\, \text{Shall}(\text{Do}(p, G) \vee \text{Do}(p, \sim G))$,

which give

$$\langle p, F \rangle \in T_3,$$
$$\langle p, G \rangle \in T_3.$$

A trivial instance of (i)–(iii) can be imagined if we suppose that the ventilation in a certain room is controlled by the door or the window being open, and that the room is in need of a change of air. If both door and window are closed, there is no ventilation; this is, accordingly, not a good alternative. If both door and window are open, there is a strong draught, and neither is this (I shall suppose) a good alternative. The remaining possibilities are that either the door or the window is open and the other closed, and I shall suppose that these alternatives are of equal value. Let p be a person responsible for airing the room and F and G be as follows:

F: that the window is closed.
G: that the door is closed.

An instance of (i)–(iii) is thereby obtained. Informally expressed,

(i′) It may be the case that p sees to it that the window is closed and p sees to it that the door is open.

(ii′) It may be the case that p sees to it that the window is open and p sees to it that the door is closed.

(iii′) It shall be the case that either

(a) p sees to it that the window is closed and p sees to it that the door is open, or

(b) p sees to it that the window is open and p sees to it that the door is closed.

(For a discussion of another example of T_3, one which is somewhat more controversial, see Appendix.)

6. *Basic types of legal positions, atomic types of rights and maximal solutions*

Before developing further the system for the seven basic types of one-agent legal positions, the construction of $T_1, ..., T_7$ will be compared with the construction of Kanger's *atomic types of right* (above, p. 54), and also briefly compared with the theory for so-called *maximal solutions* described by Charles E. Alchourrón and Eugenio Bulygin (Alchourrón & Bulygin, 1971, pp. 13 ff. and 34 ff.).

The theory of atomic types of right. Each of Kanger's 26 atomic types of right listed above (p. 56) can be defined as the intersection of certain of the so-called simple types of right *claim, freedom, power*, etc. Kanger's atomic type number 1, for example, is defined as

$$\{\langle p, q, F\rangle | \langle p, q, F\rangle \in \text{Power} \cap \text{Not immunity} \cap \text{Counter-power} \cap \text{Not counter-immunity}\},$$

Kanger's atomic type number 2 is defined as

$$\{\langle p, q, F\rangle | \langle p, q, F\rangle \in \text{Not power} \cap \text{Immunity} \cap \text{Not counter-power} \cap \text{Counter-immunity}\},$$

and so forth for the remaining twenty-four types.

The simple types of right *claim, freedom, power*, etc., are explicated by Kanger in terms of statements formulated with the help of Shall and Do. The twenty-six atomic types can therefore also be defined in terms of conditions formulated with Shall and Do. Kanger's atomic type number 1 can thus be defined as

$\{\langle p, q, F\rangle \mid$ May Do(p, F) & May Do$(q, \sim F)$ &
May Do$(p, \sim F)$ & May Do$(q, F)\}$,

his atomic type number 2 as

$\{\langle p, q, F\rangle \mid \sim$May Do$(p, F)$ & $\sim$May Do$(q, \sim F)$ &
$\sim$May Do$(p, \sim F)$ & $\sim$May Do$(q, F)\}$,

and so forth.

It can easily be shown that the list of Kanger's twenty-six atomic types defined with the help of Shall (or May) and Do as just described can be obtained by the following method of construction. Kanger refers to this method as the building of atomic types by coordination (see Kanger & Kanger, 1966, p. 96).

Beginning with the two statements

Shall Do(p, F),
Shall Do$(p, \sim F)$.

all basic conjunctions are constructed which can be obtained from them. All self-contradictory statements are then eliminated, together with redundant components of conjunctions, and the following six statements are obtained:

(i) May Do(p, F) & May Do$(p, \sim F)$.
(ii) $\sim$May Do(p, F) & $\sim$May Do$(p, \sim F)$.
(iii) Shall Do(p, F).
(iv) May Do(p, F) & $\sim$Shall Do(p, F) & $\sim$May Do$(p, \sim F)$.
(v) Shall Do$(p, \sim F)$.
(vi) $\sim$May Do(p, F) & $\sim$Shall Do$(p, \sim F)$ & May Do$(p, \sim F)$.

The corresponding statements (i′)–(vi′) are then constructed by substituting q for p everywhere in (i)–(vi). Finally, each of (i)–(vi) is combined in a conjunction with each of (i′)–(vi′) giving

(1) May Do(p, F) & May Do$(p, \sim F)$ & May Do(q, F) &
May Do$(q, \sim F)$,
(2) May Do(p, F) & May Do$(p, \sim F)$ & $\sim$May Do(q, F) &
$\sim$May Do$(q, \sim F)$,

and so forth.

In this way one obtains a list of $6 \times 6 = 36$ statements. However, ten of these are self-contradictory. The remaining twenty-six statements specify exactly those conditions which define Kanger's twenty-six atomic types of right. (Concerning the numbering of the twenty-six atomic types of right, see Kanger & Kanger, 1966, p. 96.)

If we let each of the statements (i)–(vi) define a set of ordered pairs of one agent and one state of affairs, we obtain the following six sets (or "types"), which I shall call one-agent Kanger types $K_1, ..., K_6$:

$K_1 = \{\langle p, F\rangle \mid \text{May Do}(p, F) \ \& \ \text{May Do}(p, \sim F)\}$.
$K_2 = \{\langle p, F\rangle \mid \sim\text{May Do}(p, F) \ \& \sim\text{May Do}(p, \sim F)\}$.
$K_3 = \{\langle p, F\rangle \mid \text{Shall Do}(p, F)\}$.
$K_4 = \{\langle p, F\rangle \mid \text{May Do}(p, F) \ \& \sim\text{Shall Do}(p, F) \ \& \sim\text{May Do}(p, \sim F)\}$.
$K_5 = \{\langle p, F\rangle \mid \text{Shall Do}(p, \sim F)\}$.
$K_6 = \{\langle p, F\rangle \mid \sim\text{May Do}(p, F) \ \& \sim\text{Shall Do}(p, \sim F) \ \&$
$\text{May Do}(p, \sim F)\}$.

Let us compare $\{K_1, ..., K_6\}$ with the set $\{T_1, ..., T_7\}$ of basic types of one-agent legal positions. It can be easily shown that the following holds:

$K_1 = T_1 \cup T_3$.
$K_2 = T_6$.
$K_3 = T_5$.
$K_4 = T_2$.
$K_5 = T_7$.
$K_6 = T_4$.

K_2, for example, is identical with T_6 since the statement

$$\sim\text{May Do}(p, F) \ \& \sim\text{May Do}(p, \sim F),$$

which defines K_2 is logically equivalent with the statement which defines T_6, namely

$$\text{Shall}(\sim\text{Do}(p, F) \ \& \sim\text{Do}(p, \sim F)).$$

Or, taking another example, K_4 is identical with T_2 since

$$\text{May Do}(p, F) \ \& \sim\text{Shall Do}(p, F) \ \& \sim\text{May Do}(p, \sim F)$$

is logically equivalent with

$$\text{May Do}(p, F) \;\&\; \text{May}({\sim}\text{Do}(p, F) \;\&\; {\sim}\text{Do}(p, {\sim}F)) \;\&\; {\sim}\text{May Do}(p, {\sim}F)).$$

Proof

(i) $\text{Shall}({\sim}\text{Do}(p, {\sim}F) \rightarrow \text{Do}(p, F)) \rightarrow (\text{Shall}\,{\sim}\text{Do}(p, {\sim}F) \rightarrow \text{Shall Do}(p, F)).$

(ii) $\text{Shall}\,{\sim}({\sim}\text{Do}(p, {\sim}F) \;\&\; {\sim}\text{Do}(p, F)) \rightarrow {\sim}(\text{Shall}\,{\sim}\text{Do}(p, {\sim}F) \;\&\; {\sim}\text{Shall Do}(p, F)).$

(iii) $\text{Shall}\,{\sim}\text{Do}(p, {\sim}F) \;\&\; {\sim}\text{Shall Do}(p, F)) \rightarrow \text{May}({\sim}\text{Do}(p, F) \;\&\; {\sim}\text{Do}(p, {\sim}F)).$

(iv) ${\sim}\text{May Do}(p, {\sim}F) \;\&\; {\sim}\text{Shall Do}(p, F) \rightarrow \text{May}({\sim}\text{Do}(p, F) \;\&\; {\sim}\text{Do}(p, {\sim}F)).$

(v) $\text{May}({\sim}\text{Do}(p, F) \;\&\; {\sim}\text{Do}(p, {\sim}F)) \rightarrow {\sim}\text{Shall Do}(p, F).$

It follows immediately from (iv) and (v) that the equivalence holds.

From these identities it is clear that $K_1, ..., K_6$ are, taken together, tantamount to $T_1, ..., T_7$ except that, in the cases of T_1 and T_3, the six Kanger-types do not enable us to distinguish the two distinct alternatives,

$$\langle p, F\rangle \in T_1,$$
$$\langle p,F\rangle \in T_3.$$

If T_3 were *empty*, the distinction would not be significant and we would have

$$K_1 = T_1.$$

But as was argued above (p. 97), T_3 is not empty: the "philosophy of indolence" is not a general principle.

The distinction between the list $K_1, ..., K_6$ and the list $T_1, ..., T_7$ is of significance in connection with the standard form of Boolean compounds mentioned above in connection with von Wright's theorem (above, p. 89). All statements of the general structure given in this context (which were exemplified with statements (i)–(ix) above, pp. 88 ff.) can be given standard form in terms of membership of the union of one or more of $T_1, ..., T_7$. On the other hand, all such statements cannot be expressed in terms of membership of the union of one or more of $K_1, ..., K_6$.

Consider, for example, the statement

(3) $\text{May}(\text{Do}(p, F) \vee \text{Do}(p, {\sim}F)) \rightarrow \text{May Do}(p, F)$ &
$\text{Shall}(\text{Do}(p, F) \vee \text{Do}(p, {\sim}F))$.

Using the list $T_1, ..., T_7$, (3) can be expressed in standardised form in the following way:

(3′) $\langle p, F\rangle \in T_3 \cup T_5 \cup T_6$.

Statement (3) cannot, however, be expressed in terms of membership of the union of one or more of $K_1, ..., K_6$.

That the list $K_1, ..., K_6$ is not tantamount to the list $T_1, ..., T_7$ depends, of course, on the fact that the methods of construction of each list are different. The six statements which define $K_1, ..., K_6$ (i.e., (i)–(vi) above) are obtained by a "non-recurrent" construction of basic conjunctions; the conjunctions are constructed from the two statements

Shall $\text{Do}(p, F)$,
Shall $\text{Do}(p, {\sim}F)$.

The statements defining $T_1, ..., T_7$ (i.e., statements 1–7 above, pp. 86 f.), on the other hand, are given by an "iterated" construction of basic conjunctions (see above p. 87). First the basic conjunctions are constructed from the two statements $\text{Do}(p, F)$ and $\text{Do}(p, {\sim}F)$. Then a new list of basic conjunctions is constructed, allowing the operator May to govern each of the basic conjunctions obtained on the first round.

The theory of maximal solutions. The method for constructing what Alchourrón & Bulygin call *maximal solutions* resembles this construction just described inasmuch as it contains an "iterated" construction of basic conjunctions. The basic logical apparatus, however, is different: they use a deontic operator O (for *Obligatory*) or P (for *Permitted*) together with a number of letters $p, q, r, ...$ which are interpreted

> ... as standing for propositions which describe generic actions, or better: states of affairs which are the result of an action. (Alchourrón & Bulygin, 1971, p. 35)

There is, however, no counterpart in Alchourrón & Bulygin of the Do operator, no variables for persons and no variables for arbitrary states of affairs.

According to Alchourrón & Bulygin, in order to "solve" a "normative problem" one must choose from the set of all generic actions a certain subset, namely that subset of actions which is relevant to the problem in question. The subset chosen in a given context is called *the universe of actions* (the *UA*).

A list of *maximal solutions* for a given *UA* is obtained by the same method described above for the construction of statements which define $T_1, \ldots, T_7$ but with this difference, that the first round of basic conjunctions is constructed from the action–propositions $p, q, r, \ldots$ which are elements in the *UA*. Suppose, for example, that $UA = \{p, q\}$. The first round of basic conjunctions is constructed:

$$p \mathbin{\&} q,\ p \mathbin{\&} {\sim} q,\ {\sim} p \mathbin{\&} q,\ {\sim} p \mathbin{\&} {\sim} q.$$

Then, by placing the operator P before each of these basic conjunctions, we obtain the statements:

$$P(p \mathbin{\&} q),\ P(p \mathbin{\&} {\sim} q),\ P({\sim} p \mathbin{\&} q),\ P({\sim} p \mathbin{\&} {\sim} q).$$

A list is then made of all the basic conjunctions that are obtained from these four statements:

1. $P(p \mathbin{\&} q) \mathbin{\&} P(p \mathbin{\&} {\sim} q) \mathbin{\&} P({\sim} p \mathbin{\&} q) \mathbin{\&} P({\sim} p \mathbin{\&} {\sim} q).$
2. $P(p \mathbin{\&} q) \mathbin{\&} P(p \mathbin{\&} {\sim} q) \mathbin{\&} P({\sim} p \mathbin{\&} q) \mathbin{\&} {\sim} P({\sim} p \mathbin{\&} {\sim} q).$
3. $P(p \mathbin{\&} q) \mathbin{\&} P(p \mathbin{\&} {\sim} q) \mathbin{\&} {\sim} P({\sim} p \mathbin{\&} q) \mathbin{\&} P({\sim} p \mathbin{\&} {\sim} q).$

$\vdots$

16. ${\sim} P(p \mathbin{\&} q) \mathbin{\&} {\sim} P(p \mathbin{\&} {\sim} q) \mathbin{\&} {\sim} P({\sim} p \mathbin{\&} q) \mathbin{\&} {\sim} P({\sim} p \mathbin{\&} {\sim} q).$

Finally, all self-contradictory statements are eliminated and one is left with a list of maximal solutions for the case $UA = \{p, q\}$.

The number of basic conjunctions obtained by this method is easily calculated. The number of basic conjunctions obtained from n statements is 2^n. For n elements in the *UA*, therefore, the number of basic conjunctions in the first round is 2^n. The number of statements obtained when the operator P is placed before each basic conjunction remains 2^n, and the number of basic conjunctions which can be constructed from these 2^n statements is thus 2^{2^n}. For two elements in the *UA*, $2^{2^2} = 16$ basic conjunctions are obtained; for 3 elements, $2^{2^3} = 256$, and so forth.

Of the basic conjunctions whose number is calculated according to this formula, that one according to which all alternatives are forbidden (see for example line 16 in the list above) is self-contradictory. Thus, if the elements in the *UA* are logically mutually independent of one another, the number of maximal solutions for this *UA* is $2^{2^n}-1$. For 1 element in the *UA*, therefore, there are 3 maximal solutions; for 2 elements, 15; for 3 elements, 255; and so forth. (Note that the number of maximal solutions and the formula from which this number is derived are incorrectly stated in Alchourrón & Bulygin, 1971, p. 39. The formula they give is $2^{2n}-1$, and in accordance with this the number of maximal solutions for 3 elements in the *UA* was calculated as $2^6-1=63$, for 4 elements, $2^8-1=255$, and so forth.)

The idea that gives a list of "maximal solutions" where there is just one element in the universe of actions (where the number of solutions is 3) has been expressed by Bentham (cf. above, p. 11 and below, p. 111). In consequence of the developments of the theory of disjunctive normal forms in deontic logic by von Wright (cf. above, p. 89) Alchourrón & Bulygin have been able to generalise the theory so that it holds for an arbitrary number of elements in the *UA* selected.

The theory of *basic types of one-agent legal positions* is markedly distinguishable from Alchourrón & Bulygin's theory since the combination of the two operators Shall and Do raise the possibility of distinguishing, for a person *p* and a state of affairs *F*, not less than seven "maximal solutions". Moreover, this theory can be generalised in two directions: to encompass more than one state of affairs *F*, *G*, *H*, ..., and more than one person *p*, *q*, *r*, ... Of these two possibilities it would appear that the shaping of a theory for several persons is of greater interest. In the following chapters the possibilities of developing the theory for two persons *p* and *q* and a state of affairs *F* will be explored. The theory put forward can in a trivial manner be generalised to hold for an arbitrary number of people *p*, *q*, *r*, ...

III. *The Ordering of One-Agent Types*

1. *Representation of the one-agent types by the Hasse diagram: Introduction*

The seven types T_1, ..., T_7 and their mutual relations can be graphically illustrated by the following diagram:

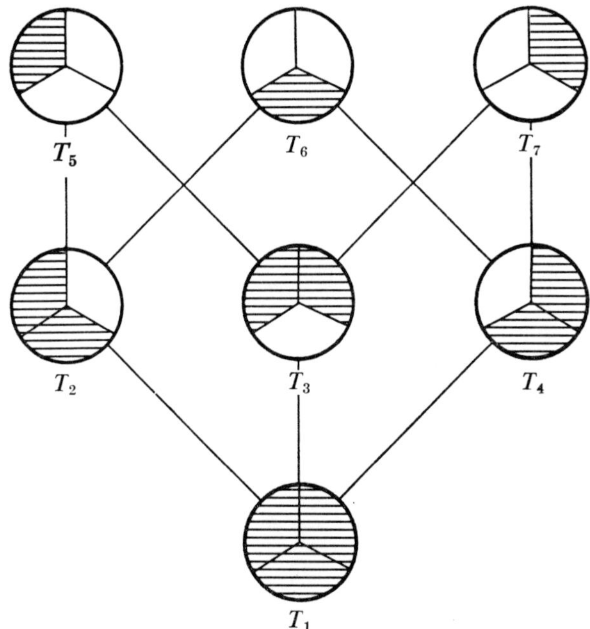

The tree is a *Hasse diagram* (so named after the German mathematician Helmut Hasse; cf. Suppes, 1957, p. 221) and represents a *partial ordering* on the set $\{T_1, ..., T_7\}$.

The remaining sections of this chapter are devoted to a development of the system for $\{T_1, ..., T_7\}$ in terms of the Hasse diagram. The concepts introduced are of significance for later chapters; in fact, they constitute the foundation on which the theory for so-called *ranges of legal action* presented in Chapters 6–9 is built.

2. *The graphic representation of each one-agent type*

Before proceeding to those concepts which concern the systematic structure for $\{T_1, ..., T_7\}$, the representation of each of the seven types by a certain circle in the Hasse diagram is herewith briefly explained.

To begin with, it should be remembered that each of the seven types $T_1, ..., T_7$ is defined as a certain set of ordered pairs comprising an agent and a state of affairs (see above, p. 92). Each circle in the diagram represents such a set of ordered pairs.

We introduce the expressions L_1, L_2 and L_3 which denote the following sets (*basic types of one-agent liberties*):

$L_1 = \{\langle p, F\rangle \mid \text{May Do}(p, F)\}$.
$L_2 = \{\langle p, F\rangle \mid \text{May}(\sim\text{Do}(p, F) \mathbin{\&} \sim\text{Do}(p, \sim F))\}$.
$L_3 = \{\langle p, F\rangle \mid \text{May Do}(p, \sim F)\}$.

Since for the present our universe of discourse is restricted to the set of all ordered pairs $\langle p, F\rangle$ comprising an agent and a state of affairs, the complement-sign is used so that $\overline{L_1}$, $\overline{L_2}$, and $\overline{L_3}$ denote as follows:

$\overline{L_1} = \{\langle p, F\rangle \mid \sim\text{May Do}(p, F)\}$.
$\overline{L_2} = \{\langle p, F\rangle \mid \sim\text{May}(\sim\text{Do}(p, F) \mathbin{\&} \sim\text{Do}(p, \sim F))\}$.
$\overline{L_3} = \{\langle p, F\rangle \mid \sim\text{May Do}(p, \sim F)\}$.

Now the following convention is adopted for how the sets L_1, L_2, L_3, $\overline{L_1}$, $\overline{L_2}$, and $\overline{L_3}$ are represented by sections of the circles in the Hasse diagram:

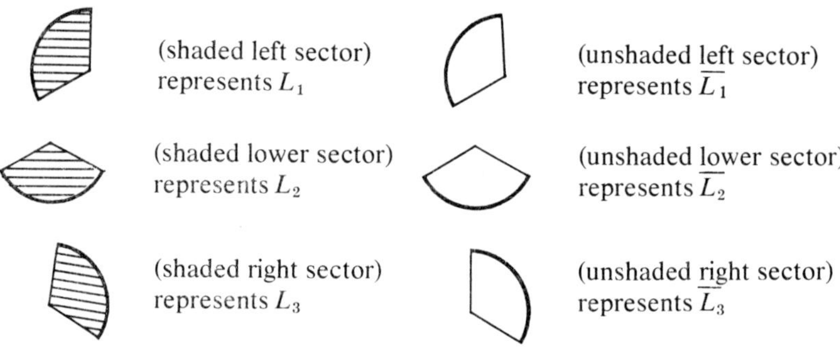

The circle in the Hasse diagram represents the intersection of those sets represented by the sectors of the circle. We obtain then:

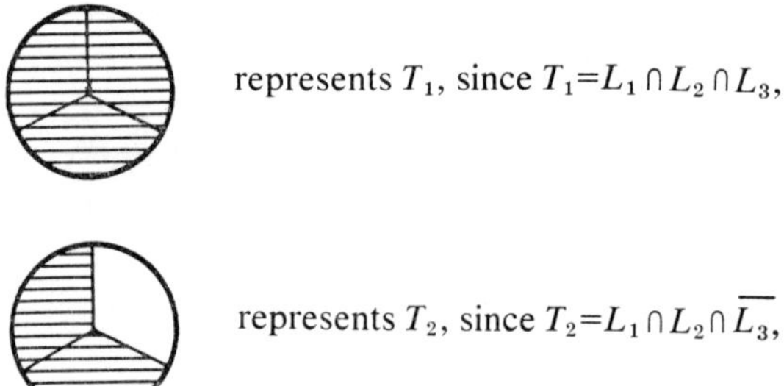

and so forth. Each of the seven types is thus graphically represented in the Hasse diagram, from which it is easily seen that the two types to the left are converses of the two types to the right, whilst the three types in the middle are neutral (cf. above, p. 92).

Subsequently, I shall need to refer to the sets whose intersection constitute a type, and for this purpose I introduce the term "factor". Thus, T_1, for example, is the intersection of L_1, L_2 and L_3, and so T_1 is said to have the factors L_1, L_2 and L_3. Similarly, $T_2 = L_1 \cap L_2 \cap \overline{L_3}$ and therefore T_2 has the factors L_1, L_2 and $\overline{L_3}$, etc. All one-agent types have exactly three factors.

3. *Liberty spaces of the one-agent types; the relation "less free than"*

Each of the seven types $T_1, ..., T_7$ corresponds to a certain set of the three basic types of one-agent liberties; i.e., a certain subset of $\{L_1, L_2, L_3\}$. The type T_1 corresponds, for example, to the set $\{L_1, L_2, L_3\}$ itself, type T_2 to $\{L_1, L_2\}$, and so forth. The set of basic types of one-agent liberties corresponding to a given type T of $T_1, ..., T_7$ we call T's *liberty space.* T's liberty space is, informally speaking, the set of those basic liberties which a person has with respect to a certain state of affairs when he is in T with respect to this state of affairs.

More formally, by *liberty space* we understand a certain function S from $\{T_1, ..., T_7\}$ to the set of non-empty subsets of $\{L_1, L_2, L_3\}$. There are seven non-empty subsets of $\{L_1, L_2, L_3\}$, called $M_1, ..., M_7$ in accordance with the following list:

$M_1 = \{L_1, L_2, L_3\}$.
$M_2 = \{L_1, L_2\}$.
$M_3 = \{L_1, L_3\}$.
$M_4 = \{L_2, L_3\}$.
$M_5 = \{L_1\}$.
$M_6 = \{L_2\}$.
$M_7 = \{L_3\}$.

A function S from $\{T_1, ..., T_7\}$ to $\{M_1, ..., M_7\}$ is defined thus:

DEFINITION 1. Let L be a variable for an arbitrary element in $\{L_1, L_2, L_3\}$, and T be a variable for an arbitrary element in $\{T_1, ..., T_7\}$.

$$S(T) =_{\text{def.}} \{L \mid T \subset L\}.$$

For T_1 it holds that:

$$T_1 = L_1 \cap L_2 \cap L_3.$$
$$T_1 \neq L_1,\ T_1 \neq L_2,\ T_1 \neq L_3.$$
$$\therefore T_1 \subset L_1 \ \&\ T_1 \subset L_2 \ \&\ T_1 \subset L_3.$$
$$\therefore S(T_1) = \{L_1, L_2, L_3\}.$$

For T_2 it holds that:

$$T_2 = L_1 \cap L_2 \cap \overline{L_3}.$$
$$T_2 \neq L_1,\ T_2 \neq L_2,\ T_2 \neq \overline{L_3}.$$
$$\therefore T_2 \subset L_1 \ \&\ T_2 \subset L_2 \ \&\ T_2 \subset \overline{L_3}.$$
$$\therefore S(T_2) = \{L_1, L_2\}.$$

and so forth. We obtain the list

$$S(T_1) = M_1.$$
$$S(T_2) = M_2.$$
$$\vdots$$
$$S(T_7) = M_7.$$

It follows immediately from the list that S is a one-one function from $\{T_1, ..., T_7\}$ to $\{M_1, ..., M_7\}$. If T, T' are variables for elements in $\{T_1, ..., T_7\}$ and M, M' variables for elements in $\{M_1, ..., M_7\}$, it holds that

$$S(T) = M \ \&\ S(T) = M' \rightarrow M = M'. \quad (S \text{ is a function.})$$
$$S(T) = S(T') \rightarrow T = T'. \quad (S \text{ is one-one.})$$

(Furthermore, it is easily seen that the inversion of S is a one-one function from $\{M_1, ..., M_7\}$ to $\{T_1, ..., T_7\}$.)

It is evident how the liberty spaces of $T_1, ..., T_7$ are depicted in the Hasse diagram. If L is an element of $\{L_1, L_2, L_3\}$ and T an element of $\{T_1, ..., T_7\}$ then L is an element of $S(T)$ if and only if the circle for T contains a sector which represents L. Thus, the circle for T_2

depicts that $\mathcal{S}(T_2)=\{L_1, L_2\}$: the circle contains a sector representing L_1 and one representing L_2, but no sector representing L_3.

If T, T' are two types from $\{T_1, ..., T_7\}$, then the question which of T, T' is less *free* and which is more *free* is to be settled by considering the liberty spaces of T and T'. Consider, for example

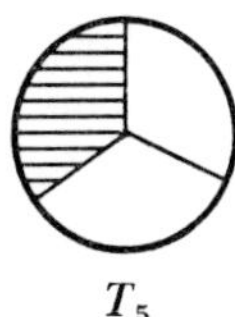
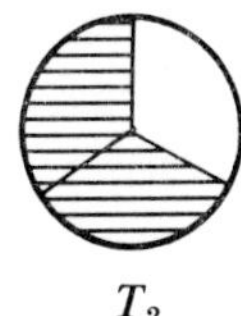

T_5 T_2 T_1

T_5 is less free than T_2, which, in turn, is less free than T_1, since $\mathcal{S}(T_5)$ is a proper subset of $\mathcal{S}(T_2)$, and similarly $\mathcal{S}(T_2)$ is a proper subset of $\mathcal{S}(T_1)$.

A relation $\mathcal{R}$ on $\{T_1, ..., T_7\}$ for "less free than" can accordingly be defined.

DEFINITION 2. Let T, T' be variables for elements of $\{T_1, ..., T_7\}$.
$$T\mathcal{R}T' =_{\text{def.}} \mathcal{S}(T) \subset \mathcal{S}(T').$$

Informally, the definition means that if T is less free than T', then for all p, q, F and G, if p is in T with respect to F and q is in T' with respect to G, then q has, with respect to G, all those basic liberties which p has with respect to F; but in addition q has, with respect to G, some basic liberty which p lacks in respect to F. Alternatively, we could say that if T is less free than T' then removing $\langle p, F\rangle$ from T' to T entails a reduction of p's basic liberties with respect to F.

It follows immediately from the definition that $\mathcal{R}$ is *irreflexive* and *transitive*. Thus $\mathcal{R}$ is a *strict partial ordering* on $\{T_1, ..., T_7\}$. Furthermore, this ordering is straightforwardly represented by the Hasse diagram (p. 105) in the following way. Let T, T' be two distinct elements in $\{T_1, ..., T_7\}$. Then the circle for T is placed above T' in the diagram and connected to it by an unbroken straight line if and only if T is less free than T' and there is no type T'' such that T is less free than T'' and T'' is less free than T'.

In addition to the relation $\mathcal{R}$ for *less free than*, the relation $\mathcal{E}$ for *as free as* can, of course, also be defined as follows:

DEFINITION 3. Let T, T' be variables for elements in $\{T_1, ..., T_7\}$.

$$T\mathcal{E}T' =_{\text{def.}} \mathcal{S}(T) = \mathcal{S}(T').$$

But this relation is not of a great deal of interest since, as already indicated,

$$\mathcal{S}(T) = \mathcal{S}(T') \rightarrow T = T' \text{ (the function } \mathcal{S} \text{ is one-one).}$$

Accordingly, there are no two distinct types T, T' in $\{T_1, ..., T_7\}$ which sustain this relation of being as free as.

Certain types in $T_1, ..., T_7$ are incomparable as regards freedom in the sense defined. We have for example:

T_2 is not less free than T_4;
T_4 is not less free than T_2;
T_2 is not as free as T_4.

If p is in T_2 with respect to F and q is in T_4 with respect to G, then certainly from one point of view p's freedom with respect to F is greater than q's freedom with respect to G, for p may see to it that F is the case, but q may not see to it that G is the case. However, from another point of view q's freedom with respect to G is greater than p's freedom with respect to F, for q may see to it that not-G obtains, whilst p may not see to it that not-F is the case. Alternatively, we could say that removing $\langle p, F\rangle$ from T_2 to T_4 means, from one point of view, an extension of p's freedom with respect to F; but from another point of view, a reduction of this freedom. The types T_2 and T_4 are therefore mutually incomparable so far as the relations $\mathcal{R}$ and $\mathcal{E}$ are concerned.

Which of the seven types are comparable and which incomparable can most easily be seen from the Hasse diagram by using the following rule. Two types T, T' are *incomparable* if and only if the circle for T' can be reached from the circle for T only via a line which goes partly upwards and partly downwards (for example, T_2 and T_4). Types T, T' are, on the other hand, *comparable* if and only if the circle for T' can be reached from the circle for T via a line going only upwards (or only downwards) in the diagram (for example, T_1 and T_5).

4. *Deontic paths: introduction and graphic representation*

The concept *deontic path* which will be formally defined in the following section can be illustrated, by way of introducing the concept, in a passage from Bentham. In a section dealing with how a *primordial* law can be changed by a *superventitious* law, Bentham cites the case of a *command* being exchanged for a *prohibition*. The superventitious provision, according to Bentham, is in this case "doubly alterative or reversive":

> Between command on the one hand and prohibition on the other, inactivity lies midway. The superventitious provision then takes in either case two steps instead of one: one from command or prohibition down to inactivity: another from inactivity up to prohibition or command. A reversive provision may accordingly be resolved into two provisions, both having for their object the same act: the one destroying the obligation imposed by the primordial provision, the other imposing a new obligation but of the opposite nature. (1970*b*, p. 111)

For the sake of simplicity let Shall *F* be the expression of a command in Bentham's sense. Then, according to Bentham, the following three alternatives can be distinguished (as mutually exclusive and jointly exhaustive):

(1) (*Command*) Shall *F*, i.e., May F & ~May~*F*.
(2) (*Inactivity*) ~Shall *F* & ~Shall~*F*, i.e., May *F* & May~*F*.
(3) (*Prohibition*) Shall~*F*, i.e., ~May *F* & May~*F*.

With the help of a construction similar to that described in the preceding section, these alternatives (1)–(3) can be represented by the following Hasse diagram (the details of interpretation of the diagram are evident and need not be repeated here):

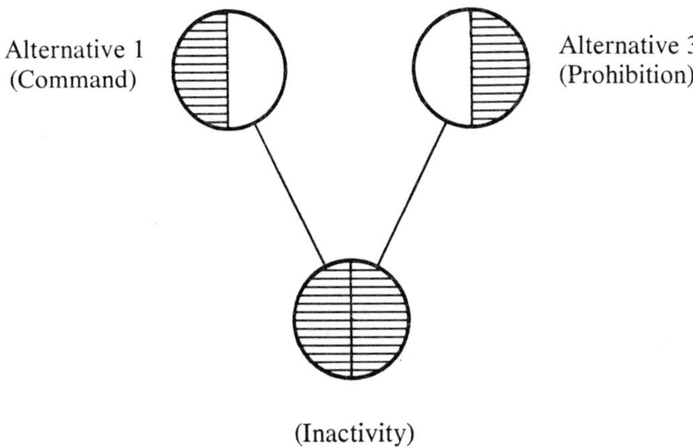

According to Bentham, the path between alternatives 1 and 3 goes via alternative 2:

Between command on the one hand and prohibition on the other, inactivity lies midway. (1970*b*, p. 111)

Alternative 2 is, so to speak, an "intermediate station" between the alternatives 1 and 3.

The quotation from Bentham occurs in a section dealing with how a legislator can change the content of the law. The corresponding question in the theory of basic types of one-agent legal positions is how a pair $\langle p, F \rangle$ comprising a person and a state of affairs can be moved from one of the seven types $T_1, ..., T_7$ to another: through the decree of some authority, by promise, contract, and so forth.

By analogy with Bentham's train of thought, I shall speak of "the deontic path" or, as we shall see, "the deontic paths", between two types T, T' of the seven $T_1, ..., T_7$. The following extracts from the Hasse diagram exemplify some deontic paths:

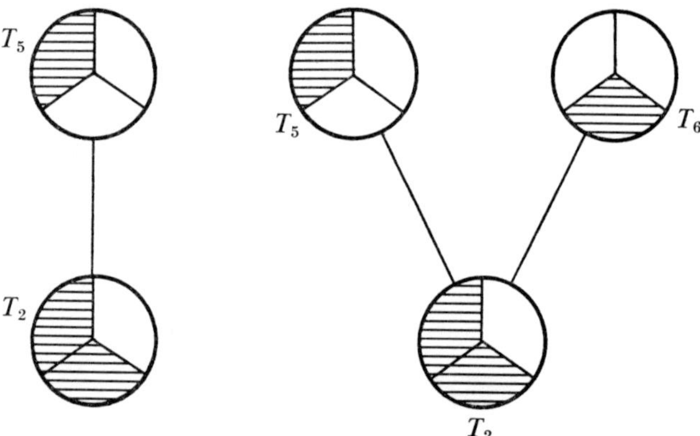

The left-hand diagram shows a path between T_2 and T_5—a path with no intermediate stations. The right-hand diagram shows a path between T_5 and T_6—a path passing through T_2 as an intermediate station.

Bentham distinguishes only between *command*, *inactivity*, and *prohibition*. In the theory of one-agent legal positions, on the other hand, we have available for consideration no less than seven types, i.e., $T_1, ..., T_7$. The pattern of deontic paths is therefore much richer in this theory, and we need to be able to distinguish between different kinds of paths. A deontic path between two types can be either *straight* or *non-straight*, and it can be *minimal* or *non-minimal.*

The path represented by the following extract of the Hasse diagram:

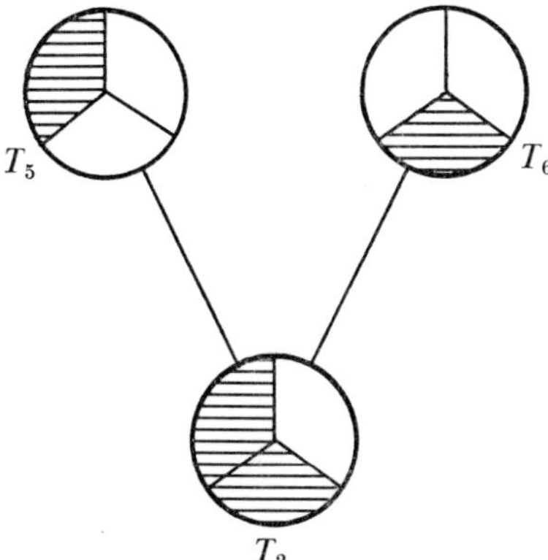

goes partly downwards and partly upwards. The movement between the end stations via an intermediate station means first an expansion and thereafter a reduction of the sphere of freedom; similarly with the position as regards the deontic path which Bentham mentions and which is represented by:

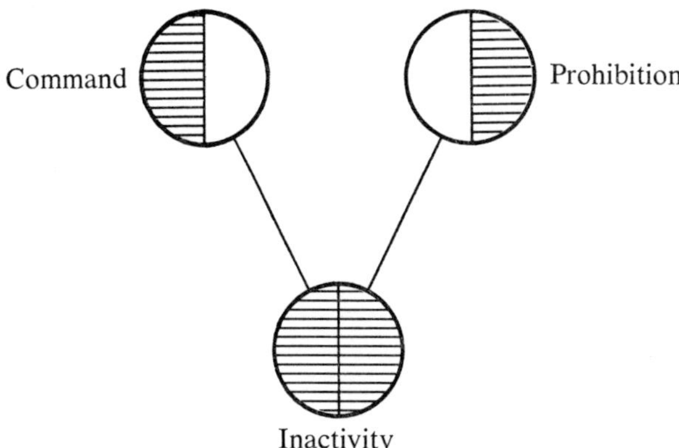

The intermediate station T_2 lies "midway" between T_5 and T_6 in the same sense that according to Bentham, *inactivity* lies "midway" between *command* and *prohibition.*

Consider, on the other hand, the deontic path represented by the diagram:

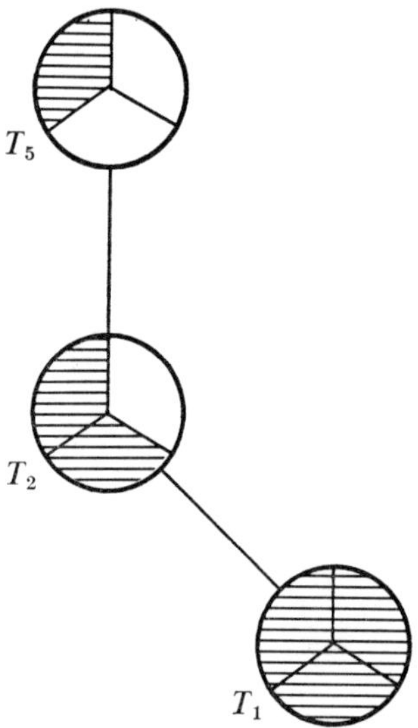

This path goes entirely upwards (entirely downwards). A movement between the end stations via the intermediate station entails a successive contraction of the sphere of freedom or a successive expansion of the sphere of freedom. But just as before, we can say that the intermediate station T_2 lies "midway" between the end stations. T_2 is less free than T_1 but more free than T_5.

The path between T_1 and T_5 is an example of a deontic path which is *straight;* the path between T_5 and T_6, on the other hand, is *non-straight.* A deontic path is *straight* if it goes entirely upwards (entirely downwards) in the diagram, and is *non-straight* if it goes partly upwards, partly downwards.

There is always more than one deontic path between two types T, T'. The two diagrams on the next page, for example, illustrate two different paths between T_2 and T_5.

The path on the left is, according to the diagram, shorter than that on the right; and in general the paths between two types can be of different length. I shall say that a path between T and T' is *minimal* if there is no other path between T and T' which is shorter. The path between T_2

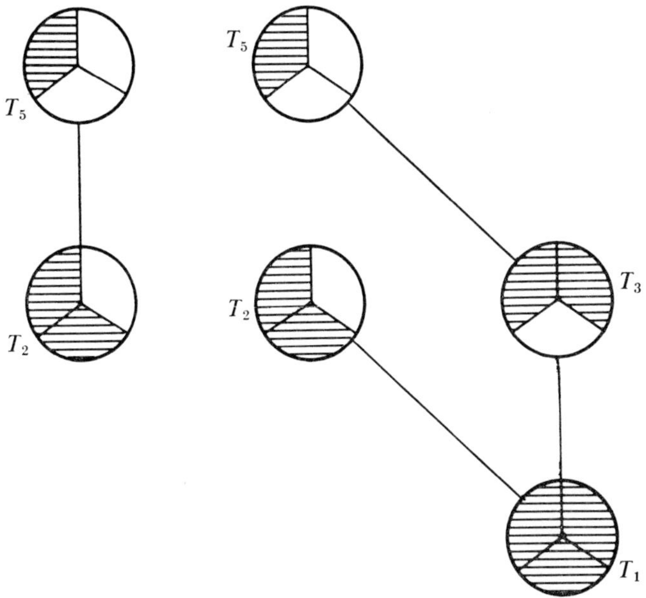

and T_5 represented in the left-hand diagram above is obviously minimal since it contains no intermediate station and thus there cannot be a shorter path.

5. *Deontic paths: formal definitions*

In this section I shall give more formal definitions of those concepts informally explained just now in connection with the Hasse diagram. In order to facilitate the definitions I introduce the concept *cover* (cf. Stoll, 1963, p. 50).

DEFINITION 1. Let T, T' be variables for elements of $\{T_1, ..., T_7\}$ and let $\mathcal{R}$ be the relation *less free than*. *T covers* T' in $\{T_1 ..., T_7\}$ with respect to $\mathcal{R} =_{\text{def.}} T'\mathcal{R}T$ and there is no type $T'' \in \{T_1, ..., T_7\}$ such that $T'\mathcal{R}T''$ and $T''\mathcal{R}T$.

If T covers T' according to Definition 1, then T' is placed above T in the Hasse diagram and T, T' are immediately connected with each other by a line segment. In the diagram on the following page, it can be seen, for example, that T_2 covers T_5 and T_6 in this sense.

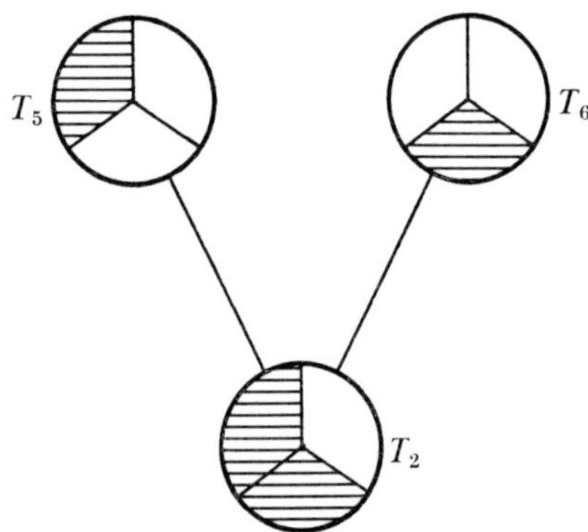

A deontic path in $\{T_1, ..., T_7\}$ is defined as a sequence $\{T^1, ..., T^n\}$ of two or more elements of $\{T_1, ..., T_7\}$. The superscripts 1, ..., n indicate the ordering of the types in the sequence and should not be confused with the subscripts 1, ..., 7 which distinguish the seven types according to the list above (p. 92).

In order that a sequence $\{T^1, ..., T^n\}$ should be a deontic path it is required that each pair of types T, T', where T' follows immediately after T in the sequence, is such that T covers T' or T' covers T according to Definition 1.

DEFINITION 2. Let $\{T^1, ..., T^n\}$ be a sequence of two or more elements of $\{T_1, ..., T_7\}$ and $\mathcal{R}$ the relation *less free than*. $\{T^1, ..., T^n\}$ is a *deontic path* in $\{T_1, ..., T_7\} =_{\text{def.}}$ For each pair $\{T^i, T^{i+1}\}$ in the sequence, T^i covers T^{i+1} in $\{T_1, ..., T_7\}$ with respect to $\mathcal{R}$ or T^{i+1} covers T^i in $\{T_1, ..., T_7\}$ with respect to $\mathcal{R}$.

Example. The sequence $\{T^1_5, T^2_2, T^3_6\}$ is a deontic path in $\{T_1, ..., T_7\}$, since for the pair $\{T^1, T^2\}$, it holds that T^2 covers T^1, and for the pair $\{T^2, T^3\}$, T^2 covers T^3.

In order that a sequence $\{T^1, ..., T^n\}$ should be a *straight deontic path* it is required that either, for each type T in the sequence, T covers the type immediately following, or, for each type T in the sequence, T covers the type immediately preceding in the sequence.

DEFINITION 3. Let $\{T^1, ..., T^n\}$ be a sequence of two or more elements of $\{T_1, ..., T_7\}$ and $\mathcal{R}$ be the relation *less free than*. $\{T^1, ..., T^n\}$ is a *straight deontic path* in $\{T_1, ..., T_7\} =_{\text{def.}}$ For each pair $\{T^i, T^{i+1}\}$ in the sequence, T^i covers T^{i+1} in $\{T_1, ..., T_7\}$ with respect to $\mathcal{R}$ or for each pair $\{T^i, T^{i+1}\}$ in the sequence, T^{i+1} covers T^i in $\{T_1, ..., T_7\}$ with respect to $\mathcal{R}$.

Example. The sequence $\{T_1^1, T_2^2, T_5^3\}$ is a straight deontic path in $\{T_1, ..., T_7\}$, since for the pair $\{T^1, T^2\}$ it holds that T^1 covers T^2, and for $\{T^2, T^3\}$, T^2 covers T^3.

A deontic path $\{T^1, ..., T^n\}$ is said to be *from* T^1 *to* T^n, and is *minimal* if there is no other path from T^1 to T^n which is shorter.

DEFINITION 4. Let $\{T^1, ..., T^n\}$ be a sequence of two or more elements of $\{T_1, ..., T_7\}$. $\{T^1, ..., T^n\}$ is a *minimal deontic path* in $\{T_1, ..., T_7\} =_{\text{def.}}$ $\{T^1, ..., T^n\}$ is a deontic path in $\{T_1, ..., T_7\}$ and there is no sequence W from T^1 to T^n such that W is a deontic path in $\{T_1, ..., T_7\}$ and such that the number of elements in W is less than the number of elements in $\{T^1, ..., T^n\}$.

It is easily seen from the Hasse diagram that if a deontic path is *straight*, it is also minimal in $\{T_1, ..., T_7\}$. Furthermore, it is easily seen that for certain pairs of types there are several minimal paths between them. For example, each of the sequences $\{T_1^1, T_2^2, T_5^3\}$ and $\{T_1^1, T_3^2, T_5^3\}$ is a minimal deontic path in $\{T_1, ..., T_7\}$.

Given these formal definitions, a simplified notation can be introduced when referring to deontic paths by using the usual notation $\langle\ \rangle$ for ordered sets and dropping the superscripts. Thus, if $T, T', ...$ are elements of $\{T_1, ..., T_7\}$ and $\{T^1, ..., T^n\}$ is a deontic path in $\{T_1, ..., T_7\}$ such that $T^1 = T$, $T^2 = T'$, and so forth, we refer to this deontic path as an ordered set $\langle T, T', ...\rangle$. The ordered set $\langle T_5, T_2, T_6\rangle$, for example, is a deontic path from T_5 to T_6.

6. *Deontic distance*

The concept *deontic path* together with the variations explained and defined in the previous sections leads directly to the idea of *measuring the distance* between two types T, T'. A similar idea has already been suggested above (p. 111), again deriving from Bentham. Bentham speaks of just *one* step being required to go from Command to Inactivity or from Prohibition to Inactivity, whilst *two* steps are required to go from Command to Prohibition:

Between command on the one hand and prohibition on the other, inactivity lies midway. The superventitious provision then takes in either case two steps instead of one: one from command or prohibition down to inactivity: another from inactivity up to prohibition or command. (1970*b*, p. 111)

The distance between two of Bentham's alternatives can obviously be defined as the *number of intermediate stations* on the deontic path between the alternatives *plus one;* or, what amounts to the same thing, as the *number of elements* in the deontic path *minus one*. The number of intermediate stations between Command and Inactivity, for example, is 0, and the distance between them is thus $0+1=1$. Alternatively, we can arrive at the same result by taking the number of elements in the deontic path from Command to Inactivity (i.e., 2) and calculate the distance between them as $2-1=1$.

The distance, or as I shall say, the *deontic distance* between two of the seven types T_1, ..., T_7 is determined in a similar way. But as noted above, it must be remembered that there is always more than one deontic path between two of these types, and accordingly the distance between two types will be understood to be the distance along a deontic path, which is *minimal* in $\{T_1, ..., T_7\}$.

When it comes to defining *deontic distance* three alternatives present themselves. Two of these have just been mentioned in the comments on Bentham, namely

(1) The deontic distance between T and T' = the number of intermediate stations plus 1 on a deontic path from T to T' which is minimal in $\{T_1, ..., T_7\}$.

(2) The deontic distance between T and T' = the number of elements minus 1 in a deontic path from T to T' which is minimal in $\{T_1, ..., T_7\}$.

A third alternative exists, however. I have talked about the *factors* (p. 107) which a one-agent type has, and a glance at the large Hasse diagram (p. 105) serves to show that the deontic distance can be determined according to:

(3) The deontic distance between T and T' = the number of T's factors which are not factors of T'.

I shall refer to the number of factors of T which are not factors of T' as the *numerical difference* between T and T'. According to (3), then, the deontic distance is the same as the numerical difference; and this figure can vary between 1 and 3 (that the maximum is 3 is explained by each one-agent type having exactly three factors).

Example. T_1 has the factors L_1, L_2 and L_3, whilst T_2 has the factors L_1, L_2 and $\overline{L_3}$; the deontic distance between T_1 and T_2 is 1. T_5 has the factors L_1, $\overline{L_2}$ and $\overline{L_3}$ whilst T_6 has the factors $\overline{L_1}$, L_2 and $\overline{L_3}$; the deontic distance between T_5 and T_6 is 2. T_2 has the factors L_1, L_2 and $\overline{L_3}$, whilst T_7 has the factors $\overline{L_1}$, $\overline{L_2}$ and L_3; the distance between T_2 and T_7 is 3.

The alternatives (1)–(3) all lead to the same result and therefore it does not matter which we choose. However, when we come to the corresponding stage in the development of individualistic two-agent types (Chapter 4), the analogue of definition (3) sometimes yields different results from the analogues of definitions (1) and (2). For the sake of consistency, then, we shall opt for one of these, and let us choose (2). Formally, the definition is:

DEFINITION. Let T, T' be variables for elements of $\{T_1, ..., T_7\}$ and let n be a variable for elements of $\{1, 2, 3\}$. Dist (for deontic distance) is a function from $\{\langle T, T'\rangle | T \neq T'\}$ to $\{1, 2, 3\}$. Dist $(T, T') = n =_{\text{def}}$. There is a sequence $\langle T, ..., T'\rangle$ such that $\langle T, ..., T'\rangle$ is a minimal deontic path in $\{T_1, ..., T_7\}$ and such that the number of elements in $\langle T, ..., T'\rangle = n+1$.

7. *The notion of intermediate*

An important notion in the latter part of the book is that of a type T *lying between* the types T' and T''; T is said to be *intermediate.* Once again, several alternative courses present themselves for defining this notion all yielding identical results. Let T, T', T'' be distinct elements of $\{T_1, ..., T_7\}$; then it is easily seen from the Hasse diagram that the following statements are equivalent

(1) There is a sequence $\langle T', ..., T, ..., T''\rangle$ such that $\langle T', ..., T, ..., T''\rangle$ is a minimal deontic path in $\{T_1, ..., T_7\}$.

(2) $\text{Dist}(T', T'') = \text{Dist}(T, T') + \text{Dist}(T, T'')$.

(3) The numerical difference between T', T'' = the numerical

difference between T and T' + the numerical difference between T and T''.

(4) Each factor of T is a factor of T' or a factor of T''.

To illustrate: It is true that

(5) T_1 is intermediate between T_2 and T_7,

and it is easily verified that

(i) $\langle T_2, T_1, T_4, T_7\rangle$ is a minimal deontic path in $\{T_1, ..., T_7\}$;

(ii) $\text{Dist}(T_2, T_7) = \text{Dist}(T_1, T_2) + \text{Dist}(T_1, T_7)$

(since $\text{Dist}(T_2, T_7) = 3$, $\text{Dist}(T_1, T_2) = 1$ and $\text{Dist}(T_1, T_7) = 2$);

(iii) The numerical difference between T_2 and T_7 = the numerical difference between T_1 and T_2 + the numerical difference between T_1 and T_7

(the numbers here are the same as in (ii));

(iv) Each factor of T_1 is a factor of T_2, or a factor of T_7.

(T_1 has the factors L_1, L_2 and L_3; L_1 and L_2 are factors of T_2 and L_3 of T_7.) On the other hand

(6) It is not the case that T_1 is intermediate between T_5 and T_7.

We have here

(i) There is no sequence $\langle T_5, ..., T_1, ..., T_7\rangle$ such that $\langle T_5, ..., T_1, ..., T_7\rangle$ is a minimal deontic path in $\{T_1, ..., T_7\}$;

(ii) $\text{Dist}(T_5, T_7) \neq \text{Dist}(T_1, T_5) + \text{Dist}(T_1, T_7)$

($\text{Dist}(T_5, T_7) = 2$, $\text{Dist}(T_1, T_5) = 2$, $\text{Dist}(T_1, T_7) = 2$);

(iii) The numerical difference between T_5 and $T_7 \neq$ the numerical difference between T_1 and T_5 + the numerical difference between T_1 and T_7

(the numbers are the same as in (ii));

(iv) There is a factor of T_1 which is not a factor either of T_5 or of T_7

(L_2 is one of the factors of T_1, whilst $\overline{L_2}$ is a factor of T_5 and T_7).

When it comes to defining "intermediate" it again does not much matter which of the alternatives is chosen; moreover, the analogues of (1)–(4) for two-agent types (Chapters 4 and 5) are also equivalent to one another. I shall opt for a definition according to (4):

DEFINITION. Let T, T' and T'' be three distinct elements of $\{T_1, ..., T_7\}$. T is intermediate between T' and $T'' =_{\text{def.}}$ Each factor of T is a factor of T' or a factor of T''.

In view of what follows subsequently (Chapters 8–9), I shall finally give two theorems which are corollaries of the definition of "intermediate". Analogous theorems hold good within the theory of two-agent types (Chapters 4 and 5).

THEOREM 1. *Let T, T' and T'' be elements of $\{T_1, ..., T_7\}$. If T', T'' have no factor in common, then for each T distinct from T' and T'', T is intermediate between T' and T''.*

Proof

If T' and T'' have no factor in common, then for each factor V of T', $\overline{V}$ is a factor of T''. Accordingly, if U is a factor of any type T, U is a factor either of T' or of T''. Thus, if T is distinct from T' and from T'', T lies between them.

Example. T_2 and T_7 have no factor in common and so every other one-agent type lies between them.

THEOREM 2. *Let T, T' and T'' be three distinct elements of $\{T_1, ..., T_7\}$. If $V_1, ..., V_n (n \geqslant 1)$ are the factors which T' and T'' have in common, then T is intermediate between T' and T'' if and only if $V_1, ..., V_n$ are factors of T.*

Proof

By definition, if both T' and T'' have the factors $V_1, ..., V_n$ $(n \geqslant 1)$ and T lies between T' and T'', then these factors also number amongst T's factors (if one of $\overline{V_1} ..., \overline{V_n}$ were a factor of T, T could not lie between T' and T''). It furthermore follows from the definition that if both T' and T'' have amongst their factors $V_1, ..., V_n$ $(n \geqslant 1)$ and T too, then T lies between T' and T'' if and only if each remaining factor (V_{n+1}, etc.)

of T is to be found amongst T''s or amongst T'''s factors. It follows immediately that if (as was supposed) $V_1, \ldots, V_n$ are the only factors T' and T'' have in common, then each remaining factor of T is either one of T''s or one of T'''s (if T' has $\overline{V_{n+1}}$ then T'' has V_{n+1}, etc.).

Example. T_2 and T_4 have just one factor in common, namely L_2. Now L_2 is also a factor of T_1 and T_6. Accordingly, T_1 and T_6 both lie between T_2 and T_4.

CHAPTER 4

Individualistic Two-Agent Types

I. *Introduction*

This chapter and the next are devoted to what I call *basic types of two-agent legal positions*, or, in short, *two-agent types*. The theory for these types is a further development of the theory of one-agent types as presented in Chapter 3.

The seven types of one-agent positions $T_1, ..., T_7$ are defined as sets of ordered pairs comprising *one* agent and a state of affairs. A statement of membership of a one-agent type thus has the form

$$\langle p, F \rangle \in T,$$

or, more informally,

> *p* has a legal position of type *T* with respect to the state of affairs that *F*.

Those types classified within the theory for two-agent types, on the other hand, are defined as sets of ordered triples comprising *two agents* and a state of affairs. Statements expressing membership of two-agent types therefore have the form

$$\langle p, q, F \rangle \in R$$

or, more informally,

> *p* has a legal position versus *q* of type *R* with respect to the state of affairs that *F*.

From what has been said, two-agent types are clearly *defined as relations between two parties*, as "legal relations" (cf. above, p. 85), which cannot be said for one-agent types.

In order to avoid misunderstanding, however, it ought to be said that even the statement

$$\langle p, F \rangle \in T$$

(where T is one of T_1, ..., T_7) can be interpreted so that it involves a relation between parties; but though it *can*, it *need not* be so interpreted. Everything depends on the interpretation of the variable F—whether F is interpreted as involving an agent other than the one designated by the variable p.

For example, consider the statement

(1) $\langle p, F \rangle \in T_5$

which, according to the definition of T_5 (above, p. 92), is equivalent to

(1′) Shall Do(p, F).

If *John* is substituted for p and *Peter receives £50 from John* for F, we obtain

(2) It shall be the case that John sees to it that Peter receives £50 from John.

It is clear that (2) concerns a legal relation between John and Peter. This is because the state of affairs *Peter receives £50 from John* involves another agent apart from John.

That statement (2) deals with a relation between parties is not made explicit when (2) appears in the general form (1), (1′), where the variable F represents an arbitrary state of affairs. If one wants to express (2) in a general form where the relation between the parties is made explicit, this is easily accomplished: the variables F, G, ... are replaced by a notation which makes explicit which parties are involved.

The theory of basic types of legal positions presented in this study abstracts from different sorts of states of affairs uniformly designated by the variables F, G, ..., including the fact that a state of affairs can involve one, two, or more agents, or perhaps none at all. The theory obtained in this way is more general than would otherwise be the case.

This sort of abstracting from the distinction between different kinds of states of affairs occurs not only within the theory for one-agent types. For those types I call basic types of *two-agent* legal positions are *explicitly defined as relations between two parties*, but their properties are independent of the kind of state of affairs designated by the variables F, G, ..., where again they represent arbitrary states of affairs.

The system of individualistic two-agent types presented in this chapter contains, for example, a two-agent type R_5 so defined that the statement

(3) $\langle p, q, F\rangle \in R_5$

is equivalent to

(3′) Shall Do(p, F) & Shall Do(q, F).

In statements (3) and (3′) there occur two agent variables, and the type R_5 is therefore explicitly defined as a relation between two parties in spite of F's denoting an arbitrary state of affairs.

The distinction in the area of application between the system of one-agent types and the system of two-agent types is as follows. A statement of the form

$$\langle p, F\rangle \in T,$$

where T is a one-agent type, says that *p's behaviour* with respect to F is normatively controlled in a certain way. A statement of the form

$$\langle p, q, F\rangle \in R,$$

where R is a two-agent type, always expresses something about the normative control of *p's and q's behaviour* with respect to F. Compare, for example, statements (1) and (1′) with statements (3) and (3′).

When talking about "legal relations" between two people, one sometimes pays attention only to the normative restrictions governing one party's behaviour. It is said, for example, that John shall see to it that Peter receives £50 without considering what Peter may or may not do in respect of receiving the money. The system of one-agent types is adequate for cases considered in this way.

A statement dealing only with how *one* agent's behaviour is regulated, however, is often insufficient to express all one wants to say—particularly when the state of affairs considered involves another agent. Consider, for example, the statement

(4) John may pick flowers in the forest that belongs to Peter.

This statement is logically consistent with each of the following two mutually contradictory statements:

(5) Peter may not prevent John from picking flowers in the forest that belongs to Peter.

(6) Peter may prevent John from picking flowers in the forest that belongs to Peter.

Statement (4) says simply that John will not break the law if he picks flowers in Peter's forest. Nothing is thereby said about whether Peter would break the law if he were to prevent John picking flowers there—for example, by erecting a fence. But if a statement is to be made to this effect, then (4) must be complemented with one of the statements (5) or (6). If (4) is combined by (5), we obtain a statement of permission together with a forbidding of interference on Peter's part. And if (4) is combined with (6), John's legal position becomes weaker since Peter is permitted to interfere.

In this context it is well to remember Bentham's distinction between *vested* liberty and *naked* liberty (above, p. 17). According to Bentham, a person has a vested liberty to act only if permission to act is combined with a general forbidding of interference:

> How can I possess the *right* of going into all the streets of a city? It is because there exists no obligation which hinders me, and because everybody is bound by an obligation not to hinder me. (Bentham, 1962, p. 181, see above p. 18)

A statement saying that a person belongs to a certain one-agent type with respect to a given state of affairs is clearly not sufficient for the purpose of stating the implications of "right" (vested liberty) which Bentham intends here.

According to the logic for Shall and Do it is possible, in certain cases, to infer, from the regulating of one party's behaviour with respect to a state of affairs, certain statements concerning the regulation of another party's behaviour. From the statement

(7) Shall Do(p, F)

it follows that

(8) $\sim$May Do(q, $\sim F$),

from which it follows that

(9) May$\sim$Do(q, $\sim F$),

(see the schema above, p. 53). But the possibilities of such conclusions are severely restricted according to the logical rules introduced above. From the statement

(10) May Do(p, F)

it is not possible, according to these rules, to conclude that interference is forbidden in the sense of

(11) $\sim$May Do(q, $\sim F$).

If the logical rules were to be made "stronger" so as to sanction such an inference as concluding (11) from (10), it would already be excluded on logical grounds that a person could have *naked liberty*—that is, that it would be permitted to act without interference being forbidden. But as already mentioned (pp. 30 f.), Hohfeld has emphasised the danger of such conclusions. The question of whether a person's liberty (privilege) to act is in some way connected with a right to non-interference by others is, as Hohfeld says, not decided beforehand by the rules of logic but rather is dependent on "justice and policy" (above, p. 30; cf. also Williams, 1956, pp. 1142 ff.). Concerning the conjunction of (10) and (11), then, it is not sufficient to formulate the matter simply as in statement (10), which concerns *p's behaviour;* statement (11) is also required which states the constraints on *q's behaviour.*

Some such understanding of the situation as Hohfeld's was one of the inspirations for Kanger's construction of his system of *atomic types of right* (above, pp. 54 ff.). Kanger's atomic types are defined as relations between two parties with respect to a given state of affairs. For each type, the defining condition states a certain normative regulation of the behaviour of *both* parties. Kanger's starting point is that relations defined in this way are needed in many cases for the explication of juridical concepts.

In this study I shall present two different systems of *two-agent types:* a system $R_1, ..., R_{35}$ of *individualistic* types and a system $S_1, ..., S_{127}$ of *collectivistic* types. The system of individualistic types is presented in the present chapter and the system of collectivistic types in Chapter 5. The distinction between the areas of application of the two systems will be taken up in the introduction to Chapter 5.

II. *The Construction of Individualistic Two-Agent Types*

1. *The method of coordination*

In the construction of the individualistic types $R_1, ..., R_{35}$ I begin with the following two lists of statements (where $T_1, ..., T_7$ denote the seven *one-agent* types defined in chapter 3; see above, p. 92):

1.	$\langle p, F\rangle \in T_1$	1′. $\langle q, F\rangle \in T_1$
2.	$\langle p, F\rangle \in T_2$	2′. $\langle q, F\rangle \in T_2$
3.	$\langle p, F\rangle \in T_3$	3′. $\langle q, F\rangle \in T_3$
4.	$\langle p, F\rangle \in T_4$	4′. $\langle q, F\rangle \in T_4$
5.	$\langle p, F\rangle \in T_5$	5′. $\langle q, F\rangle \in T_5$
6.	$\langle p, F\rangle \in T_6$	6′. $\langle q, F\rangle \in T_6$
7.	$\langle p, F\rangle \in T_7$	7′. $\langle q, F\rangle \in T_7$

Each of the statements 1–7 (dealing with *p*'s legal position with respect to *F*) is combined in a conjunction with each of the statements 1′–7′ (dealing with *q*'s legal position with respect to *F*).

Of the 49 conjunctions thereby obtained, 14 are self-contradictory according to the logic for Shall and Do. These self-contradictory statements are, in particular, conjunctions of the following pairs of statements:

1, 5′	1, 7′	2, 7′	3, 5′	3, 7′	4, 5′	5, 7′
5, 1′	7, 1′	7, 2′	5, 3′	7, 3′	5, 4′	7, 5′

Consider, for example, the conjunction of 1 and 5′, i.e.,

$$\langle p, F\rangle \in T_1 \ \& \ \langle q, F\rangle \in T_5,$$

which according to the definitions of T_1 and T_5 can be rewritten as

$$\text{May Do}(p, F) \ \& \ \text{May}(\sim\text{Do}(p, F) \ \& \sim\text{Do}(p, \sim F)) \ \& \\ \text{May Do}(p, \sim F) \ \& \ \text{Shall Do}(q, F).$$

According to the logic for Shall and Do, the two components of the conjunction

$$\text{May Do}(p, \sim F),$$
$$\text{Shall Do}(q, F),$$

are incompatible (see the implication schema above, p. 53). Consequently the conjunction of 1 and 5′ is self-contradictory.

Each of the remaining 35 conjunctions defines an individualistic two-agent type. The conjunction of 1 and 1′, for example, defines the two-agent type R_1 as follows:

$$R_1 = \{\langle p, q, F\rangle | \langle p, F\rangle \in T_1 \;\&\; \langle q, F\rangle \in T_1\}.$$

Or, taking another example, the conjunction of 7 and 6′ defines the two-agent type R_{35} thus

$$R_{35} = \{\langle p, q, F\rangle | \langle p, F\rangle \in T_7 \;\&\; \langle q, F\rangle \in T_6\}.$$

In this way we obtain a list of 35 individualistic two-agent types, where each type is defined as a set of ordered triples comprising two people and a state of affairs.

The thiry-five types $R_1, ..., R_{35}$ are characterised by different combinations of $T_1, ..., T_7$ occurring in the definitions. Therefore, we might say that each of $R_1, ..., R_{35}$ is an *ordered pair* of two (not necessarily distinct) elements in $\{T_1, ..., T_7\}$. R_1 is thus the ordered pair $\langle T_1, T_1\rangle$ and R_{35} the ordered pair $\langle T_7, T_6\rangle$. In accordance with this mode of expression, each of $R_1, ..., R_{35}$ can be represented as a point of intersection of two coordinates in a Cartesian coordinate system: as the point of intersection of a $\langle p, F\rangle$ coordinate and a $\langle q, F\rangle$ coordinate, where the $\langle p, F\rangle$ coordinate is the first coordinate and the $\langle q, F\rangle$ coordinate the second. The two-agent type R_{35}, for example, is the point of intersection of T_7 on the $\langle p, F\rangle$ axis and T_6 on the $\langle q, F\rangle$ axis.

The first coordinate here—i.e., the $\langle p, F\rangle$ axis—I take to be the *vertical* axis and the other (the $\langle q, F\rangle$ axis) the *horizontal* axis (cf. Kanger & Kanger, 1966, p. 94, 96; the opposite choice of axes is often made). The definitions of the thirty-five types of individualistic two-agent types, together with the numbering assigned here, are clearly portrayed in the diagram on the subsequent page, which shows how the types were constructed by coordination.

As an example to assist in the reading of the diagram, consider R_{34}. This is an ordered pair $\langle T_7, T_4\rangle$ comprising T_7 on the $\langle p, F\rangle$ axis and T_4 on the $\langle q, F\rangle$ axis. This means that R_{34} is defined as follows:

$$R_{34} = \{\langle p, q, F\rangle | \langle p, F\rangle \in T_7 \;\&\; \langle q, F\rangle \in T_4\}.$$

This definition, in turn, can be rewritten (see above, p. 92) as follows:

$$R_{34} = \{\langle p, q, F\rangle \mid \text{Shall Do}(p, \sim F) \;\&\; \text{May}(\sim \text{Do}(q, F) \;\&\; \sim \text{Do}(q, \sim F)) \;\&\; \text{May Do}(q, \sim F)\}.$$

(The conjunct $\sim$May Do(q, F) has been omitted since it is implied by Shall Do(p, $\sim F$) and is therefore redundant.)

$\langle p,F\rangle$axis							
T_7	–	–	–	R_{34}	–	R_{35}	R_7
T_6	R_{28}	R_{29}	R_{30}	R_{31}	R_{32}	R_6	R_{33}
T_5	–	R_{26}	–	–	R_5	R_{27}	–
T_4	R_{21}	R_{22}	R_{23}	R_4	–	R_{24}	R_{25}
T_3	R_{17}	R_{18}	R_3	R_{19}	–	R_{20}	–
T_2	R_{12}	R_2	R_{13}	R_{14}	R_{15}	R_{16}	–
T_1	R_1	R_8	R_9	R_{10}	–	R_{11}	–
$\langle q,F\rangle$axis	T_1	T_2	T_3	T_4	T_5	T_6	T_7

The diagram shows clearly at a glance how the numbering of the individualistic two-agent types depends on their construction as ordered pairs of one-agent types. Thus, $R_1, \ldots, R_7$ (which are *symmetric*—see immediately below), have the same indices as the corresponding one-agent type from which they are constructed. The remainder are numbered in the following order: $\langle T_i, T_m\rangle, \langle T_i, T_{m+1}\rangle, \ldots, \langle T_{i+1}, T_m\rangle, \langle T_{i+1}, T_{m+1}\rangle$, and so forth.

2. *Inversion and conversion; symmetrical and neutral types*

Following Kanger (see above, pp. 57 ff.) I define the *inverse* and *converse*, and the properties *symmetric* and *neutral*, of our thirty-five types.

DEFINITIONS. Let R, R' be variables for elements of $\{R_1, \ldots, R_{35}\}$.

(1) R is the *inverse* of $R' =_{\text{def.}}$ For each p, q and F, $\langle p, q, F\rangle \in R$ if and only if $\langle q, p, F\rangle \in R'$.

(2) R is the *converse* of $R' =_{\text{def.}}$ For each p, q and F, $\langle p, q, F\rangle \in R$ if and only if $\langle p, q, \sim F\rangle \in R'$.

(3) R is *symmetric* $=_{\text{def.}}$ For each p, q and F, $\langle p, q, F\rangle \in F$ if and only if $\langle q, p, F\rangle \in R$. ($R$ is its own inverse.)

(4) R is *neutral* $=_{\text{def.}}$ For each p, q and F, $\langle p, q, F\rangle \in R$ if and only if $\langle p, q, \sim F\rangle \in R$. ($R$ is its own converse.)

As an easy key to finding both the inverse and converse of each two-agent type, the following diagram is more useful than that given above:

R_{5}	R_{26}	R_{27}				R_{27}		
R_{15}	R_{2}	R_{16}	R_{13}	R_{12}	R_{13}	R_{16}	R_{14}	
R_{32}	R_{29}	R_{6}	R_{30}	R_{28}	R_{30}	R_{6}	R_{31}	R_{33}
	R_{18}	R_{20}	R_{3}	R_{17}	R_{3}	R_{20}	R_{19}	
	R_{8}	R_{11}	R_{9}	R_{1}	R_{9}	R_{11}	R_{10}	
	R_{18}	R_{20}	R_{3}	R_{17}	R_{3}	R_{20}	R_{19}	
R_{32}	R_{29}	R_{6}	R_{30}	R_{28}	R_{30}	R_{6}	R_{31}	R_{33}
	R_{22}	R_{24}	R_{23}	R_{21}	R_{23}	R_{24}	R_{4}	R_{25}
		R_{35}				R_{35}	R_{34}	R_{7}

In order to read the diagram, the following principles should be followed:

1. *Coordination.* The ordered pair $\langle T_i, T_j\rangle$ with T_i on the $\langle p, F\rangle$ axis and T_j on the $\langle q, F\rangle$ axis occurs in the square lying on the same line as the two-agent type R_i and in the same column as the two-agent type R_j.

For example, $R_{26} = \langle T_5, T_2 \rangle$, since the square for R_{26} occurs in the line for R_5 and the column for R_2.

2. *Inverse Pair.* The inverse of a two-agent type R occurs in the square which is the mirror image of R's square along the dotted diagonal line. For example, R_{15} is the inverse of R_{26}.

3. *Converse Pair.* The converse of a two-agent type R occurs in the square reached from R's square by rotating through 180 degrees about the central square in the diagram (i.e., R_1's square). For example, R_{26} is the converse of R_{34}.

The latter diagram is also helpful in showing that none of the thirty-five individualistic two-agent types is *empty*. To show this, it is not necessary to consider all thirty-five cases individually; it suffices to consider fourteen, provided they are appropriately chosen. A choice of fourteen types sufficient to cover the cases of all thirty-five can easily be found using the diagram just given. Consider the following extract of it, which follows the diagonal to the midpoint:

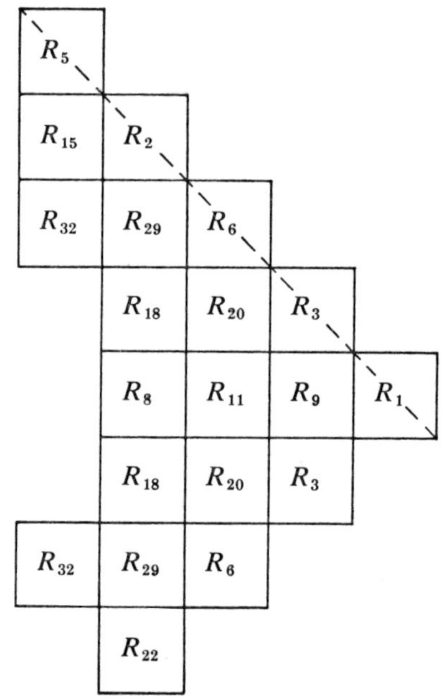

This diagram contains fourteen distinct two-agent types (the number of squares is greater since certain types occur twice). From the large diagram it is clear that for each individualistic type, it is (i) identical with one of the fourteen in the latter diagram, or it is (ii) the *inverse* of one of the fourteen, or it is (iii) the *converse* of one of the fourteen, or, finally, it is (iv) the *inverse of the converse* of one of the fourteen. For example, R_{27} is the inverse of R_{32} (which occurs in the latter diagram), R_{33} is the converse of R_{32} and R_{35} is the inverse of the converse of R_{32}.

In order to cover the case of an arbitrarily chosen type from the thirty-five it is obviously sufficient to cover the inverse, the converse or the inverse of the converse of the types in question (cf. the analogous question in the theory of atomic types of right, Kanger & Kanger, 1966, p. 95). Suppose, for example, that R_{32} is shown to be non-empty. It would then have been shown that there are p, q, F such that

(1) $\langle p, q, F\rangle \in R_{32}$

is true. (1) is logically equivalent to

(2) $\langle q, p, \sim F\rangle \in R_{35}$.

Consequently, it follows that R_{35} is not empty since (2) is satisfied for a given p, q and F.

3. *Elements of individualistic two-agent types: Illustrations*

In this section a number of examples will be described illustrating some of the fourteen types in the diagram above, and thereby indicating at the range of application of all thirty-five types R_1, ..., R_{35}. (I refer the reader to Helle Kanger's forthcoming thesis for a more detailed discussion of applications; cf. above, p. 62.)

Example 1. Suppose John is a Swedish citizen and F the state of affairs that a certain manuscript of John's is published in Sweden (cf. Kanger & Kanger's example, 1966, p. 86). If the manuscript does not contain anything unlawful, then John has a legal position of type R_{11} against the Swedish state with respect to F. This means that he may publish, and he may prevent publication; moreover, he may remain passive with respect to its publication. The Swedish state, on the other hand, may neither bring about nor prevent publication.

It is noteworthy that this example relates nicely to a problem discussed earlier concerning the "forbidding of interference" (p. 126). Using the parlance of Bentham, Austin and Hohfeld, John's "liberty" or "privilege" to publish the manuscript or to prevent publication is connected with a prohibition to interfere directed against the Swedish State. (The relation obtaining here between John and the Swedish State with respect to F also holds between John and several—perhaps all—other agents.)

Example 2. Suppose again that John is a Swedish citizen but this time F is the state of affairs that he receives medical care. John then has a position of type R_8 against the Swedish State (or the local community) with respect to F. John may both see to it and prevent his receiving medical care; and he may do neither. The state (or community) may see to it that he receives medical care, but may not prevent it; however, the state (or community) is not obliged to see to it (suppose, for example, that John refused attention).

Example 3. Assume that John and Mary are a childless married Swedish couple, residing in Sweden and subject to Swedish law. Let F be the state of affairs that a divorce is granted. Several relations obtain here. John has a position of type R_2 against Mary with respect to F; i.e., John may see to it that a divorce is granted, but he may not prevent it. Of course, he may also remain passive, neither seeing to nor preventing the divorce. The situation is precisely the same for Mary (R_2 is symmetric). On the other hand, John's mother or father has a position of type R_{29} against John with respect to F, so that, whilst John has the power to act just described, his mother or father may neither bring about nor prevent the divorce. Finally, John's mother or father has a position of type R_6 against Mary's mother or father: neither of them may bring about or prevent the divorce.

Example 4. Suppose John has had the misfortune to have encountered hard times and become insolvent, and F is the state of affairs that John is bankrupt. Peter and Henry, I shall suppose, are two of John's creditors. Looking at the legal relation between these two creditors, Peter has a position of type R_1 versus Henry: he may see to it that John becomes bankrupt or he may prevent it (for example, by paying off the debts). He may also, of course, remain passive. The same holds for Henry. The question of the relation between John and his creditors is rather complicated, however, and will be left aside. Instead, we can consider the relation between one of the creditors and a third party—John's father, for example—who is not a creditor. Each creditor has a position of type R_{10} against such a party. Whilst Peter, for example, has those powers, just attributed to him, John's father may not see to it that John becomes bankrupt, though he may prevent it or simply remain passive.

Example 5. Suppose John has lent Peter and Henry £50 between them, and F is the state of affairs that the money is returned to him (the debt is, as jurists say, "joint and several"; cf. for example Treitel, 1962, pp. 384 ff.). John then has a position of the type R_{15} against each of Peter and Henry with respect to F. That is to say, John may see to it that he gets his money back; he may also remain passive if he so wishes, but he may not prevent repayment. Each of Henry and Peter shall see to it that the money is repaid, and the relation between the two debtors is of type R_5 (a symmetric type).

Two points should be noted concerning this example. Firstly, type R_{15} (the relation between John and each of his debtors) is the individualistic two-agent type usually in question when one person has, according to legal parlance, a *claim* against another person. (An explication of *claim* in terms of R_{15}, however, is not exhaustive. I shall return to this point in Chapter 8.) Secondly, the supposition

(1) $\text{Shall Do}(p, F) \,\&\, \text{Shall Do}(q, F)$,

which means that p has a position of type R_5 against q with respect to F (cf. the relation between Peter and Henry), should be distinguished from what is expressed by

(2) $\text{May} \sim \text{Do}(p, F) \,\&\, \text{May} \sim \text{Do}(q, F) \,\&$
$\text{Shall}(\text{Do}(p, F) \vee \text{Do}(q, F))$.

(to which I shall return in Chapter 5). According to (1), each of p and q shall see to it that F, whereas according to (2) it is not the case that either of p or q shall see to it that F, though *at least one* shall. If (2) is maintained instead of (1) in the example, the relations which would then obtain are of different types. For it follows from (2) that

(3) $\text{May Do}(p, F) \,\&\, \text{May}(\sim \text{Do}(p, F) \,\&\, \sim \text{Do}(p, \sim F)) \,\&$
$\sim \text{May Do}(p, \sim F)$,

(4) $\text{May Do}(q, F) \,\&\, \text{May}(\sim \text{Do}(q, F) \,\&\, \sim \text{Do}(q, \sim F)) \,\&$
$\sim \text{May Do}(q, \sim F)$,

and accordingly the supposition of (2) rather than (1) entails that John has a position of type R_2 against each of Peter and Henry, and a position of the same type also holds between Peter and Henry themselves.

When deciding which of (1) and (2) obtains in a given case it should be borne in mind that a statement of the kind Do(p, F) may be true even though p does not actively take any measures to bring about F, for there is the possibility of a *null action* (p. 70). Consequently, if (1) holds for Peter and Henry, this does not imply that each of them shall send money to John. If Peter sends £50, for example, it is not necessary for Henry to do anything since each party's obligation is fulfilled; provided, of course, that Henry would have sent the money had it been necessary.

In view of the possibility of a null action, the distinction between (1) and (2) becomes rather a subtle point. The distinction should nevertheless be maintained for there are cases where it is of decisive importance from the standpoint of jurisprudence. For example, suppose two sentries, p and q, are guarding a certain military area and F is the state of affairs that no unauthorized person is allowed inside. It is of considerable significance which of (1) and (2) obtains. If (1) is the case then p has not fulfilled his obligation if he sleeps in his sentry box—irrespective of whether or not the other sentry q guards the area against unauthorized persons by actively taking the appropriate measures. If (2) is the case, however, the orders could have been obeyed even if p had slept or gone to the local dance or whatever so long as q remained at his post seeing to it that no unauthorized person entered.

Example 6. Let F be the state of affairs that the form on which John has declared his income for purposes of taxation is signed by him. John's wife then has a legal position of type R_{32} against John, since she may neither bring about the signature nor prevent it, whilst John shall himself see to it that he signs.

Example 7. The subject of this example is football: United are playing City, with the United team defending the goal at the scoreboard end and the City team defending the Stretford end goal at the kick-off. F is the state of affairs that the ball lies at the back of United's goal net and as a result City are $1-0$ up. Any member of the United team then has a position of type R_{22} against any member of the City team with respect to F; i.e., United players may not see to it that the ball lands in their own goal, but they may of course, prevent it. City players, on the other hand, may see to it that the ball lands in the United goal, but may not prevent it. And it is open to all players that they may neither see to nor prevent the ball landing in United's goal. (This supposition, that players from both sides may remain passive concerning whether the ball lands in United's net, is the only reasonable one to make. Otherwise, if it were supposed that the members of United's team *shall* see to it that the ball does not land in their own goal, and that the members of City's team *shall* see to it that it does, there results a contradiction in the rules of football: Shall(F & $\sim F$) for the given value of F.)

Example 8. In this example and the next, the one-agent type T_3 is involved. First, I return to the simple, albeit trivial, example of Chapter 3 concerning the ventilation of a room (p. 97). As in Chapter 3, F and G are again:

F that the window is closed,
G that the door is closed,

and once more, F & G and $\sim F$ & $\sim G$ describe two "bad" alternatives whilst F & $\sim G$ and $\sim F$ & G are two equally preferable, better alternatives. If John and Peter are two caretakers, both having responsibility for keeping the room aired, then John has a position of type R_3 against Peter both with respect to F and with respect to G. In other words (cf. pp. 97 f.), it may be so that John sees to it that the window is closed and the door is open, or that the window is open and the door is closed. Moreover, it shall be the case that John either sees to it that the window is closed and that the door is open, or sees to it that the window is open and the door closed. Exactly the same holds for Peter.

Note that in this case we can be doubly sure that the room is aired according to the directions (cf. what was said in example 5)—each of John and Peter has an independent obligation, and it may not be the case that either of them neglects to see to it that the room is aired. On the other hand, this might not require active participation; a null action on the part of Peter whilst John opens the window when the door is closed suffices.

A small modification of the present case provides an example of another individualistic two-agent type. A third person, Henry, is introduced into the situation. He is a visitor, holding a temporary position in the same institution that employs John and Peter and that owns the room in question. Henry may see to it that the room is aired (in accordance with the directions) but he need not, and he has a position of type R_9 against both John and Peter.

Example 9. In this final example I shall take up a discussion of a more complicated kind, the example involving what is referred to in the literature on jurisprudence as the question of "gaps in the law" (cf. from the more recent literature Alchourrón & Bulygin, 1971, pp. 116–180). Suppose that the municipal Court in Loughborough has to decide a civil case between John, the plaintiff, and Peter, the defendant. The parties dispute the ownership of a certain property called Glenroy and John pleads that he shall be declared the owner. F and G are as follows:

F that judgement is passed in favour of John (the plaintiff),
G that judgement is passed in favour of Peter (the defendant).

Letting p denote the court, the first supposition is that

(1) $\text{Shall}[(\text{Do}(p, F) \mathbin{\&} \text{Do}(p, \sim G)) \vee (\text{Do}(p, G) \mathbin{\&} \text{Do}(p, \sim F))]$,

is the case. (1)'s being true depends on the legal rule that the court shall decide the case, and it means that it shall be the case that one of the following obtains:

(a) The court sees to it that judgement is passed in favour of John
and
the court sees to it that judgement is not passed in favour of Peter.

(b) The court sees to it that judgement is passed in favour of Peter
and
the court sees to it that judgement is not passed in favour of John.

Given (1) various possibilities are to be distinguished. The first,

(2) $\text{Shall}(\text{Do}(p, F) \mathbin{\&} \text{Do}(p, \sim G))$,

means that the court shall decide in favour of John and against Peter. The second,

(3) $\text{Shall}(\text{Do}(p, G) \mathbin{\&} \text{Do}(p, \sim F))$,

means that, conversely, the court shall decide in favour of Peter and against John. A third and final possibility is

(4) May(Do(p, F) & Do(p, $\sim G$)) & May(Do(p, G) & Do(p, $\sim F$)),

which means that the court may decide in favour of John and against Peter, but also in favour of Peter and against John. I will not involve myself here in a discussion of the possible situations in which it is reasonable to choose one of (2), (3) and (4) (cf. the discussion of the one-agent type T_3 in the Appendix). Rather, it will suffice for my purposes simply to point to a plausible further specification of the situation in the example in which (1) and (4) obtain. I shall suppose that the court has adequate information on previous dealings between Peter and John, on the history of the Glenroy property, etc., but that the statutory texts, precedents and other so-called sources of law are obscure or contradictory so that the following obtains:

(5) The court cannot see to it that it becomes convinced that John is the owner of Glenroy, and nor can it become convinced that John does not own Glenroy.

Such a situation is by no means unusual, and in such cases there is said to be a gap in the law. Jurists often suppose in cases of this kind that it is equally permissible for the court to pass judgement in favour of the plaintiff as it is to decide in favour of the defendant (cf. Alchourrón & Bulygin, 1971, pp. 156 f.), and this amounts to (1) and (4) obtaining in the example.

Given a situation in which (1) and (4) are true, it is possible to illustrate two more individualistic types, R_{20} and R_{18}. It should, for example, be supposed that the court has a position of type R_{20} against the (British) government with respect to F and to G. This means that, whilst (1) and (4) hold for the court, the government may neither see to nor hinder judgement's being passed in favour of John, and similarly for Peter; the government may not become involved in a civil suit between private parties at court. The second of the two types is illustrated in the relation sustained between Peter and the court with respect to F. It ought to be assumed that the court has a position of type R_{18} against Peter with respect to F. Whilst (1) and (4) hold for the court, Peter may not prevent their passing judgement in favour of John. He may, however, positively see to it that such a judgement is given; this is brought about if, for example, he concedes as defendant to John's plea (which he may, of course, do if he so desires). Furthermore, Peter may remain passive in so far as he neither brings about nor prevents the court's passing judgement in favour of John.

If these nine cases are accepted as illustrations of the types mentioned, all of the types occurring in the second diagram of the previous section (p. 132) are thereby shown to be non-empty. Consequently, all of the individualistic two-agent types $R_1, ..., R_{35}$ are non-empty.

4. *Individualistic two-agent types and atomic types of rights*

The system of thirty-five two-agent types strongly resembles Kanger's system of atomic types of rights. The relation between the two is displayed in the following table (where $K_1, K_2, ..., K_{26}$ denote Kanger's twenty-six atomic types of right according to the numbering above, p. 56):

$K_1 = R_1 \cup R_3 \cup R_9 \cup R_{17}$	$K_{14} = R_{33}$
$K_2 = R_6$	$K_{15} = R_{24}$
$K_3 = R_5$	$K_{16} = R_{10} \cup R_{19}$
$K_4 = R_2$	$K_{17} = R_{22}$
$K_5 = R_{11} \cup R_{20}$	$K_{18} = R_{28} \cup R_{30}$
$K_6 = R_{15}$	$K_{19} = R_{26}$
$K_7 = R_{32}$	$K_{20} = R_{27}$
$K_8 = R_{16}$	$K_{21} = R_{29}$
$K_9 = R_8 \cup R_{18}$	$K_{22} = R_{12} \cup R_{13}$
$K_{10} = R_{14}$	$K_{23} = R_{34}$
$K_{11} = R_7$	$K_{24} = R_{35}$
$K_{12} = R_4$	$K_{25} = R_{31}$
$K_{13} = R_{25}$	$K_{26} = R_{21} \cup R_{23}$

It is apparent from this table that the system of individualistic two-agent types is "stronger" than Kanger's system; for all that can be said in the latter can also be expressed in terms of the thirty-five types of the former, but not conversely.

The distinction between the two systems arises because no distinction is made between T_1 and T_3 in Kanger's system (see above, p. 100). Thus, Kanger's two-agent type K_1 is equivalent to the union of not less than four individualistic types, namely $\langle T_1, T_1\rangle$, i.e., R_1; $\langle T_3, T_3\rangle$, i.e., R_3; $\langle T_1, T_3\rangle$, i.e., R_9; and $\langle T_3, T_1\rangle$, i.e., R_{17}.

The possibility of T_3's being empty ("the philosophy of indolence", p. 96 above) was discussed in Chapter 3. This discussion is also decisive for a comparison between Kanger's system of twenty-six types and the system proposed here. If T_3 were empty, nine of the thirty-five types would be empty and each of the remaining twenty-six individualistic types would be identical with one of Kanger's twenty-six. The following statements can be proved valid:

1. $\langle p, F\rangle \in T_3 \leftrightarrow \langle p, q, F\rangle \in (R_3 \cup R_{17} \cup R_{18} \cup R_{19} \cup R_{20})$.
2. $\langle q, F\rangle \in T_3 \leftrightarrow \langle p, q, F\rangle \in (R_3 \cup R_9 \cup R_{13} \cup R_{23} \cup R_{30})$.
3. $T_3 = \varnothing \leftrightarrow (R_3 \cup R_9 \cup R_{13} \cup R_{17} \cup R_{18} \cup R_{19} \cup R_{20} \cup R_{23} \cup R_{30}) = \varnothing$.
4. $T_3 = \varnothing \leftrightarrow (K_1 = R_1 \;\&\; K_5 = R_{11} \;\&\; K_9 = R_8 \;\&\; K_{16} = R_{10} \;\&\; K_{18} = R_{28} \;\&\; K_{22} = R_{12} \;\&\; K_{26} = R_{21})$.

That T_3 is not empty does not itself exhaust the possibility of some of the nine two-agent types constructed from T_3 as first or second coordinate being empty. But the examples given in the preceding section illustrating these nine types remedy the deficiency.

III. *The Ordering of Individualistic Two-Agent Types*

1. *The ordering and its graphic representation*

It has been shown in Chapter 3 how the relation *less free than* gives a strict partial ordering of the one-agent types $T_1, ..., T_7$ (p. 109). I go on now to define the relation *less free than* as a relation between individualistic two-agent types; i.e., between elements of $\{R_1, ..., R_{35}\}$. The definition is constructed along the lines of the corresponding relation of one-agent types, but allowing for the representation of each individualistic two-agent type as an ordered pair of one-agent types.

Thus, we define a relation $\mathcal{R}$ on $\{R_1, ..., R_{35}\}$ standing for *less free than*.

DEFINITION. Let T, T', T'', T''' be variables for elements of $\{T_1, ..., T_7\}$ such that $\langle T, T' \rangle$, $\langle T'', T''' \rangle$ are elements of $\{R_1, ..., R_{35}\}$.

$$\langle T, T' \rangle \mathcal{R} \langle T'', T''' \rangle =_{\text{def.}} (T \mathcal{R} T'' \ \& \ T' \mathcal{R} T''') \lor$$
$$(T \mathcal{R} T'' \ \& \ T' = T''') \lor (T = T'' \ \& \ T' \mathcal{R} T''').$$

The idea underlying the definition can be expressed in the following one of several possible ways (cf. above, p. 109). If R and R' are individualistic two-agent types and R' is less free than R, then moving a triple $\langle p, q, F \rangle$ from R to R' entails one of the following alternatives:

1. both p and q have less freedom with respect to F than before.
2. p has less freedom, whilst q's freedom remains as before.
3. q has less freedom, but p's freedom is as before.

An example of how different elements in $\{R_1, ..., R_{35}\}$ are ordered by the relation $\mathcal{R}$ is most easily given with the help of a graphic representation where each type is represented by a circle divided into two, with each half further divided into three. The following conventions are introduced.

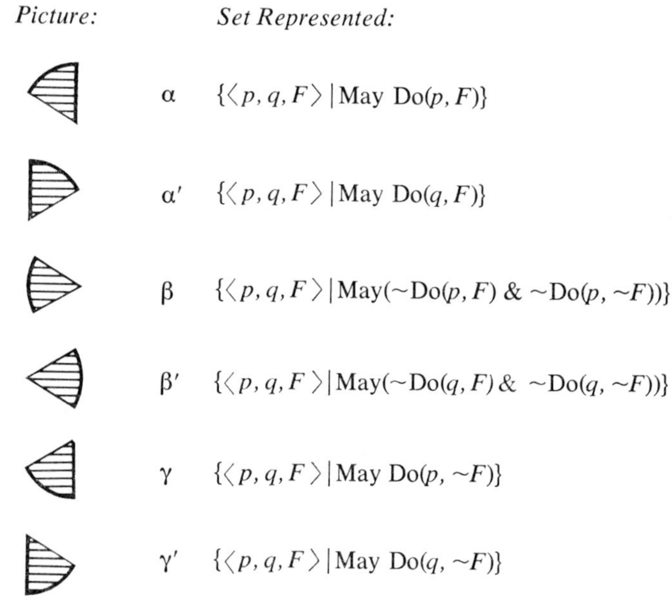

Picture:		*Set Represented:*
	α	$\{\langle p, q, F \rangle \mid \text{May Do}(p, F)\}$
	α'	$\{\langle p, q, F \rangle \mid \text{May Do}(q, F)\}$
	β	$\{\langle p, q, F \rangle \mid \text{May}(\sim\text{Do}(p, F) \ \& \ \sim\text{Do}(p, \sim F))\}$
	β'	$\{\langle p, q, F \rangle \mid \text{May}(\sim\text{Do}(q, F) \ \& \ \sim\text{Do}(q, \sim F))\}$
	γ	$\{\langle p, q, F \rangle \mid \text{May Do}(p, \sim F)\}$
	γ'	$\{\langle p, q, F \rangle \mid \text{May Do}(q, \sim F)\}$

Unshaded regions of the sectors represent the complements of sets mentioned here (i.e., $\bar{\alpha}$, $\bar{\beta}$, $\bar{\gamma}$, etc.).

Each complete circle represents the intersection of the sets represented by these sectors. Then we obtain

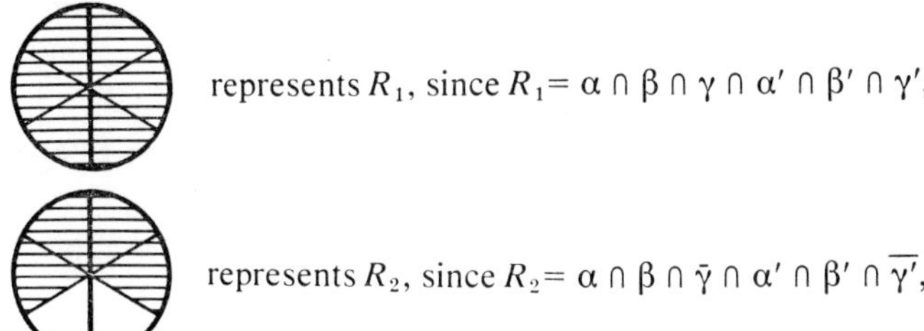

and so forth. It is easily seen that the left half circle represents the first coordinate and the right half the second coordinate for the type in question. (As in Chapter 3, p. 107, I shall speak here of the *factors* which a given type has; thus, R_1 has the factors α, β, γ, α', β' and γ'; R_2 has α, β, $\bar{\gamma}$, α', β' and $\overline{\gamma'}$; etc.)

The following three diagrams provide examples of how some of the elements in $\{R_1, \ldots, R_{35}\}$ are ordered by $\mathcal{R}$:

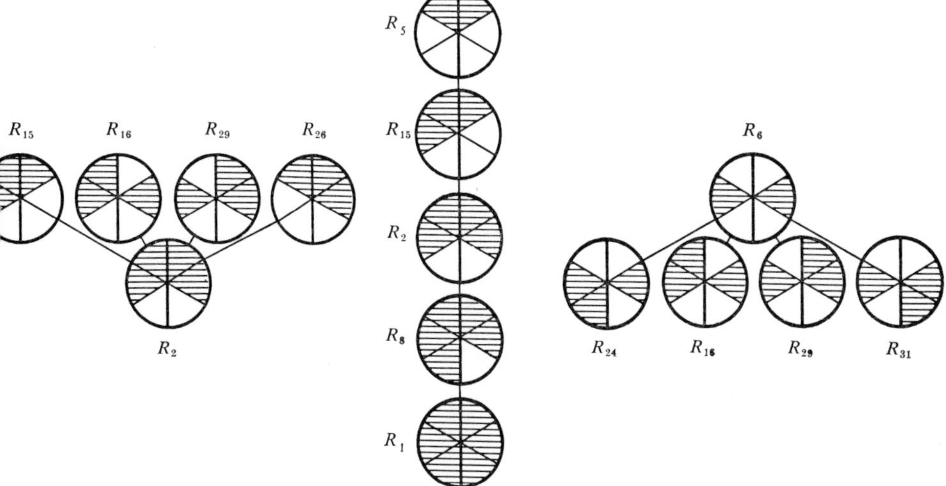

The left-hand diagram shows that each of R_{15}, R_{16}, R_{26} and R_{29} is less free than R_2. R_{15} and R_{16} have the same first coordinate as R_2 (represented by the left-hand half circle). The second coordinate for R_{15} and R_{16}, respectively (represented by the right half circle), is, on the other hand, less free than the second coordinate for R_2. Conversely, for R_{26} and R_{29} the second coordinate is identical with the second coordinate of R_2. The first coordinates of R_{26} and R_{29} are less free than the first coordinate of R_2. The right-hand diagram shows, in a corresponding way, that R_6 is less free than each of R_{16}, R_{24}, R_{29} and R_{31}. Finally, the centre diagram shows that R_5 is less free than R_{15}, which is less free than R_2, which is less free than R_8, which is less free than R_1.

These three diagrams can be considered as part of a complete Hasse diagram for the partial ordering on $\{R_1, ..., R_{35}\}$ (cf. above, p. 105). The complete Hasse diagram is rather unwieldy, but in its place we have a graphic "frame diagram" representation (see p. 145). The diagram is constructed in the following way:

(i) Each of $R_1, ..., R_{35}$ is designated by its index (i.e., R_1 is denoted simply by 1, R_2 by 2, and so forth).

(ii) Each rectangular frame represents that two-agent type indicated at the opening of the frame. Thus, the outermost frame represents R_1, and so forth.

(iii) If R, R' are two types represented by different frames, then the R frame encloses the R' frame if and only if R' is less free than R. (Thus, the R_1 frame encloses the R_9 frame; consequently R_9 is less free than R_1.)

(iv) If a type R occurs in an innermost frame, there is no type R' less free than R. (For example, there is no type less free than R_5 and no type less free than R_{32}.)

It can easily be verified that the diagram is so constructed that it has the following properties:

(v) The *converse* of a type R occurs at that point which is the mirror image about the vertical axis of symmetry of R's position. (Thus, R_8 is the converse of R_{10}.)

(vi) The *inverse* of a type R occurs as the mirror image to R's position about the horizontal axis of symmetry. (Thus, R_8 is the inverse of R_{12}.)

This "frame diagram" gives a complete picture of how the thirty-five individualistic two-agent types are related to one another according to their relative freedom. In order to illustrate the use of the diagram, I refer first to the three diagrams above (p. 143) where the types are represented by circles. It can be seen immediately from the frame diagram

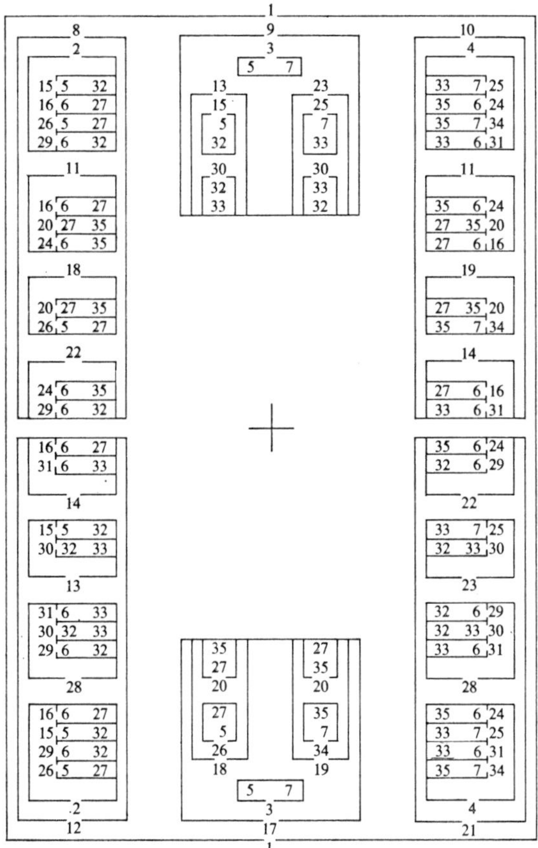

that the R_2 frame encloses the R_{15} frame, the R_{16} frame, the R_{26} frame and the R_{29} frame. Thus, each of R_{15}, R_{16}, R_{26} and R_{29} is less free than R_2 (cf. the left-hand diagram above, p. 143). Furthermore, it is apparent from the frame diagram that R_6 is enclosed by the R_{16} frame, the R_{24} frame, the R_{29} frame and the R_{31} frame. Thus, R_6 is less free than each of R_{16}, R_{24}, R_{29} and R_{31} (cf. the right-hand diagram above, p. 143). Finally, it can be seen from the frame diagram that the R_1 frame encloses the R_8 frame, which in turn encloses the R_2 frame which encloses the R_{15} frame which encloses R_5. Thus, R_5 is less free than R_{15} which is less free than R_2 which is less free than R_8 which is less free than R_1 (cf. the middle diagram above, p. 143).

Suppose that R, R' are two distinct types such that

(1) R is not less free than R' and R' is not less free than R.

In this case, R and R' are *incomparable* so far as their freedom (in the sense intended here) is concerned. Which types are incomparable in this way can easily be seen from the frame diagram. For if R and R' are incomparable, it is not possible to reach R''s position from R's position simply by moving "inwards" or "outwards" in the diagram. Consider, for example, the types R_8 and R_9. In the diagram, R_8's frame does not enclose R_9's frame and neither does R_9's frame enclose R_8's frame. Therefore R_8 and R_9 are incomparable in respect to their relative freedom.

2. *Deontic paths, deontic distance and intermediateness*

In connection with one of Bentham's ideas, the concept *deontic path* was introduced in Chapter 3 in the theory for one-agent types. This concept with its variations—*straight*, *non-straight* and *minimal* deontic paths—can be applied analogously in the theory of two-agent types. Some examples of different types of deontic paths between two-agent types are given in the following four diagrams:

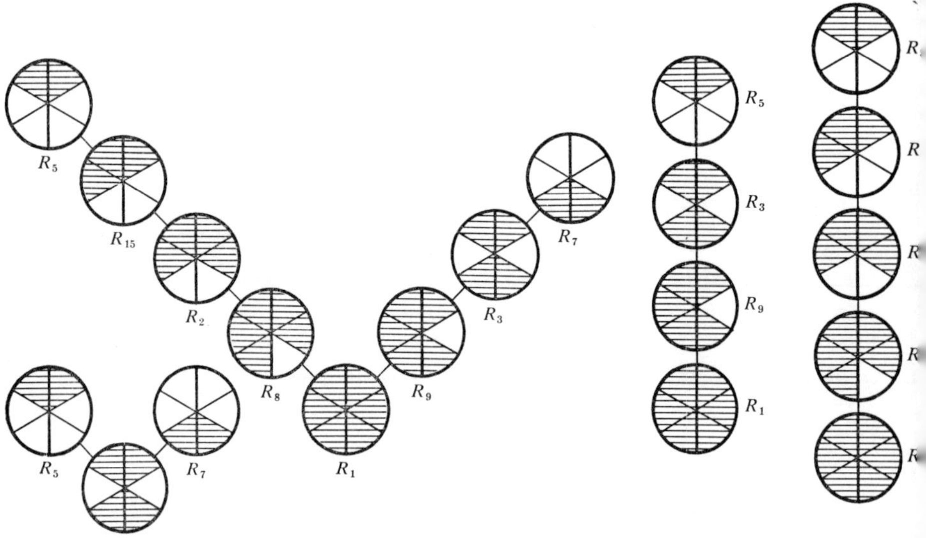

The two diagrams on the left show paths from R_5 to R_7 (or conversely). Since R_5 and R_7 are mutually incomparable with respect to freedom, all paths between them are *non-straight*, i.e., go partly upwards and partly downwards (cf. above, p. 114). One of the two paths shown is shorter than the other. In fact, the path $\langle R_5, R_3, R_7\rangle$ is *minimal* in $\{R_1, ..., R_{35}\}$: there is no other sequence $\langle R_5, ..., R_7\rangle$ which is a deontic path in $\{R_1, ..., R_{35}\}$ and which has a smaller number of elements.

The two diagrams on the right show paths between R_1 and R_5. Since R_5 is less free than R_1, there are *straight* paths, i.e., paths which go upwards only, such as the two shown. Now, of these two paths, one is shorter than the other; in fact, in the theory of two-agent types it is possible for a path to be straight without being minimal (cf., on the other hand, above, p. 117, concerning one-agent types). The path $\langle R_1, R_9, R_3, R_5\rangle$ is straight and minimal in $\{R_1, ..., R_{35}\}$; the path $\langle R_1, R_8, R_2, R_{15}, R_5\rangle$, on the other hand, is straight but non-minimal.

The various deontic paths between two types R and R' can always be found with the help of the frame diagram above (p. 145). In moving from R to R' in the diagram each distinct step of the path takes us either outwards from an inner frame or inwards from an outer frame (in other words, each step is taken between *comparable* types; see above, p. 146). For example, it is clear from the top of the diagram that $\langle R_2, R_8, R_1, R_{10}, R_4\rangle$ is a deontic path from R_2 to R_4. R_4 can be reached from R_2 in the following steps: from R_2 outwards to R_8, then outwards again to R_1, then inwards to R_{10}, and then finally inwards again to R_4. In order to find all of the paths between two types R and R', however, it must be borne in mind that most types occur in more than one place in the diagram, and one must therefore consider how each place occupied by R can be reached from each position occupied by R'.

The formal definitions of the concept *deontic path* and the variations *straight* and *minimal* deontic paths are analogous to those given in Chapter 3 for one-agent types. The definitions in question for two-agent types are obtained simply by substituting R for T and $\{R_1, ..., R_{35}\}$ for $\{T_1, ..., T_7\}$ in the definitions given in Chapter 3 (above, pp. 115 f.).

The notions of *deontic distance* and *intermediate* have analogous applications in the theory of individualistic two-agent types. "Intermediate" is defined by making the same substitutions in the definition on p. 121 as were just made above in the definition of "deontic path"; and the definition of "deontic distance" is also obtained in the same way (p. 119), but with the additional substitution of $\{1, 2, ..., 6\}$ for $\{1, 2, 3\}$ (i.e., the distance can vary between 1 and 6).

An example of how the deontic distance varies between different two-agent types is given in the following diagram:

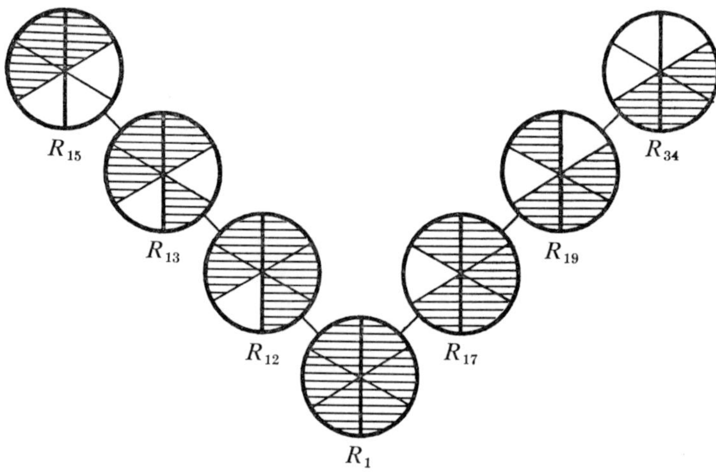

The diagram, or rather, parts of it, show deontic paths in $\{R_1, ..., R_{35}\}$ between, amongst others, the following types:

between R_{15} and R_{34};
between R_{15} and R_{19};
between R_{13} and R_{19};
between R_{13} and R_{17};
between R_{12} and R_{17};
between R_{12} and R_1.

All of these paths are minimal.

The deontic distance between two types R and R' is equal to the number of intermediate stations between R and R' plus one (on a path which is minimal in $\{R_1, ..., R_{35}\}$). It follows accordingly from the diagram that:

$\text{Dist}(R_{15}, R_{34}) = 6$;
$\text{Dist}(R_{15}, R_{19}) = 5$;

$\text{Dist}(R_{13}, R_{19}) = 4;$
$\text{Dist}(R_{13}, R_{17}) = 3;$
$\text{Dist}(R_{12}, R_{17}) = 2;$
$\text{Dist}(R_{12}, R_1) \ = 1.$

Thus, the diagram illustrates how the deontic distance can vary between 1 and 6.

A movement of a triple $\langle p, q, F \rangle$ along a deontic path entails, according to what has been said, one or more steps, each occurring upwards or downwards in the tree diagram (alternatively, inwards or outwards, respectively, in the frame diagram). It is appropriate to say something about p's and q's freedom with respect to F at each distinct step.

A step upwards in the tree diagram (inwards in the frame diagram) entails a movement of $\langle p, q, F \rangle$ from a type R to a type R' less free than R and such that R covers R' in $\{R_1, ..., R_{35}\}$ with respect to the relation "less free than". (Concerning the notion *cover*, see Definition 1, p. 115, which can be applied analogously.) Such a single-step movement upwards (or inwards) usually entails that *one* party's freedom with respect to F is diminished whilst the *other* party's freedom remains as before. Such is the case for a movement from R_1 to R_8. This movement can be represented as a movement upwards in the following diagram:

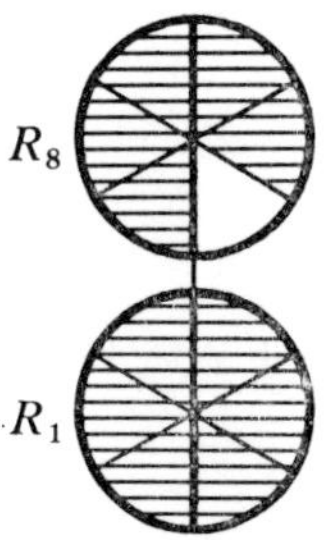

It is clear from the diagram that the movement involves a diminishing of q's freedom with respect to F whilst p's freedom remains as it was.

A single step movement upwards entails a reduction of freedom for both parties, however, in certain cases. Such is the case, for example, for a movement from R_3 to R_5. This movement can be represented as a movement upwards in the following diagram:

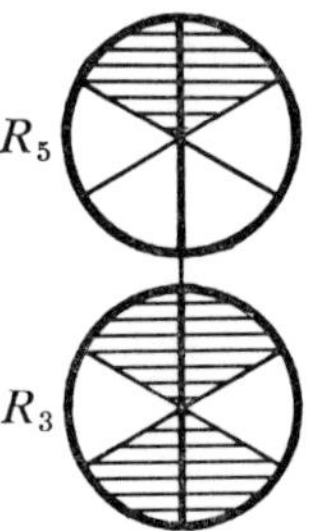

The diagram shows that the movement involves a decrease in both p's and q's freedom with respect to F. Expressed in terms of factors and numerical difference (cf. p. 119), this means that R_3 has two factors which R_5 does not (R_3 has γ and γ' whilst R_5 has $\overline{\gamma}$ and $\overline{\gamma'}$); the numerical difference between R_3 and R_5 is thus 2, whilst the deontic distance is 1.

That there is no intermediate station between R_3 and F_5 depends on the logic for Shall and Do. For it follows from their construction by coordination that:

$$R_3 = \langle T_3, T_3 \rangle,$$
$$R_5 = \langle T_5, T_5 \rangle,$$

(see above, p. 130). If there were a two-agent type R which was an intermediate station between R_3 and R_5, R would be constructed by coordination of T_3 with T_5 or of T_5 with T_3; we should have then

$$R = \langle T_3, T_5 \rangle$$

or

$$R = \langle T_5, T_3 \rangle.$$

According to the logic for Shall and Do, however, the following statement is valid:

(1) $\text{Shall Do}(p, F) \rightarrow \sim \text{May Do}(q, \sim F).$

It follows from (1) that there is no non-empty type R constructed as an ordered pair $\langle T_3, T_5 \rangle$ or $\langle T_5, T_3 \rangle$. In fact it holds for T_3 and T_5 (see above, p. 92) that:

(2) $\langle p, F \rangle \in T_3 \;\&\; \langle q, F \rangle \in T_5 \rightarrow \text{May Do}(p, \sim F) \;\&$ $\text{Shall Do}(q, F);$

(3) $\langle p, F \rangle \in T_5 \;\&\; \langle q, F \rangle \in T_3 \rightarrow \text{Shall Do}(p, F) \;\&\; \text{May Do}(q, \sim F).$

From (1) it follows, therefore, that

(4) $\langle p, F\rangle \in T_3 \rightarrow \sim(\langle q, F\rangle \in T_5)$;

(5) $\langle p, F\rangle \in T_5 \rightarrow \sim(\langle q, F\rangle \in T_3)$.

The possibility of a single step movement upwards entailing, in certain cases, a reduction in only one party's freedom, whilst in other cases a diminution of both parties' freedom, provides an explanation of the fact mentioned above (p. 147) that a deontic path in $\{R_1, ..., R_{35}\}$ can be straight and yet not minimal. Thus, consider the two deontic paths from R_1 to R_5 given in the two diagrams to the right in the figure above (p. 146). The longer path, represented by the diagram on the extreme right, is such that each step entails a diminution of only one party's freedom. The shorter path, on the other hand, is such that the last step (between R_3 and R_5) entails a reduction of both parties' freedom.

IV. *Addendum: The Theory of Structure Types*

1. *Introduction*

It is easily seen that the theory of individualistic two-agent types can be generalised, so that the method of constructing types from coordinates can be extended to three-agent types, four-agent types, etc. The types of such systems can be ordered by the "less free than" relation and the concepts "deontic path" and "deontic distance" are analogous to those developed for two-agent types.

So far as the regulating of several agents' actions is concerned, there is, however, further reason for drawing attention to the theory of what will here be called *position structures*. I shall complete the present chapter with a short account of the basis of this theory.

The term "position structure" occurs in Kanger & Kanger as part of the expression "government position structure" (1966, pp. 103 f.) meaning the right relations obtaining between the head of state, the prime minister, the parliament and other parties so far as the appointment and discharging of members of the government and dissolving of parliament is concerned. The basis of a more general theory is outlined in what follows—a theory for "types of position structure" or *structure types* for short.

2. *The definition of "structure type"*

First the concept "position class" is defined.

DEFINITION 1. Let Z be a set of agents and F be a condition. Y is a *position class in Z with respect to* $F =_{\text{def.}}$ Y is a non-empty subset of Z such that

$$\begin{aligned} &Y = \{p \in Z \mid \langle p, F \rangle \in T_1\} \vee \\ &Y = \{p \in Z \mid \langle p, F \rangle \in T_2\} \vee \\ &\qquad \vdots \\ &Y = \{p \in Z \mid \langle p, F \rangle \in T_7\}. \end{aligned}$$

For each pair $\langle Z, F \rangle$ of a non-empty set of agents and a condition F there is exactly one partition of Z into cells such that each cell is a position class in Z with respect to F. Each such cell is obviously assigned a certain one-agent type; i.e., one element of $\{T_1, ..., T_7\}$. Consequently, each pair $\langle Z, F \rangle$ of a non-empty set of agents together with a condition is assigned a certain *set* of one-agent types. The set of one-agent types assigned to a certain pair $\langle Z, F \rangle$ is called the *structure type* of Z with respect to F.

DEFINITION 2. Let $\{T_i, ..., T_m\}$ be a non-empty subset of $\{T_1, ..., T_7\}$, Z be a variable for sets of agents and F a variable for conditions. The *structure type* of Z with respect to $F = \{T_i, ..., T_m\} =_{\text{def.}}$

(i) For each $p \in Z$, $\langle p, F \rangle \in T_i \vee ... \vee \langle p, F \rangle \in T_m$; and

(ii) For some $p \in Z$, $\langle p, F \rangle \in T_i$ & ... & For some $p \in Z$, $\langle p, F \rangle \in T_m$.

It is clear that the expression "structure type" as just defined denotes a function: for given values of Z and F there is exactly one non-empty set $\{T_i, ..., T_m\}$ of one-agent types which is the structure type of Z with respect to F. "Structure type" is, however, not a one-one function, since there are, of course, Z, Z', F and F' such that

> $Z \neq Z'$, $F \neq F'$, and the structure type of Z with respect to $F =$ the structure type of Z' with respect to F'.

"Structure type" can also be used as a one-place predicate; we can simply say that a certain set $\{T_i, ..., T_m\}$ of one-agent types is a structure type. The intention behind this move is clear from the following definition:

DEFINITION 3. Let $\{T_i, ..., T_m\}$ be a non-empty subset of $\{T_1, ..., T_7\}$, Z a variable for sets of agents and F a variable for conditions. $\{T_i, ..., T_m\}$ is a *structure type* $=_{\text{def.}}$ For some Z and some F, the structure type of Z with respect to $F = \{T_i, ..., T_m\}$.

3. *The thirty-nine possible structure types*

Since $\{T_1, ..., T_7\}$ has seven elements, the number of its subsets is $2^7 = 128$. Certain of these subsets, however, are for reasons of logic precluded from being structure types. Consider, for example, the set $\{T_5, T_7\}$ and suppose:

(1) The structure type of Z with respect to $F = \{T_5, T_7\}$.

From (1) it follows that

(2) For some p, $\langle p, F\rangle \in T_5$, and for some p, $\langle p, F\rangle \in T_7$.

Statement (2) is self-contradictory according to the logic of Shall and Do, and so $\{T_5, T_7\}$ is clearly not a structure type.

Having eliminated those subsets which cannot, for this reason, be structure types, there remain thirty-nine subsets, $P_1, ..., P_{39}$, which are represented in the following diagram:

	T_1	T_2	T_3	T_4	T_5	T_6	T_7
P_1	+	+	+	+		+	
P_2	+	+	+	+			
P_3	+	+	+			+	
P_4	+	+		+		+	
P_5	+		+	+		+	
P_6		+	+	+		+	
P_7	+	+	+				
P_8	+	+		+			
P_9	+	+				+	
P_{10}	+		+	+			
P_{11}	+		+			+	
P_{12}	+			+		+	
P_{13}		+	+	+			
P_{14}		+	+			+	
P_{15}		+		+		+	
P_{16}		+			+	+	
P_{17}			+	+		+	
P_{18}				+		+	+
P_{19}	+	+					
P_{20}	+		+				

	T_1	T_2	T_3	T_4	T_5	T_6	T_7
P_{21}	+			+			
P_{22}	+					+	
P_{23}		+	+				
P_{24}		+		+			
P_{25}		+			+		
P_{26}		+				+	
P_{27}			+	+			
P_{28}			+			+	
P_{29}				+		+	
P_{30}				+			+
P_{31}					+	+	
P_{32}						+	+
P_{33}	+						
P_{34}		+					
P_{35}			+				
P_{36}				+			
P_{37}					+		
P_{38}						+	
P_{39}							+

(The occurrence of "+" in a square indicates that the one-agent type at the head of the column to which the square belongs is an element of the set at the head of the row to which the square belongs.)

4. *Converse and neutral structure types*

$P_1, ..., P_{39}$ can be classified in converse pairs and neutral types.

DEFINITIONS. Let P and P' be variables for elements of $\{P_1, ..., P_{39}\}$, Z a variable for sets of agents and F a variable for conditions.

(1) P is the *converse* of $P' =_{\text{def.}}$ For each Z and each F, P is the structure type of Z with respect to F if and only if P' is the structure type of Z with respect to not-F.

(2) P is *neutral* $=_{\text{def.}}$ For each Z and each F, P is the structure type of Z with respect to F if and only if P is the structure type of Z with respect to not-F. (P is its own converse.)

The converse and neutral types are presented in the following table (note that the relation "converse" is symmetric):

Converse types:		*Neutral types:*		
P_3, P_5	P_{23}, P_{27}	P_1	P_8	P_{22}
P_7, P_{10}	P_{25}, P_{30}	P_2	P_{11}	P_{24}
P_9, P_{12}	P_{26}, P_{29}	P_3	P_{13}	P_{28}
P_{14}, P_{17}	P_{31}, P_{32}	P_4	P_{15}	P_{33}
P_{16}, P_{18}	P_{34}, P_{36}	P_6	P_{20}	P_{35}
P_{19}, P_{21}	P_{37}, P_{39}			

5. P_1, P_{16} *and the number of structure types*

Since $P_1, ..., P_{39}$ are the only subsets of $\{T_1, ..., T_7\}$ which can be structure types, for each non-empty set of agents Z and each state of affairs F, the structure type of Z with respect to F must be one of $P_1, ..., P_{39}$. However, it is not thereby decided that all of $P_1, ..., P_{39}$ are structure types in the sense defined; i.e., for every $P \in \{P_1, ..., P_{39}\}$, it is not clear that there is a Z and F such that the structure type of Z with respect to F is P. That this is in fact the case must be shown by example.

In this connection, P_1 and P_{16} are of crucial importance, because of the following theorem.

THEOREM. *If P_1 and P_{16} are structure types, then so are the other elements of* $\{P_1, ..., P_{39}\}$.

The proof of this theorem is given in three steps. 1. To begin with, since P_{18} is the converse of P_{16}, it is evident that if P_{16} is a structure type, then so is P_{18}. 2. The next step in the argument rests on the following general statement (where P and P' are elements of $\{P_1, ..., P_{39}\}$):

> For each P, P', if $P' \subseteq P$, and P is a structure type, then P' is a structure type.

It is easily seen that this holds true. Let the set $\{T_i, ..., T_j, ..., T_m\}$ be one of the structure types $P_1, ..., P_{39}$ and suppose the following is true (for a given Z and F):

> The structure type of Z with respect to $F = \{T_i, ..., T_j, ..., T_m\}$.

In that case there is a partition of Z into cells $c_i, ..., c_j, ..., c_m$ such that each cell is assigned exactly one element of $\{T_i, ..., T_j, ..., T_m\}$—$T_i$ is assigned to c_i, etc. By constructing the union of the cells $c_i, ..., c_j$ a non-empty set Z' of agents can be constructed such that Z' is a subset of Z and

> The structure type of Z' with respect to $F = \{T_i, ..., T_j\}$.

3. It is easily shown that each element of $\{P_1, ..., P_{39}\}$ is a subset of one of P_1, P_{16} or P_{18}; in fact we have:

Subsets of P_1:	*Subsets of P_{16}*:	*Subsets of P_{18}*:
P_1–P_{15}	P_{16}	P_{18}
P_{17}	P_{25}–P_{26}	P_{29}–P_{30}
P_{19}–P_{24}	P_{31}	P_{32}
P_{26}–P_{29}	P_{34}	P_{36}
P_{33}–P_{36}	P_{37}–P_{38}	P_{38}–P_{39}
P_{38}		

6. P_1 *and* P_{16} *as structure types: The outlines of an illustration*

In this section I shall briefly consider the question whether P_1 and P_{16} are structure types. I shall begin by making explicit what this would imply in the two cases.

1. By definition, P_1 is a structure type if and only if there is a non-empty set Z of agents and a condition F such that Z can be partitioned into the following five cells c_1, ..., c_5, which are all non-empty:

c_1: $\{p \in Z | \langle p, F \rangle \in T_1\}$.
c_2: $\{p \in Z | \langle p, F \rangle \in T_2\}$.
c_3: $\{p \in Z | \langle p, F \rangle \in T_3\}$.
c_4: $\{p \in Z | \langle p, F \rangle \in T_4\}$.
c_5: $\{p \in Z | \langle p, F \rangle \in T_6\}$.

2. Similarly, P_{16} is a structure type if and only if there is a non-empty set Z of agents and a condition F such that Z can be partitioned into the following three non-empty cells c_1, c_2 and c_3:

c_1: $\{p \in Z | \langle p, F \rangle \in T_2\}$.
c_2: $\{p \in Z | \langle p, F \rangle \in T_5\}$.
c_3: $\{p \in Z | \langle p, F \rangle \in T_6\}$.

It is not too easy to find everyday illustrations of these two partitions, and particularly not of the first one. Position structures which are as complicated as these might, however, be found by considering the composition of an organisation; for example, how the employees in a company or an authority can be classified into different categories. I shall be content to suggest how two examples could be constructed along these lines.

Since P_1 involves the one-agent type T_3, I shall once more assume (cf. above, pp. 97 f., 137 ff.) that the following holds true for a given p, F and G:

(i) May(Do(p, F) & Do(p, $\sim G$)).
(ii) May(Do(p, G) & Do(p, $\sim F$)).
(iii) Shall[(Do(p, F) & Do(p, $\sim G$)) v (Do(p, G) & Do(p, $\sim F$))].

The variable p is now interpreted as a company, an authority or some such, rather than an individual person. An example could be obtained by assuming that there are within this organisation different categories of employees, each having a particular legal position with respect to F and G. In particular, we can assume that the legal positions of members of the different categories are as follows:

Category:	*F:*	*G:*
F-executive agents	T_2	T_4
G-executive agents	T_4	T_2
All round agents	T_1	T_1
Supervisory agents	T_3	T_3
Others	T_6	T_6

I shall be content to comment briefly on this schema without trying to elaborate the example in detail. The schema establishes some kind of "division of labour" among the *F-executive* and the *G-executive agents:* those who belong to the former category may see to it that F, while the latter may see to it that G, but not conversely. An *all round agent* has greater authority and can be thought of as someone who is competent to take over the work of the F-executives or of the G-executives as required. A *supervisory agent* is in the same legal position with respect to F and G as the organisation (the company, etc.) itself. It is by no means unusual, for example, that in a company there are certain administrative personnel who bear responsibility for the organisation's acting in accordance with given regulations. It is especially presupposed, however, that the carrying out of this duty incumbent upon such people manifests itself as so-called *null action* (see above, p. 70), and their active intervention is required only in exceptional cases. Finally, those falling under the heading *others* are the employees who are completely "unauthorised" both with respect to F and with respect to G.

P_{16} can be illustrated by an example of the same kind with one or two changes. Consider a situation in which the statement

(iv) Shall Do(p, F)

is true for a given p and F and where, as before, p is an organisation—a company or an authority, etc. The employees are divided into three groups in view of their legal position with respect to F as follows:

Category:	*F:*
F-executive agents	T_2
Supervisory agents	T_5
Others	T_6

This schema can be understood without further comment in view of what has been said previously.

CHAPTER 5

Collectivistic Two-Agent Types

I. *Introduction*

The characteristic feature of the system of two-agent types presented in Chapter 4 was that the types $R_1, ..., R_{35}$ were *individualistic*. Each statement

$$\langle p, q, F\rangle \in R$$

(where $R \in \{R_1, ..., R_{35}\}$) is equivalent to the conjunction of a statement

$$\langle p, F\rangle \in T,$$

which describes individually p's legal position with respect to F, and a statement

$$\langle q, F\rangle \in T'$$

individually describing q's legal position with respect to F (where T, $T' \in \{T_1, ..., T_7\}$). This chapter will be concerned with another system of two-agent types—a system of *collectivistic* types.

Like the individualistic types, the collectivistic types are defined as sets of ordered triples $\langle p, q, F\rangle$ comprising two agents and a state of affairs. The types are thus defined as legal relations between two parties, notwithstanding the variable F for an arbitrary state of affairs (cf. above, p. 124). A statement

$$\langle p, q, F\rangle \in S,$$

where S is what I shall call a genuinely collectivistic type, cannot, however, be split up into statements individually describing the regulation of p's and q's behaviour with respect to F. Rather, the statement describes a certain "collective" regulation of p's and q's behaviour with respect to F.

Suppose that John and Peter are employed in Henry's firm. Amongst other things the daily work includes seeing to it that the post is dealt with and letters answered, that clients are received and that the daily takings are deposited in the bank. Suppose, moreover, that concerning these tasks Henry prescribes that at least one of John and Peter shall see to it that they are done; but John and Peter may decide themselves how the tasks are to be distributed between them. For example, John and Peter may decide whether each of them shall see to it that the letters are answered, or John shall see to it and Peter need not, or Peter shall see to it while John need not. The prescription laid down by Henry concerning each of these tasks can be represented as a conjunction of the following statements:

(1) Shall(Do(p, F) v Do(q, F));
(2) May(Do(p, F) & Do(q, F));
(3) May(Do(p, F) & ~Do(q, F));
(4) May(~Do(p, F) & Do(q, F)).

For example, if the task is answering the firm's letters, then F is the state of affairs that the letters are answered, p could be John and q Peter.

What is expressed by the conjunction of (1)–(4) cannot be expressed in terms of statements to the effect that $\langle p, q, F\rangle$ belongs to a certain individualistic two-agent type. (1)–(4) express a certain regulation of the *coordination of p's and q's behaviour* with respect to F, but this cannot be done separately for p and q We might therefore say that (1)–(4) express a collective regulation of p's and q's behaviour with respect to F.

The system of collectivistic two-agent types is intended to facilitate a survey of the various such collective regulations of two agents' behaviour, of which the conjunction of (1)–(4) is just one among many. In particular, the conjunction is equivalent to

(5) $\langle p, q, F\rangle \in S_{67}$,

where S_{67} is type number 67 of those contained in the system.

The system of collectivistic two-agent types is the stronger of the two systems of two-agent types: all that can be said in terms of individualistic types can also be expressed in terms of collectivistic types, but not conversely. Take, for instance, the above example of the conjunction of (1)–(4). It follows from this conjunction, according to the logic of Shall and Do, that

(6) $\text{May Do}(p, F)\ \&\ \text{May}(\sim\text{Do}(p, F)\ \&\ \sim\text{Do}(p, \sim F))\ \&$
$\sim\text{May Do}(p, \sim F);$

(7) $\text{May Do}(q, F)\ \&\ \text{May}(\sim\text{Do}(q, F)\ \&\ \sim\text{Do}(q, \sim F))\ \&$
$\sim\text{May Do}(q, \sim F).$

Proof

(i) $\text{Shall}(\text{Do}(p, F) \vee \text{Do}(q, F)) \rightarrow \sim\text{May Do}(p, \sim F)\ \&$
$\sim\text{May Do}(q, \sim F).$

(ii) $\text{May}(\text{Do}(p, F)\ \&\ \sim\text{Do}(q, F)) \rightarrow \text{May Do}(p, F)\ \&$
$\text{May} \sim\text{Do}(q, F).$

(iii) $\text{May}(\sim\text{Do}(p, F)\ \&\ \text{Do}(q, F)) \rightarrow \text{May} \sim\text{Do}(p, F)\ \&$
$\text{May Do}(q, F).$

(iv) $\text{May} \sim\text{Do}(p, F)\ \&\ \sim\text{May Do}(p, \sim F) \rightarrow \text{May}(\sim\text{Do}(p, F)\ \&$
$\sim\text{Do}(p, \sim F)).$

(v) $\text{May} \sim\text{Do}(q, F)\ \&\ \sim\text{May Do}(q, \sim F) \rightarrow \text{May}(\sim\text{Do}(q, F)\ \&$
$\sim\text{Do}(q, \sim F)).$

The conjunction of (6) and (7) is equivalent to

(8) $\langle p, q, F\rangle \in R_2,$

where R_2 is type number 2 of the individualistic two-agent types. Here we have an example of a statement saying that $\langle p, q, F\rangle$ belongs to a certain individualistic type, which is a logical consequence of a statement saying that $\langle p, q, F\rangle$ belongs to a certain collectivistic type, since (8) follows from (5). The example is a special case of a general rule according to which a statement

$$\langle p, q, F\rangle \in S,$$

where S is a given collectivistic type, logically implies a statement

$$\langle p, q, F\rangle \in R,$$

where R is a given individualistic type. Conversely, it does not always hold that a statement of the kind

$$\langle p, q, F\rangle \in R$$

implies one of the kind

$$\langle p, q, F\rangle \in S$$

(where R and S are as before). (5), for example, does not follow from (8); it is obvious that (6) and (7) do not suffice to render the entire content of (1)–(4). However, a few of the collectivistic types are identical with certain individualistic types. For example, the types R_5 and S_{121} are defined by

$$R_5 = \{\langle p, q, F\rangle \mid \text{Shall Do}(p, F) \;\&\; \text{Shall Do}(q, F)\};$$
$$S_{121} = \{\langle p, q, F\rangle \mid \text{Shall}(\text{Do}(p, F) \;\&\; \text{Do}(q, F))\}.$$

Now, according to the logic of Shall,

$$\text{Shall Do}(p, F) \;\&\; \text{Shall Do}(q, F) \leftrightarrow \text{Shall}(\text{Do}(p, F) \;\&\; \text{Do}(q, F)),$$

and R_5 is thus identical with S_{121}. In view of this, S_{121}, although belonging to the collectivistic system, will be said not to be a *genuinely* collectivistic type; for to say

$$\langle p, q, F\rangle \in S_{121}$$

is not to specify a regulation of p's and q's behaviour which is collective in the sense that it cannot be specified by separately describing p's and q's legal position with respect to F.

II. *The Construction and Application of Collectivistic Types*

1. *Deontic basic conjunctions*

The method of constructing one-agent types was described in Chapter 3 as an iterated construction of basic conjunctions. The first step was to build the basic conjunctions obtained from the two statements

$$\text{Do}(p, F), \text{Do}(p, \sim F).$$

Next, a second round of basic conjunctions is constructed from those statements obtained by letting the operator May govern each of the basic conjunctions resulting from the first round (see above, pp. 87 f., 102 f.).

The method for constructing collectivistic two-agent types is just the same, except that the first round of basic conjunctions is constructed, not from $\mathrm{Do}(p, F)$ and $\mathrm{Do}(p, \sim F)$, but from the four statements

$$\mathrm{Do}(p, F),\ \mathrm{Do}(p, \sim F),\ \mathrm{Do}(q, F),\ \mathrm{Do}(q, \sim F).$$

Apart from this difference, the collectivistic two-agent types are constructed in the same way as one-agent types. The details are as follows: in the first round, $2^4 = 16$ basic conjunctions are obtained, nine of which are contradictory. Eliminating redundant conjuncts of the remaining seven, we obtain

(i) $\mathrm{Do}(p, F)\ \&\ \mathrm{Do}(p, F)$
(ii) $\mathrm{Do}(p, F)\ \&\ \sim\mathrm{Do}(q, F)$
(iii) $\mathrm{Do}(p, \sim F)\ \&\ \mathrm{Do}(q, \sim F)$
(iv) $\mathrm{Do}(p, \sim F)\ \&\ \sim\mathrm{Do}(q, \sim F)$
(v) $\sim\mathrm{Do}(p, F)\ \&\ \mathrm{Do}(q, F)$
(vi) $\sim\mathrm{Do}(p, \sim F)\ \&\ \mathrm{Do}(q, \sim F)$
(vii) $\sim\mathrm{Do}(p, F)\ \&\ \sim\mathrm{Do}(p, \sim F)\ \&\ \sim\mathrm{Do}(q, F)\ \&\ \sim\mathrm{Do}(q, \sim F)$.

In the interests of brevity and economy, the expression

$$\mathrm{Pass}(p, F)$$

("p is passive with respect to F") will be used as an abbreviation for

$$\sim\mathrm{Do}(p, F)\ \&\ \sim\mathrm{Do}(p, \sim F).$$

Statement (vii) can accordingly be more briefly expressed by

(vii′) $\mathrm{Pass}(p, F)\ \&\ \mathrm{Pass}(q, F)$.

The operator May is now introduced, governing each of (i)–(vi) and (vii′), and giving

(1) $\mathrm{May}(\mathrm{Do}(p, F)\ \&\ \mathrm{Do}(q, F))$;
(2) $\mathrm{May}(\mathrm{Do}(p, F)\ \&\ \sim\mathrm{Do}(q, F))$;
(3) $\mathrm{May}(\mathrm{Do}(p, \sim F)\ \&\ \mathrm{Do}(q, \sim F))$;
(4) $\mathrm{May}(\mathrm{Do}(p, \sim F)\ \&\ \sim\mathrm{Do}(q, \sim F))$;
(5) $\mathrm{May}(\sim\mathrm{Do}(p, F)\ \&\ \mathrm{Do}(q, F))$;
(6) $\mathrm{May}(\sim\mathrm{Do}(p, \sim F)\ \&\ \mathrm{Do}(q, \sim F))$;
(7) $\mathrm{May}(\mathrm{Pass}(p, F)\ \&\ \mathrm{Pass}(q, F))$.

Finally, the last round of basic conjunctions is constructed; i.e., all the basic conjunctions which can be obtained from (1)–(7). Of the $2^7=128$ conjunctions so obtained, just one is contradictory, namely the one in which all the conjuncts are negations (i.e., where all alternatives are forbidden). The remaining 127 conjunctions are called *deontic basic conjunctions* of the four statements Do(p, F), Do(p, $\sim F$), Do(q, F) and Do(q, $\sim F$) (cf. above, p. 88). Each of these 127 conjunctions defines a collectivistic two-agent type.

2. *Collectivistic types as represented by their liberty spaces*

The 127 collectivistic types are denoted by S_1, ..., S_{127}. In order to present the definitions of S_1, ..., S_{127} in a minimum of space, I shall avail myself of the notion of *liberty space* introduced in Chapter 3 (above, p. 107).

First, seven sets are defined with the help of statements (1)–(7) of section 1, denoted by a, b, ..., g (*basic types of collectivistic two-agent liberties*, cf. above, p. 106).

a $= \{\langle p, q, F\rangle \mid$ May(Do(p, F) & Do(q, F))$\}$.
b $= \{\langle p, q, F\rangle \mid$ May(Do(p, F) & $\sim$Do(q, F))$\}$.
c $= \{\langle p, q, F\rangle \mid$ May(Do(p, $\sim F$) & Do(q, $\sim F$))$\}$.
d $= \{\langle p, q, F\rangle \mid$ May(Do(p, $\sim F$) & $\sim$Do(q, $\sim F$))$\}$.
e $= \{\langle p, q, F\rangle \mid$ May($\sim$Do(p, F) & Do(q, F))$\}$.
f $= \{\langle p, q, F\rangle \mid$ May($\sim$Do(p, $\sim F$) & Do(q, $\sim F$))$\}$.
g $= \{\langle p, q, F\rangle \mid$ May(Pass(p, F) & Pass(q, F))$\}$.

By analogy with the procedure of Chapter 3 (p. 107), a function $\mathcal{S}$ (for *liberty space*) is defined from the set of collectivistic two-agent types to the set of non-empty subsets of {a, b, ..., g}.

DEFINITION. Let S be a variable for collectivistic two-agent types and L a variable for elements of {a, b, ..., g}.

$$\mathcal{S}(S) =_{\text{def.}} \{L \mid S \subset L\}.$$

It follows from the construction of collectivistic types that both $\mathcal{S}$ and its inverse are one-one functions (cf. p. 108). In other words, each non-empty subset of {a, b, ..., g} corresponds uniquely to a certain collectivistic two-agent type, and vice versa. In view of this, the key to the definitions of S_1, ..., S_{127} is given simply by listing all the non-empty subsets of {a, b, ..., g} and stating for each subset which collectivistic two-agent type corresponds to it. As we shall soon see, the list provides all the information needed to spell out a definition of any type in terms of Shall and Do. With the numbering of the collectivistic types used throughout this book, the list is as follows:

S_{1}. abcdefg
S_{2}. abcdef
S_{3}. abcdeg
S_{4}. abcdfg
S_{5}. abcefg
S_{6}. abdefg
S_{7}. acdefg
S_{8}. bcdefg
S_{9}. abcde
S_{10}. abcdf
S_{11}. abcdg
S_{12}. abcef
S_{13}. abceg
S_{14}. abcfg
S_{15}. abdef
S_{16}. abdeg
S_{17}. abdfg
S_{18}. abefg
S_{19}. acdef
S_{20}. acdeg
S_{21}. acdfg
S_{22}. acefg
S_{23}. adefg
S_{24}. bcdef
S_{25}. bcdeg
S_{26}. bcdfg
S_{27}. bcefg
S_{28}. bdefg
S_{29}. cdefg
S_{30}. abcd
S_{31}. abce
S_{32}. abcf
S_{33}. abcg
S_{34}. abde
S_{35}. abdf
S_{36}. abdg
S_{37}. abef
S_{38}. abeg
S_{39}. abfg
S_{40}. acde
S_{41}. acdf
S_{42}. acdg
S_{43}. acef
S_{44}. aceg
S_{45}. acfg
S_{46}. adef
S_{47}. adeg
S_{48}. adfg
S_{49}. aefg
S_{50}. bcde
S_{51}. bcdf
S_{52}. bcdg
S_{53}. bcef
S_{54}. bceg
S_{55}. bcfg
S_{56}. bdef
S_{57}. bdeg
S_{58}. bdfg
S_{59}. befg
S_{60}. cdef
S_{61}. cdeg
S_{62}. cdfg
S_{63}. cefg
S_{64}. defg
S_{65}. abc
S_{66}. abd
S_{67}. abe
S_{68}. abf
S_{69}. abg
S_{70}. acd
S_{71}. ace
S_{72}. acf
S_{73}. acg
S_{74}. ade
S_{75}. adf
S_{76}. adg
S_{77}. aef
S_{78}. aeg
S_{79}. afg
S_{80}. bcd
S_{81}. bce
S_{82}. bcf
S_{83}. bcg
S_{84}. bde
S_{85}. bdf
S_{86}. bdg
S_{87}. bef
S_{88}. beg
S_{89}. bfg
S_{90}. cde
S_{91}. cdf
S_{92}. cdg
S_{93}. cef
S_{94}. ceg
S_{95}. cfg
S_{96}. def
S_{97}. deg
S_{98}. dfg
S_{99}. efg
S_{100}. ab
S_{101}. ac
S_{102}. ad
S_{103}. ae
S_{104}. af
S_{105}. ag
S_{106}. bc
S_{107}. bd
S_{108}. be
S_{109}. bf
S_{110}. bg
S_{111}. cd
S_{112}. ce
S_{113}. cf
S_{114}. cg
S_{115}. de
S_{116}. df
S_{117}. dg
S_{118}. ef
S_{119}. eg
S_{120}. fg
S_{121}. a
S_{122}. b
S_{123}. c
S_{124}. d
S_{125}. e
S_{126}. f
S_{127}. g

As an example of the use of the list, the collectivistic type S_{67} is assigned the letters "abe", meaning that S_{67} has the liberty space {a, b, e}. This in turn means that

$$S_{67} = a \cap b \cap e \cap \bar{c} \cap \bar{d} \cap \bar{f} \cap \bar{g}.$$

(S_{67} has the *factors* a, b, $\bar{c}$, $\bar{d}$, e, $\bar{f}$, $\bar{g}$; cf. above, p. 107, 143.) This definition can be spelt out so that S_{67} is the set of all $\langle p, q, F\rangle$ such that

(1) May(Do(p, F) & Do(q, F));
(2) May(Do(p, F) & ~Do(q, F));
(3) May(~Do(p, F) & Do(q, F));
(4) ~May(Do(p, ~F) & Do(q, ~F));
(5) ~May(Do(p, ~F) & ~Do(q, ~F));
(6) ~May(~Do(p, ~F) & Do(q, ~F));
(7) ~May(Pass(p, F) & Pass(q, F)).

From the information given in the list placing "abe" by S_{67}, we can conclude that the statement

$$\langle p, q, F\rangle \in S_{67}$$

is equivalent to the conjunction of (1)–(7).

Note that the conjunction of (1)–(7) can be more briefly expressed. The conjunction of (4) and (5) gives

(8) ~May Do(p, ~F);

the conjunction of (4) and (6) gives

(9) ~May Do(q, ~F);

and the conjunction of (7)–(9) gives

(10) Shall(Do(p, F) v Do(q, F)).

Statement (10) is thus a logical consequence of the conjunction of (4)–(7). It is easily seen that, conversely, the conjunction of (4)–(7) is a logical consequence of (10), and (4)–(7) can therefore be more briefly expressed as (10).

3. *Inversion and conversion; symmetrical and neutral types*

The concepts *inverse*, *converse*, *symmetrical* and *neutral* are defined for collectivistic types in completely analogous fashion to the corresponding terms for individualistic types defined in Chapter 4 (p. 130), and the definitions are not spelt out here in detail; they are obtained from those given on pp. 130 f. by substituting everywhere S for R and $\{S_1, ..., S_{127}\}$ for $\{R_1, ..., R_{35}\}$.

From the list of collectivistic two-agent types it can be seen that $\{S_1, ..., S_{127}\}$ can be divided into seven cells such that the types in any of these cells have the same number of elements in their liberty spaces. The division is summarised in the following table:

Cell	*Elements in the cell*	*Number of elements in the corresponding liberty spaces*
C_1	S_1	7
C_2	S_2–S_8	6
C_3	S_9–S_{29}	5
C_4	S_{30}–S_{64}	4
C_5	S_{65}–S_{99}	3
C_6	S_{100}–S_{120}	2
C_7	S_{121}–S_{127}	1

It is apparent that the inverse and the converse of any given type always belongs to the same cell. Accordingly, the inverses and converses, together with the symmetrical and neutral types, can be summarised and presented in seven diagrams, one for each cell, as follows:

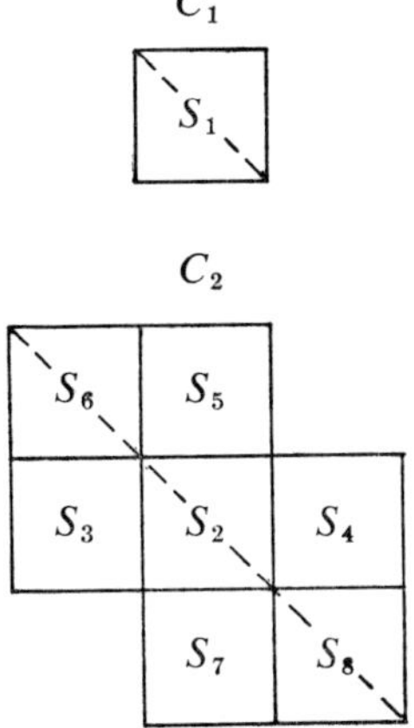

C_3

S_{15}	S_9	S_{18}	S_{23}	
S_{12}	S_{13}	S_{22}	S_{20}	S_{25}
S_{16}	S_{11}	S_{28}	S_{11}	S_{26}
S_{17}	S_{14}	S_{22}	S_{21}	S_{19}
	S_{27}	S_{29}	S_{10}	S_{24}

C_4

S_{48}	S_{46}	S_{49}	S_{47}			
S_{35}	S_{38}	S_{37}	S_{44}	S_{59}		
S_{36}	S_{34}	S_{31}	S_{43}	S_{40}	S_{58}	
S_{39}	S_{33}	S_{30}	S_{56}	S_{30}	S_{42}	S_{61}
	S_{57}	S_{32}	S_{43}	S_{41}	S_{51}	S_{52}
		S_{64}	S_{45}	S_{60}	S_{62}	S_{50}
			$S_{55.}$	S_{63}	S_{53}	S_{54}

C_5

S_{88}	S_{78}	S_{79}	S_{99}			
S_{69}	S_{75}	S_{74}	S_{77}	S_{87}		
S_{76}	S_{68}	S_{67}	S_{71}	S_{97}	S_{85}	
S_{86}	S_{66}	S_{65}	S_{73}	S_{70}	S_{80}	S_{86}
	S_{84}	S_{89}	S_{72}	S_{91}	S_{90}	S_{83}
		S_{96}	S_{93}	S_{82}	S_{81}	S_{92}
			S_{99}	S_{94}	S_{95}	S_{98}

C_6

S_{108}	S_{103}	S_{104}	S_{119}	
S_{100}	S_{105}	S_{118}	S_{115}	S_{117}
S_{102}	S_{107}	S_{101}	S_{107}	S_{106}
S_{110}	S_{109}	S_{118}	S_{114}	S_{111}
	S_{120}	S_{112}	S_{113}	S_{116}

C_7

S_{121}	S_{125}	
S_{122}	S_{127}	S_{124}
	S_{126}	S_{123}

As before, the inverse of a given type is the mirror image about the dotted diagonal, and the converse is reached by rotating through 180 degrees about the central point.

4. *The expressive power of the collectivistic system*

Consider the following statement:

(1) $\text{Shall}(\text{Do}(p, F) \leftrightarrow \text{Do}(q, F))$ & $\text{Shall}(\text{Do}(p, \sim F) \leftrightarrow \text{Do}(q, \sim F))$.

It can be shown that (1) is equivalent to

(1′) $\langle p, q, F\rangle \in (S_{73} \cup S_{101} \cup S_{105} \cup S_{114} \cup S_{121} \cup S_{123} \cup S_{127})$.

Statement (1) can thus be expressed in a standard form in terms of the membership of $\langle p, q, F\rangle$ to the union of certain types from the list $S_1, ..., S_{127}$. The list of collectivistic types can in fact be used for the purpose of giving the standard form of statements of the same general structure as (1) in view of the following result:

THEOREM. *Let A be a non-contradictory Boolean compound of one or more components $A_1, ..., A_n$, which are statements in which* Shall *or* May *governs a Boolean compound of one or more of* $\text{Do}(p, F)$, $\text{Do}(p, \sim F)$, $\text{Do}(q, F)$ *and* $\text{Do}(q, \sim F)$. *Then A is equivalent to a statement of the form* $\langle p, q, F\rangle \in (S \cup ... \cup S')$, *where* $S, ..., S'$ *occur in the list* $S_1, ..., S_{127}$.

An analogous theorem was presented in Chapter 3 for one-agent types. Both theorems are applications of von Wright's general theorem on disjunctive normal form in deontic logic (pp. 89 f.). But the theorem just formulated, comprising as it does statements involving two agents, is, as we shall soon see, of much greater interest than the earlier theorem.

5. *Basic types of two-agent collectivistic dependence*

In order to elucidate the theorem of the preceding section and to illustrate the use of the collectivistic types $S_1, ..., S_{127}$, I shall consider some legal relations characteristic of the collectivistic system which distinguish it from the system discussed in the preceding chapter. These relations I call *basic types of two-agent collectivistic dependence* and are seven in number, denoted by $D_1, ..., D_7$. As a preliminary to the description of their construction, it should first be remembered that the seven liberty spaces a–g were defined (p. 164) by the following conditions:

(C.a) $\text{May}(\text{Do}(p, F) \,\&\, \text{Do}(q, F))$;
(C.b) $\text{May}(\text{Do}(p, F) \,\&\, {\sim}\text{Do}(q, F))$;
(C.c) $\text{May}(\text{Do}(p, {\sim}F) \,\&\, \text{Do}(q, {\sim}F))$;
(C.d) $\text{May}(\text{Do}(p, {\sim}F) \,\&\, {\sim}\text{Do}(q, {\sim}F))$;
(C.e) $\text{May}({\sim}\text{Do}(p, F) \,\&\, \text{Do}(q, F))$;
(C.f) $\text{May}({\sim}\text{Do}(p, {\sim}F) \,\&\, \text{Do}(q, {\sim}F))$;
(C.g) $\text{May}(\text{Pass}(p, F) \,\&\, \text{Pass}(q, F))$.

The conditions (C.b) and (C.d)–(C.f) are equivalent, respectively, to

(C.b′) $\text{May}(\text{Do}(p, F) \,\&\, \text{Pass}(q, F))$;
(C.d′) $\text{May}(\text{Do}(p, {\sim}F) \,\&\, \text{Pass}(q, F))$;
(C.e′) $\text{May}(\text{Pass}(p, F) \,\&\, \text{Do}(q, F))$;
(C.f′) $\text{May}(\text{Pass}(p, F) \,\&\, \text{Do}(q, {\sim}F))$.

The construction of $D_1, \ldots, D_7$ starts from the list of the negations of these seven conditions, taking the equivalent forms just mentioned where appropriate; that is, the list

(NC.a) ${\sim}\text{May}(\text{Do}(p, F) \,\&\, \text{Do}(q, F))$;
(NC.b) ${\sim}\text{May}(\text{Do}(p, F) \,\&\, \text{Pass}(q, F))$;
(NC.c) ${\sim}\text{May}(\text{Do}(p, {\sim}F) \,\&\, \text{Do}(q, {\sim}F))$;
(NC.d) ${\sim}\text{May}(\text{Do}(p, {\sim}F) \,\&\, \text{Pass}(q, F))$;
(NC.e) ${\sim}\text{May}(\text{Pass}(p, F) \,\&\, \text{Do}(q, F))$;
(NC.f) ${\sim}\text{May}(\text{Pass}(p, F) \,\&\, \text{Do}(q, {\sim}F))$;
(NC.g) ${\sim}\text{May}(\text{Pass}(p, F) \,\&\, \text{Pass}(q, F))$.

Now, let

$${\sim}\text{May}(A \,\&\, B)$$

be a schema representing the form of any one of (NC.a)–(NC.g); for each of these seven statements, the statement

(1) $\text{May } A \,\&\, \text{May } B \,\&\, {\sim}\text{May}(A \,\&\, B)$

is constructed. The statements so constructed each define one of the seven sets which are the basic types of two-agent collectivistic dependence; thus

$D_1 = \{\langle p, q, F\rangle \mid \text{May Do}(p, F)\ \&\ \text{May Do}(q, F)\ \&\ {\sim}\text{May}(\text{Do}(p, F)\ \&\ \text{Do}(q, F))\}$;
$D_2 = \{\langle p, q, F\rangle \mid \text{May Do}(p, F)\ \&\ \text{May Pass}(q, F)\ \&\ {\sim}\text{May}(\text{Do}(p, F)\ \&\ \text{Pass}(q, F))\}$;
$D_3 = \{\langle p, q, F\rangle \mid \text{May Do}(p, {\sim}F)\ \&\ \text{May Do}(q, {\sim}F)\ \&\ {\sim}\text{May}(\text{Do}(p, {\sim}F)\ \&\ \text{Do}(q, {\sim}F))\}$;
$D_4 = \{\langle p, q, F\rangle \mid \text{May Do}(p, {\sim}F)\ \&\ \text{May Pass}(q, F)\ \&\ {\sim}\text{May}(\text{Do}(p, {\sim}F)\ \&\ \text{Pass}(q, F))\}$;
$D_5 = \{\langle p, q, F\rangle \mid \text{May Pass}(p, F)\ \&\ \text{May Do}(q, F)\ \&\ {\sim}\text{May}(\text{Pass}(p, F)\ \&\ \text{Do}(q, F))\}$;
$D_6 = \{\langle p, q, F\rangle \mid \text{May Pass}(p, F)\ \&\ \text{May Do}(q, {\sim}F)\ \&\ {\sim}\text{May}(\text{Pass}(p, F)\ \&\ \text{Do}(q, {\sim}F))\}$;
$D_7 = \{\langle p, q, F\rangle \mid \text{May Pass}(p, F)\ \&\ \text{May Pass}(q, F)\ \&\ {\sim}\text{May}(\text{Pass}(p, F)\ \&\ \text{Pass}(q, F))\}$.

The notions of *inverse* and *converse* are again applicable, and these relations together with the symmetrical and neutral types are represented in the following diagram (read in the by now familiar way; see p. 169):

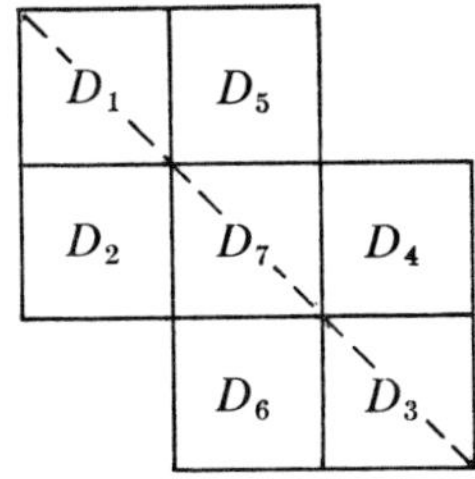

It is apparent from the diagram that each of $D_1, \ldots, D_7$ can be obtained from D_1, D_2 and D_7 by certain substitutions in the defining conditions—by interchanging p and q (inversion), by substituting ${\sim}F$ for F (conversion), or by combining both these operations of inversion and conversion.

A statement of the kind

(2) $\langle p, q, F\rangle \in D$

(where D is one of $D_1, \ldots, D_7$) always means that a certain kind of conduct is permitted for p with respect to F and a certain conduct permitted for q with respect to F, but also that p and q must coordinate their behaviour in a certain way. A statement of this kind provides a *collectivistic* regulation because it cannot be analysed in terms of statements individually regulating p's and q's behaviour (cf. above, p. 159). Moreover, such a statement says that the behaviour of one party is *dependent* on the other's—their behaviour must be coordinated in a certain way. This is why $D_1, ..., D_7$ are called types of *collectivistic dependence.*

It is possible to distinguish, on the basis of $D_1, ..., D_7$, three sorts of dependence between the parties' behaviour. In the cases

$$\langle p, q, F\rangle \in D_1, \langle p, q, F\rangle \in D_3,$$

there is a *prescribed maximum* so far as p's and q's action with respect to F is concerned: it may not be the case that *both* parties act in a certain way; in case D_1, for example,

> Each of p and q may see to it that F, but it must not be the case that both of them do.

In the cases

$$\langle p, q, F\rangle \in D_2, \langle p, q, F\rangle \in D_4, \langle p, q, F\rangle \in D_5, \langle p, q, F\rangle \in D_6,$$

there is a *prescribed congruence* concerning p's and q's action with respect to F: both parties shall act in the same way; in case D_2, for example,

> It may be the case that p sees to it that F, and it may be the case that q is passive, but it must not be the case that p sees to it that F, while q is passive.

In the case

$$\langle p, q, F\rangle \in D_7,$$

finally, there is a *prescribed minimum* concerning p's and q's action with respect to F: at least one of them must do something, and in this case

> Each of p and q may be passive with respect to F, but it must not be the case that both of them are.

The seven liberty types a, b, ..., g and their complements ā, b̄, ..., ḡ were used earlier in defining the collectivistic system's types $S_1, ..., S_{127}$

(p. 165), and these same seven liberty types together with their complements can also be used to define $D_1, \ldots, D_7$, for it is a theorem that

$$D_1 = \bar{\mathrm{a}} \cap \mathrm{b} \cap \mathrm{e};$$
$$D_2 = \mathrm{a} \cap \bar{\mathrm{b}} \cap (\mathrm{d} \cup \mathrm{g});$$
$$D_3 = \bar{\mathrm{c}} \cap \mathrm{d} \cap \mathrm{f};$$
$$D_4 = \mathrm{c} \cap \bar{\mathrm{d}} \cap (\mathrm{b} \cup \mathrm{g});$$
$$D_5 = \mathrm{a} \cap \bar{\mathrm{e}} \cap (\mathrm{f} \cup \mathrm{g});$$
$$D_6 = \mathrm{c} \cap \bar{\mathrm{f}} \cap (\mathrm{e} \cup \mathrm{g});$$
$$D_7 = \bar{\mathrm{g}} \cap (\mathrm{b} \cup \mathrm{d}) \cap (\mathrm{e} \cup \mathrm{f}).$$

These identities are easily proven. Consider, for example, the first. The statement

$$\langle p, q, F \rangle \in D_1$$

means, in terms of Shall and Do,

(3) May Do(p, F) & May Do(q, F) & ~May(Do(p, F) & Do(q, F)).

The statement

$$\langle p, q, F \rangle \in \bar{\mathrm{a}} \cap \mathrm{b} \cap \mathrm{e}$$

is equivalent to the conjunction of the following statements:

(4) ~May(Do(p, F) & Do(q, F));
(5) May(Do(p, F) & ~Do(q, F));
(6) May(~Do(p, F) & Do(q, F)).

But (3) is equivalent to the conjunction of (4)–(6).

6. $D_1, \ldots, D_7$ *as unions of collectivistic two-agent types*

It follows from the theorem of section 4 (p. 169) that each of $D_1, \ldots, D_7$ is identical with the union of certain elements of $\{S_1, \ldots, S_{127}\}$; in particular, the following holds:

D_1 = the union of:
S_8, S_{24}, S_{25}, S_{27}, S_{28}, S_{50}, S_{53}–S_{54}, S_{56}–S_{57}, S_{59}, S_{81}, S_{84}, S_{87}–S_{88}, S_{108}.

D_2 = the union of:
S_7, S_{19}–S_{23}, S_{40}–S_{42}, S_{44}–S_{49}, S_{70}, S_{73}–S_{76}, S_{78}–S_{79}, S_{102}, S_{105}.

D_3 = the union of:
S_6, S_{15}, S_{17}, S_{23}, S_{28}, S_{35}, S_{46}, S_{48}, S_{56}, S_{58}, S_{64}, S_{75}, S_{85}, S_{96}, S_{98}, S_{116}.

D_4 = the union of:
S_5, S_{12}–S_{14}, S_{22}, S_{27}, S_{31}–S_{33}, S_{44}–S_{45}, S_{53}–S_{55}, S_{63}, S_{65}, S_{73}, S_{81}–S_{83}, S_{94}–S_{95}, S_{106}, S_{114}.

D_5 = the union of:
S_4, S_{10}–S_{11}, S_{14}, S_{17}, S_{21}, S_{32}–S_{33}, S_{35}–S_{36}, S_{39}, S_{41}–S_{42}, S_{45}, S_{48}, S_{68}–S_{69}, S_{72}–S_{73}, S_{75}, S_{76}, S_{79}, S_{104}–S_{105}.

D_6 = the union of:
S_8, S_9, S_{11}, S_{13}, S_{20}, S_{25}, S_{31}, S_{33}, S_{40}, S_{42}, S_{44}, S_{50}, S_{52}, S_{54}, S_{61}, S_{71}, S_{73}, S_{81}, S_{83}, S_{90}, S_{92}, S_{94}, S_{112}, S_{114}.

D_7 = the union of:
S_2, S_9–S_{10}, S_{12}, S_{15}, S_{19}, S_{24}, S_{31}–S_{32}, S_{34}–S_{35}, S_{37}, S_{40}–S_{41}, S_{46}, S_{50}–S_{51}, S_{53}, S_{56}, S_{60}, S_{67}–S_{68}, S_{74}–S_{75}, S_{81}–S_{82}, S_{84}–S_{85}, S_{87}, S_{90}–S_{91}, S_{96}, S_{108}–S_{109}, S_{115}–S_{116}.

Ninety-two of the collectivistic types $S_1, ..., S_{127}$ are subsets of one or more of $D_1, ..., D_7$, leaving thirty-five that are not. The supposition (to which I shall return later) that $D_1, ..., D_7$ are empty implies that the collectivistic system reduces to the system of individualistic types $R_1, ..., R_{35}$ discussed in Chapter 4.

7. *Intersections of $D_1, ..., D_7$*

Several of the intersections of $D_1, ..., D_7$ are empty according to the logic of Do and Shall .Take, for example, the types D_1 and D_2; it is easily seen that

(1) $\langle p, q, F \rangle \in D_1 \;\&\; \langle p, q, F \rangle \in D_2$

is a contradiction. For according to the definitions of D_1 and D_2, (1) is equivalent to the conjunction of

(2) May Do(p, F);
(3) May Do(q, F);
(4) May Pass(q, F);
(5) ~May(Do(p, F) & Do(q, F));
(6) ~May(Do(p, F) & Pass(q, F));

and from (5) and (6), it follows that

(7) ~May Do(p, F),

which is just the negation of (2). Similarly, it can be shown that the following hold:

$$D_1 \cap D_2 = \emptyset;$$
$$D_1 \cap D_5 = \emptyset;$$
$$D_3 \cap D_4 = \emptyset;$$
$$D_3 \cap D_6 = \emptyset;$$
$$D_2 \cap D_4 \cap D_7 = \emptyset;$$
$$D_5 \cap D_6 \cap D_7 = \emptyset.$$

If, instead, non-empty intersections are considered, it follows from the theorem in section 4 (p. 169) that each such intersection is identical with the union of one or more of $S_1, ..., S_{127}$; for example,

(8) $D_1 \cap D_4 \cap D_6 \cap D_7 = S_{81}$;
(9) $D_1 \cap D_4 \cap D_6 = S_{54} \cup S_{81}$.

(8) is easy to prove by considering how $D_1, ..., D_7$ are defined in terms of the seven liberty types and their complements (p. 164). We have

$$D_1 = \bar{a} \cap b \cap e;$$
$$D_4 = c \cap \bar{d} \cap (a \cup b \cup e \cup g);$$
$$D_6 = c \cap \bar{f} \cap (a \cup b \cup e \cup g);$$
$$D_7 = \bar{g} \cap (b \cup d) \cap (e \cup f).$$

Accordingly,

$$D_1 \cap D_4 \cap D_6 \cap D_7 = \bar{a} \cap b \cap c \cap \bar{d} \cap e \cap \bar{f} \cap \bar{g}.$$

Now, the definition of S_{81} (p. 165) gives

$$S_{81} = \bar{a} \cap b \cap c \cap \bar{d} \cap e \cap \bar{f} \cap \bar{g},$$

and (8) is thereby proven. Similarly for (9), we obtain in the same way

$$D_1 \cap D_4 \cap D_6 = (\bar{a} \cap b \cap c \cap \bar{d} \cap e \cap \bar{f} \cap g) \cup (\bar{a} \cap b \cap c \cap \bar{d} \cap e \cap \bar{f} \cap \bar{g}),$$

and the definitions of S_{54} and S_{81} give

$$S_{54} \cup S_{81} = (\bar{a} \cap b \cap c \cap \bar{d} \cap e \cap \bar{f} \cap g) \cup (\bar{a} \cap b \cap c \cap \bar{d} \cap e \cap \bar{f} \cap \bar{g}).$$

Statement (9) is therefore valid.

8. *Applications of the system of collectivistic types*

If all of S_1, ..., S_{127} are non-empty, there are for each statement A satisfying the conditions of the theorem in section 4 (p. 169) values of p, q and F such that A is true for p, q and F. In order to show that all of them are non-empty, it is not necessary to illustrate each of the one hundred and twenty-seven types by separate example. In view of the relations of inverse and converse amongst the types it suffices to consider forty-seven types, provided these are suitably chosen (cf. the similar situation in Chapter 4, p. 133). A selection of forty-seven suitable types is easily found with the help of the seven diagrams of the cells C_1, ..., C_7 of collectivistic types (p. 167). However, since even examples of forty-seven types would require a good deal of space, I shall restrict myself to illustrating just a few cases and suggest a general method for constructing examples in so doing.

Let us begin with the type S_1, which is defined by the conjunction of

(i) May(Do(p, F) & Do(q, F));
(ii) May(Do(p, F) & ~Do(q, F));
(iii) May(Do(p, ~F) & Do(q, ~F));
(iv) May(Do(p, ~F) & ~Do(q, ~F));
(v) May(~Do(p, F) & Do(q, F));
(vi) May(~Do(p, ~F) & Do(q, ~F));
(vii) May(Pass(p, F) & Pass(q, F)).

(i)–(vii) can be illustrated by finding a division of the logical possibilities into seven cases c_1, ..., c_7 according to the scheme

Case	*Appropriate behaviour for p and q with respect to F*
c_1	Do(p, F) & Do(q, F).
c_2	Do(p, F) & ~Do(q, F).
⋮	⋮
c_7	Pass(p, F) & Pass(q, F).

For example, let F be that a certain person is reimbursed for an official journey on behalf of a local authority, and p and q are officials of the authority. The following situations can then be imagined:

Case	*Appropriate behaviour for p and q with respect to F*
Application is made, p is on duty, q is on duty	$\text{Do}(p, F)$ & $\text{Do}(q, F)$.
Application is made, p is on duty, q is not on duty.	$\text{Do}(p, F)$ & $\sim\text{Do}(q, F)$.
Application is not made, p is on duty, q is on duty.	$\text{Do}(p, \sim F)$ & $\text{Do}(q, \sim F)$.
Application is not made, p is on duty, q is not on duty.	$\text{Do}(p, \sim F)$ & $\sim\text{Do}(q, \sim F)$.
Application is made, p is not on duty, q is on duty.	$\sim\text{Do}(p, F)$ & $\text{Do}(q, F)$.
Application is not made, p is not on duty, q is on duty.	$\sim\text{Do}(p, \sim F)$ & $\text{Do}(q, \sim F)$.
Application is made or not made, p is not on duty, q is not on duty.	$\text{Pass}(p, F)$ & $\text{Pass}(q, F)$.

Within this sort of context it is easy to construct plausible statements from which (i)–(vii) are formally deducible. First, the following abbreviations are introduced:

A for Application is made;
P for p is on duty;
Q for q is on duty.

Statements (i)–(vii) can then be deduced if we suppose that

May(A & P & Q), Shall(A & P & $Q \leftrightarrow \text{Do}(p, F)$ & $\text{Do}(q, F)$);
May(A & P & $\sim Q$), Shall(A & P & $\sim Q \leftrightarrow \text{Do}(p, F)$ & $\sim\text{Do}(q, F)$);
May($\sim A$ & P & Q), Shall($\sim A$ & P & $Q \leftrightarrow \text{Do}(p, \sim F)$ & $\text{Do}(q, \sim F)$);
May($\sim A$ & P & $\sim Q$), Shall($\sim A$ & P & $\sim Q \leftrightarrow \text{Do}(p, \sim F)$ & $\sim\text{Do}(q, \sim F)$);
May(A & $\sim P$ & Q), Shall(A & $\sim P$ & $Q \leftrightarrow \sim\text{Do}(p, F)$ & $\text{Do}(q, F)$);

$\text{May}({\sim}A \mathbin{\&} {\sim}P \mathbin{\&} Q)$, $\text{Shall}({\sim}A \mathbin{\&} {\sim}P \mathbin{\&} Q \leftrightarrow {\sim}\text{Do}(p, {\sim}F) \mathbin{\&} \text{Do}(q, {\sim}F))$;
$\text{May}({\sim}P \mathbin{\&} {\sim}Q)$, $\text{Shall}({\sim}P \mathbin{\&} {\sim}Q \leftrightarrow \text{Pass}(p, F) \mathbin{\&} \text{Pass}(q, F))$.

Variations on this example serve as illustrations of other types. For example, if we suppose (with the remaining assumptions unchanged)

$${\sim}\text{May}(A \mathbin{\&} {\sim}P) \mathbin{\&} {\sim}\text{May}({\sim}P \mathbin{\&} {\sim}Q),$$

(i. e., one of p or q must always be on duty, but applications are to be made only when p is on duty), then (i)–(iv) and (vi) are obtained as before, but instead of (v) and (vii) their negation

(viii) ${\sim}\text{May}({\sim}\text{Do}(p, F) \mathbin{\&} \text{Do}(q, F)) \mathbin{\&} {\sim}\text{May}(\text{Pass}(p, F) \mathbin{\&} \text{Pass}(q, F))$.

The conjunction of (i)–(iv), (vi) and (viii) is equivalent to

$$\langle p, q, F\rangle \in S_{10}.$$

Another possible variation of the original example is that q is a substitute or proxy for p, and that therefore it holds that

$$\text{Shall}(P \rightarrow \text{Pass}(q, F));$$

that is, that it may not be the case that q is active while p is on duty. Then the following might obtain:

$\text{May}(A \mathbin{\&} P)$, $\text{Shall}(A \mathbin{\&} P \leftrightarrow \text{Do}(p, F) \mathbin{\&} {\sim}\text{Do}(q, F))$;
$\text{May}({\sim}A \mathbin{\&} P)$, $\text{Shall}({\sim}A \mathbin{\&} P \leftrightarrow \text{Do}(p, {\sim}F) \mathbin{\&} {\sim}\text{Do}(q, {\sim}F))$;
$\text{May}(A \mathbin{\&} {\sim}P \mathbin{\&} Q)$, $\text{Shall}(A \mathbin{\&} {\sim}P \mathbin{\&} Q \leftrightarrow {\sim}\text{Do}(p, F) \mathbin{\&} \text{Do}(q, F))$;
$\text{May}({\sim}A \mathbin{\&} {\sim}P \mathbin{\&} Q)$, $\text{Shall}({\sim}A \mathbin{\&} {\sim}P \mathbin{\&} Q \leftrightarrow {\sim}\text{Do}(p, {\sim}F) \mathbin{\&} \text{Do}(q, {\sim}F))$;
$\text{May}({\sim}P \mathbin{\&} {\sim}Q)$, $\text{Shall}({\sim}P \mathbin{\&} {\sim}Q \leftrightarrow \text{Pass}(p, F) \mathbin{\&} \text{Pass}(q, F))$;

from which it can be deduced that

(i′) ${\sim}\text{May}(\text{Do}(p, F) \mathbin{\&} \text{Do}(q, F))$;
(ii′) $\text{May}(\text{Do}(p, F) \mathbin{\&} {\sim}\text{Do}(q, F))$;

(iii′) $\sim$May(Do(p, $\sim F$) & Do(q, $\sim F$));
(iv′) May(Do(p, $\sim F$) & $\sim$Do(q, $\sim F$));
(v′) May($\sim$Do(p, F) & Do(q, F));
(vi′) May($\sim$Do(p, $\sim F$) & Do(q, $\sim F$));
(vii′) May(Pass(p, F) & Pass(q, F)).

The conjunction of (i′)–(vii′) is equivalent to

$$\langle p, q, F\rangle \in S_{28}.$$

Again with this last variation the further variation that

$$\sim\text{May}(\sim P \,\&\, \sim Q)$$

can be introduced, from which the negation of (vii′) follows. The conjunction of (i′)–(vi′) and the negation of (vii′) is equivalent to

$$\langle p, q, F\rangle \in S_{56}.$$

This procedure for constructing examples can be generally characterised in the following way: Suppose S is the type to be illustrated. The statement

$$\langle p, q, F\rangle \in S$$

says that one or more alternative courses of action are permitted for p and q with respect to F. (The number of alternative courses of action is the number of elements in S's liberty space and can therefore vary between 1 and 7.) Each of the permitted courses of action is supposed to be appropriate if and only if a certain permitted case occurs. Those cases that are permitted (and assigned alternative courses of action) are so construed that they are logically mutually incompatible, and moreover, either exhaust the set of logical possibilities (cf. the examples of S_1 and S_{28}) or together with the prohibited cases exhaust the set of logical possibilities (cf. the examples of S_{10} and S_{56}).

9. *Collectivistic types, individualistic types, and atomic types of right*

As already indicated (p. 160), the system of collectivistic types $S_1, \ldots, S_{127}$ is stronger than the system $R_1, \ldots, R_{35}$ of individualistic types, which is in turn stronger than Kanger's system of atomic types of right $K_1, \ldots, K_{26}$. Each of $R_1, \ldots, R_{35}$ is identical with the union of one or more of $S_1, \ldots,$

S_{127}, and each of K_1, ..., K_{26} is identical with the union of one or more of R_1, ..., R_{35}. The relation between the three systems is presented in the following summary:

K_1 = the union of:	R_1 = the union of:	S_1–S_{15}, S_{17}, S_{19}–S_{25}, S_{27}–S_{28}, S_{31}–S_{33}, S_{35}, S_{40}–S_{42}, S_{44}–S_{46}, S_{48}, S_{50}, S_{53}–S_{54}, S_{56}, S_{73}, S_{75}, S_{81}.
	R_3 =	S_{101}.
	R_9 = the union of:	S_{43}, S_{71}, S_{72}.
	R_{17} = the union of:	S_{30}, S_{65}, S_{70}.
K_2 =	R_6 =	S_{127}.
K_3 =	R_5 =	S_{121}.
K_4 =	R_2 = the union of:	S_{38}, S_{67}, S_{69}, S_{78}, S_{88}, S_{105}, S_{108}.
K_5 = the union of:	R_{11} =	S_{86}.
	R_{20} =	S_{107}.
K_6 =	R_{15} =	S_{103}.
K_7 =	R_{32} =	S_{125}.
K_8 =	R_{16} =	S_{110}.
K_9 = the union of:	R_8 = the union of:	S_{16}, S_{34}, S_{36}, S_{47}, S_{57}, S_{74}, S_{76}, S_{84}.
	R_{18} = the union of:	S_{66}, S_{102}.
K_{10} =	R_{14} = the union of:	S_{89}, S_{109}.
K_{11} =	R_7 =	S_{123}.
K_{12} =	R_4 = the union of:	S_{62}, S_{91}–S_{92}, S_{95}, S_{98}, S_{114}, S_{116}.
K_{13} =	R_{25} =	S_{113}.
K_{14} =	R_{33} =	S_{126}.
K_{15} =	R_{24} =	S_{117}.
K_{16} = the union of:	R_{10} = the union of:	S_{26}, S_{51}, S_{52}, S_{55}, S_{58}, S_{82}, S_{83}, S_{85}.
	R_{19} = the union of:	S_{80}, S_{106}.
K_{17} =	R_{22} = the union of:	S_{97}, S_{115}.
K_{18} = the union of:	R_{28} =	S_{99}.
	R_{30} =	S_{118}.
K_{19} =	R_{26} =	S_{100}.
K_{20} =	R_{27} =	S_{122}.
K_{21} =	R_{29} =	S_{119}.
K_{22} = the union of:	R_{12} = the union of:	S_{18}, S_{37}, S_{39}, S_{49}, S_{59}, S_{68}, S_{79}, S_{87}.
	R_{13} = the union of:	S_{77}, S_{104}.
K_{23} =	R_{34} =	S_{111}.
K_{24} =	R_{35} =	S_{124}.
K_{25} =	R_{31} =	S_{120}.
K_{26} = the union of:	R_{21} = the union of:	S_{29}, S_{60}–S_{61}, S_{63}–S_{64}, S_{90}, S_{94}, S_{96}.
	R_{23} = the union of:	S_{93}, S_{112}.

It is apparent from this summary that the collectivistic system contains twenty types which are not genuinely collectivistic (cf. p. 162 above). Consider, for example, the type S_{100} for which

$$S_{100} = R_{26} = K_{19}$$

holds. The statement

$$\langle p, q, F \rangle \in S_{100}$$

says the following

(i) May(Do(p, F) & Do(q, F));
(ii) May(Do(p, F) & ~Do(q, F));
(iii) ~May(Do(p, ~F) & Do(q, ~F));
(iv) ~May(Do(p, ~F) & ~Do(q, ~F));
(v) ~May(~Do(p, F) & Do(q, F));
(vi) ~May(~Do(p, ~F) & Do(q, ~F));
(vii) ~May(Pass(p, F) & Pass(q, F)).

The conjunction of (iii)–(vii) is equivalent to

(viii) Shall[(Do(p, F) & Do(q, F)) v (Do(p, F) & ~Do(q, F))],

which is in turn equivalent to

(ix) Shall Do(p, F).

The conjunction of (i), (ii) and (ix) is equivalent to

(x) Shall Do(p, F) & May Do(q, F) & May Pass(q, F),

that is, to the conditions defining R_{26} and K_{19}.

It is also apparent from the summary that, particularly, statements of membership of R_1 and K_1 can be made more precise in many ways within the collectivistic system. R_1 is, in fact, identical with the union of forty-three collectivistic types and K_1 with the union of fifty.

10. *The problem of reduction of the set of collectivistic types*

A comparison between on the one hand $\{S_1, ..., S_{127}\}$ and on the other $\{R_1, ..., R_{35}\}$ and $\{K_1, ..., K_{26}\}$ leads naturally to the question of which conditions or principles would be needed to effect a reduction of the number of elements in $\{S_1, ..., S_{127}\}$ so that the collectivistic system reduces either to the individualistic or to Kanger's system.

If all the seven types of collectivistic dependence $D_1, ..., D_7$ were empty, the set $\{S_1, ..., S_{127}\}$ would, as already mentioned, be reduced so that only thirty-five non-empty types remain, each being identical with a distinct one of the individualistic types (p. 174). This supposition amounts to the same as accepting the following three statements as general principles (where $\sim F$ can be substituted for F and p and q interchanged):

P1. May Do(p, F) & May Do(q, F) → May(Do(p, F) & Do(q, F)),

P2. May Do(p, F) & May Pass(q, F) → May(Do(p, F) & Pass(q, F)),

P3. May Pass(p, F) & May Pass(q, F) → May(Pass(p, F) & Pass(q, F)).

P1 holds if and only if D_1 and D_3 are empty; P2 if and only if D_2, D_4, D_5 and D_6 are empty; and P3 if and only if D_7 is empty. Acceptance of P1–P3 implies the identities

$$\begin{array}{lllll}
R_1 = S_1, & R_8 = S_{16}, & R_{15} = S_{103}, & R_{22} = S_{97}, & R_{29} = S_{119}, \\
R_2 = S_{38}, & R_9 = S_{43}, & R_{16} = S_{110}, & R_{23} = S_{93}, & R_{30} = S_{118}, \\
R_3 = S_{101}, & R_{10} = S_{26}, & R_{17} = S_{30}, & R_{24} = S_{117}, & R_{31} = S_{120}, \\
R_4 = S_{62}, & R_{11} = S_{86}, & R_{18} = S_{66}, & R_{25} = S_{113}, & R_{32} = S_{125}, \\
R_5 = S_{121}, & R_{12} = S_{18}, & R_{19} = S_{80}, & R_{26} = S_{100}, & R_{33} = S_{126}, \\
R_6 = S_{127}, & R_{13} = S_{77}, & R_{20} = S_{107}, & R_{27} = S_{122}, & R_{34} = S_{111}, \\
R_7 = S_{123}, & R_{14} = S_{89}, & R_{21} = S_{29}, & R_{28} = S_{99}, & R_{35} = S_{124},
\end{array}$$

and the remaining collectivistic types are empty.

In Chapter 3 (p. 96) we encountered a statement which encompassed a view that was there called the philosophy of indolence, namely

P4. May Do(p, F) & May Do(p, $\sim F$) → May Pass(p, F).

If P4 is accepted in addition to P1–P3, then $\{S_1, ..., S_{127}\}$ reduces to just twenty-six non-empty types, each being identical with one of Kanger's twenty-six atomic types of right (p. 141).

Besides P1–P4 other principles of similar structure can be constructed; in particular

P5. May $\sim$Do(p, F) & May $\sim$Do(p, $\sim F$) & May $\sim$Do(q, F) & May $\sim$Do(q, $\sim F$) → May(Pass(p, F) & Pass(q, F));

P6. May $\sim$Do(p, F) & May $\sim$Do(q, F) → May($\sim$Do(p, F) & $\sim$Do(q, F));

P7. May($\sim$Do(p, F) & $\sim$Do(q, F)) & May($\sim$Do(p, $\sim F$) & $\sim$Do(q, $\sim F$)) → May(Pass(p, F) & Pass(q, F)).

However, these principles are not logically independent of P1–P4 as can be shown by the implications and equivalences in the following schemata:

Most of these theorems are easily seen, and I shall only outline the proof of one that is, perhaps, not so obvious, namely that P6 is a logical consequence of P3. Thus, it has to be shown that

(1) $[\text{May Pass}(p, F) \;\&\; \text{May Pass}(q, F) \rightarrow \text{May}(\text{Pass}(p, F) \;\&\; \text{Pass}(q, F))] \rightarrow [\text{May} \sim \text{Do}(p, F) \;\&\; \text{May} \sim \text{Do}(q, F) \rightarrow \text{May}(\sim \text{Do}(p, F) \;\&\; \sim \text{Do}(q, F))]$.

Two lemmas are proved first.

LEMMA 1. *The statement*

(2) $\text{May}(\sim \text{Do}(p, F) \;\&\; \sim \text{Do}(q, F))$

follows from the conjunction of the two statements

(3) $\text{May Pass}(p, F) \;\&\; \text{May Pass}(q, F) \rightarrow \text{May}(\text{Pass}(p, F) \;\&\; \text{Pass}(q, F))$;

(4) $\text{May}(\sim \text{Do}(p, F) \;\&\; \sim \text{Do}(q, F)) \vee [\text{May}(\text{Do}(p, F) \;\&\; \sim \text{Do}(q, F)) \;\&\; \text{May}(\sim \text{Do}(p, F) \;\&\; \text{Do}(q, F))]$.

LEMMA 2. *The statement*

(5) $\text{May} \sim \text{Do}(p, F) \;\&\; \text{May} \sim \text{Do}(q, F)$

is equivalent to (4).

From lemmas 1 and 2 it is clear that (2) follows from (3) in conjunction with (5), and hence (1) is proved given the proofs of the two lemmas, which are as follows:

Proof of Lemma 1

(i) May(Do(p, F) & ~ Do(q, F)) → May Pass(q, F).
(ii) May(~ Do(p, F) & Do(q, F)) → May Pass(p, F).
(iii) May(Pass(p, F) & Pass(q, F)) → May(~ Do(p, F) & ~ Do(q, F)).
(iv) [[May Pass(p, F) & May Pass(q, F) → May(Pass(p, F) & Pass(q, F))] & [May(Do(p, F) & ~ Do(q, F)) & May(~ Do(p, F) & Do(q, F))]] → May(~ Do(p, F) & ~ Do(q, F)).
(v) [[May Pass(p, F) & May Pass(q, F) → May(Pass(p, F) & Pass(q, F))] & [May(~ Do(p, F) & ~ Do(q, F)) v [May(Do(p, F) & ~ Do(q, F)) & May(~ Do(p, F) & Do(q, F))]]] → May(~ Do(p, F) & ~ Do(q, F)).

Statement (v) says the same as Lemma 1.

Proof of Lemma 2

(i) ~ Do(p, F) ↔ (~ Do(p, F) & Do(q, F)) v (~ Do(p, F) & ~ Do(q, F)).
(ii) ~ Do(q, F) ↔ (Do(p, F) & ~ Do(q, F)) v (~ Do(p, F) & ~ Do(q, F)).
(iii) May ~ Do(p, F) & May ~ Do(q, F) ↔ May[(~ Do(p, F) & Do(q, F)) v (~ Do(p, F) & ~ Do(q, F))] & May[(Do(p, F) & ~ Do(q, F)) v (~ Do(p, F) & ~ Do(q, F))].
(iv) May ~ Do(p, F) & May ~ Do(q, F) ↔ [May(~ Do(p, F) & Do(q, F)) v May(~ Do(p, F) & ~ Do(q, F))] & [May(Do(p, F) & ~ Do(q, F)) v May(~ Do(p, F) & ~ Do(q, F))].
(v) May ~ Do(p, F) & May ~ Do(q, F) ↔ May(~ Do(p, F) & ~ Do(q, F)) v [May(Do(p, F) & ~ Do(q, F)) & May(~ Do(p, F) & Do(q, F))].

Statement (v) says the same as Lemma 2.

It is not difficult, however, to find counter-examples for each of P1–P7. In fact, among the various examples already given in the present chapter and in Chapter 3 there are to be found counter-instances for all these principles. Concerning P1–P3, the illustrations of the types S_{10}, S_{28} and S_{56} (pp. 178 f.) suffice. There we had

$$S_{10} \subseteq D_5 \cap D_7,\ S_{28} \subseteq D_1 \cap D_3,\ S_{56} \subseteq D_1 \cap D_3 \cap D_7,$$

and so the examples of S_{10}, S_{28}, and S_{56} are accordingly counter-examples to all of P1–P3. Concerning P4, a counter-instance for "the philosophy of indolence" has already been given in Chapter 3 (p. 97). And from the implication diagram above (p. 183), a counter-example to P4 also serves as a counter-example to P5 and P7. Finally, the example used to illustrate S_{67} (p. 160) can be used concerning P6; that there are situations exemplifying S_{67} shows that P6 is not a general principle.

That P1–P7 are not acceptable as general principles does not preclude the possibility, however, of there being interesting classes of triples $\langle p, q, F\rangle$ for which one or more of the principles hold true. But I shall not go into this here.

III. *The Ordering of Collectivistic Two-Agent Types*

1. *The ordering by the relation "less free than"*

The notions pertaining to the ordering of the collectivistic types by the relation *less free than* can be dealt with briefly. Using the notion of liberty space a relation $\mathcal{R}$ can be defined on $\{S_1, ..., S_{127}\}$ standing for *less free than:*

DEFINITION. Let S, S' be variables for elements in $\{S_1, ..., S_{127}\}$.

$$S\mathcal{R}S' =_{\text{def.}} \mathcal{S}(S) \subset \mathcal{S}(S').$$

$\mathcal{R}$ is a strict partial ordering on $\{S_1, ..., S_{127}\}$, which can be graphically represented by a Hasse diagram. Representing each collectivistic type by the sequence of letters indicating its liberty space (p. 165), the following three diagrams show how some of the elements in $\{S_1, ..., S_{127}\}$ are ordered by the relation $\mathcal{R}$:

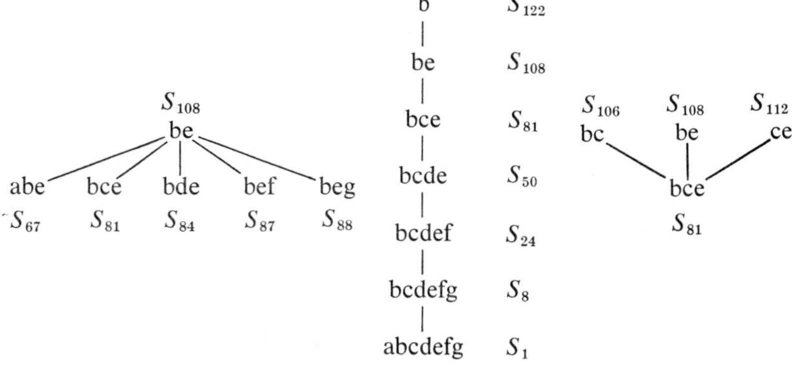

The left-hand diagram shows that S_{108} is less free than each of S_{67}, S_{81}, S_{84}, S_{87}, and S_{88}, while the right-hand diagram shows that each of S_{106}, S_{108} and S_{112} is less free than S_{81}. The centre diagram, finally, shows that of the types shown, those higher on the page are less free than those lower down; so that, for example, S_{122} is less free than S_{108}, which is in turn less free than S_{81}, and so on.

It is of interest to consider in some detail what the movement of a triple $\langle p, q, F\rangle$ from a *more* to a *less free* collectivistic type means for the two parties p and q. If S, S' are two collectivistic types such that $S\mathcal{R}S'$, a movement of $\langle p, q, F\rangle$ from S' to S always involves one, and perhaps both, of the following changes:

1. After the transfer, $\langle p, q, F\rangle$ belongs to a less free individualistic two-agent type;
2. Among the seven types $D_1, \ldots, D_7$ there is one to which $\langle p, q, F\rangle$ belongs after the transfer which it did not belong to before.

The import of these two changes can in turn be explained in the following way. A change of the first kind entails one of the following alternatives (see above, Chapter 4, p. 149).

1a. Each of p and q belongs to a less free one-agent type than before;
1b. p belongs to a less free one-agent type than before, but q remains in the same one-agent type.
1c. p remains in the same one-agent type, while q belongs to one less free than before.

Accordingly, the first change entails that at least one of the parties becomes *individually* less free than before. A change of the second kind, on the other hand, entails an increase in the degree of *collectivistic dependence:* a type of collectivistic dependence obtains between the parties which did not do so before.

It is easy to understand why a change of one of these kinds always occurs when a triple $\langle p, q, F\rangle$ is moved from a more to a less free collectivistic type. Suppose

$$(A \,\&\, B)$$

is a schema representing the form of one of the following seven alternative courses of action

$$\begin{aligned}
&\mathrm{Do}(p, F) \mathbin{\&} \mathrm{Do}(q, F);\\
&\mathrm{Do}(p, F) \mathbin{\&} {\sim}\mathrm{Do}(q, F);\\
&\mathrm{Do}(p, {\sim}F) \mathbin{\&} \mathrm{Do}(q, {\sim}F);\\
&\mathrm{Do}(p, {\sim}F) \mathbin{\&} {\sim}\mathrm{Do}(q, {\sim}F);\\
&{\sim}\mathrm{Do}(p, F) \mathbin{\&} \mathrm{Do}(q, F);\\
&{\sim}\mathrm{Do}(p, {\sim}F) \mathbin{\&} \mathrm{Do}(q, {\sim}F);\\
&\mathrm{Pass}(p, F) \mathbin{\&} \mathrm{Pass}(q, F).
\end{aligned}$$

If $S\mathcal{R}S'$, then a movement of $\langle p, q, F\rangle$ from S' to S always entails that at least one statement of the kind

$$\mathrm{May}(A \mathbin{\&} B)$$

is replaced by its negation

$${\sim}\mathrm{May}(A \mathbin{\&} B).$$

Suppose such a replacement of the statement of permission by its negation occurs. Before the replacement, the statement

$$\mathrm{May}\, A \mathbin{\&} \mathrm{May}\, B$$

is true, which means that a certain kind of behaviour is permitted for p individually and a certain behaviour is permitted for q individually. There are, on the other hand, four alternative possibilities for p and q individually after the change, namely

(i) ${\sim}\mathrm{May}\, A \mathbin{\&} {\sim}\mathrm{May}\, B;$
(ii) ${\sim}\mathrm{May}\, A \mathbin{\&} \mathrm{May}\, B;$
(iii) $\mathrm{May}\, A \mathbin{\&} {\sim}\mathrm{May}\, B;$
(iv) $\mathrm{May}\, A \mathbin{\&} \mathrm{May}\, B.$

The first of these means that each party is individually less free than before (i.e., case 1a obtains). Alternatives (ii) and (iii) mean that exactly one of the parties is individually less free than before (i.e., case 1b or 1c occurs). Finally, alternative (iv) means that, individually, the two parties are as free as before (so far as A and B are concerned), but a new kind of collectivistic dependence obtains between them. Before the change,

$$\text{May } A \ \& \text{ May } B \ \& \text{ May}(A \ \& \ B)$$

was true (where the first two conjuncts are redundant, following from the third); but afterwards, according to alternative (iv),

$$\text{May } A \ \& \text{ May } B \ \& \sim\text{May}(A \ \& \ B)$$

holds—precisely that sort of statement which indicates collectivistic dependence (see the definitions of $D_1, \ldots, D_7$ above, p. 171).

All this can be nicely illustrated by a few examples. Consider the following diagram:

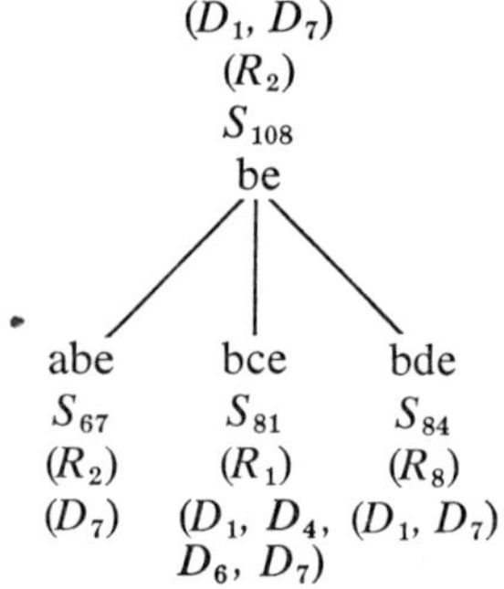

Membership of individualistic two-agent types and types of collectivistic dependence is shown in the diagram in brackets. For example, if $\langle p, q, F\rangle$ belongs to S_{108}, it also belongs to the individualistic two-agent type R_2 and to the types D_1 and D_7 of collectivistic dependence (and only to these).

It is apparent from the diagram that the movement of a triple $\langle p, q, F\rangle$ from S_{67} to S_{108} involves no change of individualistic type, but does involve an increased collectivistic dependence. On the other hand, a movement from S_{81} to S_{108}, or from S_{84} to S_{108}, involves a movement to a less free individualistic type (since $R_2 \mathcal{R} R_1$ and $R_2 \mathcal{R} R_8$) but no increase in collectivistic dependence.

2. *Deontic paths, deontic distance and intermediateness*

The concept *deontic path*, together with its variants, can be applied analogously in the theory of collectivistic two-agent types. The following diagrams illustrate some deontic paths in the set $\{S_1, ..., S_{127}\}$:

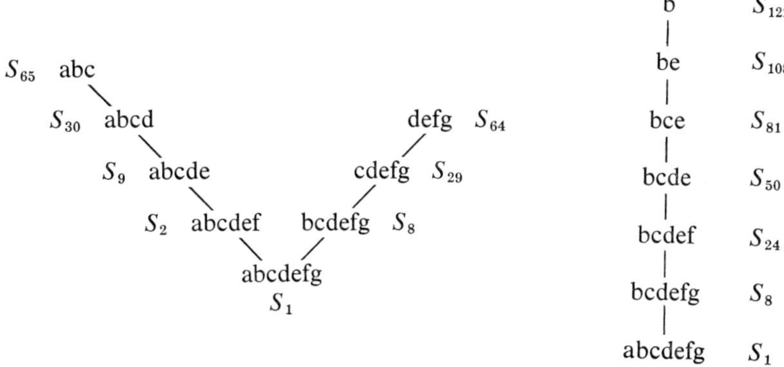

The left-hand diagram shows a path between S_{65} and S_{64} which is *non-straight*, whilst the right-hand diagram shows a *straight* path between S_1 and S_{122}. Both paths are *minimal* in $\{S_1, ..., S_{127}\}$. (In the theory of collectivistic types, if a path $\langle S, ..., S' \rangle$ is straight, it is also minimal in $\{S_1, ..., S_{127}\}$; it is otherwise in the case of individualistic types, cf. p. 147.)

The notions of *deontic distance* and *intermediate* also have analogous application. If S and S' are two collectivistic types, then the deontic distance between them equals the numerical difference between them; i.e., the number of factors of S which are not factors of S'. Since each collectivistic type has seven factors (p. 166), the distance can vary between 1 and 7.

It is superfluous to formalise here the definitions of "deontic path", and its variants, "deontic distance" and "intermediate", for collectivistic types, as they are easily obtained by appropriate substitutions in the definitions given in Chapter 3 (pp. 115 ff.).

PART II

Change of Position and Ranges of Legal Action

CHAPTER 6

Traditions of Legal Power and a New Departure

I. Introduction

Towards the end of Chapter 1 (p. 65), I mentioned an important problem area which concerns how the legal situation involving one or more people can change from one time to another—for example, by promise, contract, decision of an authority, and so forth. What is involved here is the movement of a pair $\langle p, F\rangle$ or a triple $\langle p, q, F\rangle$ from one type to another, and it is movements of this kind which constitute the subject of the remaining part of the book.

Just as the theory of legal positions presented in Chapters 3–5 was set in historical perspective, the "dynamics" of the theory of legal positions should also be seen against the historical background of the tradition within jurisprudence and legal philosophy. In this connection, the work of Hohfeld is perhaps best known. He introduced a conceptual framework for discussing what he called "changes in legal relations"; I refer here to the last four of his eight basic concepts, namely *power*, *liability*, *disability* and *immunity* (see above, p. 25). But Bentham had something to say on the subject, and more recently, von Wright, Hart and Alf Ross have added to the discussion. Hohfeld's account of the four concepts just mentioned was intended as a contribution to the theory of *legal relations*, for he takes as his starting point the question of which relations can obtain between two parties. Bentham, von Wright and Hart, on the other hand, see their work as a contribution to the theory of *legal validity* and *norm-creating action* within the general theory of norms and normative systems (see Bentham, 1970*b*, pp. 21 ff.; von Wright, 1963, pp. 189 ff.; Hart, 1961, pp. 26 ff.; Ross, 1968, pp. 130 ff. See also Kelsen, 1945, pp. 123 ff.). However, they all emphasise the concept of *legal power* or *competence*. A brief summary of these earlier theories is presented in this chapter, though it is mainly concerned with the theories of legal power as presented by Bentham and Hohfeld. In the final section the concept *range of action* is introduced which is central to the theory developed in the following chapters.

II. Some Traditional Theories of Legal Power or Competence

1. *Three concepts of legal power or competence*

Within the Anglo-Saxon tradition (Bentham, Hohfeld, Hart and others), the term *power* is central to the discussion of "legal change". It occurs, for example, in statements such as the following:

(i) John has the power to bring about that John has an obligation to Peter to pay him £50.

(ii) The municipal court of Loughborough has the power to bring about that John has an obligation to the state to pay £50 to the state in fines for speeding.

Scandinavian authors such as von Wright and Ross prefer the term *competence* rather than *power*, and statements such as the following are obtained:

(i′) John has the competence to bring about that John has an obligation to Peter to pay him £50.

(ii′) The municipal court of Loughborough has the competence to bring about that John has an obligation to the state to pay £50 to the state in fines for speeding.

The use of the terms *power* and *competence* in statements such as these will be considered in what follows. In general, I shall be considering statements of the kind

(1) *p* has the *power* to bring about that *F*,

(1′) *p* has the *competence* to bring about that *F*,

where *F* stands for a deontic statement (i.e., a statement formulated in terms of Shall or May, or in terms of Obligation, Privilege or other so-called legal relations). Within these terms of reference three different variants of *power* or *competence* can be distinguished. The first can be explained in terms of May or *permission;* the second in terms of Can, interpreted as an expression of *practical possibility* (this is indicated by writing "can^{P}"); and finally the third variant is what in German is called "rechtliches Können", which is held to be an expression of *possibility* in a special technical *legal* sense (written as "can^{J}"). Accordingly, there are at least three different interpretations of statements (1) and (1′) above, which are distinguished here by writing:

(1a) *p* may bring about that *F*;
(1b) *p* can^{P} bring about that *F*;
(1c) *p* can^{J} bring about that *F*.

Let us look at (1a) and (1b) first. (1b) is constructed using the concept May which is defined in this book in terms of Shall and which, according to what I have maintained earlier, acquires an intelligible, if somewhat vague, sense according to this definition (cf. p. 77). Similarly, the concept Can^{P} in (1b) can be defined along the same lines in terms of the concept Unavoidable ($\text{Can}^{\text{P}} F =_{\text{def.}} \sim \text{Unavoidable} \sim F$) and has a correspondingly intelligible meaning (cf. Kanger, 1972, pp. 107 ff.). From the everyday meaning of May and Can^{P} it is fairly clear that (1a) and (1b) can have different truth values, for, so far as concerns bringing about a certain legal change, someone can have power or competence in one sense but not in the other. Cases where (1a) is true whilst (1b) is false are, however, not of much practical interest. If a person cannot bring about a certain legal change (for example, if he finds himself on a desert island or is physically paralysed) it is not so important that he *may* bring it about; the change will still not occur as a result of his action. Of more interest are cases where (1b) is true but (1a) false. It can be the case that someone has the practical possibility to bring about a certain legal change although he may not do so. Suppose, for example, that *p* is a private person and *q* a policeman on duty. It is then easily imagined that the following is the case:

(2) It is not the case that *p* may bring about that *q* may knock *p* down.
(3) *p* can^{P} bring about that *q* may knock *p* down.

(For example, by violent assault on *q*.) In this case *p* has the power or competence according to (1b) but lacks the power (competence) according to (1a).

The analysis of statement (1c), where "can^{J}" stands for the so-called *rechtliches Können*, is dependent on the rather unclear concept of *act-in-the-law* (*Rechtsgeschäft*, *acte juridique*). I shall content myself here simply by quoting some representative passages which hint at the sort of ideas lying behind these concepts. The lack of clarity will at the same time become apparent from the quotations.

The concept *act-in-the-law* is a classic bone of contention in European jurisprudence. However, a representative sample of examples is provided by the following passage from Ross:

> ... *actes juridiques*, or acts-in-the-law, or, in private law, dispositive declarations. Examples are: a promise, a will, a judgment, an administrative license, a statute. (Ross, 1968, p. 130)

Other sorts of examples also occur in the literature:

> ... acts-in-the-law ... encompass, for example, payment of a debt, delivery of a thing or of a quantity of goods in fulfilment of a purchase contract, return of property borrowed, hired or deposited, and, in general, all acts which are performed in fulfilment of an obligation incumbent on the person who is acting. (Swedish Contracts Act Committee, 1914, p. 117; my translation.)

A general characteristic is given in the following statement of a well-known German jurist:

> ... acts-in-the-law, i.e., in the widest sense of the word ... such acts which are imposed or adopted by the law for achieving its invisible legal effects. (Brinz, 1873, p. 211; my translation.)

The concept *rechtliches Können* is dependent on the concept *act-in-the-law* as is apparent from the following definition:

> Beside the *simple legal permission* [das einfache rechtliche Dürfen], the content of which is, in essence, purely negative, [i.e.,] not being legally forbidden ... stands, according to the prevailing opinion, the so-called *legal ability* [das rechtliche Können], i.e., the ability, following from some provision of positive law, to produce certain legal effects by "acts-in-the-law". (Bierling, 1883, p. 50; my translation.)

Ross' definition of competence is also essentially of the same kind:

> Competence is the legally established ability to create legal norms (or legal effects) through and in accordance with enunciations to this effect ... Those enunciations in which competence is exercised are called *actes juridiques*, or acts-in-the-law, or, in private law, dispositive declarations. (Ross, 1968, p. 130)

It has been suggested in the Scandinavian literature that *rechtliches Können* (or "competence") should be analysed in terms of a non-truth-functional conditional (Sundby 1974, p. 414; cf. Moritz, 1960, p. 90). As a first attempt we might try a formulation along the lines

If ... *p* ..., then *p* brings about that *F*

(where *F* stands for a deontic state of affairs). But there remains the problem of finding an acceptable statement which can be substituted for the schema ... *p* ... in the antecedent. Statements such as "*p* performs an act imposed or adopted by the law for achieving that *F*" (cf. Brinz) or "*p* enunciates that *F*" (cf. Ross) are clearly unacceptable in what purports to be an analysis.

Since *rechtliches Können* in (1c) is an unclear concept, difficult to analyse, there is good reason to ask whether (1c) is really necessary for giving important information over and above what can be said in terms of (1a) and (1b) by one of the following statements:

(i) *p* can^P bring about that *F* and *p* may bring about that *F*.
(ii) *p* can^P bring about that *F* but it is not the case that *p* may bring about that *F*.
(iii) It is not the case that *p* can^P bring about that *F*, but *p* may bring about that *F*.
(iv) It is not the case that *p* can^P bring about that *F* and it is not the case that *p* may bring about that *F*.

Inspection of (i)–(iv) shows that in no case is further important information given by adding one or the other of the sentences

(1c) *p* can^J bring about that *F*,
(1c′) It is not the case that *p* can^J bring about that *F*.

If it is assumed that

(1b) *p* can^P bring about that *F*

then the essential distinction appears to be between the cases

(1a) *p* may bring about that *F*,
(1a′) It is not the case that *p* may bring about that *F*.

On the other hand, if it is assumed that

(1b′) It is not the case that *p* can^P bring about that *F*, it is immaterial which of (1c) or (1c′) is true: As a result of *p*'s action, *F* does not obtain in either case.

Finally, there is nothing to prevent one using the expression "rechtliches Können" to refer to case (1b) rather than (1c). Case (1b) is described in terms of Can^{P} and thus represents a *Können;* and it represents a *rechtliches Können* since *F* is deontic.

The distinction between (1a), (1b) and (1c) as interpretations of the concept of *power* or *competence* was introduced here mainly to facilitate understanding of the definitions which occur in the literature on jurisprudence. All three variants will be illustrated in the next section.

2. *Bentham on legal power*

Bentham's theory of power and "legal change" (cf. with the following Hart's detailed essay, 1972, pp. 799 ff.) begins with the notions of power of *imperation* and power of *de-imperation.* These concepts can be explained by the following pairs of synonyms, where *F* represents an arbitrary state of affairs:

(1) *p* has a power of imperation with respect to *F;*
(1′) *p* has the power to bring about that it is commanded that *F.*
(2) *p* has a power of de-imperation with respect to *F;*
(2′) *p* has the power to bring about that it is not commanded that *F.*

A basic idea of Bentham's is that the complete power of imperation and de-imperation in a developed society is divided between several people, and he speaks of the innumerable ways in which the complete power of imperation may be "broken into shares" (1970*b*, p. 26, n. h). The power is divided between, on the one hand, the sovereign of the society, and on the other, a collection of so-called subordinate power-holders.

According to Bentham, there are primarily two kinds of subordinate power to be distinguished. A subordinate power-holder can have *power to issue mandates*, and this kind of subordinate power can be explained with the notion of *pre-adoption* (1970*b*, p. 21). The sovereign adopts beforehand the mandates which certain people will issue within a given area, and consequently such mandates become part of the law in the same way as those laws which are issued directly by the sovereign himself. Legal changes by pre-adopted mandate occur, Bentham maintains, to a greater extent than is commonly realised:

Trivial or important makes no difference ... The mandates of the master, the father, the husband, the guardian, are all of them the mandates of the sovereign: if not, then neither are those of the general nor of the judge. Not a cook is bid to dress a dinner, a nurse to feed a child, an usher to whip a school boy, an executioner to hang a thief, an officer to drive the enemy from a post, but it is by his orders. (1970*b*, pp. 22 f.)

More important than these rather unattractive examples, however, is Bentham's contention that the concept *pre-adoption* explains how legal changes come about by *conveyances* and *covenants* (i.e., contracts): "adopted by the sovereign, they are converted into mandates" (1970*b*, p. 25). As examples, Bentham cites someone's giving away his coat to someone else (conveyance) and of someone's engaging in mending a coat for someone else (covenant).

The other kind of subordinate power Bentham calls *accensitive power*. The adjective "accensitive" comes from the verb "accenseo"—to aggregate to a class—and accensitive power means accordingly the power to aggregate an individual to a class. That there are subordinate power-holders in a society depends on the sovereign's having, for practical reasons, to legislate *de classibus;* that is, not by reference to individuals designated by singular terms but rather by using general terms. Bentham provides the following explanation:

Conceive him [the sovereign] then on any occasion to have taken up any such generic name. By this name a class suppose of subjects (no matter what) is brought to view. This class taken at a given period is composed of a certain number of individuals. As to these individuals then, by what means is it that they have come to be aggregated to this class? ... By whatever means the event of their belonging to this class has come to pass, such event either depended or did not depend upon the will of a human being: if it did, such person has thereby a power ... The share which this person has in the entire power of imperation may be termed the *accensitive power* or power or right of *aggregation* with regard to the class in question. (Bentham, 1970*b*, pp. 82 f.)

Just as there are subordinate power-holders with accensitive power, so there are also those with *disaccensitive power:*

Conceive a person to belong to a certain class of persons, characterized by a certain name: either then there is a power in some other person or persons to cause him to belong no longer to that class, or there is not: if there is the power possessed by such person or persons may be termed *disaccensitive power*. (Bentham, 1970*b*, p. 85)

In accordance with those explanations, accensitive and disaccensitive power can be described by statements of the following sort

(3) p has the power to bring about that $\varphi(x)$,
(4) p has the power to bring about that not $\varphi(x)$,

where x denotes a certain individual and φ is a general term occurring in the law issued by the sovereign. The individual denoted by x in (4) and (5) can, but need not, be a person; x might be a physical object, an action, a place or a point in time (see 1970*b*, p. 85). (Many general terms in laws are of course relational terms, as for example the term "owner", and in such cases accensitive power can mean the power to assign an ordered pair, triple, etc., to a class. However, this way of looking at things had not been developed in Bentham's time, and throughout he always thought of accensitive power as the power to assign an individual to a class in the way described in (3) and (4).)

Of particular interest in relation to (3) and (4) are cases where φ is a deontic term; i.e., a term which can be defined with Shall and May or "It is commanded that", "It is permitted that", etc. An important kind of accensitive power is the power to invest someone with a *right* (*power of jurisdation*):

... the power of *accensing* ... or aggregating a man to some division or other in the wide-extending class of *right-holders*. (1970*b*, p. 86)

(The corresponding kind of disaccensitive power Bentham called *juris-ademptive power*.) The general terms "right" or "right-holder" are deontic since they can be defined in terms of "It is commanded that" and "It is permitted that" (see above, Chapter 1, pp. 15 ff.). Another important sort of case where φ in (3) and (4) is a deontic term is that where a person has the power to invest someone with a *power* (*power of potisdation*). Since the terms "power" and "power-holder" can be defined in terms of "It is permitted that" (I shall return to this shortly) these terms are also deontic.

I have now given an account of two sorts of subordinate power in Bentham's sense: (i) power to issue mandates (explained in terms of pre-adoption), and (ii) accensitive and disaccensitive power. It is not clear whether Bentham cared much whether these two categories are distinguished (cf. Hart 1972, p. 816). At any rate it seems that in some cases power can, according to Bentham, be described both as power in sense (i) and in sense (ii). An example of this is what is called the *power of conveyance*, illustrated here by the statement:

(5) p has the power to give away his coat to q

(cf. Bentham, 1970*b*, pp. 25 f.). Power of conveyance is explained, on the one hand, in terms of pre-adoption:

> It is in this very way [adoption] that conveyances and covenants acquire all the validity they can possess, all the connection they have with the System of the laws: adopted by the sovereign, they are converted into mandates. (1970*b*, pp. 23 ff.)

On the other hand, it is explained in terms of accensitive power:

> *Investitive power* when it regards a right (that is, when it is the power of investing a man with a right), *power of conveyance* and *power of jurisdation* are but three names for the same thing: they each of them consist in the power of *accensing* if we say so for a moment, or aggregating a man to some division or other in the wide-extending class of *right-holders*. (1970*b*, pp. 85 f.)

Finally, there remains the question of how Bentham explicates the concept of *power* itself. He touches on this question mainly in connection with the power to issue mandates and it is formulated there as the question of how pre-adoption comes about. The basic form of pre-adoption consists in the sovereign *allowing* someone to issue a mandate:

> Take any single manifestation of the sovereign's will, and all the assistance that the mandate of a subordinate power-holder can receive from it consists in bare permission ... The part thus far taken by the sovereign is, we see, merely a negative one. Nor would it be worthwhile, or indeed proper, to notice him as taking any part at all, since it is no more than what is taken by every the merest stranger, were it not for its lying so much in his way to take the contrary part; a part which he actually does take in relation to the greater number of the other members of the community. (1970*b*, p. 27)

The following statement shows that permission is both a necessary and a sufficient condition for pre-adoption:

> ... every mandate that is issued within the limits of the sovereignty and that is not illegal, is in one sense or the other the mandate of the sovereign. Take

any mandate whatsoever, either it is of the number of those which he allows or it is not: there is no medium: if it is, it is his; by adoption at least, if not by original conception: if not, it is illegal, and the issuing it an offence. Trivial or important makes no difference: if the former are not his, then neither are the latter. (1970*b*, p. 22)

It should be mentioned that Bentham takes into account the fact that pre-adoption can be realised in another way; by

... a mandate addressed immediately to those whom it is meant to subject to his [the subordinate power-holder's] power; a mandate commanding them to obey such and such mandates whensoever, if at all, he shall have thought fit to issue them. (1970*b*, p. 28)

However, this form of pre-adoption is, according to Bentham, completely equivalent to pre-adoption by permission ("it comes exactly to the same thing", 1970*b*, p. 28). Suppose that *A* is a mandate issued by someone *p* and that pre-adoption in each form can be described respectively by the statements

(7) It is permitted that *p* issues *A*,
(8) It is commanded that *A* be obeyed.

If (7) is true, then *A* is the sovereign's order. If *A* is the sovereign's order, then (8) is true. On the other hand, if (7) is false, then *A* is not the sovereign's order; and if *A* is not the sovereign's order, then (8) is false (see 1970*b*, p. 22). Thus, for Bentham, (7) is true if and only if (8) is too. Bentham maintains, consequently, that the concept *power* can generally be explicated in terms of *permission* so far as power to issue mandates is concerned. Whether the same explication should hold for accensitive and disaccensitive power, Bentham does not make too clear. However, since he draws no firm distinction between the two kinds of power—both are referred to as power of imperation (or de-imperation)—this suggests at any rate that the same explication holds here.

Amongst other authors who define *power* (or *competence*) in terms of May or *permission* I shall consider von Wright and Kanger. (Mullock, 1974, should be mentioned as also falling within this category, though he wrongly ascribes this definition to A. R. Anderson.) von Wright (whose theory strongly resembles Bentham's) defines *power* or *competence* in terms of what he calls "higher order permission":

A higher order permission is to the effect that a certain authority *may* issue norms of a certain content. It is, we could say, a norm concerning the competence of a certain authority of norms. I shall call permissive norms of higher order *competence norms.*
In the act of issuing a competence norm, *i.e.* a permissive norm of higher order, the superior authority of higher order may be said to *delegate power* to a *sub-authority* of lower order. 'Power' here means 'competence, by virtue of a norm, to act as an authority of norms'. I shall also speak of it as *normative* competence or power. (1963, p. 192)

In Kanger's theory, dealt with in Chapter 1, the statement

(9) Power(p, q, F)

is explicated by

(10) p may see to it that F

(p. 43). The variable F in (9) and (10) designates an arbitrary state of affairs, whether deontic or otherwise. If F is a deontic state of affairs, a counterpart to Bentham's power of "imperation" or "de-imperation", and to what von Wright calls "normative competence" is obtained.

3. *Hohfeld on power*

Hohfeld's account of *power* can be summarised by the following main points:
(i) The concepts *power*, *liability*, *disability* and *immunity* are interdefinable according to the following schema of opposites and correlatives (1923, p. 36; cf. above, p. 26).

Jural opposites:

{ power
disability

{ liability
immunity

Jural correlatives:

{ power
liability

{ disability
immunity

(ii) *Power*, *liability*, etc., are relations between two parties.
(iii) *Power* means *ability*, and in particular, *legal* power means the ability to bring about "a change in a given legal relation" (1923, pp. 50 f.).

I shall deal with the first two points briefly, and be content to indicate some problems here. More attention will be given to (iii) which concerns the explication of the concept *power* itself and which is a controversial point in the literature on Hohfeld.

It is apparent from Hohfeld's various examples that the thesis of inter-definability is based on observations of how such expressions as "has the power to", "is able to", "is liable to", "is disable to", "is immune from" and "is exempt from" are applied in legal usage. For example, the following statements can be regarded as synonyms:

(1) p has the power to (is able to) bring about that r has the privilege of entering on q's land;
(2) q is liable to having it brought about by p that r has the privilege of entering on q's land;
(3) p is not disable to bring about that r has the privilege of entering on q's land;
(4) q is not immune from having it brought about by p that r has the privilege of entering on q's land.

However, a problem arises in attempting to express the idiomatic statements (1)–(4) in a more general and schematic form using the relational concepts *power*, *liability*, *disability* and *immunity*. The statements alternate between the active and the passive form of the verb and the prepositions are different (e.g., liable *to* and immune *from*). There are at least two possible ways of schematically expressing the equivalence between statements such as (1)–(4). One possibility is

I

$$\begin{array}{ccc} \text{Power}(p, q, F) & \leftrightarrow & \text{Liability}(q, p, F) \\ \updownarrow & & \updownarrow \\ \sim \text{Disability}(p, q, F) & \leftrightarrow & \sim \text{Immunity}(q, p, F) \end{array}$$

Another is the following (cf. Kanger, 1957, p. 17; 1971, p. 44).

II

$$\begin{array}{ccc} \text{Power}(p, q, F) & \leftrightarrow & \text{Liability}(q, p, F) \\ \updownarrow & & \updownarrow \\ \sim \text{Disability}(p, q, \sim F) & \leftrightarrow & \sim \text{Immunity}(q, p, \sim F) \end{array}$$

The choice between schemata I and II depends on how they are read. In schema I the statements can be read along the lines

... has versus ... a ... *with respect to* ...;

but in schema II the statements should be read along the lines

... has versus ... a ... *to the effect that* ...

(cf. Kanger, 1971, p. 44). Each schema is correct, given the appropriate reading, because each of the following are synonymous pairs:

$$\begin{cases} p \text{ has versus } q \text{ no disability with respect to } F, \\ p \text{ has versus } q \text{ no disability to the effect that not } F. \end{cases}$$

$$\begin{cases} q \text{ has versus } p \text{ no immunity with respect to (or from) } F, \\ q \text{ has versus } p \text{ no immunity to the effect that not } F. \end{cases}$$

These pairs of statements explain why $\sim F$ is substituted for F in the lower line of schema II.

A second problem arises in connection with the thesis that power is a relation between two parties, a power-holder and a party who is liable. How is the party who is liable, i.e., against whom a given power-holder has the power to bring about "a change in a given legal relation", to be distinguished? Consider the following two statements:

(5) *p* has versus *q* a power to the effect that *r* has the privilege of entering on *q*'s land.

(6) *p* has versus *r* a power to the effect that *r* has the privilege of entering on *q*'s land.

One view is that (5) is true if and only if (6) is true. The reasoning behind this is that *p*'s power according to (5) and (6) concerns a change in the legal relations of *q* and *r:* if *p* has this power against *q*, he also has it against *r*, and vice versa. Another view is that one of (5) and (6) could be true and the other false. In this case, there arises the problem of giving the criteria according to which (5) and (6) can be given different truth values, but there is no hint from Hohfeld as to what these criteria might be. (An analogous problem arose in Chapter 1 in connection with Kanger's theory of *simple types of right*; see above, p. 45. But Kanger found the solution to his problem in his account of *atomic types of right*, where it is possible to explicate statements (5) and (6) so that they can have different truth values; see above, p. 61.)

Hohfeld's analysis of the concept *power* itself is problematic in a number of ways. It is usually interpreted in terms of *can*, but this interpretation is not free from controversy (cf. above, p. 51). Furthermore, the distinction must be recognised between *can* as an expression of practical possibility and *can* in the special sense of *rechtliches Können* ("can^P" and "can^J"; see above, pp. 194 ff.). Hohfeld's own statements on this question are sparse and sometimes difficult to reconcile. I shall make a somewhat more detailed comparison of two of his statements.

The first of these is the only statement of Hohfeld's intended to provide an explanation of the concept *power*; he himself says of it that it is intended as an "approximate explanation, sufficient for all practical purposes":

> A change in a given legal relation may result (1) from some superadded fact or group of facts not under the volitional control of a human being (or human beings); or (2) from some superadded fact or group of facts which are under the volitional control of one or more human beings. As regards the second class of cases, the person (or persons) whose volitional control is paramount may be said to have the (legal) power to effect the particular change of legal relations that is involved in the problem. (1923, pp. 50 f.)

The closest synonym to *power*, according to Hohfeld, is *ability*, and consequently *power* and *disability* are opposites (1923, p. 51). I shall argue here that Hohfeld's explanation speaks in favour of interpreting *power* in terms of Can^P as an expression of practical possibility.

The following extract from Hohfeld's above statement is noteworthy:

> A change ... may result ... from some superadded fact or group of facts which are under the volitional control of one or more human beings ... the person (or persons) whose volitional control is paramount may be said to have the (legal) power ...

The explanation seems to say that the statement

(7) *p* has the (legal) power to bring about that *F*

(where *F* is a deontic state of affairs) means the same as

(7′) Some fact *G*, such that *F* results from *G*, is under the volitional control of *p*.

Statement (7′) involves two important points, (i) that one state of affairs *results from* another state of affairs, and (ii) that a person has *volitional control* over a certain state of affairs. The first point can be understood in terms of the conditional connective "If ... then ...":

(8) If p brings about that G, then p brings about that F.

The second point can be understood, according to what Hohfeld himself says, as *affirmative* volitional control ("a power is one's affirmative 'control' over a given legal relation", 1923, p. 60). The point in question is expressed here in terms of Can^P (practical possibility) and *brings about that*

(9) p can^P bring about that G.

The following interpretation of (7) and (7′) is thereby obtained:

(7″) For some G,
If p brings about that G, then p brings about that F, and p can^P bring about that G.

Given a reasonable interpretation both of the connective "If ... then ..." and of Can^P in this context, statement (7″) is in turn equivalent to

(7‴) p can^P bring about that F.

This means that Hohfeld's *power* expresses a *can* in the sense of practical possibility. (The interpretation is, of course, based on an interpretation of "If ... then ..." as a stronger conditional than the usual truth functional connective. If the conditional were interpreted as the truth functional connective, the inference of (7‴) from (8) and (9) or from (7″) would be unjustified. It is noteworthy, in this connection, that the schema $(A > B) \rightarrow (\Diamond A \rightarrow \Diamond B)$ is derivable in the calculus for conditionals presented by Robert C. Stalnaker and Richmond H. Thomason, Stalnaker & Thomason, 1970, pp. 23 ff. The arrow $\rightarrow$ in the schema is the truth functional connective, $>$ is a stronger conditional and $\Diamond$ is a modal operator with the usual logical properties for Possibility; see Stalnaker & Thomason, 1970, p. 25, n. 4. The proof, though not shown here, is easily obtained from the definition of $\Diamond$, axiom schemata A3 and A6, derivation rule R1 and the theorem schema *t*4.6 of Stalnaker & Thomason, 1970, p. 25, pp. 30 f.)

This explanation of the concept *power* is based on the explanation Hohfeld presents when he introduces the concept. However, this interpretation seems at first sight not entirely in agreement with a statement Hohfeld makes in another context. An interpretation in terms of (7‴) seems to be contradicted by the following:

... it is necessary to distinguish carefully between the *legal* power, [and] the *physical* power to do the things necessary for the "exercise" of the legal power... (1923, p. 58)

This statement can, it appears, be understood in such a way that the statement

(7) *p* has the (legal) power to bring about that *F*

is compatible with

(10) *p* has not the physical power to do the things necessary for bringing about that *F*,

(cf. Corbin, 1919, p. 168). If (7) is compatible with (10), then it is not plausible to interpret (7) in accordance with (7‴): (10) and (7‴) contradict one another. However, the supposition that (7) is compatible with (10) is difficult to reconcile with Hohfeld's basic explanation of the concept *power* according to which (7) means the same as

(7′) Some fact *G*, such that *F* results from *G*, is under the volitional control of *p*.

It cannot be assumed that (7′) and (10) are true for the same value of *p* and *F*. I shall therefore argue for another reading of Hohfeld's last cited statement which does not entail that (7) is compatible with (10). One of Hohfeld's general theses in the essay *Fundamental Legal Conceptions* is that jurists have a tendency to confuse statements about "mental and physical facts" with deontic or "legal" statements; i.e., statements which should be interpreted in terms of *obligation*, *right*, etc. Such a tendency is to be found, for example, in the use of the term "contract" within the law of contract:

Passing to the field of contracts, we soon discover a similar inveterate tendency to confuse and blur legal discussions by failing to discriminate between the mental and physical facts involved in the so-called "agreement" of the parties, and the legal "contractual obligation" to which those facts give rise. Such ambiguity and confusion are peculiarly incident to the use of the term "contract". One moment the word may mean *the agreement* of the parties; and then, with a rapid and unexpected shift, the writer or speaker may use the term to indicate the *contractual obligation* created by law as a result of the agreement (1923, p. 31)

What Hohfeld seems to be saying in this example can be developed in a somewhat different form in the following way. Let F denote a deontic state of affairs (e.g., that p has an obligation towards q to pay £50 to q). Two different kinds of conditionals can be distinguished, where F is the consequent. First, one might consider a conditional of the kind

(11) If G_1, then F

such that G_1 also denotes a deontic state of affairs and such that (11) is an analytic truth or logically valid. Second, one can consider a conditional of the kind

(12) If G_2, then F

such that G_2 denotes a non-deontic state of affairs and such that (12) is not analytic and can be either true or false. The following deductions are then not of the same kind:

	I		II
(i)	If G_1, then F,	(i)	If G_2, then F,
(ii)	G_1,	(ii)	G_2,
(iii)	F.	(iii)	F.

Since premise (i) of deduction I is analytic, mention of it can be suppressed and it could be said that F follows directly from G_1 (F is an "analytical consequence" of G_1). In the case of deduction II, however, premise (i) is not analytic and must therefore be explicitly stated. Consequently, it would be a mistake to infer F directly from G_2. Such a mistake would have very serious consequences in law, since it would lead to neglect of the important considerations needed in any given case in order to establish the truth value of premise (i): the interpretation of statutes and precedents, considerations of justice and policy, etc. The mistake is easily made if G_1 is confused with G_2, and there is a great risk of this happening in those cases where one and the same linguistic expression is used to denote both G_1 and G_2.

(Within the legal tradition the expression *Begriffsjurisprudenz* is sometimes used as a pejorative term for the activity of deducing deontic statements as analytic consequences of statements containing traditional legal terms such as *property*, *trust*, *contract*, etc. The criticism directed against the *Begriffsjurisprudenz* is, of course, justified insofar as the deductions have the appearance of being both relevant to the point and logically valid by equivocating between a deontic and a non-deontic sense of the terms in question. More recently, in philosophical literature, John Searle's well-known attempt to deduce "ought" from "is", 1964, pp. 43 ff., has been criticised on similar grounds; see Hintikka, 1971, pp. 93 ff. and Danielsson, 1973, pp. 47 f.)

Returning to the earlier quotation from Hohfeld, where he says that "the *legal* power" and "the *physical* power to do the things necessary for the 'exercise' of the legal power" should be distinguished, a natural interpretation is to say that he is warning us of the mistake of considering

(13) p has the power to bring about that F,

where F denotes a deontic state of affairs, as an analytical consequence of

(14) p has the power to bring about that G,

where G denotes a non-deontic state of affairs. According to Hohfeld's terminology, (14) is a statement of "physical power" whilst (13) is a statement of "legal power". (14) is not sufficient grounds from which to infer (13); a further non-analytic premise is required and the considerations relevant to establishing the truth value of this premise must not be overlooked.

This interpretation of Hohfeld is entirely compatible with the explication of *power* in terms of Can^{P}. With this explication we obtain instead of (13) and (14) the two statements

(13′) p can^{P} bring about that F,
(14′) p can^{P} bring about that G.

The same is true for (13′) and (14′) as for (13) and (14): (13′) is not an analytical consequence of (14) and a further non-analytic premise—the same as that required for the deduction of (13) from (14)—is required for the deduction to be carried out.

4. *Brinz on rechtliches Können*

In Section 1 I mentioned the notion of "legal power" or "competence" (p. 195), for which I gave the German term *rechtliches Können* ("can^J"), and as was said there, this is usually explained in terms of the notion of *act-in-the-law*. Here, I shall simply draw attention to some authors who have laid emphasis on this sense of "power" or "competence".

Several variants of the concept *rechtliches Können* occur in the literature and some authors have maintained that this concept corresponds better than do May and Can^P to what jurists mean when they use the terms "power" and "competence". From the more recent literature, for example, Hart's theory of power and power-conferring rules and Ross' similar theory of competence and norms of competence are both based on this concept (Hart, 1961, pp. 27 ff.; 1972, pp. 816 ff.; Ross, 1968, pp. 130 ff.; cf. also Ross, 1953, p. 45, 65). But the concept was used long before in the German literature. Bierling's definition has already been mentioned (p. 196). The classic reference, however, is to Alois Brinz (1857, pp. 49 f.; 1873, pp. 211 ff.). A number of distinctions emphasised by later writers are expressed in the following passage:

> Legal permission and legal ability (*licere, posse*), though linguistically indistinct, are different from each other. Permission, or license, is something that occurs in both kinds of acts, ordinary acts and acts-in-the-law; legal ability, or legal power, on the other hand, occurs only in acts-in-the-law, i.e., in the widest sense of the word, only to such acts which are imposed or adopted by the law for achieving its invisible legal effects. Where the legal power exists for an act-in-the-law, there usually is also a license for it; yet, sometimes the former exists where the latter is missing. Physical ability is different both from permission and from ability in our sense, though neither the latter nor the former can be made use of without physical power; yet, ordinary acts can occur by physical power also without permission (*vi, clam facere, Delict*); acts-in-the-law without legal power are null and void. (Brinz, 1873, pp. 211 f.; my translation.)

The dependence of the definition of the just quoted term "legal ability" (*rechtliches Können*) on the notion of *act-in-the-law* is apparent from this statement of Brinz's, as is the contention that *rechtliches Können* should be distinguished both from *permission* and from *physical* ability, and, finally, that acts-in-the-law without *rechtliches Können* are "void". These points have been constantly repeated in subsequent accounts.

III. *The Theory of Ranges of Action*

1. *Some introductory distinctions*

The theory of *basic types of legal positions* as developed above in Chapters 3–5 was built on the foundations of an earlier tradition culminating in Kanger's system of atomic types of right. The theory to be presented in the following chapters has not had much of an impulse from the earlier tradition of "legal change" or "changes in legal relations" (Bentham, Hohfeld, etc.). Rather, the theory is built on the results given in Chapters 3–5, and in particular, the partial orderings induced by the relations *less free than* represented by Hasse diagrams.

As before, the basic apparatus consists of the two operators Shall (or May) and Do, and the basic idea here is to further exploit the possibilities of combining these operators. More precisely, statements of the kinds

(1) May Do$(p, \langle q, F\rangle \in T)$;
(2) May Do$(p, \langle q, r, F\rangle \in R)$;
(3) May Do$(p, \langle q, r, F\rangle \in S)$.

are used. As before, the variables p, q and r denote arbitrary agents (a person or a collective agent) and F denotes an arbitrary state of affairs. T stands for any one of $T_1, ..., T_7$ (one-agent types; Chapter 3), R for one of $R_1, ..., R_{35}$ (individualistic two-agent types; Chapter 4) and S for one of $S_1, ..., S_{127}$ (collectivistic two-agent types; Chapter 5). In a certain sense, statements of the kind (1)–(3) can be said to be statements of *legal power*. This is to presuppose that the expression "legal power" is interpreted in terms of May or *permission* in accordance with the views of Bentham, von Wright and Kanger (see pp. 201 ff.). However, in what follows, no stress is laid on the use of the term "power"; statements to be used are expressed directly in terms of May along the lines of (1)–(3).

The information conveyed by (1)–(3) can be supplemented by saying whether p *can* or *cannot* bring it about that a pair $\langle q, F\rangle$ belongs to a certain one-agent type, or that a triple $\langle q, r, F\rangle$ belongs to a given two-agent type (cf. above, pp. 194 ff., 207 ff.). However, I shall disregard this in what follows. The construction of a theory for combinations of the three operators Can, Shall and Do falls outside the scope of this book.

It is noteworthy that (1)–(3) cover two cases: first, that p may see to it that the pair $\langle q, F\rangle$ or triple $\langle q, r, F\rangle$ *is moved* to a given type, and second, that p may see to it that $\langle q, F\rangle$ or $\langle q, r, F\rangle$ *remains* in a certain type. It is easy to distinguish explicitly between these two cases. In the case of (1), we have

(1′) $\langle q, F\rangle \in T'$ & May Do$(p, \langle q, F\rangle \in T)$,
(1″) $\langle q, F\rangle \in T$ & May Do$(p, \langle q, F\rangle \in T)$,

(where T, T' are distinct two-agent types). (1′) means that p may move $\langle q, F\rangle$ from T' to T (for example, by releasing q from a promise). (1″) says that p may see to it that $\langle q, F\rangle$ remains in T (for example, by preventing q's obligation due to a certain promise expiring by prescription). Similarly, concerning (2) we can distinguish between the two statements

(2′) $\langle q, r, F\rangle \in R'$ & May Do$(p, \langle q, r, F\rangle \in R)$,
(2″) $\langle q, r, F\rangle \in R$ & May Do$(p, \langle q, r, F\rangle \in R)$,

and concerning (3), we have

(3′) $\langle q, r, F\rangle \in S'$ & May Do$(p, \langle q, r, F\rangle \in S)$,
(3″) $\langle q, r, F\rangle \in S$ & May Do$(p, \langle q, r, F\rangle \in S)$.

In the cases (1′), (2′) and (3′) where a transfer is at issue, the types involved can be related in three ways: the first type can be *more* or *less free* than the second, or they can be incomparable with respect to freedom (see p. 109, 142, 186). Suppose, for example, that the types are T and T'; if T is less free than T' then, according to (1′), p has permission to restrict q's freedom with respect to F (by command, order, decree, etc.). If T is more free than T' then p has permission to increase q's freedom with respect to F (by, for example, releasing q from a promise). If T and T' are incomparable then p has permission both to increase and to restrict q's freedom with respect to F (see p. 110).

Concerning the parties named in (1)–(3), a number of cases can be distinguished. In the case of (1), p can be either identical with or distinct from q. In the former case, p alters his own legal situation and in the latter, another person's, by, for example, giving a command or granting permission. (Cf. Ross' distinction between heteronomous and autonomous competence, 1968, pp. 132 f.) p can alter his own situation, for example, by *promising* to see to it that a certain state of affairs obtains; this is a case of *commitment*, and an account of this sort of case is given in Chapter 9. A similar distinction can be drawn for (2) and (3), but here there are the possibilities of p being distinct from both q and r and p being identical with one of q and r.

A case meriting special attention is that where p denotes a collective agent. By a collective agent is understood here any unit that may be chosen as an agent formed by some operation on a set $\{p, q, r, ...\}$ or an ordered n-tuple $\langle p, q, r, ...\rangle$ of people. (Note that the expression "collective agent" is, in this sense, not synonymous with the expression "legal personality" as used by jurists.) There are many different operations generating a variety of collective agents: Smith & Co. Ltd., the Swedish Government, the public meeting in the Loughborough town square on 1st June, 1976, etc. In what follows, however, only one simple, though important, operation for building collective agents will be considered in any detail, namely "together with", which generates collective agents from two or more people cooperating together to achieve some result. The operation is important in legal contexts when, for example, two people make a contract; thus, q and r together see to it that $\langle q, F\rangle$ belongs to the one-agent type T of basic legal positions, or q and r together see to it that $\langle q, r, F\rangle$ belongs to the two-agent type R or S. In these cases, the variable p in (1)–(3) designates the collective agent *q together with r*. This operation "together with" is discussed in Chapter 7, laying the foundation for the discussion of contracts in Chapter 9.

2. *The concept of range of action*

For given p, q and F, just one of the following statements is true for each type T of the seven one-agent types $T_1, ..., T_7$:

(1) May Do$(p, \langle q, F\rangle \in T)$,

(2) $\sim$ May Do$(p, \langle q, F\rangle \in T)$.

The set $\{T_1, ..., T_7\}$ can, accordingly, be divided into two parts for each set of values for p, q and F, namely

$$K = \{T | \text{May Do}(p, \langle q, F\rangle \in T)\},$$
$$\overline{K} = \{T | \sim \text{May Do}(p, \langle q, F\rangle \in T)\}.$$

Which of $T_1, ..., T_7$ belong to K and which to $\overline{K}$ depends, of course, on the choice of values for p, q and F. For a given set of values it might, for example, be that K comprises all of $T_1, ..., T_7$ whilst $\bar{K}$ is empty. In this case p has maximum authority to influence which of $T_1, ..., T_7$ $\langle q, F\rangle$ will belong to. Or again, for another choice of p, q, and F, K could be empty and $\bar{K}$ contain all seven types, in which case p would have no authority whatsoever over the placing of $\langle q, F\rangle$. The set K is said to be p's *range of legal action* (Swedish *spelrum*) with respect to $\langle q, F\rangle$. (Where the context allows, the expression "range of legal action" may be shortened to "range of action" or simply to "range", and explicit reference to a pair $\langle q, F\rangle$ dropped where this is clearly to be understood.)

From what has been said, for each choice of p, q and F there is exactly one subset K of $\{T_1, ..., T_7\}$ which is p's range of action with respect to $\langle q, F\rangle$. Accordingly, a function $\mathcal{A}$ is defined for *range of (legal) action* such that:

(i) The first argument domain of $\mathcal{A}$ = the set of agents.
(ii) The second argument domain of $\mathcal{A}$ = the cartesian product of the set of agents and the set of states of affairs.
(iii) The range of $\mathcal{A}$ = the power set of $\{T_1, ..., T_7\}$.

DEFINITION 1. Let T be a variable ranging over elements of $\{T_1, ..., T_7\}$. Then $\mathcal{A}(p, \langle q, F\rangle) =_{\text{def.}} \{T \mid \text{May Do}(p, \langle q, F\rangle \in T)\}$.

Informally, p's range of action with respect to $\langle q, F\rangle$ is the set of all T such that p may see to it that $\langle q, F\rangle$ belongs to T.

This explanation and definition of *range of action* can be applied analogously to individualistic and collectivistic two-agent types. The arguments are now of the kind $\langle p, \langle q, r, F\rangle\rangle$ and the range is the power set either of $\{R_1, ..., R_{35}\}$ or of $\{S_1, ..., S_{127}\}$. Formally, functions $\mathcal{A}^R$ and $\mathcal{A}^S$ are defined as follows

DEFINITION 2. Let R be a variable ranging over elements of $\{R_1, ..., R_{35}\}$. Then $\mathcal{A}^R(p, \langle q, r, F\rangle) =_{\text{def.}} \{R \mid \text{May Do}(p, \langle q, r, F\rangle \in R)\}$.

That is, p's *range of action*^{R} with respect to $\langle q, r, F\rangle$ is the set of all R such that p may see to it that $\langle q, r, F\rangle$ belongs to R.

DEFINITION 3. Let S be a variable ranging over elements of $\{S_1, ..., S_{127}\}$. Then $\mathcal{A}^S(p, \langle q, r, F\rangle) =_{\text{def.}} \{S \mid \text{May Do}(p, \langle q, r, F\rangle \in S)\}$.

And so, p's *range of action*^{S} with respect to $\langle q, r, F\rangle$ is the set of all S such that p may see to it that $\langle q, r, F\rangle$ belongs to S.

I shall frequently use the notion of a *range of action* as though it were a one-place predicate. The following definitions show what is intended by this:

DEFINITIONS. Let T, T', ... be variables for one-agent types, R, R', ... be variables for individualistic two-agent types and S, S', ... be variables for collectivistic two-agent types.

4. $\{T, T', ..\}$ is a *range of action* $=_{\text{def.}}$ For some p, q and F, $\mathcal{A}(p, \langle q, F\rangle) = \{T, T', ...\}$.
5. $\{R, R', ...\}$ is a *range of action* $=_{\text{def.}}$ For some p, q, r and F, $\mathcal{A}^{R}(p, \langle q, r, F\rangle) = \{R, R', ...\}$.
6. $\{S, S', ...\}$ is a *range of action* $=_{\text{def.}}$ For some p, q, r and F, $\mathcal{A}^{S}(p, \langle q, r, F\rangle) = \{S, S', ...\}$.

3. *The justification for a theory of ranges of action*

So far as I know, there is no counterpart to the notion of *range of action* as defined here within the earlier theories of legal change or "changes in legal relations". It is therefore appropriate at this point to motivate the introduction of the concept which will then be developed in Chapters 8 and 9. First, *range of action* captures what would otherwise have to be expressed in long and complicated sentences on legal relations. Consider

(1) $\mathcal{A}^{S}(p, \langle q, r, F\rangle) = \{S_1, S_2, S_9, S_{30}, S_{65}, S_{100}, S_{121}\}$.

In view of the definitions given above, (1) can be reformulated step by step into a very thorough description of p's authority to influence legal relations between q and r with respect to F. As a first step, (1) can be translated into a sentence with a hundred and twenty-seven conjuncts of the kind

$$\text{May Do}(p, \langle q, r, F\rangle \in S_1),$$
$$\text{May Do}(p, \langle q, r, F\rangle \in S_2),$$
$$\sim\text{May Do}(p, \langle q, r, F\rangle \in S_3),$$

and so forth. Then, each of the terms

$$\langle q, r, F\rangle \in S_1,$$
$$\langle q, r, F\rangle \in S_2,$$
$$\vdots$$
$$\langle q, r, F\rangle \in S_{127},$$

occurring in the conjuncts can in turn be formulated in terms of Shall and Do according to the definitions of $S_1, ..., S_{127}$. The advantage of (1) over the cumbersome result of these reformulations is apparent.

Efficiency of expression cannot alone be sufficient motivation, of course, in the absence of some further point to the concept expressed by the abbreviation, and this further point lies in the possibility of developing the theory of legal change by considering properties of various *sets* of one- or two-agent types. Given a set K of such types, the set can be characterised by the relations amongst the various elements, and the ordering of the set as a whole, generated by the relation *less free than* (p. 109, 142, 186). A Hasse diagram perspicuously expresses these features of K. Consider, for example, the range of action given in (1) above—i.e., $\{S_1, S_2, S_9, S_{30}, S_{65}, S_{100}, S_{121}\}$—which can be graphically represented by the following diagram (cf. Chapter 5):

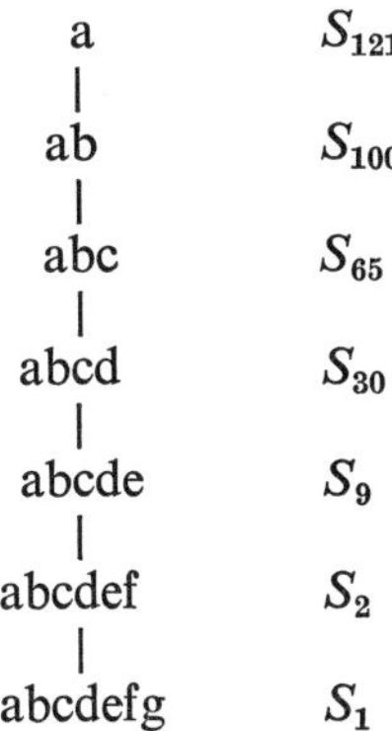

S_{121}

S_{100}

S_{65}

S_{30}

S_9

S_2

S_1

The types here are linearly ordered: for each pair of types in the range, the one with the higher index is the less free. When the theory is properly developed in Chapters 8 and 9, the general principles governing the relations amongst the elements in a range of action will play a prominent role. At the same time it should be remembered that considerations of properties of ranges of action and their internal ordering are of a high level of abstraction, and the central principles must be checked by reformulation to statements of a lower level of abstraction—statements dealing with what an agent may or may not do, etc. (i.e., statements formulated directly in terms of Shall and Do). In fact, the basic principles of the theory formulated in Chapters 8 and 9 are expressed on this lower level of abstraction. It is then shown that from principles formulated in this way certain theorems can be deduced about the properties of ranges of action, and these theorems can be perspicuously illustrated by Hasse diagrams.

4. *The logical basis of the theory*

If the number of elements in a set K is n, the number of subsets is 2^n, and consequently

the number of subsets of $\{T_1, ..., T_7\} = 2^7$;
the number of subsets of $\{R_1, ..., R_{35}\} = 2^{35}$;
the number of subsets of $\{S_1, ..., S_{127}\} = 2^{127}$.

It would appear, then, that there is an enormous number of possible values of the three functions $\mathcal{A}$, $\mathcal{A}^{\mathrm{R}}$ and $\mathcal{A}^{\mathrm{S}}$. A central problem, accordingly, is to find rules or principles which preclude some of these subsets being ranges of action. Are there, for example, principles according to which a set K of one- or two-agent types can be a range of action only if the elements of K are related in a certain way? (Cf. the end of the preceding section.) As long as we just adhere to the rules for Shall and Do introduced in Chapter 2 (RI–RII and A1–A3, p. 68), any subset of $\{T_1, ..., T_7\}$, $\{R_1, ..., R_{35}\}$ and $\{S_1, ..., S_{127}\}$ can be a range of action. In what follows, a number of supplementary rules are introduced, designed to cope with combinations of the operators Shall and Do. The most important of these for the theory of ranges of action are not, however, logical rules, but rather *rules of feasibility;* though what exactly the latter is will be left until the end of the next chapter.

As a final point, note that if the logic for the operator Shall were strengthened by the addition of the axioms

(I) Shall $F \rightarrow$ Shall Shall F,
(II) May $F \rightarrow$ Shall May F,

corresponding to the so-called S4 and S5 axioms of alethic modal logic, the development of a theory of ranges of action in the sense described would be rendered pointless. For the following three statements are consequences of axioms (I) and (II):

(1) $T \in \mathcal{A}(p, \langle q, F\rangle) \rightarrow \langle q, F\rangle \in T;$
(1′) $R \in \mathcal{A}^{\mathrm{R}}(p, \langle q, r, F\rangle) \rightarrow \langle q, r, F\rangle \in R;$
(1″) $S \in \mathcal{A}^{\mathrm{S}}(p, \langle q, r, F\rangle) \rightarrow \langle q, r, F\rangle \in S;$

and these statements imply that every non-empty range of action has exactly one element.

That (1)–(1″) follow from I–II can easily be shown. Assume the negation of one of (1)–(1″) is true. Then there are, in one of the sets $\{T_1, ..., T_7\}$, $\{R_1, ..., R_{35}\}$ or $\{S_1, ..., S_{127}\}$ two distinct types Q and Q' such that

(2) $\quad$ May Do(p, $\langle q, F\rangle \in Q$) & $\langle q, F\rangle \in Q'$,

or,

(2′) $\quad$ May Do(p, $\langle q, r, F\rangle \in Q$) & $\langle q, r, F\rangle \in Q'$.

Either of (2) or (2′) means (according to the construction of one- and two-agent types, see Chapters 3–5) that a statement of one of the following general kinds is true:

(3) $\quad$ May Do(p, (May A & ...)) & ($\sim$May A & ...);
(4) $\quad$ May Do(p, ($\sim$May A & ...)) & (May A & ...).

From (3) it follows that

(5) $\quad$ May May A & $\sim$May A,

which is equivalent to the negation of I. From (4) it follows that

(6) $\quad$ May $\sim$ May A & May A,

which is equivalent to the negation of II.

I and II mar any would-be theory of ranges of action because, basically, they contradict the idea that a person can have legal power (in the sense of permission) to bring about a change in a legal situation. Consider, for example, the statements

(7) $\quad$ May Do(p, May Do(q, F)) & $\sim$May Do(q, F),
(8) $\quad$ May Do(p, $\sim$May Do(q, F)) & May Do(q, F).

According to (7) it is forbidden that q performs a certain action, but p may change the legal situation so that it becomes permitted that q performs the action. According to (8), conversely, it is permitted that q performs a certain action, but p may change the legal situation so that it is forbidden that q performs the action. Both statements characterise everyday situations; but if I and II are accepted, they become self-contradictory: from I the negation of (7) can be deduced, and from II the negation of (8).

CHAPTER 7

Symbols and Logical Rules (Continued)

I. *Introduction*

In this chapter I shall add to the logical apparatus already in use and introduce a distinction between logical rules and rules of feasibility. First, the symbols of Chapter 2 will be supplemented with a new operator and some logical rules governing its behaviour; this addition will be of particular relevance when I come to discuss legal change by *contract*. Then, the notion of a *rule of feasibility* is briefly explained.

II. *The Logical Apparatus*

1. *A new operator and some logical rules*

The following operator is now added to the existing symbolism:

$+$ ("together with")

This is a binary operation yielding an agent $p+q$ by operating on two agents p and q, and is read "p and q together" or "p together with q". Expressions such as $p_1+(p_2+p_3)$, $p_1+(p_2+(p_3+p_4))$, $(p_1+p_2)+(p_3+p_4)$, etc. are generated by iteration. Each expression designating an individual person or collective agent I call an *agent designator*, and falling within this category are both agent variables $p, q, r, ..., p_1, p_2, ...$ and expressions generated by the $+$ operator.

The formation rules are supplemented by the following two:

(1) If s and s' are agent designators, then $s=s'$ is a well-formed statement.

(2) If A is a well-formed sentence and s is an agent designator, then Do(s, A) is a well-formed statement.

Accordingly, a statement of the kind $p+q=r$, identifying r with the collective agent $p+q$, and a statement of the kind Do($p+q$, F), saying that p and q together see to it that F, are both well-formed.

In addition to the rules RI and RII, and the axiom schemata A1–A3 of Chapter 2, five further axiom schemata are now to be added (where A is a well-formed statement and s, s', and s'' are agent designators):

Rules for $+$:

A4. $s+s'=s'+s$. (Commutative property)
A5. $s+(s'+s'')=(s+s')+s''$. (Associative property)

Rules for Do:

A6. $s=s'\rightarrow(\text{Do}(s, A)\leftrightarrow\text{Do}(s', A))$.

Rules for the combination of Shall *and* Do:

A7. $s=s'\rightarrow(\text{Shall Do}(s, A)\leftrightarrow\text{Shall Do}(s', A))$.
A8. $s=s'\rightarrow(\text{Shall}\sim\text{Do}(s, A)\leftrightarrow\text{Shall}\sim\text{Do}(s', A))$.

Given these axioms, the agent designators occurring in an expression for a collective agent with one or more occurrences of $+$ can be written in any order and brackets are unnecessary. Thus, $q+(p+r)$ can also be written $p+q+r$, and Do($q+(p+r)$, F) can also be written Do($p+q+r$, F), and so forth.

In addition to A4 and A5 there are a number of other plausible axiom schemata which come to mind; for example,

A.i. $s+s=s$.
A.ii. $(s+s'=s+s'')\rightarrow(s'=s'')$.
A.iii. $(s'=s'')\rightarrow(s+s'=s+s'')$.

However, these do not play any role in what follows, and therefore are simply discarded here.

2. *The notion of "together with"*

Cases that can be described as being of the kind

(1) Do($p+q$, F)

are well-known from a variety of familiar situations: p and q together see to it that a certain stone is moved from one place to another, p and q together see to it that p is married to q, and so on. Clearly, (1) is not equivalent to

(2) Do(p, F) & Do(q, F).

Suppose that four grammes of a certain poison is the minimum quantity sufficient to kill a person r. Now compare the two cases: (i) p and q each give r two grammes of the poison at the same time; (ii) p and q each simultaneously give four grammes of poison to r. Let F denote the state of affairs that r dies. In case (i) statement (1) is true but (2) false; but in case (ii) both are true, so that each of p and q sees to it that r dies though they both do together as well. The distinction between (1) and (2) is also apparent from familiar situations that can be described as of the following kinds

(3) $\quad$ Can Do$(p+q, F)$ & ~Can Do(p, F) & ~Can Do(q, F),

(4) $\quad$ May Do$(p+q, F)$ & ~May Do(p, F) & ~May Do(q, F).

It is often situations of these kinds that lead to cooperation between two people; for example, suppose F in (3) says that a certain stone is moved and in (4) that p is married to q.

A particularly important case in the field of law which can be described by (1) is that form of cooperation known as *making a contract*, where the cooperation of the parties results in a certain deontic state of affairs being the case. A trivial example to illustrate: suppose there is a contract according to which p shall pay, on q's behalf, £50 to r from q's account, as described by the statement

(9) $\quad$ p and q together see to it that it shall be the case that p sees to it that £50 is paid to r from q's account.

(9) has the form

(10) $\quad$ Do$(p+q$, Shall Do$(p, F))$.

Both A4 and A5 are satisfied when a contract is made: p and q making a contract is the same as q and p making the contract; and where three parties are involved, they can be written in any order; and so forth.

The significance of the cooperation which is the characteristic feature of a contract is brought out in (4), namely, that two people may together be allowed to do what they otherwise would not be permitted to do individually. To illustrate the point, the previous example will be developed somewhat. Let F denote the state of affairs that £50 is paid to r from q's account. Suppose that it is the case, before the contract is made between p and q, that

(11) $\quad$ ~May Do(p, F) & ~May Do$(p, \sim F)$,

that is, p may neither see to nor prevent the money being paid. p's legal position with respect to F is represented by

(12) $\langle p, F \rangle \in T_6$

where T_6 is one-agent type number 6. Suppose, furthermore, that after the contract is made,

(13) Shall Do(p, F),

that is, p shall see to it that the money is paid. (13) is equivalent to

(14) $\langle p, F \rangle \in T_5$;

consequently, the result of the contract's being made is that $\langle p, F \rangle$ is moved from T_6 to T_5. The relation between T_5 and T_6 is represented by the following extract of the Hasse diagram for one-agent types:

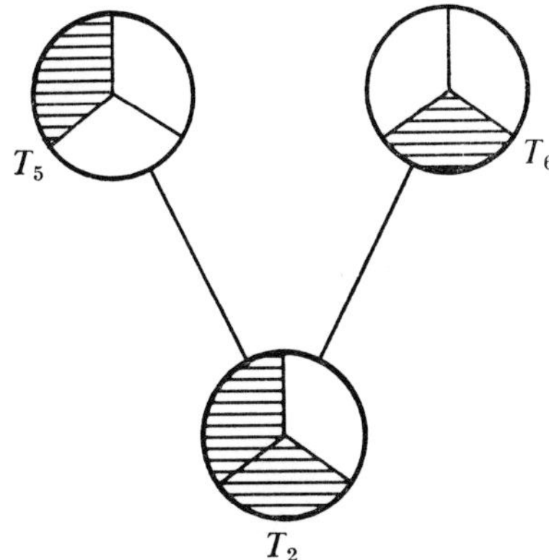

It is easily seen from the diagram just why a contract is required in such a situation. If p and q are ordinary citizens with no previous employment contracts or suchlike existent between them then neither p nor q may move $\langle p, F \rangle$ from T_6 to T_5. But at the same time q may move $\langle p, F \rangle$ from T_6 to T_2: q may, by permitting p to make the payment, increase the shaded area of $\langle p, F \rangle$ to cover the left-hand section too. Moreover, if $\langle p, F \rangle$ is in T_2 then p may move $\langle p, F \rangle$ to T_5, i.e., p may (by committing himself to taking care of the payment) decrease the shaded area for $\langle p, F \rangle$ so that only the left-hand section is covered. The movement can therefore come about as the result of two successive actions: first, q moves $\langle p, F\rangle$ to T_2, and then p moves $\langle p, F\rangle$ to T_5. When p and q cooperate by making a contract, however, both movements occur at the same time and in this sense p and q jointly see to it that $\langle p, F\rangle$ is moved from T_6 to T_5. Before the contract is made,

(15) $\sim$May Do$(p, \langle p, F\rangle \in T_5)$ & $\sim$May Do$(q, \langle p, F\rangle \in T_5)$ & May Do$(p+q, \langle p, F\rangle \in T_5)$,

obtains, which is a special case of the general situation described by (4) in which cooperation is required.

3. *Some concepts differing from "together with"*

There are a number of concepts rather similar to "together with" but which do not satisfy A4 and A5 in combination with A6–A8. For example, the two statements

(1) p sees to it that F after consultation with q,
(2) q sees to it that F after consultation with p,

are not equivalent: "after consultation with" does not have the commutative property expressed by A4. Similarly, the two statements

(3) p sees to it that F with the help of q,
(4) q sees to it that F with the help of p,

are not equivalent since "with the help of" is not commutative either. The order in which the agent variables occur in each of (1)–(4) is of significance, and none of them can therefore be expressed in the form Do$(p+q, F)$.

Kanger & Kanger (1966, p. 103) have a notion of a *joint party*, by which they understand two or more parties "in union" and denote the joint party of n parties $p_1, ..., p_n$ by the sequence $p_1p_2 ... p_n$. They lay down the following *principles of joint parties* (I have substituted Do for "causes" in accordance with Kanger, 1971 and 1972; cf. above, p. 38):

(5a) Do$(p, F) \rightarrow$ Do(pq, F),
(5b) Do$(p, F) \rightarrow$ Do(qp, F),
(5c) Do$(pq, F) \rightarrow$ Do(prq, F).

The analogue of (5a) for the operator + would be

(6) $\mathrm{Do}(p, F) \rightarrow \mathrm{Do}(p+q, F)$,

and it is clear what the analogues of (5b) and (5c) would be. These principles are not incompatible with A4 and A5, but then neither do they follow from them. Bearing in mind particularly the kind of situation discussed above where cooperation is required to achieve certain ends, however, it can be seen that these are not suitable principles for the operator "together with". To state the reason concisely, I shall for the moment avail myself of an operator S for *supports* used by Pörn (1971, pp. 9 ff.) and write $\mathrm{S}(p, F)$ for "p supports that F" or "p contributes to F's being the case". Of the axioms governing S we have

(7) $\mathrm{Do}(p, F) \rightarrow \mathrm{S}(p, F)$

(cf. Pörn, 1971, p. 12). S is not, however, a so-called success operator: $\mathrm{S}(p, F)$ is compatible with $\sim F$. A natural rule for the operator + can now be formulated as follows:

(8) $\mathrm{Do}(p_1 + \ldots + p_n, F) \rightarrow \mathrm{S}(p_1, F) \ \& \ \ldots \ \& \ \mathrm{S}(p_n, F)$.

In other words, all of $p_1, \ldots, p_n$ together see to it that F only if each of them supports or contributes to F's being the case. (Think of them cooperating to lift a stone between them.) However, it follows from (6)–(8) that

(9) $\mathrm{Do}(p, F) \rightarrow \mathrm{S}(q, F)$,

that is, if one agent sees to it that F, then anybody whosoever contributes to the bringing about of F. (9) is obviously unacceptable—if I move a stone, it does not follow that someone half way around the world has helped me! In the light of (7) and (8), it would seem then that (6) is not an acceptable principle.

III. *Logical Rules and Rules of Feasibility*

Apart from the operator + and those axioms governing its use already introduced in the present chapter, I shall make no further addition to the logical apparatus established in Chapter 2. The system consists, therefore, of the usual logic of the predicate calculus and elementary set theory together with axiom schemata A1–A8 and rules RI–RII. In calling these rules and axioms *logical* rules I mean that they partially define the meaning of the three operators Do, Shall and +; if these rules did not hold, then Do, Shall and + would stand for concepts other than those intended here. However, as distinct from the logical rules for Do, Shall and +, another group of rules can be distinguished which I call *rules of feasibility*. Within the larger set of logical possibilities there are a number of cases which are *not feasible*, i.e., possibilities which need not in practice be considered; and a rule of feasibility excludes a number of such cases.

The expression "rule of feasibility" is borrowed from Kanger & Kanger (1966, p. 107, 112) where it occurs in connection with an analysis of what they call government position structures (by which they understand the system of rights relations obtaining between the head of state, the prime minister, the parliament, etc., and concerning appointment and dismissal of members of the government, and the dissolution of parliament; cf. above, p. 151). In this connection, Kanger & Kanger consider as rules of feasibility

> Political principles which hold in every feasible position structure of the type here in question. These principles are in most cases too obvious to be worth explicit statement in a document like the constitution, but they are often implicitly assumed in interpretations of the constitution. (1966, p. 107)

With the help of certain such rules, they are able to reduce the great number of logically possible government position structures to a manageable number of *feasible* government position structures.

The theory of government position structures is just one of those areas where the use of rules of feasibility is of importance. It is a well-known fact, both in everyday and scientific contexts, that of the various solutions that arise in discussing a given problem certain alternatives are immediately excluded, which, although logically possible, are either unreasonable or in practice completely without interest. The elimination of alternatives is often based on rules of feasibility of one kind or another, though the principles actually used are often not made explicit. General principles having the character of feasibility rules can also occur in formalised theories based upon a logical apparatus where the results are formally deduced. There are many areas of applied logic where a fruitful development of the theory cannot be attained solely on the basis of the standard logical apparatus (predicate logic, set theory, etc.) together with uncontroversial logical rules for the primitive terms of the theory. Rather than strengthening the logical rules in a controversial way, a number of rules of feasibility might be introduced expressly for the purpose of disregarding a number of logically possible but otherwise uninteresting cases.

CHAPTER 8

The General Theory of Ranges of Legal Action

I. *Introduction*

The theory of ranges of action as developed here includes both a general and a more specialised part; the former is discussed in the present chapter and the latter in Chapter 9. As these terms themselves suggest, principles and theorems developed for the general part also hold for the more specialised part, but not conversely. The area of application of the special part will be described in Chapter 9.

The concept of *range of action* was presented towards the end of Chapter 6 (pp. 215 f.), and in accordance with what was said there each of the expressions within the following groups are synonymous:

I. $\begin{cases} \{T \mid \text{May Do}(p, \langle q, F\rangle \in T)\}, \\ \mathcal{A}(p, \langle q, F\rangle), \\ p\text{'s range of action with respect to } \langle q, F\rangle. \end{cases}$

II. $\begin{cases} \{R \mid \text{May Do}(p, \langle q, r, F\rangle \in R)\}, \\ \mathcal{A}^{\text{R}}(p, \langle q, r, F\rangle), \\ p\text{'s range of action}^{\text{R}} \text{ with respect to } \langle q, r, F\rangle. \end{cases}$

III. $\begin{cases} \{S \mid \text{May Do}(p, \langle q, r, F\rangle \in S)\}, \\ \mathcal{A}^{\text{S}}(p, \langle q, r, F\rangle), \\ p\text{'s range of action}^{\text{S}} \text{ with respect to } \langle q, r, F\rangle. \end{cases}$

The expressions in the first group denote, for a given value of p, q and F, a certain subset of $\{T_1, ..., T_7\}$; similarly, expressions in the second group denote subsets of $\{R_1, ..., R_{35}\}$ and in the third group, subsets of $\{S_1, ..., S_{127}\}$.

Unless otherwise explicitly stated, the range of values of the agent variables $p, q, r, ...$ and statement variables $F, G, H, ...$ is unrestricted. In particular, agent variables may denote distinct or identical agents, be they individual or collective (cf. pp. 213 f.). The results for the general theory are based on the logical rules given in Chapters 2 and 7, together with certain rules of feasibility to be introduced in this chapter.

II. *Ranges of Action for One-Agent Types*

1. *Ranges of action and the distribution of* May Do

The theory of ranges of action for one-agent types deals with conjunctions of statements of the kind

(1) May Do(p, $\langle q, F\rangle \in T$),
(2) May Do(p, $\langle q, F\rangle \in T'$),
(3) $\sim$May Do(p, $\langle q, F\rangle \in T''$),

etc., where T, T', T'', ... are elements of $\{T_1, ..., T_7\}$. Statements of the kind (1)–(3) describe p's legal power (in the sense of *permission*; cf. p. 212) in connection with influencing q's legal position with respect to F. If we reflect for a moment on everyday legal reasoning, such as is presented, for example, by judges and solicitors, descriptions of this kind seem unusual. If we set T equal to T_1, T' to T_2 and T'' to T_5, for example, we obtain the statements

(1′) May Do(p, May Do(q, F) & May Pass(q, F) & May Do(q, $\sim F$)),
(2′) May Do(p, May Do(q, F) & May Pass(q, F) & $\sim$May Do(q, $\sim F$)),
(3′) $\sim$May Do(p, Shall Do(q, F)).

Clearly, it would be a rare occasion that we came across a statement to the effect that the conjunction of (1′)–(3′) is true for given values of p, q and F in a book on law. On the other hand, statements often arise in everyday legal talk that can be schematically expressed by one of the following statements or their negation:

(4) May Do(p, May Do(q, F)),
(5) May Do(p, May Pass(q, F)),
(6) May Do(p, May Do(q, $\sim F$)),
(7) May Do(p, $\sim$May Do(q, F)),
(8) May Do(p, $\sim$May Pass(q, F)),
(9) May Do(p, $\sim$May Do(q, $\sim F$)).

Suppose for example, p is a police superintendent, q a private person who finds himself at a police station and F the state of affairs that q leaves the police station. The truth of (4) entails that p may allow q to leave the police station; (5) means that p may allow q to remain passive in respect to the question of his leaving the police station; (6) means that p may allow q to remain there; and so forth for (7)–(9).

In what follows I shall suppose that there is a connection between statements of the kind (1′)–(3′) and statements of the kind (4)–(9) or their negations. Compare, for example, statement (1′) with

(10) May Do(p, May Do(q, F)) & May Do(p, May Pass (q, F)) & May Do(p, May Do(q, $\sim F$)),

which is just the conjunction of (4)–(6). The difference is that whereas in (1′) the first occurrence of the combination May Do governs the whole conjunction, in (10) this same combination of operators is distributed throughout the conjunction so that each conjunct is directly governed by May Do. My assumption in a case of this sort amounts to the supposition that the question whether (10) is true is relevant to the truth of (1′), and conversely. Exactly what this relation consists in is expressed in the form of a rule of feasibility, described in the next section. Before going into details, it is useful to appreciate that the logical rules RI and RII together with axioms A1–A8 (p. 68, p. 221) are not sufficient to enable us to deduce (10) from (1′) or conversely. In fact it holds quite generally that there are no non-contradictory Boolean compounds of one or more of (4)–(9) from which it is possible, with RI, RII and A1–A8, to deduce a (non-tautological) statement of the kind (1′)–(3′). And so conversely: there is no non-contradictory statement of the kind (1′)–(3′) from which a non-tautological Boolean compound of (4)–(9) can be deduced using the same rules.

2. *The rule of feasibility* FI

To facilitate the formulation of the feasibility rule for one-agent types I shall introduce some notational conventions as follows:

1. s, s' are arbitrary agent designators (p. 220) and A is an arbitrary well-formed statement.

2. X_1, X_2, X_3 are schemata such that

X_1 stands for one of the statements:	X_2 stands for one of the statements:	X_3 stands for one of the statements:
May Do(s', A),	May Pass(s', A),	May Do(s', $\sim A$),
$\sim$May Do(s', A).	$\sim$May Pass(s', A).	$\sim$May Do(s', $\sim A$).

The rule can then be formulated as

FI. May Do$(s, X_1 \& X_2 \& X_3) \leftrightarrow$ May$(X_1 \& X_2 \& X_3)$ & May Do(s, X_1) & May Do(s, X_2) & May Do(s, X_3).

For the sake of constructing an example, suppose

s stands for p,
s' stands for q,
A stands for F,
X_1 stands for May Do(q, F),
X_2 stands for $\sim$May Pass(q, F),
X_3 stands for $\sim$May Do$(q, \sim F)$.

The following instance of FI is thereby obtained:

(1) May Do(p, May Do(q, F) & $\sim$May Pass(q, F) & $\sim$May Do$(q, \sim F)$) $\leftrightarrow$ May(May Do(q, F) & $\sim$May Pass(q, F) & $\sim$May Do$(q, \sim F)$) & May Do(p, May Do(q, F)) & May Do(p, $\sim$May Pass(q, F)) & May Do(p, $\sim$May Do$(q, \sim F)$).

The most obvious feature of (1)—its length, with the consequent difficulty of reading—can be ameliorated by reformulation, taking advantage of a result from Chapter 3, namely that

(2) May Do(q, F) & $\sim$May Pass(q, F) & $\sim$May Do$(q, \sim F)$

is equivalent to each of

(2′) Shall Do(q, F),
(2″) $\langle q, F\rangle \in T_5$.

Statement (1) is therefore equivalent to each of

(1′) May Do(p, Shall Do(q, F)) $\leftrightarrow$ May Shall Do(q, F) & May Do(p, May Do(q, F)) & May Do(p, $\sim$May Pass(q, F)) & May Do(p, $\sim$May Do$(q, \sim F)$),

(1″) May Do(p, $\langle q, F\rangle \in T_5$) $\leftrightarrow$ May($\langle q, F\rangle \in T_5$) &
May Do(p, May Do(q, F)) &
May Do(p, $\sim$May Pass(q, F)) &
May Do(p, $\sim$May Do(q, $\sim F$)).

The content of (1″) can be seen with the help of the diagrammatic representation of T_5:

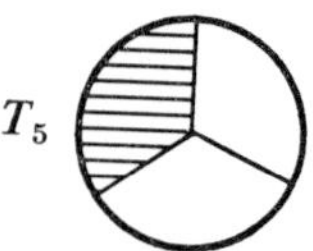

(cf. p. 106). (1″) says that p may see to it that $\langle q, F\rangle$ belongs to T_5 if and only if the following holds true: it is not forbidden that $\langle q, F\rangle$ belongs to T_5, p may see to it that $\langle q, F\rangle$ belongs to the shaded left-hand sector (the factor L_1), p may see to it that $\langle q, F\rangle$ belongs to the unshaded lower sector (the factor $\overline{L_2}$) and p may see to it that $\langle q, F\rangle$ belongs to the unshaded right-hand sector (the factor $\overline{L_3}$). (Concerning the notion "factor", see above p. 107.)

The example used in Chapter 7, where p and q made a contract (p. 222), can be used to illustrate FI. I supposed there that q needed someone who's responsibility it would be to see to it that £50 is paid to r and that q turned to p for this purpose. p and q made a contract according to which p would see to it that the money was paid to r. F denoted the state of affairs that £50 is paid to r from q's account, and I supposed that $\langle p, F\rangle$ was moved from T_6, i.e.,

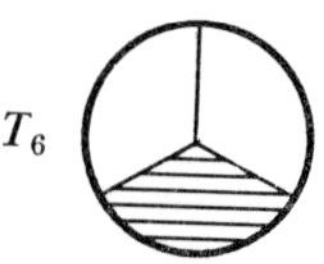

to T_5 upon the action of entering into contract. It was presupposed that no earlier contract obtained between p and q when the contract just described was made, and it therefore seemed reasonable to suppose that, at the time the contract was made, the following was the case:

(2) $\sim$May Do(p, $\langle p, F\rangle \in T_5$),
(3) $\sim$May Do(q, $\langle p, F\rangle \in T_5$),
(4) May Do($p+q$, $\langle p, F\rangle \in T_5$).

It is easier to appreciate the appropriateness of (2)–(4) in the light of FI. Since p is a private person not employed by either of q or r, q should not be permitted to impose upon p to be active in any way with respect to F; in other words, we should suppose that

(5) $\sim$May Do(q, $\sim$May Pass(p, F)).

(5) means that q may not see to it that $\langle p, F\rangle$ belongs to the lower, unshaded sector of T_5. It follows from FI and (5) that q may not see to it that $\langle p, F\rangle$ belongs to T_5; i.e., it follows that (2) is true. Since p was, before the drawing up of the contract, an independent private person having nothing to do with q's affairs, it should furthermore be supposed that p may not himself see to it that p may see to it that F; it should thus be supposed that

(6) $\sim$May Do(p, May Do(p, F)).

(6) means that p may not see to it that $\langle p, F\rangle$ belongs to the left-hand shaded sector in T_5. It follows from FI and (6) that p may not see to it that $\langle p, F\rangle$ belongs to T_5; i.e., it follows that (3) is true. Finally, it should be supposed that the legal power that p and q enjoy together in the example should be of more consequence than that which each of p and q had separately. More precisely, it should normally (i.e., when it is a question of the usual sort of payment where the money is not intended to be used for illegal purposes or suchlike) be possible to suppose that

(7) May Do($p+q$, May Do(p, F)),
(8) May Do($p+q$, $\sim$May Pass(p, F)),
(9) May Do($p+q$, $\sim$May Do(p, $\sim F$)).

are the case. (7)–(9) mean that p and q may together see to it that $\langle p, F\rangle$ is a member of each sector of T_5. Given (7)–(9), where (7) is already based on the assumption that the money is not intended for illegal purposes or suchlike, it is clear that in an example of the present kind it may also be supposed that

(10) May($\langle p, F\rangle \in T_5$).

It follows from FI and (7)–(10) that p and q together may see to it that $\langle p, F\rangle$ belongs to T_5; i.e., it follows that (4) is true.

As was apparent from (1″) and further clarified by the example, FI means that an agent p may see to it that a pair $\langle q, F\rangle$ belongs to a given one-agent type T if and only if $\langle q, F\rangle$ may belong to T and, for each sector (or factor) from which T is constituted, p may see to it that $\langle q, F\rangle$ belongs to this sector (factor). In the next two sections I shall discuss the content of this rule in more detail.

3. *The left-to-right implication of the rule* FI

FI is formulated as a bi-conditional. The implication from left to right says that for those possible values of X_1, X_2 and X_3 given above (where q now replaces s' and F replaces A)

(1) $$\text{May Do}(p, X_1 \,\&\, X_2 \,\&\, X_3) \rightarrow \text{May}(X_1 \,\&\, X_2 \,\&\, X_3)$$

and

(2) $$\text{May Do}(p, X_1 \,\&\, X_2 \,\&\, X_3) \rightarrow \text{May Do}(p, X_1) \,\&\, \text{May Do}(p, X_2) \,\&\, \text{May Do}(p, X_3).$$

Statement (1) needs no comment at this stage since it follows from the rules introduced in Chapter 2. But the same is not true of (2). (2) would be logically valid if the operator Do obeyed the axiom

(3) $$\text{Do}(p, F \,\&\, G) \rightarrow \text{Do}(p, F),$$

where F and G denote arbitrary states of affairs. Some authors have in fact adopted (3), reading Do as "sees to it that" (Pörn, 1970, pp. 9 f. adopts it for his operator D_i, though in Pörn, 1974, he does not adopt it for his E_a). However, a consequence of (3)'s being logically valid is that we obtain as a rule of deduction

(4) $$\text{If} \vdash (F \rightarrow G), \text{then} \vdash (\text{Do}(p, F) \rightarrow \text{Do}(p, G))$$

and the theorem

(5) $$\text{Do}(p, F) \rightarrow \text{Do}(p, G \vee \sim G).$$

(5) means that if, for some F, p sees to it that F, then p sees to it that each tautology is the case. For reasons already discussed (Chapter 2, p. 76), this is unacceptable.

A weaker axiom, more plausible than (3), is

(6) $$\text{May Do}(p, F \,\&\, G) \rightarrow \text{May Do}(p, F),$$

from which follows the rule

(7) If $\vdash (F \rightarrow G)$, then $\vdash$ (May Do$(p, F) \rightarrow$ May Do(p, G))

and the theorem

(8) May Do$(p, F) \rightarrow$ May Do$(p, G \vee \sim G)$.

(8) says that if p may see to it that some state of affairs F is the case, then p may see to it that every tautology is the case. (8) might be regarded less dubious than (5) since, if it is maintained that in practice an agent never brings about a tautology, then it is a quite harmless supposition that an agent *may* see to it that a tautology is the case. On the other hand, (6)–(8) can be positively harmful in so far as they restrict further development of the logic of the Do operator. For some one might well want to introduce the rule

(9) If $\vdash F$, then $\vdash \sim$Do(p, F),

according to which it is absurd to say that an agent brings about a tautology, and though (9) has not been adopted in this book, it is by no means implausible. But (6) and (9) cannot stand side by side in the same logical system since, given the remaining rules for Do and Shall, it follows from (9) that

(10) $\sim$May Do$(p, G \vee \sim G)$,

which, if (8) were in the system, would in turn imply

(11) $\sim$May Do(p, F).

In other words, (6) and (9) together entail that no agent may ever bring about a state of affairs!

However, none of these drawbacks for (3) and (6) apply to (2) since X_1, X_2 and X_3 are statements of a special kind; in fact no untoward consequences result from (2), making its adoption as a rule of feasibility non-controversial. The case for (2) could perhaps be pressed to give it the status of a logical axiom; however I maintain it only as a rule of feasibility because of its relatively complicated structure given the restrictions on X_1, X_2 and X_3. Logical rules should be simple.

4. *The right-to-left implication of the rule* FI

The implication from right to left in FI means that, for permitted values of X_1, X_2 and X_3 (where again q replaces s' and F replaces A),

(1) May(X_1 & X_2 & X_3) & May Do(p, X_1) & May Do(p, X_2) & May Do(p, X_3)$\rightarrow$May Do(p, X_1 & X_2 & X_3).

This rule is both less obviously appropriate and more interesting than the one discussed in the previous section. I shall begin by considering a putative counter-example. Suppose p is a despotic king, q a prime minister and r a commander-in-chief, all of the land Ruritania; and let F be the state of affairs that the country's army is mobilised. The point of the example revolves around the legal power (in the sense of permission) which p and q have concerning the movement of $\langle r, F\rangle$ between two one-agent types. King p, being the despot he is, may of course move $\langle r, F\rangle$ between different types according to his inclination, even to the extent that

(2) May Do(p, May Do(r, F) & May Pass(r, F) & May Do(r, $\sim F$))

is true. Suppose, moreover, that so far as q is concerned, we have

(3) May Do(q, Shall Do(r, F)),
(4) May Do(q, Shall Pass(r, F)),
(5) May Do(q, Shall Do(r, $\sim F$)).

In other words, q may order r to mobilise the army, to remain passive, or to ensure that the army is not mobilised. From (2)–(5) it follows, given FI, that

(6) May Do(q, May Do(r, F) & May Pass(r, F) & May Do(r, $\sim F$)).

Proof

From (3)–(5) it follows from the left-to-right implication of FI that

(i) May Do(q, May Do(r, F)) & May Do(q, May Pass(r, F)) & May Do(q, May Do(r, $\sim F$)).

From (2) we have according to the logic for Do and Shall

(ii) May(May Do(r, F) & May Pass(r, F) & May Do(r, $\sim F$)).

And from (i) and (ii) we get (6), this time by the right-to-left implication of FI.

But is it not possible in an example of this kind that whilst (2)–(5) are true, (6) is false? Is it not possible that p, the despotic king, has legal power according to (2) whilst q, a mere prime minister, does not have the same kind of legal power as he would have according to (6)? Before proceeding further, a more convenient formulation is obtained by replacing (2) and (6) with their respective equivalents

(2′) May $\text{Do}(p, \langle r, F\rangle \in T_1)$,
(6′) May $\text{Do}(q, \langle r, F\rangle \in T_1)$.

The question is then whether (2′) and (3)–(5) can all be true whilst (6′) is false. Now note that (6′) is equivalent to the disjunction of the two statements

(7) $\text{May}(\text{Do}(p, \langle r, F\rangle \in T_1) \;\&\; \text{Do}(q, \langle r, F\rangle \in T_1))$,
(8) $\text{May}(\sim\text{Do}(p, \langle r, F\rangle \in T_1) \;\&\; \text{Do}(q, \langle r, F\rangle \in T_1))$.

Accordingly, the denial of (6′) in the example is tantamount to denying both (7) and (8). As the example was formulated, it is quite possible to deny (8): it is possible that q may not *alone* see to it that $\langle r, F\rangle$ belongs to the free type T_1. Such a supposition is, of course, compatible with

(9) $\text{May}(\text{Do}(p, \langle r, F\rangle \in T_1) \;\&\; \sim\text{Do}(q, \langle r, F\rangle \in T_1))$

which means that it may be the case that p sees to it that $\langle r, F\rangle \in T_1$ without q also seeing to it. (8)'s being false and (9)'s being true mean that king p has, in a certain respect, greater legal power than q. On the other hand, it is not appropriate to deny (7) in the same sense, and it is difficult to find an adequate motivation for a system of legal rules where (2)–(5) are all true but both of (7) and (8) false. In the particular example under discussion it is difficult to see why it could possibly be forbidden that the prime minister q coordinates his behaviour with the king's so that q also sees to it that $\langle r, F\rangle \in T_1$ given p also brings about the same thing. (Remember q's seeing to it that $\langle r, F\rangle \in T_1$ need not necessarily occur as a result of q's actively taking steps in that direction; it might also occur by *null action* (cf. p. 70)). From (7) it follows, however, that (6′) and (6) are true, and so the supposition of the truth of (7) means there is no counter-example to FI.

(There are, of course, many variations on this example. A similar situation in the area of the rights of private individuals is, for example, easily obtained if (2)–(5) are reinterpreted, letting F be an action relating to an object owned by p, and q and r are two people employed in p's service.)

The argument I used in considering this example can be generally described as an argument to the effect that a certain supposition which prima facie seems to be of the kind

(10) $\sim$May Do(q, G)

is in fact more accurately described as being of the kind

(11) $\sim$May($\sim$Do(p, G) & Do(q, G)).

In this way a legal regulation is seen to be better described in collectivistic rather than individualistic terms (cf. Chapter 5, pp. 172 f.). That (10) appears to be the appropriate formulation may well have to do with the fact that jurists arguing in everyday language often fail to distinguish between the different kinds of collectivistic regulation of two parties' behaviour.

A similar argument can be used in other prima facie counter-examples to the right-to-left implication in FI. In what follows I shall disregard cases so constructed that FI does not hold: FI is, after all, a rule of feasibility. As we shall see, this is in fact favourable to the ensuing theory construction.

5. *Ranges of action and intermediate stations*

I shall now concentrate on the application of FI to the theory of ranges of action of one-agent types, where FI, together with the logical rules, yields an important theorem. This theorem deals with cases where T is intermediate between two one-agent types T' and T'' (cf. Chapter 3, p. 121). Consider, for the sake of illustration, the following extract of the Hasse diagram for one-agent types appearing on the next page. The diagram shows a deontic path between T_1 and T_5, which is minimal in $\{T_1, ..., T_7\}$ and where T_2 is intermediate. In this case the theorem says that if T_1 and T_5 belong to p's range of action with respect to $\langle q, F\rangle$ and it is not forbidden that $\langle q, F\rangle$ belongs to T_2, then T_2 also

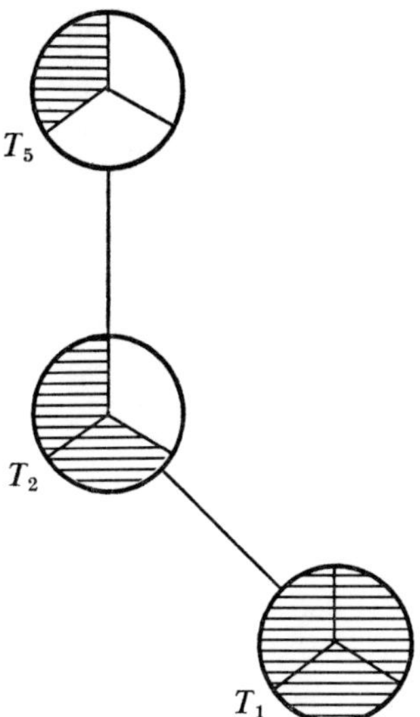

belongs to p's range of action with respect to $\langle q, F\rangle$. This means, among other things, that if T_2 is in any way a permitted type for $\langle q, F\rangle$, then it is precluded that p's legal power is restricted in such a way that p may only, for example, move $\langle q, F\rangle$ between the two types T_1 and T_5. Or again, consider the following diagram:

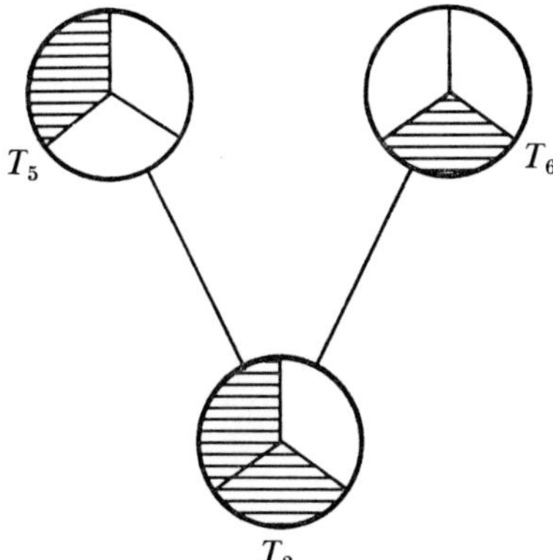

which shows a minimal deontic path between T_5 and T_6, and T_2 as an intermediate station. According to the theorem, if T_5 and T_6 belong to p's range of action with respect to $\langle q, F\rangle$, and it is not forbidden that

$\langle q, F \rangle$ belongs to T_2, then T_2 belongs to p's range of action too. The theorem is as follows (where T, T', T'', denote elements of $\{T_1, ..., T_7\}$):

THEOREM 1. *If T is intermediate between T' and T''*, T' and T'' *are members of $\mathcal{A}(p, \langle q, F \rangle)$, and May$(\langle q, F \rangle \in T)$, then T is a member of $\mathcal{A}(p, \langle q, F \rangle)$.*

(Informally expressed, if T is intermediate between T' and T'', both T' and T'' belong to p's range of action with respect to $\langle q, F \rangle$, and it may be the case that $\langle q, F \rangle$ belongs to T, then T belongs to p's range of action with respect to $\langle q, F \rangle$.)

Proof

(i) According to the definition of *intermediate* (p. 121), if T is intermediate between T' and T'', then each factor of T is a factor of T' or of T''.
(ii) From the left-to-right implication of FI it follows that if p may see to it that $\langle q, F \rangle \in T'$ and p may see to it that $\langle q, F \rangle \in T''$, then for each factor V of T', p may see to it that $\langle q, F \rangle \in V$, and, similarly, for each factor V of T'', p may see to it that $\langle q, F \rangle \in V$.
(iii) It follows from (i) and (ii) that if T is intermediate between T' and T'', p may see to it that $\langle q, F \rangle \in T'$, and p may see to it that $\langle q, F \rangle \in T''$, then for each factor V of T, p may see to it that $\langle q, F \rangle \in V$.
(iv) From the right-to-left implication of FI it follows that if it is permitted that $\langle q, F \rangle \in T$ and p may see to it that $\langle q, F \rangle$ belongs to each factor V of T, then p may see to it that $\langle q, F \rangle \in T$.

The theorem can be illustrated by the example concerning a contract which was used in Chapter 7 (see pp. 222 ff. for a description of the situation). It is plausible to suppose that, at the point in time when p and q have decided to make a contract, we have

(1) May Do$(p+q, \langle p, F \rangle \in T_5)$,
(2) May Do$(p+q, \langle p, F \rangle \in T_6)$,
(3) May $(\langle p, F \rangle \in T_2)$.

Supposition (1) has already been motivated (p. 224); (2) means that p and q may see to it that $\langle p, F \rangle$ *remains* in T_6 rather than being moved (a contract can, of course, be made to the effect that the legal situation is not changed); finally (3) says that it is not forbidden that $\langle p, F \rangle \in T_2$, which is obvious, given the state of affairs that F denotes. Under these conditions, it follows from the theorem that

(4) $\text{May Do}(p+q, \langle p, F\rangle \in T_2)$.

The example affirms the theorem since it is clear that in the situation of the example (4) is true. If, by the action of entering into contract, p and q move $\langle p, F\rangle$ from T_6 (where p is unauthorised to concern himself with the payment), the movement need not be to T_5 (where p is duty-bound to take care of the payment). If p and q so desire, they may content themselves with a movement of $\langle p, F\rangle$ to T_2, where p may bring about the payment, but is not duty-bound to do so.

6. *Restricted and unrestricted movement*

In this and the following section I shall consider the question of the possibility of reducing the number of ranges of action of one-agent types and then proceed to characterise those ranges remaining after the reduction. (The maximum possible number of ranges of one-agent types is 2^7; see Chapter 6, p. 218.). The result, which is an application of the theorem just proved dealing with ranges and intermediate stations, depends on a partition into two cells of the set of all ordered pairs $\langle p, F\rangle$ comprising an agent and a state of affairs. I shall give two different partitions. The first, to be presented in this section, is both natural and important from the viewpoint of jurisprudence. In the next section this partition is replaced by another which gives a greater breadth of results and which is more interesting from the point of view of legal philosophy.

The first division then, of interest from the point of view of jurisprudence, yields a class K and its complement as follows

$$\mathrm{K} = \{\langle p, F\rangle \mid \text{For each } T, \text{ May } (\langle p, F\rangle \in T)\},$$
$$\overline{\mathrm{K}} = \{\langle p, F\rangle \mid \text{For some } T, \sim\text{May } (\langle p, F\rangle \in T)\},$$

(where T is as usual an element of $\{T_1, ..., T_7\}$). K is the class of all $\langle p, F\rangle$ with *unrestricted movement*, whilst $\overline{\mathrm{K}}$ is the class of all $\langle p, F\rangle$ with *restricted movement*. A special subset of $\overline{\mathrm{K}}$ is then the class of *non-moveable* $\langle p, F\rangle$s:

$$\{\langle p, F\rangle \mid \text{For some } T, \text{ Shall } (\langle p, F\rangle \in T)\}.$$

The question whether a given pair $\langle p, F \rangle$ belongs to K or $\overline{\mathrm{K}}$ depends partly on the character of the F in question, and partly on properties of the agent p. I shall try to elaborate on this with the help of a few examples. Suppose first that F is the sort of state of affairs involved in everyday business transactions; for example, that a sum of money is paid from a bank account to a certain person, that certain goods are delivered, that a building is constructed at a certain place, etc. If F is of this kind and p is an accountable adult, there is in general no one-agent type T of which it is forbidden that $\langle p, F \rangle$ belongs to T. Which one-agent type $\langle p, F \rangle$ belongs to is here dependent on what one or more individuals or collective agents decide according to their own choice. For each T there is always some individual or collective agent who may place $\langle p, F \rangle$ in T. What is important in these cases is rather that different agents' ranges of action are distinguished in respect of the placing of $\langle p, F \rangle$. Certain agents, for example, simply have no legal power to place $\langle p, F \rangle$ anywhere; the range of action of these agents with respect to $\langle p, F \rangle$ is empty. Other agents perhaps have a non-empty, albeit small, range of action; there are, for example, two types T and T' such that they may move $\langle p, F \rangle$ between T and T' and only between these two. Still other agents might have a larger range of action; possibly the range includes all of $T_1, \ldots, T_7$. Suppose, on the other hand, that F is the state of affairs that q is killed by p, that q is maltreated by p, or suchlike; i.e., F is a state of affairs for which there exist strong legal preferences in favour of F or of $\sim F$. In that case it holds for certain one-agent types T that it is categorically forbidden that $\langle p, F \rangle$ belongs to T, and if T is such a type, then there is no agent whatsoever who may place $\langle p, F \rangle$ in T. If F is the state of affairs that q is killed by p we can, for example, take it that

$$(1) \qquad \sim \text{May}(\langle p, F \rangle \in T_5)$$

holds (i.e., it is not permitted that it shall be the case that p kills q). From (1) follows

$$(2) \qquad \sim (\exists r) \text{May Do}(r, \langle p, F \rangle \in T_5).$$

This means that, informally speaking, there is no agent r who may see to it that p is duty-bound to kill q.

The question whether a given pair $\langle p, F \rangle$ belongs to K or $\overline{\mathrm{K}}$ is, it might be thought, largely dependent on the character of F. But properties of p are also of significance. Suppose that F is of the same kind as exemplified above concerning payment of money, delivery of goods, and so forth; i.e., where there is no strong legal preference in favour of F or of $\sim F$. It might nevertheless be the case that certain one-agent types are forbidden for $\langle p, F\rangle$ because p has certain qualities. If p is a child or an irresponsible person it is possible that, for example, (1) and (2) are true, even if F concerns an ordinary payment of money. The reason is that children and irresponsible people may not be bound to make payments of money or other such business.

7. *Regular and irregular movement*

The class of $\langle p, F\rangle$ with unrestricted movement, where the decisive question is "Who is to be the master?" should a pair $\langle p, F\rangle$ be moved from one type to another, is a very significant and interesting class from the viewpoint of jurisprudence. But this class is a subset of a greater class I call the class of $\langle p, F\rangle$ with *regular movement*, to which a number of $\langle p, F\rangle$ with restricted movement also belong. The definition is as follows (let it be remembered that each one-agent type is the intersection of three factors taken from $\{L_1, L_2, L_3, \overline{L_1}, \overline{L_2}, \overline{L_3}\}$; cf. pp. 106 f.):

DEFINITION. Let T be a variable for elements of $\{T_1, ..., T_7\}$ and V a variable for elements of $\{L_1, L_2, L_3, \overline{L_1}, \overline{L_2}, \overline{L_3}\}$. The movement of $\langle p, F\rangle$ is *regular* $=_{\text{def}} (\forall T)[\sim \text{May}(\langle p, F\rangle \in T) \rightarrow (\exists V)(T \subseteq V \ \& \ \sim \text{May}(\langle p, F\rangle \in V))]$.

Informally expressed, the movement of $\langle p, F\rangle$ is regular if and only if for each one-agent type T, if it is not permitted that $\langle p, F\rangle$ belongs to T, then there is a factor V of T to which it is not permitted that $\langle p, F\rangle$ belongs. The movement of $\langle p, F\rangle$ is said to be *irregular* if and only if it is not regular.

It is obvious that for any pair $\langle p, F\rangle$, if the movement of $\langle p, F\rangle$ is unrestricted, it is also regular. According to the usual rules of predicate logic, we have

(1) $(\forall T)[\text{May}(\langle p, F\rangle \in T) \rightarrow [\sim \text{May}(\langle p, F\rangle \in T) \rightarrow (\exists V)(T \subseteq V \ \& \ \sim \text{May}(\langle p, F\rangle \in V))]]$,

from which it follows that

(2) $(\forall T)(\text{May}(\langle p, F\rangle \in T))$

implies

(3) $(\forall T)[\sim\text{May}(\langle p,F\rangle \in T) \rightarrow (\exists V)(T \subseteq V \,\&\, \sim\text{May}(\langle p,F\rangle \in V))]$.

However, a number of $\langle p, F\rangle$ with *restricted* movement also belong to the class of those with regular movement. Suppose, for example, that F is the state of affairs that q is killed by p. As in the previous section, it is reasonable to assume in this situation that

(4) $\sim$May Shall Do(p, F),

or, informally expressed, it may not be the case that p is duty-bound to see to it that q is killed by p. Expressed in terms of one-agent types, (4) means the same as

(5) $\sim\text{May}(\langle p, F\rangle \in T_5)$.

and the movement of $\langle p, F\rangle$ is thus restricted in this case. It ought further to be supposed that, for this p and F,

(6) $\sim$May May Do(p, F)

and

(7) Shall May Do(p, $\sim F$).

(6) says that it is not permitted that p may see to it that q is killed by p, and (7) says that it shall be the case that p may see to it that q is not killed by p. (6) and (7) are equivalent, respectively, to the following statements expressed in terms of factors:

(6′) $\sim\text{May}(\langle p, F\rangle \in L_1)$,
(7′) $\sim\text{May}(\langle p, F\rangle \in \overline{L_3})$,

(see p. 106). Since T_5 is the intersection of L_1, $\overline{L_2}$ and $\overline{L_3}$, each of (6′) and (7′) implies

(8) $(\exists V)(T_5 \subseteq V \,\&\, \sim\text{May}(\langle p, F\rangle \in V))$;

that is to say, it follows both from (6′) and from (7′) that there is a factor V of T_5 to which it is not permitted that $\langle p, F\rangle$ belongs. Proceeding with what may be reasonable suppositions concerning the relation between $\langle p, F\rangle$ and the remaining one-agent types T_1, T_2, T_3, T_4, T_6 and T_7, it turns out that for each T it remains the case that either

(11) $\quad \text{May}(\langle p, F\rangle \in T)$

is true (this is reasonable if T is T_7) or

(12) $\quad \sim\text{May}(\langle p, F\rangle \in T)\ \&\ (\exists V)(T \subseteq V\ \&\ \sim\text{May}(\langle p, F\rangle \in V))$

is true (this is reasonable if T is T_1, T_2, T_3, T_4, T_5 or T_6). (3) above is therefore true for the given value of F and the movement of $\langle p, F\rangle$ is regular, albeit restricted.

That the movement of a given pair $\langle p, F\rangle$ is *irregular* means, according to the definition, that

(13) $\quad (\exists T)[\sim\text{May}(\langle p, F\rangle \in T)\ \&\ (\forall V)(T \subseteq V \rightarrow \text{May}(\langle p, F\rangle \in V))]$

is the case. That is to say, for some one-agent type T it is not permitted that $\langle p, F\rangle$ belongs to T, but it is permitted that $\langle p, F\rangle$ belongs to each of T's factors. An illustration of (13) can be obtained by developing further the example of the football match in Chapter 4 (Example 7, p. 136). To begin with, suppose the same assumptions are made as in the original example. A football match is to be played between United and City, United defending the scoreboard end goal, City defending the Stretford end goal, and F is the state of affairs that the ball rests at the back of the scoreboard end goal. Suppose, in addition, that the players on each side are to be chosen from a certain set of people, and that no one has as yet been selected. There is a person, I shall suppose, (a coach, for example) who divides the players into two teams according to his own choice. Let p be one of the players to be assigned either to United's or City's team; the following are then reasonable assumptions:

(14) $\quad \text{May}(\langle p, F\rangle \in T_4)$;
(15) $\quad \text{May}(\langle p, F\rangle \in T_2)$;
(16) $\quad \sim\text{May}(\langle p, F\rangle \in T_1)$.

If p belongs to United's team, $\langle p, F\rangle$ will belong to T_4, and since p may belong to this team, (14) is a reasonable supposition. If, on the other hand, p belongs to City's team, $\langle p, F\rangle$ belongs to T_2 (the converse of T_4) instead, and since p may be selected for this team (15) is also an appropriate supposition. Finally, (16) is appropriate. For $\langle p, F\rangle \in T_1$ means that p may see to it that the ball lands in United's goal, but he may also prevent that occurring (and he may, moreover, remain passive). However, such a supposition about p's legal position seems to go against the spirit of the rules of football since it means that p is somehow playing for both sides simultaneously. Accordingly, it must be presumed that $\langle p, F\rangle$ is not permitted to belong to T_1; in other words, (16) is true. It is easily shown that (13) is a logical consequence of (14)–(16), and thus that the movement of $\langle p, F\rangle$ is irregular. T_2 is the intersection of L_1, L_2 and $\overline{L_3}$, and T_4 is the intersection of $\overline{L_1}$, L_2 and L_3. It follows from (14) and (15), therefore, (according to the logical rules governing the distribution of May in a conjunction), that

(17) $\quad \text{May}(\langle p, F\rangle \in L_1)\ \&\ \text{May}(\langle p, F\rangle \in L_2)\ \&\ \text{May}(\langle p, F\rangle \in L_3)$.

Since T_1 is the intersection of L_1, L_2 and L_3, (17) is equivalent to

(17′) $\quad (\forall V)(T_1 \subseteq V \rightarrow \text{May}(\langle p, F\rangle \in V))$.

It follows immediately that (13) is a logical consequence of (16) and (17′).

This example of the football match seems to be representative of the cases where the movement of $\langle p, F\rangle$ is irregular. There is in the example a rigid system of roles which can be distributed amongst a certain class of agents. For each role, he who plays that role has beforehand certain immoveably fixed relations to the players of the other roles; the precise way in which roles are distributed amongst the agents, however, is of less significance. This is often the case with various traditional games and activities involving role-playing.

I shall not speculate now on the possibility of developing a general theory of role-playing of this particular kind since it lies outside the scope of this book. The results that follow are confined to the class of pairs $\langle p, F\rangle$ with regular movement; but this class does include all such pairs with unrestricted movement as well as a considerable number with restricted movement.

The following theorem concerns classes with regular movement and it is of importance for what is to come in the next section; it is a generalisation of Theorem 1 (p. 240). T, as usual, is a variable over one-agent types.

THEOREM 2. *If T is intermediate between T' and T'', T' and T'' are members of $\mathcal{A}(p, \langle q, F\rangle)$ and the movement of $\langle q, F\rangle$ is regular, then T is a member of $\mathcal{A}(p, \langle q, F\rangle)$.*

Proof

(i) If T' and T'' are members of $\mathcal{A}(p, \langle q, F\rangle)$, it follows from the logical rules for Do and Shall that for each factor V of T', May($\langle q, F\rangle \in V$), and also for each factor V of T'', May($\langle q, F\rangle \in V$).
(ii) If T is intermediate between T' and T'', it follows by definition that each factor V of T is a factor either of T' or of T''.
(iii) From (i) and (ii), if T' and T'' are members of $\mathcal{A}(p, \langle q, F\rangle)$ and T is intermediate between T' and T'', then for each factor V of T, May($\langle q, F\rangle \in V$).
(iv) If the movement of $\langle q, F\rangle$ is regular, and for each factor V of T, May($\langle q, F\rangle \in V$), then May($\langle q, F\rangle \in T$).
(v) It follows from (iii) and (iv) that if T' and T'' are members of $\mathcal{A}(p, \langle q, F\rangle)$, T is intermediate between T' and T'', and the movement of $\langle q, F\rangle$ is regular, then May($\langle q, F\rangle \in T$). Theorem 2 follows immediately from (v) together with Theorem 1.

8. *Regular ranges of action*

When the expression "range of action" was first introduced towards the end of Chapter 6 (p. 215) it was defined as being a function whose value for a given argument is a subset of $\{T_1, ..., T_7\}$. Further, it was apparent that the expression could also be treated as a one-place predicate for the purpose of saying that a certain subset of $\{T_1, ...,, T_7\}$ is a range of action (p. 216). In the same way, the expression *regular range of action* can be used as a one-place predicate in accordance with the following definition:

DEFINITION. Let E be a variable over subsets of $\{T_1, ..., T_7\}$. E is a *regular range of action* $=_{\text{def.}}$ For some p, q and F, the movement of $\langle q, F\rangle$ is regular and $\mathcal{A}(p, \langle q, F\rangle) = E$.

Given the rule of feasibility FI, a number of results follow concerning regular ranges of action. The following theorem is a spring-board for what follows (T, T' and T'' are variables for one-agent types):

THEOREM 3. *If E is a regular range of action, T' and T'' are members of E and T is intermediate between T' and T'', then T is a member of E.*

This theorem is a corollary to Theorem 2 in the previous section given the definition of *regular range of action.* For consider the negation of Theorem 3, according to which there is a p, a q and an F such that T' and T'' are members of $\mathcal{A}(p, \langle q, F\rangle)$, the movement of $\langle q, F\rangle$ is regular and T is intermediate between T' and T''; but T is not a member of $\mathcal{A}(p, \langle q, F\rangle)$. Clearly this contradicts Theorem 2.

Theorem 3 means that a regular range of action cannot be an arbitrary subset of $\{T_1, ..., T_7\}$; only those subsets whose elements are related in a definite way ought to be considered. For example, consider the set $\{T_1, T_2, T_4\}$. It is easily seen that this is not a regular range of action since T_6 is intermediate between T_2 and T_4 (cf. the large Hasse diagram, p. 105), and therefore, if T_2 and T_4 belong to the range of action, so also must T_6 if the range of action is regular. The minimal range of action is therefore $\{T_1, T_2, T_4, T_6\}$, and this set is a regular range of action.

The following two theorems are useful in eliminating subsets of $\{T_1, ..., T_7\}$ which cannot be regular ranges of action. (The analogues of these theorems concerning ranges of action for two-agent types are of greater practical value where the number of ranges of action is greater and therefore less easily surveyed.)

THEOREM 4. *If E is a regular range of action, T' and T'' are members of E and T' and T'' have no factor in common, then $E = \{T_1, ..., T_7\}$.*

THEOREM 5. *If E is a regular range of action, T' and T'' are members of E, and $V_1, ..., V_n$ ($n \geqslant 1$) are the factors which T' and T'' have in common and $V_1, ..., V_n$ are factors of T, then T is a member of E.*

The proof of these theorems need not be presented here since they follow immediately from Theorem 3 together with the two theorems on intermediate stations given in Chapter 3 (p. 121).

Eliminating subsets of $\{T_1, ..., T_7\}$ which are not regular ranges of action, the following twenty-four sets remain (denoted by $E_1, ..., E_{24}$):

E_1. $\{T_1, ..., T_7\}$	E_9. $\{T_1, T_3\}$	E_{17}. $\{T_1\}$
E_2. $\{T_1, T_2, T_3, T_5\}$	E_{10}. $\{T_1, T_4\}$	E_{18}. $\{T_2\}$
E_3. $\{T_1, T_2, T_4, T_6\}$	E_{11}. $\{T_2, T_5\}$	E_{19}. $\{T_3\}$
E_4. $\{T_1, T_3, T_4, T_7\}$	E_{12}. $\{T_2, T_6\}$	E_{20}. $\{T_4\}$
E_5. $\{T_2, T_5, T_6\}$	E_{13}. $\{T_3, T_5\}$	E_{21}. $\{T_5\}$
E_6. $\{T_3, T_5, T_7\}$	E_{14}. $\{T_3, T_7\}$	E_{22}. $\{T_6\}$
E_7. $\{T_4, T_6, T_7\}$	E_{15}. $\{T_4, T_6\}$	E_{23}. $\{T_7\}$
E_8. $\{T_1, T_2\}$	E_{16}. $\{T_4, T_7\}$	E_{24}. $\varnothing$

9. *Greatest members, range converses and neutral ranges*

It is easily verified that each of the non-empty ranges of action $E_1, ..., E_{23}$ has a *greatest member* (cf. Stoll, 1963, p. 53) with respect to the relation "less free than".

DEFINITION 1. Let T and T' be variables for elements of $\{T_1, ..., T_7\}$ and E a variable for elements of $\{E_1, ..., E_{23}\}$. T is the *greatest member* of E with respect to the relation "less free than" $=_{\text{def.}}$ T is a member of E, and for each T', if T' is a member of E distinct from T, then T' is less free than T.

The following are the greatest members of the twenty-three non-empty ranges of action:

Range	*Greatest member*
E_1–E_4, E_8–E_{10}, E_{17}	T_1
E_5, E_{11}, E_{12}, E_{18}	T_2
E_6, E_{13}, E_{14}, E_{19}	T_3
E_7, E_{15}, E_{16}, E_{20}	T_4
E_{21}	T_5
E_{22}	T_6
E_{23}	T_7

That each of $E_1, ..., E_{23}$ has a greatest member means that the diagrammatic representation takes the form of a Hasse diagram (a "tree") in which there is just one lowest circle from which the tree spreads out upward. In some cases the tree has just one branch; in other cases there are several branches, which may come together in one uppermost circle or there may be several circles at the top. Consider, for example, the diagrams for E_8, E_5 and E_2:

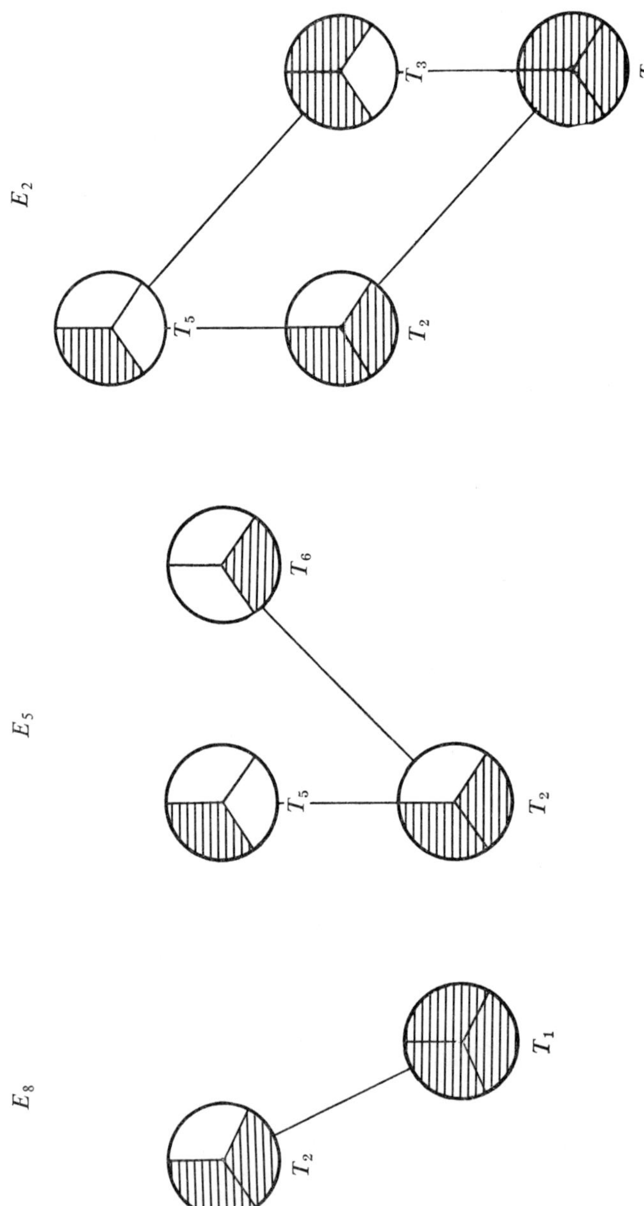
E_2
T_3
T_1
T_5
T_2
E_5
T_6
T_5
T_2
E_8
T_1
T_2

E_8 has just one branch, whilst E_5 has two branches terminating in two separate circles, and the two branches of E_2 come together in the same circle at the top.

That each of $E_1, ..., E_{23}$ has a greatest member is a consequence of FI and the logical rules for Do and Shall:

THEOREM 6. *Every non-empty and regular range of action for one-agent types has a greatest member with respect to the relation "less free than".*

Proof

(i) Let T, T' and T'' be variables over one-agent types. That T' and T'' are incomparable in respect to freedom means that they are distinct, T' is not less free than T'' and neither is T'' less free than T' (p. 110). Clearly, for each T' and T'', if they are incomparable then there is a one-agent type T which is intermediate between T' and T'', and more free than both of them.

(ii) It follows from (i) together with Theorem 3 that if E is a regular range of action, T' and T'' are members of E and incomparable in respect to freedom, then there is a T more free than both T' and T'' which is a member of E.

(iii) Suppose the negation of Theorem 6 is true. Then there is a regular range of action E with two members, T' and T'', such that no member of E is more free than either of T' or T'' and T' and T'' are incomparable. Obviously (iii) contradicts (ii).

The ranges of action $E_1, ..., E_{24}$ can be systematized by appealing to notions of *converse* and *neutral* analogous to those used for basic types of legal position (Chapters 3–5, p. 92, 131, 166).

DEFINITION 2. Let E and E' be subsets of $\{T_1, ..., T_7\}$. E is the *range converse* of E' $=_{\text{def.}}$ For every p, q and F, $\mathcal{A}(p, \langle q, F\rangle) = E$ if and only if $\mathcal{A}(p, \langle q, \sim F\rangle) = E'$.

DEFINITION 3. Let E be a subset of $\{T_1, ..., T_7\}$. E is *range neutral* $=_{\text{def.}}$ For every p, q and F, $\mathcal{A}(p, \langle q, F) = E$ if and only if $\mathcal{A}(p, \langle q, \sim F\rangle) = E$ (i.e., E is its own range converse).

The following classification is obtained:

Range converses		*Range neutral sets*	
E_2, E_4	E_{12}, E_{15}	E_1	E_{17}
E_5, E_7	E_{13}, E_{14}	E_3	E_{19}
E_8, E_{10}	E_{18}, E_{20}	E_6	E_{22}
E_{11}, E_{16}	E_{21}, E_{23}	E_9	$\varnothing$

10. *Regular ranges of action: Some examples*

Each regular range of action is identical with one of the sets $E_1, ..., E_{24}$. That, conversely, each of $E_1, ..., E_{24}$ is a regular range of action must, however, be shown by example. I shall do no more here than illustrate a few points, leaving the task of finding suitable examples to the reader.

In those cases where p is distinct from q and where p's range of action with respect to $\langle q, F\rangle$ includes all of $T_1, ..., T_7$, p has a thoroughgoing "power of command" over q with respect to F. To illustrate this point, consider the following examples: p is the captain of a ship, q is an able seaman and F a state of affairs concerning the navigation of the ship; or, p is a military commander with the right to exercise command over q, and F is a state of affairs brought about in the line of duty; or, in legal systems of a capitalist kind, q is employed by p to look after a certain object owned by p; etc.

Apart from the employer – employee relation, the military chain of command, and suchlike, it is not easy to find examples where p has such thoroughgoing power of command over q. But there are many examples to be found where p, within the framework of a smaller range of action, may move $\langle q, F\rangle$ just a few stages up the tree to a less free type. To illustrate, consider the situation of offer and acceptance in the law of contract. Suppose q has made an offer of a certain sum of money to p for some consideration—delivery of goods, for example. p may then, by accepting the offer, see to it that q is obliged to pay the sum agreed. For example, let F be the state of affairs that £50 is credited to p's bank account on 1st July 1976. Provided no previous contract exists between them, it is reasonable to suppose that q has a legal position of type T_2 with respect to F. In other words, q may see to it that £50 is credited to p's account on 1st July 1976, but he may not prevent its occurrence; he may, on the other hand, remain passive, neither seeing to nor preventing the money being deposited. It can also be reasonably supposed that p's range of action with respect to $\langle q, F\rangle$

contains T_2 as its only element. Suppose, then, that it is in this situation that q makes an offer to p: q offers to credit £50 to p's account on the 1st July if p promises to deliver certain goods to q subsequently. When p hears of the offer, q's legal position with respect to F is the same as before: $\langle q, F\rangle \in T_2 \cdot p$, on the other hand, has a greater range of action with respect to $\langle q, F\rangle$ as a consequence of receiving the offer: p may see to it that q shall see to it that £50 is credited to his account on the day agreed. This means that p may move $\langle q, F\rangle$ upwards in the tree from T_2 to T_5, p's range of action now including both T_2 and T_5. The value of the offer to p lies precisely in increasing his range of action from $\{T_2\}$ to $\{T_2, T_5\}$.

There are also many examples where p may move $\langle q, F\rangle$ downwards in the tree to a more free type. For example, consider a simple case of debt arising from a loan. Suppose q has borrowed £50 from p, promising to repay it by crediting p's account on 1st July 1976. Let F be, as in the previous example, that £50 is credited to p's account on the date in question. To begin with, then, q shall see to it that the money is paid in; i.e., $\langle q, F\rangle \in T_5$. As is usual with monetary debts, however, p may, by remitting the debt, move $\langle q, F\rangle$ downwards in the tree to T_2, in which case p's range of action is reduced from $\{T_2, T_5\}$ to $\{T_2\}$.

Another kind of example is obtained if F is the state of affairs that p is not killed by q. Even here, it is appropriate to assume that $\langle q, F\rangle \in T_5$; i.e., it shall be the case that q sees to it that p is not killed by q. In that case p's range of action is reasonably supposed to comprise just T_5: p may see to it that $\langle q, F\rangle$ remains in T_5 (which can occur by *null action*), but p may not move $\langle q, F\rangle$ downwards in the tree to a more free type. (The difference between this case and the previous one has a certain connection with the difference between unrestricted and restricted movement, and I shall return to these examples in the next section.)

As a final illustration I shall take up the question of p's range of action with respect to $\langle q, F\rangle$ where F is a tautology or a contradiction. This may seem of little direct interest for jurisprudence, but is of some interest in connection with the logic of Shall and Do. I have already had cause to mention that

(1) If $\vdash F$, then $\vdash \sim \mathrm{Do}(p, F)$

would not be an inappropriate strengthening of the logical rules for Do, saying as it does that it would be absurd to say of a person that he brought about a tautology. From (1), together with the rules for Shall and Do introduced in Chapter 3 and the definitions of $T_1, ..., T_7$ and the function $\mathcal{A}$, it can be deduced that

(2) If $\vdash F$, then $\vdash \langle q, F \rangle \in T_6$

and

(3) If $\vdash F$, then $\vdash \mathcal{A}(p, \langle q, F \rangle) = \varnothing$.

(The proof is straightforward and therefore omitted here.) According to (2) and (3), if F is a tautology or a contradiction (T_6 is neutral), then for each q, $\langle q, F \rangle$ is and remains in T_6, and every agent's range of action with respect to $\langle q, F \rangle$ is empty. This consequence is quite plausible.

11. *Ranges of legal action and different subtypes of duty and right*

The theory of ranges of action can be used to throw some light on certain distinctions between various subtypes of the relations *duty* (*obligation*) and *right* (*claim*). Two of the examples from the preceding section can be used as illustrations. The following assumptions were made in a case of a money debt where F stands for the state of affairs that £50 is credited to p's account on 1st July 1976:

(1) $\langle q, F \rangle \in T_5$,
(2) $\mathcal{A}(p, \langle q, F \rangle) = \{T_2, T_5\}$.

In the example that followed, where F stands for the state of affairs that p is not killed by q, the following assumptions were made:

(3) $\langle q, F \rangle \in T_5$,
(4) $\mathcal{A}(p, \langle q, F \rangle) = \{T_5\}$.

According to (1) and (3), q can be said to have a duty or obligation with respect to F. Comparing (2) and (4), on the other hand, brings to light a clear distinction between the examples concerning p's range of action with respect to $\langle q, F \rangle$. In the first example, p has a certain degree of "control" over the placing of $\langle q, F \rangle$ within the one-agent types: p may, by remitting the debt, move $\langle q, F \rangle$ to T_2. But in the second case p

does not have this range of action. In fact $\langle q, F\rangle$ could be said to be *non-moveable* (cf. p. 241) in this latter case.

This distinction, expressed here in terms of ranges of action, can also be expressed in such a way as to illustrate two different subtypes of the relation *duty*. Understanding the situation in this way has, in fact, already been suggested on several occasions by Hart (1973, pp. 191 ff.; cf. 1962, p. 315 and 1953, pp. 16 f.). Hart says that he prefers to reserve the expression *relative duty* (which denotes a relation "correlative" to the relation *right*) for "the obligations of the civil law, such as those which arise under contracts or under the law of tort, and other civil wrongs" (1973, p. 191). If q has a relative duty and p a correlative right, the situation is characterised, according to Hart, by p having "control" over q's duty:

> The idea is that of one individual being given by the law exclusive control, more or less extensive, over another person's duty so that in the area of conduct covered by that duty the individual who has the right is a small-scale sovereign to whom the duty is owed. (1973, p. 192)

Hart would say that this control entails, first and foremost, that "the right holder may waive or extinguish the duty or leave it in existence" (1973, p. 192). If, on the other hand, q has an *absolute duty*, which covers "most duties under the criminal law" (1973, p. 191), the situation is characterised by there not being any right holder who has "control" over q's duty in the manner described.

Clearly, this distinction of Hart's is much the same as that drawn here and expressed as the distinction between, on the one hand (1) and (2), and on the other hand, (3) and (4) (leaving aside the question of the interpretation of the expressions "control" and "may" in the quotation from Hart). And as the theory of ranges of action also clearly makes it possible to distinguish a large number of cases concerning both the range of p's control over $\langle q, F\rangle$ and the direction—upwards or downwards in the tree—in which p may move $\langle q, F\rangle$, the theory can also be used in this way as an instrument for the analysis of various other modifications of the notions of duty and right, though I shall not spell out the details here.

III. *Ranges of Action for Two-Agent Types*

1. *Introduction*

The general theory of ranges of action for one-agent types as presented here can be summarised in the following points: 1. The basis of the theory lies in the logical rules of Chapter 3 and the feasibility rule FI. 2. A number of terms were defined, the most important being *regular* and *irregular movement* of a pair $\langle p, F \rangle$, *regular range of action* and *greatest member* (p. 243. 247 and 249). 3. Of the theorems derived from the rules and definitions, the most important are the theorem on regular ranges of action and intermediate types (p. 248), which effects the reduction in the number of regular ranges of action, and the theorem that each regular range of action has a greatest member with respect to the relation "less free than" (p. 251).

Turning now to two-agent types, the account of ranges of action there deals with the movement of a triple $\langle q, r, F \rangle$, either within the set $\{R_1, ..., R_{35}\}$ of individualistic types or within the set $\{S_1, ..., S_{127}\}$ of collectivistic types. I shall argue that analogues of the feasibility rule FI can be motivated and maintained here for two-agent types. All the definitions can also be maintained with obvious modifications to suit these cases, and given this, the corresponding analogues of the theorems for one-agent types can be derived.

In view of this close analogy, my account of ranges of action for two-agent types will be brief and summary. I shall, in fact, concentrate on two points. The first concerns the formulation and motivation of the feasibility rules analogous to FI, which are the basis of the whole theory for two-agent types. Second, some brief comments are in order on the distinction between *regular* and *irregular movement*. This leads to problems which cannot be dealt with here, requiring further investigation outside the scope of this book.

2. *The rules of feasibility* FI′ *and* FI″

The feasibility rule for *individualistic* types, FI′, is formulated in terms of the following notation:

1. s, s' and s'' are arbitrary agent designators and A is an arbitrary well-formed statement.

2. $Y_1, Y_2, \ldots, Y_6$ are schemata given by:

Y_1 stands for one of:	Y_2 stands for one of:	Y_3 stands for one of:
May Do(s', A),	May Pass(s', A),	May Do(s', $\sim A$),
$\sim$May Do(s', A).	$\sim$May Pass(s', A).	$\sim$May Do(s', $\sim A$).
Y_4 stands for one of:	Y_5 stands for one of:	Y_6 stands for one of:
May Do(s'', A),	May Pass(s'', A),	May Do(s'', $\sim A$),
$\sim$May Do(s'', A).	$\sim$May Pass(s'', A).	$\sim$May Do(s'', $\sim A$).

The rule can now be expressed as follows:

FI′. $\text{May Do}(s, Y_1 \,\&\ldots\&\, Y_6) \leftrightarrow \text{May}(Y_1 \,\&\ldots\&\, Y_6) \,\&$
$\text{May Do}(s, Y_1) \,\&\ldots\&\, \text{May Do}(s, Y_6)$.

The analogy between FI and FI′ is apparent; the only difference lies in the replacement of X_1, X_2, and X_3 by $Y_1, \ldots, Y_6$ (an individualistic two-agent type has six factors whereas a one-agent type has just three). FI′ says that an agent p may see to it that a triple $\langle q, r, F\rangle$ belongs to a given individualistic type R if and only if it is not forbidden that $\langle q, r, F\rangle$ belongs to R and, moreover, p may see to it that $\langle q, r, F\rangle$ belongs to each factor of R.

It is as well to recall here that any individualistic type $R_1, \ldots, R_{35}$ can be construed as an ordered pair $\langle T, T'\rangle$ of two one-agent types (p. 129), because this facilitates the understanding of what it is that FI′ expresses. Suppose R is an individualistic two-agent type and T and T' are one-agent types. Then, given FI, FI′ amounts to

(1) $R = \langle T, T'\rangle \rightarrow (\text{May Do}(p, \langle q, r, F\rangle \in R) \leftrightarrow \text{May}(\langle q, r, F\rangle \in R)$
$\&\ \text{May Do}(p, \langle q, F\rangle \in T) \,\&\, \text{May Do}(p, \langle r, F\rangle \in T'))$,

which can be equivalently formulated as

(1′) $\text{May Do}(p, \langle q, r, F\rangle \in \langle T, T'\rangle) \leftrightarrow \text{May}(\langle q, r, F\rangle \in \langle T, T'\rangle) \,\&$
$\text{May Do}(p, \langle q, F\rangle \in T) \,\&\, \text{May Do}(p, \langle r, F\rangle \in T')$.

(1) and (1′) entail that an agent p may see to it that a triple $\langle q, r, F\rangle$ belongs to a given individualistic type R if and only if it is not forbidden that $\langle q, r, F\rangle$ belongs to R and, moreover, p may see to it that $\langle q, F\rangle$ belongs to the one-agent type which constitutes the first coordinate of R and may also see to it that $\langle r, F\rangle$ belongs to the second coordinate

of R. (The proof that (1) and (1′) do indeed follow from FI and FI′ is not difficult if it is borne in mind that each statement of the form $\langle q, r, F\rangle \in R$ is an instance of Y_1 & ... & Y_6, each statement of the form $\langle q, F\rangle \in T$ is an instance of X_1 & X_2 & X_3 and of Y_1 & Y_2 & Y_3, and each statement of the form $\langle r, F\rangle \in T'$ is an instance of X_1 & X_2 & X_3 and of Y_4 & Y_5 & Y_6. The details will not be spelt out here.)

The feasibility rule FI″ for collectivistic types follows the same pattern. With the notation

1. s, s' and s'' are arbitrary agent designators and A is an arbitrary well-formed statement,

2. Z_1, ..., Z_7 are schemata given by:
   Z_1 stands for one of: May(Do(s', A) & Do(s'', A)),
   ~May(Do(s', A) & Do(s'', A)),
   Z_2 stands for one of: May(Do(s', A) & ~Do(s'', A)),
   ~May(Do(s', A) & ~Do(s'', A)),
   Z_3 stands for one of: May(Do(s', ~A) & Do(s'', ~A)),
   ~May(Do(s', ~A) & Do(s'', ~A)),
   Z_4 stands for one of: May(Do(s', ~A) & ~Do(s'', ~A)),
   ~May(Do(s', ~A) & ~Do(s'', ~A)),
   Z_5 stands for one of: May(~Do(s', A) & Do(s'', A)),
   ~May(~Do(s', A) & Do(s'', A)),
   Z_6 stands for one of: May(~Do(s', ~A) & Do(s'', ~A)),
   ~May(~Do(s', ~A) & Do(s'', ~A)),
   Z_7 stands for one of: May(Pass(s', A) & Pass(s'', A)),
   ~May(Pass(s', A) & Pass(s'', A)),

the rule can be expressed as follows:

FI″. MayDo(s, Z_1 & ... & Z_7) ↔ May(Z_1 & ... & Z_7) & May Do(s, Z_1) & ... & May Do(s, Z_7).

Clearly, FI″ is also analogous to FI, X_1, X_2, and X_3 being replaced this time by Z_1, ..., Z_7 (each collectivistic type has seven factors). FI″ says that an agent p may see to it that a triple $\langle q, r, F\rangle$ belongs to a collectivistic type S if and only if it is not forbidden that $\langle q, r, F\rangle$ belongs to S and, in addition, p may see to it that $\langle q, r, F\rangle$ belongs to each factor of S.

FI, it will be remembered, was motivated by separately considering the two implications involved in the equivalence (p. 234, 236), and the same kind of argument can be brought forward in favour of FI′ and FI″. There is no relevant distinction between one-agent types and either of the systems of two-agent types that merits special comment in this connection.

3. *Regular and irregular movement*

The movement of a triple $\langle p, q, F\rangle$ which is regular within the set of individualistic types I shall call *R-regular*. The definition is completely analogous to the corresponding one for one-agent types, but I shall formulate it here explicitly in order to facilitate what follows (it should be remembered that individualistic types are intersections of six factors, p. 143).

DEFINITION 1. Let R be a variable over elements of $\{R_1, ..., R_{35}\}$ and V a variable over the factors of the elements in this set. The movement of $\langle p, q, F\rangle$ is *R-regular* $=_{\text{def.}} (\forall R)[\sim\text{May}(\langle p, q, F\rangle \in R) \rightarrow (\exists V)(R \subseteq V \,\&\, \sim\text{May}(\langle p, q, F\rangle \in V))]$.

The class of R-regular triples encompassed by this definition includes, as was the case for one-agent types, not only all $\langle p, q, F\rangle$ with unrestricted movement but an appreciable proportion of those with restricted movement too (cf. p. 243). However, I shall briefly consider some examples of triples whose movement is R-irregular. The first group of candidates are those where the movement of $\langle p, F\rangle$ and $\langle q, F\rangle$ is irregular within the system of one-agent types. It is useful here to return to the example of the football match again (p. 245). F remains as in the original example, and p and q are two players; the movement of $\langle p, q, F\rangle$ is then R-irregular since it may not be the case that p has a position of type R_1 against q with respect to F, but for each factor V of R_1, it may be the case that $\langle p, q, F\rangle$ belongs to V. I have already expressed some observations on cases of this kind (in terms of roles and role-playing; see p. 246). There is in addition another sort of case to be considered: the movement of a triple $\langle p, q, F\rangle$ can be irregular even though the movement of both $\langle p, F\rangle$ and of $\langle q, F\rangle$ is regular. This situation is characterised by the following state of affairs:

(1) $(\exists R)(\exists T)(\exists T')(R = \langle T, T' \rangle$ & $\text{May}(\langle p, F \rangle \in T)$ & $\text{May}(\langle q, F \rangle \in T')$ & $\sim\text{May}(\langle p, q, F \rangle \in R))$.

Consider cases of the kind where $\langle p, q, F \rangle$ may be moved between all *symmetric* individualistic types (p. 131) and only these. In such cases, (1) is true and the movement of $\langle p, q, F \rangle$ is R-irregular although the movements of $\langle p, F \rangle$ and $\langle q, F \rangle$ are regular.

The definition of *S-regular* movement follows a similar pattern.

DEFINITION 2. Let S be a variable over elements of $\{S_1, ..., S_{127}\}$ and V a variable over factors of the elements in this set. The movement of $\langle p, q, F \rangle$ is *S-regular* $=_{\text{def.}} (\forall S)[\sim\text{May}(\langle p, q, F \rangle \in S) \rightarrow (\exists V)(S \subseteq V$ & $\sim\text{May}(\langle p, q, F \rangle \in V))]$,

and again the familiar situation of the football match serves as the basis of an illustration. Thinking of the situation as described earlier (p. 245, 259), it is reasonable to make the following suppositions in terms of collectivistic types:

(1) $\text{May}(\langle p, q, F \rangle \in S_{89})$,
(2) $\text{May}(\langle p, q, F \rangle \in S_{97})$,
(3) $\sim\text{May}(\langle p, q, F \rangle \in S_{28})$.

(See the key to the definitions of the various types on p. 165.) It follows from (1)–(3) that the movement of $\langle p, q, F \rangle$ is S-irregular.

CHAPTER 9

Commitment, Contract and Ranges of Legal Action

I. *Introduction*

The theory presented in this chapter deals with statements of the kind

$$\begin{cases} \mathcal{A}(p, \langle p, F\rangle) = \{T, T', ...\}, \\ p\text{'s range of action with respect to } \langle p, F\rangle = \{T, T', ...\}, \end{cases}$$

$$\begin{cases} \mathcal{A}(p+q, \langle p, F\rangle) = \{T, T', ...\}, \\ \text{The range of action of } p+q \text{ with respect to } \langle p\ F\rangle = \{T, T', ...\}, \end{cases}$$

$$\begin{cases} \mathcal{A}^{\mathrm{R}}(p+q, \langle p, q, F\rangle) = \{R, R', ...\}, \\ \text{The range of action}^{\mathrm{R}} \text{ of } p+q \text{ with respect to} \\ \langle p, q, F\rangle = \{R, R', ...\}, \end{cases}$$

$$\begin{cases} \mathcal{A}^{\mathrm{S}}(p+q, \langle p, q, F\rangle) = \{S, S', ...\}, \\ \text{The range of action}^{\mathrm{S}} \text{ of } p+q \text{ with respect to} \\ \langle p, q, F\rangle = \{S, S', ...\}, \end{cases}$$

where statements in each pair here are synomymous. As before, $T, T', ...$ denote one-agent types, $R, R', ...$ individualistic two-agent types and $S, S', ...$ collectivistic two-agent types, and this notation will be understood throughout this chapter. The statements at issue here concern the area in which one or two agents may change his or their *own* legal situation with respect to a certain state of affairs. It is usual in traditional legal philosophy and jurisprudence to say that these statements deal with the *autonomy* of an agent p or $p+q$ (cf. p. 213 for Ross' distinction between heteronomous and autonomous competence). Since $\mathcal{A}$, $\mathcal{A}^{\mathrm{R}}$ and $\mathcal{A}^{\mathrm{S}}$ are functions, with a given value for a given argument, the same idea can be expressed by saying that the arguments for $\mathcal{A}$, $\mathcal{A}^{\mathrm{R}}$ and $\mathcal{A}^{\mathrm{S}}$ have a certain structure. A glance at the statements in question shows that the arguments have one of the forms

(i) $\langle p, \langle p, F\rangle\rangle$,
(ii) $\langle p+q, \langle p, F\rangle\rangle$,
(iii) $\langle p+q, \langle p, q, F\rangle\rangle$,

where each agent variable occurring in the second argument place also occurs within the first argument place. Moreover, each expression in the first argument place is either an agent variable or an expression built up from agent variables with the operator $+$.

Note that the expressions (i) and (ii) can be regarded as of the form

(iv) $\langle r, \langle p, F\rangle\rangle$,

and (iii) as of the form

(v) $\langle r, \langle p, q, F\rangle\rangle$.

These last two expressions are of the kind used for arguments of $\mathcal{A}$, $\mathcal{A}^{R}$ and $\mathcal{A}^{S}$ in Chapter 8, and accordingly the general theory developed there applies to the present special case. That is to say, the rules of feasibility, definitions and theorems of the general theory hold good within the particular branch of the theory of ranges of action concerned with arguments of the kind (i)–(iii).

The discussion of more specific assumptions, over and above those of Chapter 8, is potentially a very large area, only one of which will be pursued here. The present approach is based upon the formation of collective agents using the operator "together with" in the sense of Chapters 6 and 7 (p. 214, 221). Many other approaches are possible; for example, the notion of an organisation considered as a collective agent can involve several different joining operators (cf. Pörn, 1971, pp. 38 ff.). However, the assumptions adopted here seem to be a natural way to begin the development of this particular area of the general theory. Firstly, the simplicity of the assumptions recommend them—the structure given by (i) presupposes only identity between the agents, whilst (ii) and (iii) identify an agent with one or another of two agents who act jointly. Identity is a standard concept in logic and "together with" is an everyday notion governed by simple logical rules (p. 221). Secondly, the resulting branch of the general theory has a significant area of application and of importance in both theory and practice. The whole question of autonomy of individuals or collective agents within legal change has always been at the centre of discussion in jurisprudence and political theory—cf. the controversy between classical liberalism and theories underlying the welfare state—as well as of practical interest to the legislator and to every citizen.

The most important areas in which autonomy of this kind is exercised are *commitment* and *contract*. The first of these can be illustrated by

(1) The Swedish Government commits itself to give economic aid for the rebuilding of Vietnam,

(2) John commits himself to not preventing Peter using the road going over his (John's) land,

which can be partially explicated along the lines

(1′) $\text{Do}(p, \text{Shall Do}(p, F))$,

(2′) $\text{Do}(p, \text{Shall} \sim\text{Do}(p, \sim F))$.

Examples of how two parties can together alter their legal situation by *contract* have already been given in Chapters 7 and 8 (see p. 222, 232, 240 for details). As the example in Chapter 7 stipulated, the statement

(3) $\text{Shall Do}(p, F)$

becomes true if p and q make a contract. The cooperation that occurs between them concerning the contract can be partially described by

(4) $\text{Do}(p+q, \text{Shall Do}(p, F))$,

where the operator + plays a very important role. Therefore, commitment and contract constitute what is essentially the area of application of this branch of the theory.

II. *Legal Autonomy and One-Agent Types*

1. *Initial considerations*

I shall formulate the feasibility rule for legal autonomy relating to one-agent types in the following section, and in the present section discuss the background and motivation behind this rule. My discussion will take the form of presenting what at first sight appears to be an attractive alternative version of the theory, based on a rule which is, however, unacceptable, because it leads to an oversimplified theory.

From the feasibility rule FI of Chapter 8 it follows that

(1) $\sim\text{May Do}(p, \text{May Do}(p, F)) \rightarrow \sim\text{May Do}(p, \text{Shall Do}(p, F))$,

(2) $\sim\text{May Do}(p, \text{May Pass}(p, F)) \rightarrow \sim\text{May Do}(p, \text{Shall Pass}(p, F))$.

(Cf. p. 231. Note that $\sim F$ may be substituted for F in (1).) (1) and (2) say that a person may not *commit* himself to a course of action which he may not *cause to be permitted.* The gist of (1) and (2) is thus that certain plausible restrictions obtain on the commitments anyone may enter into. The question then naturally arises whether anything positive can be said concerning what an agent *may* commit himself to. For example, do the converse implications of (1) and (2) hold? That is to say, are

(3) May Do(p, May Do(p, F)) $\rightarrow$ May Do(p, Shall Do(p, F)),
(4) May Do(p, May Pass(p, F)) $\rightarrow$ May Do (p, Shall Pass(p, F)),

acceptable general principles? (3) and (4) make the positive statement that someone may commit himself to any course of action which he may cause to be permitted.

Statements (3) and (4) are undoubtedly attractive for the builder of theories. Suppose, for example, that T_1 belongs to p's range of action with respect to $\langle p, F\rangle$, in which case it follows from FI that

(5) May Do(p, May Do(p, F))& May Do(p, May Pass(p, F))& May Do(p, May Do(p, $\sim F$)),

and from (5), with (3) and (4) in the system, it follows that

(6) May Do(p, Shall Do(p, F))& May Do(p, Shall Pass(p, F)) & May Do(p, Shall Do(p, $\sim F$)),

which says that T_5, T_6 and T_7 all belong to p's range of action with respect to $\langle p, F\rangle$ too. Repeated application of FI then leads to the result that if T_5, T_6 and T_7 belong to this range of action of p's and the movement of $\langle p, F\rangle$ is regular, then all of $T_1, ..., T_7$ belong to this range of action. Consequently, if in our example (3) and (4) belong to the system and the movement of $\langle p, F\rangle$ is regular, then T_1 belongs to p's range of action with respect to $\langle p, F\rangle$ if and only if each of $T_1, ..., T_7$ do. Accepting (3) and (4) means, in fact, that the theory would have as a theorem

(7) If the movement of $\langle p, F\rangle$ is regular, then for each T, T is a member of p's range of action with respect to $\langle p, F\rangle$ if and only if each T' less free than T is also a member of p's range of action with respect to $\langle p, F\rangle$.

Given a regular movement of $\langle p, F\rangle$, then, the number of non-empty ranges of action for p would be seven—the same as the number of one-agent types.

Unfortunately, (3) and (4) cannot be accepted as general principles because they do not take account of what are traditionally called *inalienable rights.* In certain circumstances when someone has a freedom to choose between several courses of action, it might be the case that this freedom may not be restricted either by the agent himself or by anyone else; this freedom would then be said to be "inalienable". For some p and F, this amounts to neither p nor any other agent being permitted to move $\langle p, F\rangle$ upwards in the Hasse diagram to a less free one-agent type; for other choices of p and F, there are at least some less free types to which $\langle p, F\rangle$ may not be moved. A person's right to either vote or refrain from voting for a registered political party, for example, might be considered and inalienable right in this sense. Thus, suppose a British citizen p is an accountable adult and F the state of affairs that p votes for the Labour Party. In this case it is reasonable to suppose that

(8) $\langle p, F\rangle \in T_1$,
(9) May Do(p, $\langle p, F\rangle \in T_1$),

where (8) means

(8a) p may see to it that p votes for the Labour Party,
(8b) p may see to it that p does not vote for the Labour Party,
(8c) It may be the case that p neither sees to it that p votes for the Labour Party nor sees to it that he does not,

and where (9) means that p may see to it that he retains the freedom he has according to (8a)–(8c). From these assumptions, it follows if (3) and (4) are general principles that

(10) May Do(p, $\langle p, F\rangle \in T_5$),
(11) May Do(p, $\langle p, F\rangle \in T_6$),
(12) May Do(p, $\langle p, F\rangle \in T_7$),

which mean, roughly, that p may commit himself to voting for the Labour Party and, moreover, p may also commit himself to not voting Labour.

But statements (10)–(12) are not plausible assumptions for this particular choice of p and F: the freedom p has according to (8) is inalienable and may not be restricted, either by p or anyone else. Thus, this p and F constitute a counter-example to (3) and (4), and many similar counter-examples are easily found. The practical importance of these counter-examples is too great to be disregarded by the theory; consequently, (3) and (4) are not acceptable as rules of feasibility.

The rule of feasibility FII (as well as FIII relating to contracts), which will be advocated here, is more carefully formulated so that a person's inalienable freedom in the sense just described is not overlooked. Nevertheless, the form of the feasibility rule is much the same as that of (3) and (4), and one of the most important results will be a theorem which is a modified version of (7). As just indicated, a similar feasibility rule dealing with contracts is also introduced from which an analogous result follows concerning how p together with another agent q may move $\langle p, F\rangle$ within the set of one-agent types.

2. *The rules of feasibility* FII *and* FIII

Using the following notation:

1. s and s' are arbitrary agent designators, and A is an arbitrary well-formed statement,
2. X and Y stand for different lines of the list
   Do(s, A),
   Pass(s, A),
   Do(s, $\sim A$),

the feasibility rules can be stated as follows:

FII. May Do(s, May X) & May$\sim$May $Y \rightarrow$ May Do(s, $\sim$May Y).

FIII. May Do($s+s'$, May X) & May$\sim$May $Y \rightarrow$
May Do($s+s'$, $\sim$May Y).

Their similarity is apparent; in fact, if FII is taken to be equivalent to

(1) May Do($s+s$, May X) & May$\sim$May $Y \rightarrow$
May Do($s+s$, $\sim$May Y)

then FII follows from FIII. This equivalence would follow from the rules for Shall, Do and + accepted here together with the additional rule

(2) $s+s=s$

for + (cf. p. 221). This being made clear, however, I shall continue to speak of FII as an independent rule.

3. *The import and application of* FII

It should be borne in mind when reflecting on the meaning of FII and FIII for a given choice of X and Y that the three statements

(i) Do(p, F)
(ii) Pass(p, F),
(iii) Do(p, $\sim F$),

describe three mutually inconsistent and jointly exhaustive courses of action for p with respect to F. Saying that the course of action described by one of these statements is forbidden is therefore equivalent to saying that the disjunction of the two remaining statements shall be the case. Similarly, forbidding two of the alternatives is tantamount to saying that the third shall be brought about.

FII says that p may, under certain conditions, render one of the alternatives (i)–(iii) *forbidden.* The conditions are two, namely 1. that p does not have an inalienable right to choose the course of action in question; in other words, it *may* be the case that this course of action is *forbidden* for p, and 2. that there is, amongst (i)–(iii) an alternative course of action which *p may cause to be permitted.* Suppose, for example, we ask whether John may see to it that it is forbidden that he prevents Peter using the road over his (John's) property. In this case John has no inalienable right to prevent Peter using the road; furthermore, there is clearly a different course of action which is both permitted for John and which he may see to it that it remains permitted—namely, that he is passive. From these suppositions it is reasonable to conclude that John may see to it that it is forbidden for him to prevent Peter using the road. Our question should, therefore, be answered in the affirmative. This conclusion can also be expressed by saying that John may commit himself to not preventing Peter using the road. It is easy to see how the conclusion can be formally deduced from the premises according to FII. The first supposition—that John does not have an inalienable right to prevent Peter using the road—can be expressed by

(1) $\text{May} \sim \text{May Do}(p, \sim F)$.

The second supposition—that John may see to it that it remains permitted for him to be passive—can be expressed by

(2) $\text{May Do}(p, \text{May Pass}(p, F))$,

and the conclusion by

(3) $\text{May Do}(p, \sim \text{May Do}(p, \sim F))$.

It is then apparent that (3) follows from (1) and (2) according to FII. The plausibility of the conclusion corroborates the appropriateness of FII.

It is worth contrasting this example with two more where the conditions in the antecedent of FII are not satisfied. Consider the question whether John may see to it that it is forbidden that he tries to save his own life. Surely in this case there is an inalienable right to the effect that it *shall* be the case that John *may* try to save his life. The antecedent of FII is thus not satisfied here and FII does not lead to the conclusion that John may commit himself to not trying to save his life. Expressed formally, since the *negation of*

(4) $\text{May} \sim \text{May Do}(p, F)$,

must be accepted for this choice of p and F, i.e.,

(5) $\text{Shall May Do}(p, F)$,

FII does not imply the conclusion

(6) $\text{May Do}(p, \sim \text{May Do}(p, F))$.

(According to the logical rules for Do and Shall we can, in fact, deduce the negation of (6) from (5).) A different case, but one where the conditions in the antecedent of FII are again not satisfied, is to be found in an example used earlier in Chapters 7 and 8 (p. 222, 232). Suppose, as before, p and q are two ordinary citizens between whom there is no contract of employment or suchlike, and F again stands for the state of affairs that

£50 is paid from q's account to a third person r. Then we can assume here, as before, that

(7) Shall Pass(p, F);

that is, p may neither see to nor prevent the money being paid. We can then ask whether p may see to it that he is not permitted to remain passive. The question is, then, whether

(8) May Do(p, $\sim$May Pass(p, F))

is to be supposed true or false, and the answer ought to be that (8) is false. This is easily shown to be compatible with FII. It must be supposed, in the example, that p may not see to it that it is permitted for him to make the payment, and neither may p see to it that it is permitted for him to prevent payment. In both cases q's complicity is required, q being the owner of the account. This supposition can be expressed by

(9) $\sim$May Do(p, May Do(p, F)),
(10) $\sim$May Do(p, May Do(p, $\sim F$)).

(9) and (10) do not enable us to draw the conclusion (8) from FII. Since Do(p, F), Pass(p, F) and Do(p, $\sim F$) are the only logically possible courses of action, (9) and (10) together imply that Pass(p, F) is the only course of action that p may cause to be permitted. Therefore, if (8) is thought of as a consequent of FII, the conditions in the antecedent are not satisfied. The example illustrates, then, that the formulation of FII takes into account that an agent may cause a certain course of action to be forbidden only if there is some other course of action available to him.

With a view to what will be said in the next section, it is as well to emphasise a central point again, namely that FII deals with how an agent may change his *own* legal situation. For, given that X and Y stand for different members of the list

Do(s, A),
Pass(s, A),
Do(s, $\sim A$),

it would be entirely inappropriate to adopt as a general principle

(11) May Do(s', X) & May$\sim$May $Y \rightarrow$ May Do(s', $\sim$May Y).

(11) would allow the deduction of a number of untenable statements from statements describing quite ordinary, everyday situations, concerning how an agent may change *another* agent's legal situation. The basic idea behind FII is that an agent has the legal power to commit himself according to certain general principles, and these principles fail to hold good when it comes to the question of one agent's legal power to commit another agent.

4. *The import and application of* FIII

Although FIII is thought of as a rule about how two different agents may together change the legal situation of one of them, it is based on the same general idea as FII—that there are general principles governing how an agent may commit himself which do not govern how one agent may commit another agent. Consider an arbitrary instance of FIII:

(1) May Do($p+q$, May Do(p, F)) & May ~ May Pass(p, F) → May Do($p+q$, ~ May Pass(p, F)).

If p and q are distinct, there are many choices of p, q and F for which the antecedent of (1) is true, but which would not justify assuming

(2) May Do(q, ~ May Pass(p, F)),

which says that q may negate p's right to remain passive. The consequent of (1), however, deals with how p and q *together* may restrict p's freedom, and for this reason the consequent of (1) would be an appropriate conclusion to draw provided the antecedent were true. It was argued in Chapter 7 (p. 225) that any statement of the form

(3) Do($p+q$, F),

read as "p and q together see to it that F", should be understood to mean that F is the case as a result of p and q supporting each other in seeing to it that F. The consequent of (1), namely

(4) May Do($p+q$, ~ May Pass(p, F)),

means, accordingly, that ~ May Pass(p, F) may become true as a result of p and q supporting each other in bringing about this state of affairs. Thus, the consequent of (1) deals only with those cases where p himself cooperates in seeing to it that ~May Pass(p, F); nothing is said about q's power to change p's legal situation when p refuses to go along with the change. The acceptability of FIII, then, depends upon the requirements of cooperation between the parties expressed by the operator "together with"; an agent's freedom may be restricted in this way only if that is in accordance with his own will.

5. *Two theorems on ranges of legal action and legal autonomy*

In this section I shall present a general theorem which follows from FII (together with FI) and an analogous theorem following from FIII. These two theorems constitute the fundamental point of departure for the conclusions which will be drawn in the next two sections.

THEOREM 1. *If T is a member of $\mathcal{A}(p, \langle p, F\rangle)$, T' is less free than T and May($\langle p, F\rangle \in T'$), then T' is a member of $\mathcal{A}(p, \langle p, F\rangle)$.*

The proof of this theorem will be presented in a fairly explicit form so that it can be followed step by step. Apart from the logical rules, the proof relies on feasibility rules FI and FII, the definitions of one-agent types T_1, ..., T_7 (p. 92) and liberty types L_1, L_2, L_3 (p. 106) as well as on the definitions of *range of action* (p. 215), *factor* (p. 107) and *less free than* (p. 107).

Proof

(i) From the left-to-right implication of FI and the definitions of the one-agent types, *range of action* and *factor* it follows that

(1) If $T \in \mathcal{A}(p, \langle p, F\rangle)$ and V is a factor of T, then May Do(p, $\langle p, F\rangle \in V$).

(ii) It follows immediately from (1) that

(2) If $T \in \mathcal{A}(p, \langle p, F\rangle)$ and V is a factor of T' such that V is also a factor of T, then May Do(p, $\langle p, F\rangle \in V$).

(iii) From the definitions of the one-agent types and liberty types, *less free than* and *factor* it follows that

(3) If $T'\mathcal{R}T$ and V is a factor of T' but not of T, then $V \in \{\overline{L_1}, \overline{L_2}, \overline{L_3}\}$.

(iv) Given the logical rules, the definitions of the one-agent types and *factor* yield

(4) If V is a factor of T' and May($\langle p, F\rangle \in T'$), then May($\langle p, F\rangle \in V$).

(v) From the definitions of the one-agent types and liberty types, *less free than* and *factor* it follows that

(5) If $T'\mathcal{R}T$ and V is a factor of T' but not of T, then there is a V' such that $V' \in \{L_1, L_2, L_3\}$, $V' \neq \overline{V}$ and V' is a factor of T.

(vi) From (1) and (5) it follows that

(6) If $T \in \mathcal{A}(p, \langle p, F\rangle)$, $T'\mathcal{R}T$ and V is a factor of T' but not of T, then there is a V' such that $V' \in \{L_1, L_2, L_3\}$, $V' \neq \overline{V}$ and May Do(p, $\langle p, F\rangle \in V'$).

(vii) From FII and the definitions of the liberty types it follows that

(7) If $V \in \{\overline{L_1}, \overline{L_2}, \overline{L_3}\}$, May($\langle p, F\rangle \in V$) and there is a V' such that $V' \in \{L_1, L_2, L_3\}$, $V' \neq \overline{V}$ and May Do(p, $\langle p, F\rangle \in V'$), then May Do($p$, $\langle p, F\rangle \in V$).

(viii) From (3), (4), (6) and (7) it follows that

(8) If $T \in \mathcal{A}(p, \langle p, F\rangle)$, $T'\mathcal{R}T$, V is a factor of T' but not of T and May($\langle p, F\rangle \in T'$), then May Do($p$, $\langle p, F\rangle \in V$).

(ix) From (2) and (8) we have

(9) If $T \in \mathcal{A}(p, \langle p, F\rangle)$, $T'\mathcal{R}T$ and May($\langle p, F\rangle \in T'$), then for each factor V of T', May Do(p, $\langle p, F\rangle \in V$).

(x) The definition of *factor* together with rhe right-to-left implication of FI yield

(10) If May($\langle p, F\rangle \in T'$) and for each factor V of T', May Do(p, $\langle p, F\rangle \in V$), then May Do($p$, $\langle p, F\rangle \in T'$).

(xi) From (9) and (10) it follows that

(11) If $T \in \mathcal{A}(p, \langle p, F\rangle)$, $T'\mathcal{R}T$ and May($\langle p, F\rangle \in T'$), then May Do($p$, $\langle p, F\rangle \in T'$).

(xii) Finally, (11) and the definition of *range of action* give

(12) If $T \in \mathcal{A}(p, \langle p, F \rangle)$, $T' \mathcal{R} T$ and May$(\langle p, F \rangle \in T')$, then $T' \in \mathcal{A}(p, \langle p, F \rangle)$,

which was to be proved.

Just as Theorem 1 is the basic result for the theory of *commitment* as based on FII, an analogous result within the theory of *contract* based on FIII is forthcoming, namely

THEOREM 2. *If T is a member of $\mathcal{A}(p+q, \langle p, F \rangle)$, T' is less free than T and May$(\langle p, F \rangle \in T')$, then T' is a member of $\mathcal{A}(p+q, \langle p, F \rangle)$.*

The proof follows precisely along the same lines as that of Theorem 1; all that is necessary to obtain the proof is to make the corresponding substitutions.

6. *Irregular and restricted movement and legal autonomy*

Two focal points emerge from the theorems just proved. One such is that the theorems express general principles for delimiting feasible ranges of action within the theory of commitment and contract, without otherwise restricting the values of the variables p, q and F, and regardless of whether the movement of $\langle p, F \rangle$ is restricted or unrestricted, regular or irregular. Another, is that the theorems effect a reduction in the number of ranges of action for the class of $\langle p, F \rangle$ with unrestricted movement in delimiting those ranges which are feasible. The second point will be discussed in the next section; in this section the first point will be considered in the context of some observations on cases where the movement of a given pair $\langle p, F \rangle$ is *irregular* or *regular but restricted.*

At this point, it is convenient to introduce the following term which will facilitate our discussion:

DEFINITION. The *maximal range of movement* of $\langle p, F \rangle =_{\text{def.}} \{T \mid \text{May}(\langle p, F \rangle \in T)\}$.

In other words, the maximal range of movement of a pair $\langle p, F \rangle$ is the set of all T to which $\langle p, F \rangle$ may belong. Clearly, each agent's range of action with respect to $\langle p, F \rangle$ is a subset of the maximal range of movement of $\langle p, F \rangle$.

It is entirely compatible with the rules introduced in this book that any non-empty subset of $\{T_1, ..., T_7\}$ is a maximal range of movement for *some* $\langle p, F\rangle$ whose movement is *irregular*. For example, $\{T_1, T_5\}$ could be the maximal range of movement for some pair $\langle p, F\rangle$, $\{T_1, T_3\}$ for another, $\{T_2, T_4, T_6\}$ for yet another, etc. (cf. the large Hasse diagram, p. 105). If the movement of $\langle p, F\rangle$ is *regular*, on the other hand, the maximal range of movement of $\langle p, F\rangle$ must be one of the twenty-three non-empty subsets of $\{T_1, ..., T_7\}$ denoted by $E_1, ..., E_{23}$ in Chapter 8 (p. 249); this follows immediately from the definition of *regular movement* (p. 243).

As was pointed out in Chapter 8, the development of the theory for pairs $\langle p, F\rangle$ with *irregular* movement falls outside the scope of this book. (In fact, it might well be thought that the two theorems are of less significance for this class of pairs $\langle p, F\rangle$.) However, I shall simply illustrate a conceivable range of action for p with respect to $\langle p, F\rangle$ in a case of irregular movement. A football match is to be played for charity between the village team and the team from the nearby mustard factory. F is the state of affairs that the ball lands in the net of the goal defended by the village team. Suppose p is someone who, because he both lives in the village and works in the mustard factory may choose between the following three alternatives: (i) p joins the village team; (ii) p joins the mustard factory's team; and (iii) p is a spectator, belonging to neither side. In view of the rules of football, then,

(1) $\sim \text{May}(\langle p, F\rangle \in T_1)$,
(2) $\sim \text{May}(\langle p, F\rangle \in T_3)$,
(3) $\sim \text{May}(\langle p, F\rangle \in T_5)$,
(4) $\sim \text{May}(\langle p, F\rangle \in T_7)$,

which means that T_1, T_3, T_5 and T_6 are excluded from the maximal range of movement of $\langle p, F\rangle$. On the other hand, we also have

(5) $\text{May}(\langle p, F\rangle \in T_2)$,
(6) $\text{May}(\langle p, F\rangle \in T_4)$,
(7) $\text{May}(\langle p, F\rangle \in T_6)$,

where (5) and (6) can be motivated by p's being permitted to join either of the two sides and (7) by p's being permitted to be a spectator. It follows from (1)–(7) that the maximal range of movement of $\langle p, F\rangle$ is the set $\{T_2, T_4, T_6\}$. Now, since p may choose between (i)–(iii), it can furthermore be supposed that

(8) May Do(p, $\langle p, F\rangle \in T_2$),
(9) May Do(p, $\langle p, F\rangle \in T_4$),
(10) May Do(p, $\langle p, F\rangle \in T_6$),

and from (1)–(10) it follows that

(11) $\mathcal{A}(p, \langle p, F\rangle) = \{T_2, T_4, T_6\}$.

Clearly, (11) is completely in accord with Theorem 1 (cf. the Hasse diagram, p. 105).

In order to illustrate some ranges of action where the movement of $\langle p, F\rangle$ is *regular but restricted*, let us suppose F stands for the state of affairs that q is in mortal danger (q being a different individual from p). Then we have

(12) $\sim$May May Do(p, F),
(13) Shall May Do(p, $\sim F$),

where (12) says, in more traditional idiom, that q has an inalienable right to the negative service that p *does not see to it* that he (q) is in mortal danger, and (13) says that p has an inalienable liberty right to *see to it* that q is *not* in danger of his life. It follows from (12) and (13) that the movement of $\langle p, F\rangle$ is restricted; the one-agent types T_1, T_2, T_3, T_5 and T_6 are excluded from the maximal range of movement of $\langle p, F\rangle$. But it is also reasonable to assume that

(14) May$\sim$May Pass(p, F),
(15) May May Pass(p, F),

where (14) says that p does not have an inalienable liberty right to remain passive and (15) says, given (12), that q does not have an inalienable right to the positive service that p sees to it that q is not in danger of his life. If, as might well be assumed in this case, the movement of $\langle p, F\rangle$ is regular, it follows from (12)–(15) according to FI that

(16) The maximal range of movement of $\langle p, F\rangle = \{T_4, T_7\}$.

I shall now give some illustrations of the range of action which p

and $p+q$ have with respect to $\langle p, F\rangle$. Concerning p's range of action two cases may be distinguished. The first, which is the more common of the two cases, occurs where there are no special circumstances giving rise to a duty for p to look after q. In such cases, p has a legal position of type T_4 with respect to F; i.e.,

(17) $\langle p, F\rangle \in T_4$,

and, furthermore, p may see to it that he retains this position; that is to say,

(18) May Do$(p, \langle p, F\rangle \in T_4)$.

From (16) and (18) it follows according to FII that

(19) $\mathcal{A}(p, \langle p, F\rangle) = \{T_4, T_7\}$;

i.e., p's range of action with respect to $\langle p, F\rangle$ consists of T_4, to which $\langle p, F\rangle$ belongs, and T_7, a less free type, where p has the duty to see to it that q is not in mortal danger. The conclusion that also T_7 belongs to p's range of action is entirely appropriate since in this instance p may potentially commit himself (by making a promise to q, or to q's parents, for example) to look after q. The second case begins with the supposition that p has a duty to look after q (because he has *already* promised to do so to q or to a third party r) instead of assuming (17); in other words, it is assumed that

(20) $\langle p, F\rangle \in T_7$.

In this case three alternative ranges of action for p are compatible with FII and the rules adopted here, namely $\{T_4, T_7\}$, $\{T_7\}$ and $\varnothing$. If (20) is indeed the case because of a promise made by p, it is reasonable to assume, however, that

(21) $\mathcal{A}(p, \langle p, F\rangle) = \{T_7\}$.

The motivation behind this is that p, without consent from the promisee, may not free himself from his obligation. The promise entails, therefore, not only that $\langle p, F\rangle$ is moved from T_4 to T_7, but also that p's range of action is reduced from $\{T_4, T_7\}$ to $\{T_7\}$.

The range of action which $p+q$ has with respect to $\langle p, F\rangle$ can be described in analogous fashion, distinguishing those cases described by (17) and those described by (20). In the first case (where to begin with, p does not have a duty to look after q), it is reasonable to assume the analogue of (18), namely

(22) May Do($p+q, \langle p, F\rangle \in T_4$)

and from (16) and (22) the analogue of (19) follows according to FIII, namely

(23) $\mathcal{A}(p+q, \langle p, F\rangle) = \{T_4, T_7\}$.

(23) means that p and q together may, by entering into contract, move $\langle p, F\rangle$ from T_4 to T_7; for example, p and q make a contract according to which p is employed by q as a bodyguard. In the other case, where (20) is assumed (and p has *already* a duty to look after q), two possible alternatives may again be distinguished. One of these is that (23) is true also here, so that the range of action for $p+q$ is the same in spite of the fact that $\langle p, F\rangle \in T_7$ is assumed rather than $\langle p, F\rangle \in T_4$. If p and q have made a contract and thereby seen to it that $\langle p, F\rangle$ is moved from T_4 to T_7, they may in fact together agree to *annul* the contract and thereby see to it that $\langle p, F\rangle$ is moved back to T_4. $p+q$'s range of action is not reduced by having entered into contract because they have the prerogative of annulling it. On the other hand, if (20) obtains because of a contract p has entered into with a third party r (let us say, q's father), then (23) is no longer a reasonable assumption to make; rather,

(24) $\mathcal{A}(p+q, \langle p, F\rangle) = \{T_7\}$

is more appropriate. (24) expresses the constraint on p and q that they may not annul a contract that p has made with a third party r.

7. *Unrestricted movement and legal autonomy*

In the course of presenting the general theory in Chapter 8, the important notion of *unrestricted movement* was introduced, applying to pairs $\langle p, F\rangle$ such that for every T, May($\langle p, F\rangle \in T$). It was suggested there (p. 242) that this class covers a number of cases encountered in everyday business transactions where p is an accountable adult (or, for example, a company) and F concerns payment of money, delivery of goods, etc. It was emphasised that the important question here concerns the difference between different agents' range of action with respect to $\langle p, F\rangle$—in other words, "Who is to be the master?" concerning the movement of a given pair $\langle p, F\rangle$ within the set of one-agent types.

Within the particular area of the theory of ranges of action under discussion in the present chapter, a drastic reduction in the number of feasible ranges of action for the class of pairs $\langle p, F\rangle$ with unrestricted movement is effected as a consequence of adopting FII and FIII (together with FI). FI and FII give the following theorem:

THEOREM 3. *If the movement of* $\langle p, F\rangle$ *is unrestricted, then for each* T, T *is a member of* $\mathcal{A}(p, \langle p, F\rangle)$ *if and only if for each* T' *less free than* T, T' *is a member of* $\mathcal{A}(p, \langle p, F\rangle)$.

The proof of this theorem should be fairly clear considered in conjunction with the earlier theorems, and will be presented here in summary form.

Proof

(i) If the movement of $\langle p, F\rangle$ is unrestricted and $T \in \mathcal{A}(p, \langle p, F\rangle)$, then for each T' less free than T, $T' \in \mathcal{A}(p, \langle p, F\rangle)$. (See Theorem 1 of this chapter, p. 271).

(ii) If there is no T' less free than T, then for each T', if T' is less free than T, then $T \in \mathcal{A}(p, \langle p, F\rangle)$.

(iii) If there is a T' less free than T, then there is a T' and a T'' such that T' and T'' are incomparable in respect to freedom (p. 110) and both T', T'' are less free than T.

(iv) If there is a T' and a T'' such that T' and T'' are incomparable in respect to freedom and both T', T'' are less free than T, then T is intermediate between T' and T'' (cf. the Hasse diagram p. 105).

(v) If $T' \in \mathcal{A}(p, \langle p, F\rangle)$, $T'' \in \mathcal{A}(p, \langle p, F\rangle)$, T is intermediate between T' and T'' and the movement of $\langle p, F\rangle$ is unrestricted, then $T \in \mathcal{A}$ $(p, \langle p, F\rangle)$. (See Theorem 1 of Chapter 8, p. 240.)

FI and FIII together give an analogous theorem for $p+q$'s range of action with respect to $\langle p, F\rangle$.

THEOREM 4. *If the movement of* $\langle p, F\rangle$ *is unrestricted, then for each* T, T *is a member of* $\mathcal{A}(p+q, \langle p, F\rangle)$ *if and only if for each* T' *less free than* T, T' *is a member of* $\mathcal{A}(p+q, \langle p, F\rangle)$.

Naturally, the proof here follows along the same lines.

Theorems 3 and 4 reduce the number of non-empty ranges of action to the seven shown in the table below and denoted by $E_1', ..., E_7'$, and I shall refer to the empty range of action as E_8':

Range of action		*Greatest member*
E_1'.	$\{T_1, ..., T_7\}$	T_1
E_2'.	$\{T_2, T_5, T_6\}$	T_2
E_3'.	$\{T_3, T_5, T_6\}$	T_3
E_4'.	$\{T_4, T_6, T_7\}$	T_4
E_5'.	$\{T_5\}$	T_5
E_6'.	$\{T_6\}$	T_6
E_7'.	$\{T_7\}$	T_7
E_8'.	$\varnothing$	—

Thus, if the movement of $\langle p, F\rangle$ is unrestricted, then every range of action for either p or $p+q$ with respect to $\langle p, F\rangle$ is identical with one of $E_1', ...,$ and E_8'. It is easy to see why there is such a reduction. If the movement of $\langle p, F\rangle$ is unrestricted, each non-empty range of action with respect to $\langle p, F\rangle$ has a greatest member (cf. p. 251). It follows, then, from Theorems 3 and 4, under this supposition, that there is only one range of action for each T where T is the greatest member—namely, that range of action comprising T and every other less free one-agent type. The number of non-empty ranges cannot therefore be greater than the number of one-agent types.

To illustrate, I shall appeal to the now familiar situation where there are two individuals p and q with no contract of employment or suchlike between them and F is the state of affairs that £50 is paid from q's account to a third party r. In this case, the movement of $\langle p, F\rangle$ might well be unrestricted and the range of action each of p and $p+q$ has with respect to $\langle p, F\rangle$ is identical to one of $E_1', ...,$ and E_8'. As has already been implied earlier in this chapter (p. 269), p himself has a very small range of action with respect to $\langle p, F\rangle$; in fact, the most reasonable assumption is

(1) $\mathcal{A}(p, \langle p, F\rangle) = \{T_6\}$.

A completely different result is obtained, however, concerning the range of action p and q have *together* with respect to $\langle p, F\rangle$. A plausible set of initial suppositions is

(2) May Do($p+q$, May Do(p, F)),
(3) May Do($p+q$, May Pass(p, F)),
(4) May Do($p+q$, May Do($p \sim F$)).

Now, given that the movement of $\langle p, F\rangle$ is unrestricted, it follows from (2)–(4) that

(5) $\mathcal{A}(p+q, \langle p, F\rangle) = \{T_1, ..., T_7\}$,

which means that p and q together have the largest of the logically possible ranges. Since this range of action is even larger than q's (cf. Chapter 7, p. 223; it can be assumed that $\mathcal{A}(q, \langle p, F\rangle) = \{T_1, T_2, T_4, T_6\}$), the illustration affirms once again the significance of cooperation by contract in bringing about a change in the legal situation.

III. Legal Autonomy and Two-Agent Types

1. *Introduction*

The system of one-agent types is often inadequate for the purpose of delimiting the extent to which two agents p and q may together change their legal situation. For example, the premise

(1) May Do($p+q$, Shall Do(p, F)) &
May Do($p+q$, Shall Do(q, F))

is not sufficient to yield the conclusion

(2) May Do($p+q$, Shall Do(p, F) & Shall Do(q, F)).

For whilst (1) can be formulated in terms of how $p+q$ may move $\langle p, F\rangle$ and $\langle q, F\rangle$ within the set $\{T_1, ..., T_7\}$, (2) must be formulated in terms of how $p+q$ may move $\langle p, q, F\rangle$ within the set $\{R_1, ..., R_{35}\}$ or $\{S_1, ..., S_{127}\}$. Therefore, the theory of autonomy and contract thus far developed needs to be complemented by an account of the corresponding issues within the two systems of two-agent types. As was indicated at the beginning of the present chapter, this involves a theory of statements as follows:

$$\begin{cases} \mathcal{A}^{\mathrm{R}}(p+q, \langle p, q, F\rangle) = \{R, R', ...\}, \\ \text{The range of action}^{\mathrm{R}} \text{ of } p+q \text{ with respect to } \langle p, q, F\rangle = \{R, R', ...\}, \end{cases}$$

$$\begin{cases} \mathcal{A}^{\mathrm{S}}(p+q, \langle p, q, F\rangle) = \{S, S', ...\}, \\ \text{The range of action}^{\mathrm{S}} \text{ of } p+q \text{ with respect to } \langle p, q, F\rangle = \{S, S', ...\}. \end{cases}$$

Only a brief summary of the rules and results for two-agent types analogous to those for one-agent types was necessary in Chapter 8, and the situation is much the same here. Given the more detailed account for one-agent types, the analogous development of the theory of legal autonomy and contract for two-agent types should be apparent and not require more than an explicit formulation of the most important results and the rules from which they follow.

2. *Individualistic two-agent types and legal autonomy*

The basic result for individualistic two-agent types is the following analogue of Theorem 2. It should be noted that no new rule of feasibility is necessary to deduce the theorem; the proof is essentially based on FI′ (p. 257) and FIII (p. 266).

THEOREM 5. *If R is a member of $\mathcal{A}^{\mathrm{R}}(p+q, \langle p, q, F\rangle)$, R' is less free than R and $May(\langle p, q, F\rangle \in R')$, then R' is a member of $\mathcal{A}^{\mathrm{R}}(p+q, \langle p, q, F\rangle)$.*

The proof can be obtained from the proof of Theorem 1 (pp. 271 ff.) by making the obvious substitutions.

As a corollary, the theorem about triples $\langle p, q, F\rangle$ with *unrestricted movement* is forthcoming by analogy with Theorem 4.

THEOREM 6. *If the movement of $\langle p, q, F\rangle$ is unrestricted in $\{R_1, ..., R_{35}\}$, then for each R, R is a member of $\mathcal{A}^{\mathrm{R}}(p+q, \langle p, q, F\rangle)$ if and only if for each R' less free than R, R' is a member of $\mathcal{A}^{\mathrm{R}}(p+q, \langle p, q, F\rangle)$.*

This theorem reduces the number of non-empty ranges of action for triples with unrestricted movement to thirty-five, i.e., the number of individualistic types. These ranges of action can easily be found with the help of the large frame diagram in Chapter 4 (p. 145).

As an illustration, consider the following example. p, q, r and s are four distinct people. r owes s a certain sum of money, and F is the state of affairs that r's debt to s is paid. p and q intend to make a contract concerning the payment of this debt (a so-called contract in favour of a third party); i.e., they intend jointly to undertake an action involving the placing of the triple $\langle p, q, F\rangle$ within the set of individualistic types. Which range of action^{R}, then, does $p+q$ have with respect to $\langle p, q, F\rangle$? Reflection on the definitions of the individualistic types (p. 130) suggests that it is plausible to assume that $\mathcal{A}^{R}(p+q, \langle p, q, F\rangle)$ has a greatest member, namely R_2. With the help of the frame diagram referred to above it is easy to see that the individualistic types less free than R_2 are as follows: R_5, R_6, R_{15}, R_{16}, R_{26}, R_{27}, R_{29} and R_{32}. The triple $\langle p, q, F\rangle$ may belong to any of those types, and it can thereby be inferred according to Theorem 5 that

$$\mathcal{A}^{R}(p+q, \langle p, q, F\rangle) = \{R_2, R_5, R_6, R_{15}, R_{16}, R_{26}, R_{27}, R_{29}, R_{32}\}.$$

3. *Collectivistic two-agent types and legal autonomy*

Unlike the theory for indivualistic types, the theory for collectivistic types requires a further rule of feasibility, though this is completely analogous to FIII. Using the following notation:

1. s and s' are arbitrary agent designators and A is an arbitrary well-formed statement,

2. X and Y stand for different members of the list

$$\begin{aligned}&\text{Do}(s, A)\ \&\ \text{Do}(s', A),\\ &\text{Do}(s, A)\ \&\ {\sim}\text{Do}(s', A),\\ &\text{Do}(s, {\sim}A)\ \&\ \text{Do}(s', {\sim}A),\\ &\text{Do}(s, {\sim}A)\ \&\ {\sim}\text{Do}(s', {\sim}A),\\ &{\sim}\text{Do}(s, A)\ \&\ \text{Do}(s', A),\\ &{\sim}\text{Do}(s, {\sim}A)\ \&\ \text{Do}(s', {\sim}A),\\ &\text{Pass}(s, A)\ \&\ \text{Pass}(s', A),\end{aligned}$$

the rule can be stated thus:

FIV. May Do($s+s'$, May X) & May$\sim$May $Y\rightarrow$
May Do($s+s'$, $\sim$May Y).

Given FI″ (p. 258), two theorems analogous to Theorems 5 and 6 follow easily from FIV.

THEOREM 7. *If S is a member of* $\mathcal{A}^{S}(p+q, \langle p, q, F\rangle)$, *S′ is less free than S and* $May(\langle p, q, F\rangle \in S')$, *then S′ is a member of* $\mathcal{A}^{S}(p+q, \langle p, q, F\rangle)$.

THEOREM 8. *If the movement of* $\langle p, q, F\rangle$ *is unrestricted in* $\{S_1, ..., S_{127}\}$, *then for each S, S, is a member of* $\mathcal{A}^{S}(p+q, \langle p, q, F\rangle)$ *if and only if for each S′ less free than S, S′ is a member of* $\mathcal{A}^{S}(p+q, \langle p, q, F\rangle)$.

Just as before, a reduction in the number of ranges of action for $\langle p, q, F\rangle$ with unrestricted movement is obtained; in this case, the number of non-empty ranges is clearly one hundred and twenty-seven. Unfortunately, there is no convenient diagram specifying the elements of these one hundred and twenty-seven ranges. However, their composition can be found relatively easily by another method. The key (a combination of letters) defining collectivistic types and referring to the elements of their liberty spaces was given in Chapter 5 (p. 165). For example, type S_{67} was assigned the combination of letters abe, which means that $\mathcal{S}(S_{67})=\{a, b, e\}$. It follows, then, from the definition of "less free than" that the set of those types less free than S_{67} is the same as the set of types whose liberty spaces are a subset of {a, b, e}. S_{67} is, accordingly, the greatest element in a range of action which comprises the following types:

S_{67}.	abe
S_{100}.	ab
S_{103}.	ae
S_{108}.	be
S_{121}.	a
S_{122}.	b
S_{125}.	c

To illustrate this case, the situation described at the beginning of Chapter 5 (pp. 159 f.) serves well as an example. A company employs two people to deal with the company's business (answering letters, receiving clients, depositing the daily takings in the bank, etc.), the arrangement being that *at least one of them* should see to it that the tasks are done. Just who does what, however, is left to the two employees to agree between themselves. If F is the state of affairs that the letters are answered, or that any of the other tasks is accomplished, then the two employees are constrained to act within the limits described by the statement

(1) $\langle p, q, F\rangle \in S_{67}$.

The key to the definition of S_{67} is given by the combination of letters abe; it should be noted, however, that (1) is equivalent to the conjunction of the statements

(2) Shall(Do(p, F) v Do(q, F)),
(3) May(Do(p, F) & Do(q, F)),
(4) May(Do(p, F) & ~Do(q, F)),
(5) May(~Do(p, F) & Do(q, F)),

(cf. p. 160). In view of the foregoing, it is plausible to make the suppositions

(6) May Do($p+q$, $\langle p, q, F\rangle \in S_{67}$),
(7) ~May Do[$p+q$, ~Shall(Do(p, F) v Do(q, F))],

and the assumption that the movement of $\langle p, q, F\rangle$ is unrestricted within the set of collectivistic two-agent types. Therefore, from Theorem 8 it follows that

(8) $\mathcal{A}^{S}(p+q, \langle p, q, F\rangle) = \{S_{67}, S_{100}, S_{103}, S_{108}, S_{121}, S_{122}, S_{125}\}$,

giving the range of action which $p+q$ has with respect to $\langle p, q, F\rangle$.

Appendix

An instance of

$$\langle p, F\rangle \in T_3$$

(cf. p. 98) can be such that one shows that there are values of p, F and G such that the following statements are true:

(i) May G.
(ii) May $\sim G$.
(iii) Shall $(G \rightarrow \text{Do}(p, F))$.
(iv) Shall $(\sim G \rightarrow \text{Do}(p, \sim F))$.

It can be shown that from (i)–(iv) it follows that

$$\langle p, F\rangle \in T_3.$$

Proof:

(i) $\text{Shall}(G \rightarrow \text{Do}(p, F))\ \&\ \text{Shall}(\sim G \rightarrow \text{Do}(p, \sim F)) \rightarrow$
$\text{Shall}[(G \rightarrow \text{Do}(p, F))\ \&\ (\sim G \rightarrow \text{Do}(p, \sim F))]$.
(ii) $\text{Shall}[(G \rightarrow \text{Do}(p, F))\ \&\ (\sim G \rightarrow \text{Do}(p, \sim F))] \rightarrow$
$\text{Shall}[(G \vee \sim G) \rightarrow (\text{Do}(p, F) \vee \text{Do}(p, \sim F))]$.
(iii) $\text{Shall}[(G \vee \sim G) \rightarrow (\text{Do}(p, F) \vee \text{Do}(p, \sim F))] \rightarrow$
$[\text{Shall}(G \vee \sim G) \rightarrow \text{Shall}(\text{Do}(p, F) \vee \text{Do}(p, \sim F))]$.
(iv) $\text{Shall}(G \vee \sim G)$.
(v) $\text{Shall}(G \rightarrow \text{Do}(p, F))\ \&\ \text{Shall}(\sim G \rightarrow \text{Do}(p, \sim F)) \rightarrow$
$\text{Shall}(\text{Do}(p, F) \vee \text{Do}(p, \sim F))$.
(vi) $\text{Shall}(G \rightarrow \text{Do}(p, F)) \rightarrow \text{Shall}(\sim \text{Do}(p, F) \rightarrow \sim G)$.
(vii) $\text{Shall}(\sim \text{Do}(p, F) \rightarrow \sim G) \rightarrow (\text{Shall} \sim \text{Do}(p, F) \rightarrow \text{Shall} \sim G)$.
(viii) $(\text{Shall} \sim \text{Do}(p, F) \rightarrow \text{Shall} \sim G) \rightarrow (\text{May}\ G \rightarrow \text{May Do}(p, F))$.
(ix) $\text{Shall}(G \rightarrow \text{Do}(p, F)) \rightarrow (\text{May}\ G \rightarrow \text{May Do}(p, F))$.
(x) $\text{May}\ G\ \&\ \text{Shall}(G \rightarrow \text{Do}(p, F)) \rightarrow \text{May Do}(p, F)$.
(xi) $\text{May} \sim G\ \&\ \text{Shall}(\sim G \rightarrow \text{Do}(p, \sim F)) \rightarrow \text{May Do}(p, \sim F)$.

From (v), (x) and (xi) it follows immediately that the conjunction of (i)–(iv) above implies $\langle p, F\rangle \in T_3$.

The suppositions (iii) and (iv) can also be formulated as

(iii′) $\sim$May(G & $\sim$Do(p, F)),
(iv′) $\sim$May($\sim G$ & $\sim$Do(p, $\sim F$));

and it might be as well to stick to this latter formulation in order to avoid misunderstanding about the meaning of the truth functional conditional $\rightarrow$. Suppose, now, that John is employed by the University of Uppsala and wants to be reimbursed for a journey to Stockholm on University business. Suppose, further, that the right to reimbursement is dependent upon claiming within a month. Let p, F and G be as follows:

p: the University's cashier.
F: that John is reimbursed by the University for his journey.
G: that John submits his claim within a month.

It seems reasonable to suppose that (i)–(iv) are true given these values of the variables. Translating the operators and connectives into English in the usual way, these suppositions can be expressed as follows to facilitate reading:

(i′) It may be the case that John submits his claim within a month.
(ii′) It may be the case that John does not submit his claim within a month.
(iii″) It may not be the case that John submits his claim within a month but the cashier does not see to it that John is reimbursed.
(iv″) It may not be the case that John does not submit his claim within a month and the cashier does not prevent John's being reimbursed.

(Note, in connection with (iv″), that the cashier is responsible for the University's funds, and his seeing to it that John does not obtain reimbursement can be achieved by *null action* (cf. p. 70). An instance of

$$\langle p, F\rangle \in T_3$$

is obtained given these suppositions, which can be informally stated by:

(v) The cashier may see to it that John is reimbursed for his journey.

(vi) The cashier may see to it that John does not obtain a reimbursement for his journey.

(vii) It shall be the case that the cashier sees to it that John is reimbursed for his journey or the cashier sees to it that John is not reimbursed for his journey.

The example is, perhaps, controversial because it might be maintained that, as a background condition in this particular case, it is not in fact reasonable to suppose that both (v) and (vi) are true, but rather one of the following alternatives:

(viii) The cashier shall see to it that John is reimbursed for his journey.

(ix) The cashier shall see to it that John is not reimbursed for his journey.

(Which of these is true would depend, of course, on whether John submits his claim within a month.) Instead of the conjunction of (v)–(vi) this argument leads to the following conclusion

(x) Shall Do(p, F) v Shall Do(p, $\sim F$).

(x) can be reformulated in terms of one-agent types as

(x′) $\langle p, F\rangle \in T_5 \vee \langle p, F\rangle \in T_7$,

and in this case the example no longer serves as an illustration of one-agent type T_3.

First, it is well to be clear about which choices are available between the various suppositions before deciding the case. The premises

(i) May G,

(ii) May $\sim G$,

appear uncontroversial for the given value of G. The choice is then between the conjunction of (i)–(iv) and the conjunction of (i), (ii) and (x). I shall argue in favour of the former alternative and that the latter alternative is inappropriate in the situation of the example. From (i), (ii) and (x) it follows that

(xi) May($\sim G$ & Do(p, F)) v May(G & Do(p, $\sim F$)).

Proof:

(i) [May G & May $\sim G$ & (Shall Do(p, F) v Shall Do(p, $\sim F$))]→
[(May G & May $\sim G$ & Shall Do(p, F)) v
(May G & May $\sim G$ & Shall Do(p, $\sim F$))].

(ii) May G & May $\sim G$ & Shall Do(p, F)→
May($\sim G$ & Do(p, F)).

(iii) May G & May $\sim G$ & Shall Do(p, $\sim F$)→
May(G & Do(p, $\sim F$)).

(iv) [May G & May $\sim G$ & (Shall Do(p, F) v Shall Do(p, $\sim F$))]→
May($\sim G$ & Do(p, F)) v May(G & Do(p, $\sim F$)).

The supposition of (xi) within the context of the example means that, informally expressed, at least one of the following is true:

(xii) It is permitted that John does not submit his claim within a month, but the cashier sees to it that John is reimbursed.

(xiii) It is permitted that John submits his claim within a month, but the cashier sees to it that John is not reimbursed.

Each of these contradict the whole idea behind the example, and accordingly (xi) cannot be true in the present case. Since (xi) follows from (x) together with the original premises (i) and (ii), and since (i) and (ii) are beyond question, (x) is accordingly not a feasible supposition to be made. The original premises (i)–(iv) remain, of course, and so the example stands as an instance of

$$\langle p, F\rangle \in T_3.$$

Bibliography

(of works cited or referred to)

Alchourrón, C. E. & Bulygin, E. (1971). *Normative Systems.* Wien and New York.

Anderson, A. R. (1956). *The Formal Analysis of Normative Systems.* Technical report no. 2, contract no. SAR/nonr-609 (16), Office of Naval Research, Group Psychology Branch, New Haven, Conn. (Reprinted in *The Logic of Decision and Action*, ed. N. Rescher, Pittsburgh, 1967, pp. 147–213.)

— (1962). "Logic, Norms and Roles", *Ratio*, vol. 4, pp. 36–49.

— (1967). "Some Nasty Problems in the Formal Logic of Ethics", *Noûs*, vol. 1, pp. 345–359.

— (1971). "The Logic of Hohfeldian Propositions", *University of Pittsburgh Law Review*, vol. 33, pp. 29–38.

Austin, J. (1863). *Lectures on Jurisprudence.* Vols. II–III. London.

Bentham, J. (1945). *The Limits of Jurisprudence Defined* (ed. C. W. Everett). New York.

— (1962). *The Works of Jeremy Bentham* (ed. J. Bowring; facsimile edition reproduced from the Bowring edition of 1838–1843). Vol. III. New York.

— (1970*a*). *An Introduction to the Principles of Morals and Legislation* (ed. J. H. Burns & H. L. A. Hart). London.

— 1970*b*). *Of Laws in General* (ed. H. L. A. Hart). London.

Bierling, E. R. (1883). *Zur Kritik der juristischen Grundbegriffe.* Zweiter Teil. Gotha.

Brinz, A. (1857). *Lehrbuch der Pandekten.* Erste Abteilung. Erlangen.

— (1873). *Lehrbuch der Pandekten.* Erster Band. 2:e, veränderte Auflage. Erlangen.

Chellas, B. F. (1969). *The Logical Form of Imperatives.* Stanford.

Cook, W. W. (1938). "The Utility of Jurisprudence in the Solution of Legal Problems". In *Readings in Jurisprudence* (ed. J. Hall), Indiapolis, 1938, pp. 484–501.

Corbin, A. L. (1919). "Legal Analysis and Terminology", *Yale Law Journal*, vol. 29, pp. 163–173. (Reprinted in *Readings in Jurisprudence*, ed. J. Hall, Indianapolis, 1938, pp. 471–484.)

Danielsson, S. (1968). *Preference and Obligation: Studies in the Logic of Ethics.* Philosophical Studies published by the Philosophical Society and the Department of Philosophy, University of Uppsala. No. 7. Uppsala.

— (1973). *Some Conceptions of Performativity.* Philosophical Studies published by the Philosophical Society and the Department of Philosophy, University of Uppsala. No. 19. Uppsala.

Dickey, A. (1971). "Hohfeld's Debt to Salmond", *University of Western Australia Law Review*, vol. 10, pp. 59–64.

Eckhoff, T. (1953). *Rettsvesen of rettsvitenskap i U.S.A.* Oslo.

Fitch, F. B. (1967). "A Revision of Hohfeld's Theory of Legal Concepts", *Logique et Analyse*, vol. 10, pp. 269–276.

Fitting, M. (1969). "Logics with Several Modal Operators", *Theoria*, vol. 35, pp. 259–266.

Goble, G. W. (1928). "The Sanction of a Duty", *Yale Law Journal*, vol. 37, pp. 426–444.

Hansson, B. (1970). "Deontic Logic and Different Levels of Generality", *Theoria*, vol. 36, pp. 241–248.

Hart, H. L. A. (1953). *Definition and Theory in Jurisprudence.* Inaugural lecture delivered before the University of Oxford on 30 May 1953. Oxford.

— (1961). *The Concept of Law.* Oxford.

— (1962). "Bentham". *Proceedings of the British Academy*, vol. 48, pp. 297–320.

— (1971). "Bentham's 'Of Laws in General'", *Rechtstheorie*, vol. 2, pp. 55–66.

— (1972). "Bentham on Legal Powers", *Yale Law Jornal*, vol. 81 (1971–1972), pp. 799–822.

— (1973). "Bentham on Legal Rights". In *Oxford Essays in Jurisprudence*, Second Series (ed. A. W. B. Simpson), Oxford, 1973, pp. 171–201.

Hedenius, I. (1941). *Om rätt och moral.* Stockholm.

Hintikka, J. (1971). "Some Main Problems of Deontic Logic". In *Deontic Logic: Introductory and Systematic Readings* (ed. R. Hilpinen), Dordrecht, 1971, pp. 59–104.

Hobbes, T. (1962). *Leviathan: or The Matter, Forme and Power of a Commonwealth, Ecclesiastical and Civil* (ed. R. S. Peters). New York.

Hohfeld, W. N. (1923). *Fundamental Legal Conceptions as Applied in Judicial Reasoning and Other Legal Essays*, (ed. W. W. Cook.) New Haven.

Honoré, A. M. (1960). "Rights of Exclusion and Immunities Against Divesting", *Tulane Law Review*, vol. 34, pp. 453–468.

Hughes, G. E. & Cresswell, M. J. (1968). *An Introduction to Modal Logic.* London.

Kanger, S. (1957). *New Foundations for Ethical Theory.* Part. 1. Stockholm. (Reprinted in *Deontic Logic: Introductory and Systematic Readings*, ed. R. Hilpinen, Dordrecht, 1971, pp. 36–58.)

— (1963). "Rättighetsbegreppet". In *Sju filosofiska studier tillägnade Anders Wedberg den 30 mars 1963*. Philosophical Studies published by the Department of Philosophy, University of Stockholm. No. 9. Stockholm.

— (1971). "New Foundations for Ethical Theory". In *Deontic Logic: Introductory and Systematic Readings* (ed. R. Hilpinen), Dordrecht, 1971, pp. 36–58.

— (1972). "Law and Logic", *Theoria*, vol. 38, pp. 105–132.

Kanger, S. & Kanger, H. (1966). "Rights and Parliamentarism", *Theoria*, vol. 32, pp. 85–115.

Kelsen, H. (1945). *General Theory of Law and State*. Cambridge, Mass.

Kemeny, J. G., Snell, J. L. & Thompson, G. L. (1966). *Introduction to Finite Mathematics*. 2nd edition. Englewood Cliffs, N. J.

Leibniz, G. W. (1930). *Sämtliche Schriften und Briefe*. Hrsg. von der Preussischen Akademie der Wissenschaften. Sechste Reihe. Philosophische Schriften. Erster Band. Darmstadt.

Lemmon, E. J. (1965). "Deontic Logic and the Logic of Imperatives", *Logique et Analyse*, vol. 8, pp. 39–70.

Lyons, Dan. (1965). "Entitled to Complain", *Analysis*, vol. 26 (1965–1966), pp. 119–122.

Lyons, Dav. (1969). "Rights, Claimants and Beneficiaries", *American Philosophical Quarterly*, vol. 6, pp. 173–185.

— (1972). "Logic and Coercion in Bentham's Theory of Law", *Cornell Law Review*, vol. 57, pp. 335–362.

— (1973). *In the Interest of the Governed: A Study in Bentham's Philosophy of Utility and Law*. Oxford.

Lysaght, L. J. (1973). "Bentham on the Aspects of a Law", *Northern Ireland Legal Quarterly*, vol. 24, pp. 383–398.

Mally, E. (1926). *Grundgesetze des Sollens. Elemente der Logik des Willens*. Graz.

Moritz, M. (1960). *Über Hohfelds System der juridischen Grundbegriffe*. Lund.

Mullock, P. (1974). "The Permissiveness of Powers", *Ratio*, vol. 16, pp. 76–81.

Pound, R. (1959). *Jurisprudence*. Vol. IV. St. Paul, Minn.

Pörn, I. (1970). *The Logic of Power*. Oxford.

— (1971). *Elements of Social Analysis*. Philosophical Studies published by the Philosophical Society and the Department of Philosophy, University of Uppsala. No. 10. Uppsala.

— (1974). "Some Basic Concepts of Action". In *Logical Theory and Semantic Analysis: Essays Dedicated to Stig Kanger on His Fiftieth Birthday* (ed. S. Stenlund), Dordrecht, 1974, pp. 93–101.

Raz, J. (1970). *The Concept of a Legal System: An Introduction to the Theory of Legal System*. Oxford.

Ross, A. (1953). *Om Ret og Retfaerdighed*. København.

— (1968). *Directives and Norms*. London.

Searle, J. R. (1964). "How to Derive Ought from Is", *Philosophical Review*, vol. 73, pp. 43–58.

Stalnaker, R. C. & Thomason, R. H. (1970). "A Semantic Analysis of Conditional Logic", *Theoria*, vol. 36, pp. 23–42.

Stenius, E. (1972). "The Principles of a Logic of Normative Systems". In *Acta Philosophica Fennica*, Fasc. 25, pp. 112–128.

Stoll, R. R. (1963). *Set Theory and Logic*. San Francisco and London.

Sundby, N. K. (1973). "Benthams betydning for vår tids rettstenkning", *Tidsskrift for Rettsvitenskap*, vol. 86, pp. 676–722.

— (1974). *Om normer*. Oslo.

Suppes, P. (1957). *Introduction to Logic*. Princeton.

Swedish Contracts Act Committee (1914). *Förslag till lag om avtal och andra rättshandlingar på förmögenhetsrättens område, lag om avbetalningsköp m. m.* Stockholm.

Treitel, G. H. (1962). *The Law of Contract*. London.

Trendelenburg, A. (1855). *Historische Beiträge zur Philosophie*. Zweiter Band. Berlin.

Wedberg, A. (1969). "Konsekvensprincipen i deontisk logik och frågan om deontiska satsers sanningsvärde". In *Logik, rätt och moral: Filosofiska studier tillägnade Manfred Moritz på 60-årsdagen den 4 juni 1969*. Lund.

Williams, G. (1956). "The Concept of Legal Liberty", *Columbia Law Review*, vol. 56, pp. 1129–1150.

von Wright, G. H. (1951). "Deontic Logic", *Mind*, vol. 60, pp. 1–15.

— (1963). *Norm and Action: A Logical Enquiry*. London.

— (1972). *An Essay in Deontic Logic and the General Theory of Action*. Amsterdam.

Index of Names

Index of Subjects

SYNTHESE LIBRARY

Monographs on Epistemology, Logic, Methodology,
Philosophy of Science, Sociology of Science and of Knowledge, and on the
Mathematical Methods of Social and Behavioral Sciences

1. J. M. BOCHEŃSKI, *A Precis of Mathematical Logic.* 1959, X + 100 pp.
2. P. L. GUIRAUD, *Problèmes et méthodes de la statistique linguistique.* 1960, VI + 146 pp.
3. HANS FREUDENTHAL (ed.), *The Concept and the Role of the Model in Mathematics and Natural and Social Sciences, Proceedings of a Colloquium held at Utrecht, The Netherlands, January 1960*, 1961, VI + 194 pp.
4. EVERT W. BETH, *Formal Methods. An Introduction to Symbolic Logic and the Study of effective Operations in Arithmetic and Logic.* 1962, XIV + 170 pp.
5. B. H. KAZEMIER and D. VUYSJE (eds.), *Logic and Language. Studies dedicated to Professor Rudolf Carnap on the Occasion of his Seventieth Birthday.* 1962, VI + 256 pp.
6. MARX W. WARTOFSKY (ed.), *Proceedings of the Boston Colloquium for the Philosophy of Science, 1961–1962*, Boston Studies in the Philosophy of Science (ed. by Robert S. Cohen and Marx W. Wartofsky), Volume I. 1973, VIII + 212 pp.
7. A. A. ZINOV'EV, *Philosophical Problems of Many-Valued Logic.* 1963. XIV + 155 pp.
8. GEORGES GURVITCH, *The Spectrum of Social Time.* 1964, XXVI + 152 pp.
9. PAUL LORENZEN, *Formal Logic.* 1965, VIII + 123 pp.
10. ROBERT S. COHEN and MARX W. WARTOFSKY (eds.), *In Honor of Philipp Frank*, Boston Studies in the Philosophy of Science (ed. by Robert S. Cohen and Marx W. Wartofsky), Volume II. 1965, XXXIV + 475 pp.
11. EVERT W. BETH, *Mathematical Thought. An Introduction to the Philosophy of Mathematics.* 1965, XII + 208 pp.
12. EVERT W. BETH and JEAN PIAGET, *Mathematical Epistemology and Psychology.* 1966, XII + 326 pp.
13. GUIDO KÜNG, *Ontology and the Logistic Analysis of Language. An Enquiry into the Contemporary Views on Universals.* 1967, XI + 210 pp.
14. ROBERT S. COHEN and MARX W. WARTOFSKY (eds.), *Proceedings of the Boston Colloquium for the Philosophy of Science 1964–1966, in Memory of Norwood*

Russell Hanson, Boston Studies in the Philosophy of Science (ed. by Robert S. Cohen and Marx W. Wartofsky), Volume III. 1967, XLIX + 489 pp.

15. C. D. BROAD, *Induction, Probability, and Causation. Selected Papers.* 1968, XI + 296 pp.
16. GÜNTHER PATZIG, *Aristotle's Theory of the Syllogism. A Logical-Philosophical Study of Book A of the Prior Analytics.* 1968, XVII + 215 pp.
17. NICHOLAS RESCHER, *Topics in Philosophical Logic.* 1968, XIV + 347 pp.
18. ROBERT S. COHEN and MARX W. WARTOFSKY (eds.), *Proceedings of the Boston Colloquium for the Philosophy of Science 1966–1968*, Boston Studies in the Philosophy of Science (ed. by Robert S. Cohen and Marx W. Wartofsky), Volume IV. 1969, VIII + 537 pp.
19. ROBERT S. COHEN and MARX W. WARTOFSKY (eds.), *Proceedings of the Boston Colloquium for the Philosophy of Science 1966–1968*, Boston Studies in the Philosophy of Science (ed. by Robert S. Cohen and Marx W. Wartofsky), Volume V. 1969, VIII + 482 pp.
20. J. W. DAVIS, D. J. HOCKNEY, and W. K. WILSON (eds.), *Philosophical Logic.* 1969, VIII + 277 pp.
21. D. DAVIDSON and J. HINTIKKA (eds.), *Words and Objections. Essays on the Work of W. V. Quine.* 1969, VIII + 366 pp.
22. PATRICK SUPPES, *Studies in the Methodology and Foundations of Science. Selected Papers from 1911 to 1969*, XII + 473 pp.
23. JAAKKO HINTIKKA, *Models for Modalities. Selected Essays.* 1969, IX + 220 pp.
24. NICHOLAS RESCHER *et al.* (eds.), *Essays in Honor of Carl G. Hempel. A Tribute on the Occasion of his Sixty-Fifth Birthday.* 1969, VII + 272 pp.
25. P. V. TAVANEC (ed.), *Problems of the Logic of Scientific Knowledge.* 1969, VII + 429 pp.
26. MARSHALL SWAIN (ed.), *Induction, Acceptance, and Rational Belief.* 1970, VII + 232 pp.
27. ROBERT S. COHEN and RAYMOND J. SEEGER (eds.), *Ernst Mach: Physicist and Philosopher*, Boston Studies in the Philisophy of Science (ed. by Robert S. Cohen and Marx W. Wartofsky), Volume VI. 1970, VIII + 295 pp.
28. JAAKKO HINTIKKA and PATRICK SUPPES, *Information and Inference.* 1970, X + 336 pp.
29. KAREL LAMBERT, *Philosophical Problems in Logic. Some Recent Developments.* 1970, VII + 176 pp.
30. ROLF A. EBERLE, *Nominalistic Systems.* 1970, IX + 217 pp.
31. PAUL WEINGARTNER and GERHARD ZECHA (eds.), *Induction, Physics, and Ethics. Proceedings and Discussions of the 1968 Salzburg Colloquium in the Philosophy of Science.* 1970, X + 382 pp.
32. EVERT W. BETH, *Aspects of Modern Logic.* 1970, XI + 176 pp.
33. RISTO HILPINEN (ed.), *Deontic Logic: Introductory and Systematic Readings.* 1971, VII + 182 pp.
34. JEAN-LOUIS KRIVINE, *Introduction to Axiomatic Set Theory.* 1971, VII + 98 pp.
35. JOSEPH D. SNEED, *The Logical Structure of Mathematical Physics.* 1971, XV + 311 pp.
36. CARL R. KORDIG, *The Justification of Scientific Change.* 1971, XIV + 119 pp.
37. MILIČ ČAPEK, *Bergson and Modern Physics*, Boston Studies in the Philosophy of Science (ed. by Robert S. Cohen and Marx W. Wartofsky), Volume VII. 1971, XV + 414 pp.

38. Norwood Russell Hanson, *What I do Not Believe, and Other Essays* (ed. by Stephen Toulmin and Harry Woolf), 1971, XII + 390 pp.
39. Roger C. Buck and Robert S. Cohen (eds.), *PSA 1970. In Memory of Rudolf Carnap*, Boston Studies in the Philosophy of Science (ed. by Robert S. Cohen and Marx W. Wartofsky), Volume VIII. 1971, LXVI + 615 pp. Also available as paperback.
40. Donald Davidson and Gilbert Harman (eds.), *Semantics of Natural Language.* 1972, X + 769 pp. Also available as paperback.
41. Yehoshua Bar-Hillel (ed.), *Pragmatics of Natural Languages.* 1971, VII + 231pp.
42. Sören Stenlund, *Combinators, λ-Terms and Proof Theory.* 1972, 184 pp.
43. Martin Strauss, *Modern Physics and Its Philosophy. Selected Papers in the Logic, History, and Philosophy of Science.* 1972, X + 297 pp.
44. Mario Bunge, *Method, Model and Matter.* 1973, VII + 196 pp.
45. Mario Bunge, *Philosophy of Physics.* 1973, IX + 248 pp.
46. A. A. Zinov'ev, *Foundations of the Logical Theory of Scientific Knowledge* (*Complex Logic*), Boston Studies in the Philosophy of Science (ed. by Robert S. Cohen and Marx W. Wartofsky), Volume IX. Revised and enlarged English edition with an appendix, by G. A. Smirnov, E. A. Sidorenka, A. M. Fedina, and L. A. Bobrova. 1973, XXII + 301 pp. Also available as paperback.
47. Ladislav Tondl, *Scientific Procedures*, Boston Studies in the Philosophy of Science (ed. by Robert S. Cohen and Marx W. Wartofsky), Volume X, 1973, XII + 268 pp. Also available as paperback.
48. Norwood Russell Hanson, *Constellations and Conjectures*, (ed. by Willard C. Humphreys, Jr.) 1973, X + 282 pp.
49. K. J. J. Hintikka, J. M. E. Moravcsik, and P. Suppes (eds.), *Approaches to Natural Language. Proceedings of the 1970 Stanford Workshop on Grammar and Semantics.* 1973, VIII + 526 pp. Also available as paperback.
50. Mario Bunge (ed.), *Exact Philosophy – Problems, Tools, and Goals.* 1973, X + 214 pp.
51. Radu J. Bogdan and Ilkka Niiniluoto (eds.), *Logic, Language, and Probability.* A selection of papers contributed to Sections IV, VI, and XI of the Fourth International Congress for Logic, Methodology, and Philosophy of Science, Bucharest, September 1971. 1973, X + 323 pp.
52. Glenn Pearce and Patrick Maynard (eds.), *Conceptual Chance.* 1973, XII + 282 pp.
53. Ilkka Niiniluoto and Raimo Tuomela, *Theoretical Concepts and Hypothetico-Inductive Inference.* 1973, VII + 264 pp.
54. Roland Fraïssé, *Course of Mathematical Logic* — Volume 1: *Relation and Logical Formula.* 1973, XVI + 186 pp. Also available as paperback.
55. Adolf Grünbaum, *Philosophical Problems of Space and Time.* Second, enlarged edition, Boston Studies in the Philosophy of Science (ed. by Robert S. Cohen and Marx W. Wartofsky), Volume XII. 1973, XXIII + 884 pp. Also available as paperback.
56. Patrick Suppes (ed.), *Space, Time, and Geometry.* 1973, XI + 424 pp.
57. Hans Kelsen, *Essays in Legal and Moral Philosophy*, selected and introduced by Ota Weinberger. 1973, XXVIII + 300 pp.
58. R. J. Seeger and Robert S. Cohen (eds.), *Philosophical Foundations of Science. Proceedings of an AAAS Program, 1969.* Boston Studies in the Philosophy of Science (ed. by Robert S. Cohen and Marx W. Wartofsky), Volume XI. 1974, X + 545 pp. Also available as paperback.

59. Robert S. Cohen and Marx W. Wartofsky (eds.), *Logical and Epistemological Studies in Contemporary Physics*, Boston Studies in the Philosophy of Science (ed. by Robert S. Cohen and Marx W. Wartofsky), Volume XIII. 1973, VIII + 462 pp. Also available as paperback.
60. Robert S. Cohen and Marx W. Wartofsky (eds.), *Methodological and Historical Essays in the Natural and Social Sciences. Proceedings of the Boston Colloquium for the Philosophy of Science, 1969–1972*, Boston Studies in the Philosophy of Science (ed. by Robert S. Cohen and Marx W. Wartofsky), Volume XIV. 1974, VIII + 405 pp. Also available as paperback.
61. Robert S. Cohen, J. J. Stachel and Marx W. Wartofsky (eds.), *For Dirk Struik. Scientific, Historical and Polical Essays in Honor of Dirk J. Struik*, Boston Studies in the Philosophy of Science (ed. by Robert S. Cohen and Marx W. Wartofsky), Volume XV. 1974, XXVII + 652 pp. Also available as paperback.
62. Kazimierz Ajdukiewicz, *Pragmatic Logic*, transl. from the Polish by Olgierd Wojtasiewicz. 1974, XV + 460 pp.
63. Sören Stenlund (ed.), *Logical Theory and Semantic Analysis. Essays Dedicated to Stig Kanger on His Fiftieth Birthday*. 1974, V + 217 pp.
64. Kenneth F. Schaffner and Robert S. Cohen (eds.), *Proceedings of the 1972 Biennial Meeting, Philosophy of Science Association*, Boston Studies in the Philosophy of Science (ed. by Robert S. Cohen and Marx W. Wartofsky), Volume XX. 1974, IX + 444 pp. Also available as paperback.
65. Henry E. Kyburg, Jr., *The Logical Foundations of Statistical Inference*. 1974, IX + 421 pp.
66. Marjorie Grene, *The Understanding of Nature: Essays in the Philosophy of Biology*, Boston Studies in the Philosophy of Science (ed. by Robert S. Cohen and Marx W. Wartofsky), Volume XXIII. 1974, XII + 360 pp. Also available as paperback.
67. Jan M. Broekman, *Structuralism: Moscow, Prague, Paris*. 1974, IX + 117 pp.
68. Norman Geschwind, *Selected Papers on Language and the Brain*, Boston Studies in the Philosophy of Science (ed. by Robert S. Cohen and Marx W. Wartofsky), Volume XVI. 1974, XII + 549 pp. Also available as paperback.
69. Roland Fraïssé, *Course of Mathematical Logic* — Volume II: *Model Theory*. 1974, XIX + 192 pp.
70. Andrzej Grzegorczyk, *An Outline of Mathematical Logic. Fundamental Results and Notions Explained with All Details*. 1974, X + 596 pp.
71. Franz von Kutschera, *Philosophy of Language*. 1975, VII + 305 pp.
72. Juha Manninen and Raimo Tuomela (eds.), *Essays on Explanation and Understanding. Studies in the Foundations of Humanties and Social Sciences*. 1976, VII + 440 pp.
73. Jaakko Hintikka (ed.), *Rudolf Carnap, Logical Empiricist. Materials and Perspectives*. 1975, LXVIII + 400 pp.
74. Milič Čapek (ed.), *The Concepts of Space and Time. Their Structure and Their Development*. Boston Studies in the Philosophy of Science (ed. by Robert S. Cohen and Marx W. Wartofsky), Volume XXII. 1976, LVI + 570 pp. Also available as paperback.
75. Jaakko Hintikka and Unto Remes, *The Method of Analysis. Its Geometrical Origin and Its General Significance*. Boston Studies in the Philosophy of Science (ed. by Robert S. Cohen and Marx W. Wartofsky), Volume XXV. 1974, XVIII + 144 pp. Also available as paperback.

76. John Emery Murdoch and Edith Dudley Sylla, *The Cultural Context of Medieval Learning. Proceedings of the First International Colloquium on Philosophy, Science, and Theology in the Middle Ages — September 1973.* Boston Studies in the Philosophy of Science (ed. by Robert S. Cohen and Marx W. Wartofsky), Volume XXVI. 1975, X + 566 pp. Also available as paperback.
77. Stefan Amsterdamski, *Between Experience and Metaphysics. Philosophical Problems of the Evolution of Science.* Boston Studies in the Philosophy of Science (ed. by Robert S. Cohen and Marx W. Wartofsky), Volume XXXV. 1975, XVIII + 193 pp. Also available as paperback.
78. Patrick Suppes (ed.), *Logic and Probability in Quantum Mechanics.* 1976, XV + 541 pp.
80. Joseph Agassi, *Science in Flux.* Boston Studies in the Philosophy of Science (ed. by Robert S. Cohen and Marx W. Wartofsky), Volume XXVIII. 1975, XXVI + 553 pp. Also available as paperback.
81. Sandra G. Harding (ed.), *Can Theories Be Refuted? Essays on the Duhem-Quine Thesis.* 1976, XXI + 318 pp. Also available as paperback.
84. Marjorie Grene and Everett Mendelsohn (eds.), *Topics in the Philosophy of Biology.* Boston Studies in the Philosophy of Science (ed. by Robert S. Cohen and Marx W. Wartofsky), Volume XXVII. 1976, XIII + 454 pp. Also available as paperback.
85. E. Fischbein, *The Intuitive Sources of Probabilistic Thinking in Children.* 1975, XIII + 204 pp.
86. Ernest W. Adams, *The Logic of Conditionals. An Application of Probability to Deductive Logic.* 1975, XIII + 156 pp.
89. A. Kasher (ed.), *Language in Focus: Foundations, Methods and Systems. Essays Dedicated to Yehoshua Bar-Hillel.* Boston Studies in the Philosophy of Science (ed. by Robert S. Cohen and Marx W. Wartofsky), Volume XLIII. 1976, XXVIII + 679 pp. Also available as paperback.
90. Jaakko Hintikka, *The Intentions of Intentionality and Other New Models for Modalities.* 1975, XVIII + 262 pp. Also available as paperback.
93. Radu J. Bogdan, *Local Induction.* 1976, XIV + 340 pp.
95. Peter Mittelstaedt, *Philosophical Problems of Modern Physics.* Boston Studies in the Philosophy of Science (ed. by Robert S. Cohen and Marx W. Wartofsky), Volume XVIII. 1976, X + 211 pp. Also available as paperback.
96. Gerald Holton and William Blanpied (eds.), *Science and Its Public: The Changing Relationship.* Boston Studies in the Philosophy of Science (ed. by Robert S. Cohen and Marx W. Wartofsky), Volume XXXIII. 1976, XXV + 289 pp. Also available as paperback.
97. Myles Brand and Douglas Walton (eds.), *Action Theory. Procedings of the Winnipeg Conference on Human Action, Held at Winnipeg, Manitoba, Canada, 9–11 May 1975.* 1976, VI + 345 pp.

SYNTHESE HISTORICAL LIBRARY

Texts and Studies
in the History of Logic and Philosophy

Editors:

1. M. T. BEONIO-BROCCHIERI FUMAGALLI, *The Logic of Abelard.* Translated from the Italian. 1969, IX + 101 pp.
2. GOTTFRIED WILHELM LEIBNITZ, *Philosophical Papers and Letters.* A selection translated and edited, with an introduction, by Leroy E. Loemker. 1969, XII + 736 pp.
3. ERNST MALLY, *Logische Schriften*, ed. by Karl Wolf and Paul Weingartner. 1971, X + 340 pp.
4. LEWIS WHITE BECK (ed.), *Proceedings of the Third International Kant Congress.* 1972, XI + 718 pp.
5. BERNARD BOLZANO, *Theory of Science*, ed. by Jan Berg. 1973, XV + 398 pp.
6. J. M. E. MORAVCSIK (ed.), *Patterns in Plato's Thought. Papers arising out of the 1971 West Coast Greek Philosophy Conference.* 1973, VIII + 212 pp.
7. NABIL SHEHABY, *The Propositional Logic of Avicenna: A Translation from al-Shifā: al-Qiyās*, with Introduction, Commentary and Glossary. 1973, XIII + 296 pp.
8. DESMOND PAUL HENRY, *Commentary on De Grammatico: The Historical-Logical Dimensions of a Dialogue of St. Anselm's.* 1974, XI + 345 pp.
9. JOHN CORCORAN, *Ancient Logic and Its Modern Interpretations.* 1974, X + 208 pp.
10. E. M. BARTH, *The Logic of the Articles in Traditional Philosophy.* 1974, XXVII + 533 pp.
11. JAAKKO HINTIKKA, *Knowledge and the Known. Historical Perspectives in Epistemology.* 1974, XII + 243 pp.
12. E. J. ASHWORTH, *Language and Logic in the Post-Medieval Period.* 1974, XIII + 304 pp.
13. ARISTOTLE, *The Nicomachean Ethics.* Translated with Commentaries and Glossary by Hypocrates G. Apostle. 1975, XXI + 372 pp.
14. R. M. DANCY, *Sense and Contradiction: A Study in Aristotle.* 1975, XII + 184 pp.
15. WILBUR RICHARD KNORR, *The Evolution of the Euclidean Elements. A Study of the Theory of Incommensurable Magnitudes and Its Significance for Early Greek Geometry.* 1975, IX + 374 pp.
16. AUGUSTINE, *De Dialectica.* Translated with the Introduction and Notes by B. Darrell Jackson. 1975. XI + 151 pp.